Counseling
and Therapy
for Children

Counseling and Therapy for Children

Jim Gumaer

THE FREE PRESS
A Division of Macmillan, Inc.
NEW YORK
Collier Macmillan Publishers
LONDON

The Free Press
A Division of Macmillan, Inc.
866 Third Avenue, New York, N. Y. 10022

Collier Macmillan Canada, Inc.

Printed in the United States of America

printing number
       5   6   7   8   9   10

Library of Congress Cataloging in Publication Data

Gumaer, Jim.
   Counseling and therapy for children.

   Includes index.
   1. Child psychotherapy. 2. Children—Counseling of.
I. Title.
RJ504.G86 1984   618.92'8914   83-48683
ISBN 0-02-913350-5

To

Lynda Marie Gumaer
James Jeffrey Gumaer
Christopher Wayne Gumaer

My wife and children, who help me learn about life and love each day; and

Iris G. Wilson

My mother, who is the most child-centered person I have known.

Contents

Preface

ALTHOUGH THERE ARE MANY BOOKS that deal with counseling children, few focus effectively on theory, key concepts of theoretical approaches, and basic therapeutic techniques as they are integrated in practice. The purpose of this book is to provide counselors with a volume that will make a definitive transition from child counseling theories into practice. With the exception of two chapters, the entire book is based on my personal experiences as an elementary school counselor, counselor educator, and counselor in private practice.

Specifically, the text focuses on counseling children in the age range from 5 to 13. The text should possess wide appeal to all mental health practitioners who work with children either individually or in groups and who are concerned with helping children cope with the increasing anxieties and stress from a rapidly changing society.

Because the counselor's role with children has frequently been defined as being made up primarily of individual counseling, group counseling, and consultation, I chose these three functions to differentiate parts of the book. However, the reader is encouraged to keep in mind that, although the book is separated into parts, all the material discussed in Part I is important to Part II and Part III. All fundamental concepts and skills are progressive in nature and importance of learning. By this statement, I mean to imply to the reader that one cannot be an effective counselor of children without an adequate understanding of child growth and development and a skilled group counselor must be a skilled individual counselor.

Each chapter in all three parts is structured essentially the same, beginning with an introduction and rationale for the chapter and followed by key theoretical concepts, basic techniques, counseling activities, and recommended supplementary resources.

Part One focuses on information that is essential to the successful counselor of individual child clients. It consists of nine chapters, which cover child development and counseling, child-centered counseling, play therapy and play process, developmental play, art therapy, music therapy, bibliotherapy, behavioral counseling, and relaxation and guided fantasy. In Part II, many of the ideas discussed in Part I are explored in relation to counseling children in groups. Part II includes four chapters on the following: child-centered group counseling, growth-centered group counseling, problem-centered group counseling, and family counseling. In Part III, consultation procedures are discussed as an integral part of the overall counseling process.

Who will benefit from this book? It is for undergraduate and graduate students majoring in counseling, psychology, sociology, and education who are working with children or who anticipate working with children and families. Any mental health practitioner who is involved with children, parents, and families will also find this book a practical and helpful resource in handling everyday counseling concerns.

Two editorial concerns developed as I prepared this text. First, the need to decide how to avoid the repetitious and awkward use of the third person gender specific pronouns (he, she) when referring to child clients. To evade this problem, I have made extensive use of plural nouns and only utilized the asexist language when absolutely necessary. It is my desire that the style of writing not generate an adverse emotional response in the reader so as to devaluate the material being read. Secondly, although there have been many efforts to clarify and define the terms *counseling* and *therapy*, I find personally that their differences are far outweighed by their similarities. Because of this lack of distinction, I will use either term to encompass the other throughout the text in an alternating fashion. Wherever possible, terms are written consistently according to historical usage.

I wish to express my appreciation to Dr. George Giacobbe, Dr. Richard Graham, and Mr. Frederick Patrick for contributing their chapter on music therapy; to Dr. Thomas Tavantzis for his chapter on family counseling; and to Mrs. Karen Anthony, nurse/clinician, for her research and advice on diet and drugs in Chapter 1.

I also wish to express my special gratitude to Dr. Robert Myrick, mentor and friend, who provided many of the ideas and content background for this text through his teaching and supervision at the University of Florida. Words of thanks in a preface seem insufficient to cover the wealth of experience that my students and clients have given me. In many instances, I think I have learned and gained more from helping than I have given. To all who have contributed to me in this fashion, thank you.

Lastly, I am especially indebted to Ms. Kitty Moore, editor, The Free Press, for her patience, support, encouragement, and expertise; and to Mrs. Charlotte Angle for typing and proofreading the final manuscript.

About the Author

Jim Gumaer, Associate Professor of Counselor Education at Virginia Commonwealth University in Richmond and licensed professional counselor, received his doctorate in counselor education from the University of Florida. He is a member of the American Personnel and Guidance Association, American School Counselors Association, American Mental Health Counselors Association, Association for Counselor Education and Supervision, and the Association for Specialists in Group Work. Professor Gumaer has taught a variety of counseling courses at the graduate level and has identified specific areas of expertise as counseling with children, group counseling, consultation strategies, peer counseling, and clinical supervision. In the past six years, he has conducted approximately 100 training workshops for counselors, mental health workers, and educators. In addition, he has authored or coauthored over 20 articles that have been published in nationally refereed journals, authored and coauthored several book chapters, and coedited a book titled *Developmental Groups for Children*, published by Charles C Thomas in 1980. Professor Gumaer has also served as editorial board member of the *Personnel and Guidance Journal*, the *Journal for Specialists in Group Work*, and the *Elementary Guidance and Counseling* journal. In addition, he was president of the Association for Specialists in Group Work in 1981–1982. He is currently devoting more of his free time to his private practice in Richmond.

Counseling and Therapy for Children

Part I

COUNSELING CHILDREN INDIVIDUALLY

Chapter 1

Child Development and Counseling

RECENTLY I EXPERIENCED for the second time one of the natural wonders of the world—the birth of a child. Only during the last decade have hospitals in most states throughout the United States relaxed operating room procedures to allow fathers to witness and be a part of this most significant event in human life. The nervous anticipation during the long hours of labor and seemingly brief half hour of delivery ended when the physician held the infant up for parental inspection and then placed him on his mother's abdomen. My wife's first statement was "it's a boy!" We both then checked quickly to make sure that Christopher was all right. After the umbilical cord was severed and tied, I was allowed to hold the baby for about 10 minutes. I realized that, as parents, my wife and I had begun to interact with our child and he with us. As we were beginning to learn about Christopher, he was beginning to learn from us. We had begun a reciprocal learning process in which we as parents, would influence our family, and the family interactions in the home would influence most the psychosocial growth of Christopher. Although I recognize the importance of family influence on child growth and development, I cannot ignore the impact that schools and society will also have in shaping my children.

Since Alvin Toffler (1970) wrote his now-famous book, *Future Shock*, public awareness about the significant and rapid changes in society and the impact on children has reached an unparalleled high level. Recent statistics cited as supporting evidence for the Elementary School Guidance and Counseling Incentive Act (1981) included the following problems of contemporary life that affect children:

3

1. Since 1970 almost half of all Americans aged five and over have changed residency, often moving to a new school district. These children frequently need assistance in adjusting to their new school and community.
2. For every two marriages in 1975, there was one divorce. Current predictions claim one of every six children is living with one or neither parent. Frequently, these children come home from school to empty homes with little or no supervision.
3. Current estimates state that between 10% and 15% of our adolescents have suffered child abuse and/or neglect during their early childhood—and these figures are rising.
4. The dramatic increase in the use of alcohol by parents and older children produces devastating effects on younger children and family relationships.
5. Thousands of children under the age of 18 die annually as a result of drug usage. Recent studies indicate that the age at which drug experimenting takes place is steadily being lowered.
6. Integration and desegregation are currently being implemented in many communities.
7. An increasing number of children are dropping out of school and/or running away from home.
8. Estimates are that 10–15% of children in every school suffer from emotional disorders serious enough to require special intervention. (p. 34)

Other statistics are also startling. Frank, Simons, Abramson, and Zabarasky (1980) pointed out that one million children a year are affected by divorce, a number that has tripled in the last 20 years. Because of divorce, an estimated 45 percent of all children born in any given year will live with only one parent before reaching the age of 18. For 80 percent of these children, no warning will be received from their parents that the divorce is imminent.

In the early 1970s, the United States Children's Bureau estimated that 100,000 incidents of child abuse occurred in this country each year and 6,000 of these children died. These numbers have increased each year. According to the National Center of Child Abuse, there were 1 million estimated cases in 1979 and a projection for 3 million cases by 1980 (Goodwin, 1979). It was suggested that child abuse was the number one killer of children at that time. In addition, Elkind (1982) has cited teenage suicide as the third leading cause of death in teenagers. Currently, about 5,000 teenagers take their lives each year. These figures have more than doubled in the last decade.

The Department of Health, Education and Welfare revealed that 1 million juvenile delinquency cases, excluding traffic violations, are handled by juvenile courts in the United States. These children constitute almost 3 percent of all children in the country in the 10-to-17 age range. Arrests of juveniles accused of violent crimes has increased 247 percent during the past decade. Children between the ages of 10 and 17 account for 16 percent of the population; yet the same age group accounts for 45 percent of all arrests for serious crimes. Elkind (1982) cites 12,762 children aged 16 and under arrested in New York City on felony charges in 1980 and 18,754 in Chicago for the same year. In Virginia where one forcible rape is reported every 7½ hours, the average age range of convicted rapists is between 15 and 19 years old.

Professors Melvin Zelnick and John Kater of John Hopkins University in Baltimore, Maryland, have concluded that 50 percent of girls between the ages of 15 and 19 (over 10 million and increasing in number) have had premarital sex. They report this percentage has nearly doubled in the last decade. A consequence of this increase in sexual liberation is teenage pregnancy. One million teenage girls (about 10 percent) become pregnant each year—and this number is increasing. The greatest increase occurred in girls 14 and under. A second consequence of this sexual liberation is the increase in venereal disease in teenagers, who now account for 25 percent of the approximately one million cases of gonorrhea each year.

What is happening? The children of today have become unwilling and unknowing victims of our fast-paced, pressure-cooked society where frustration, anxiety, and constant stress have approached "normal" emotional states. "Boys and girls both are under extraordinary pressure to achieve, to succeed, to please. They are constantly being hurried. . . . Harried children are forced to take on the physical, psychological, and social trappings of adulthood before they are ready to do so." (Elkind, 1982, p. 16) It is with little wonder that our society has realized an increased need for counselors of children. Many counseling professionals and other mental health care providers of children in the 80s have assumed a developmental counseling approach, to help children cope effectively.

KEY CONCEPTS

Developmental Counseling

Developmental counseling as a theoretical approach emerged in the 1960s. Contrary to my own beliefs, as described in the preface of this book, that little difference exists between counseling and therapy, Dinkmeyer (1966) explained developmental counseling by differentiating the two:

> Developmental counseling, which can be contrasted with adjustment or crises counseling, is not always problem oriented in assuming that the child has a difficult problem. Instead, the goals are the development of self-understanding, awareness of one's potentiality, and methods of utilizing one's capacity. Developmental counseling truly focuses on helping the individual know and understand and accept himself. This type of counseling, then, becomes personalized learning, not individualized teaching. The child learns not only to

understand himself but to become ultimately responsible for his choices and actions. (p. 264.)

Blocher (1966) also attempted to explain developmental counseling by describing its focus as education-oriented, in contrast with therapy which is remedial in nature. It is my orientation that developmental counseling is educative and preventive, yet, in some instances, remediative in construct.

Because developmental counseling is preventive, its basic premise is to impede the occurrence of severe problems by planning for children's learning at all developmental levels, thus enhancing children's growth and potential. If difficult problems do occur at any stage, then the developmental counselor's position is to *prevent* an exacerbation of the situation while beginning to *remediate* the causal factors of the immediate, predominant concern. Developmental counselors recognize that all children will encounter personal conflict as they grow and that children will need to master certain developmental tasks to successfully resolve these conflicts as they pass through critical life stages. A developmental task or skill which must be mastered was defined by Havighurst (1972) as one:

> . . . which arises at or about a certain period in the life of an individual, successful achievement of which leads to his happiness and to success with later tasks, while failure leads to unhappiness in the individual, disapproval by the society, and difficulty with later tasks. (p. 2)

Tasks are, therefore, created through interactions of each child's physical maturation, societal change, environmental stress, and the individual personality.

As a result, the counselor must have a thorough knowledge and understanding of children's developmental, social, emotional, and learning patterns. Personality theory and learning theory provide a framework for counselors to structure their work with children. This structure includes the processes and procedures by which therapists diagnose conflicts; create hypotheses for intervention in problem areas; develop goals, objectives, and strategies of intervention for enhancing the personal growth of children; and evaluate and follow up on client progress.

Personality Theory and Child Development

In examining the lives of children, sometimes it may be helpful to keep in mind that children, like all animal organisms, exist in a threatening environment. Survival is basic to children in their environment, and the child's need to maintain self or survive becomes the most dominant influence in learning of physical behavior and in shaping psychological growth. In fact, the development of a child's identity or "self" probably assumes a position of primary importance in the survival process. Three theorists who have contributed greatly to the understanding of children and their development are Freud, Erikson, and Maslow.

Sigmund Freud was the first theorist to stress the developmental aspects of personality and the role of early childhood in the overall development of the person. Briefly and simplistically stated, Freud hypothesized that the personality consisted of the id, ego, and superego. According to Freud, the id contained everything psychological that was inherited at birth. It also influenced the child's impulse or zest for living or, to interpret it differently, the child's motivations for behaving in terms of survival to satisfy basic needs through reduction of tension. The id contains the "pleasure principle," that is, it acts to "please" the needs of the individual. The ego is identified as the objective, realistic-thinking, decision-maker which tries to maintain a balance between the pleasure-seeking id and the moralistic superego. The superego acts to inhibit the impulsive behavior of the id and attempts to persuade the ego to adopt more-moralistic behavior.

Freud postulated the three parts of the personality were complete in children by age 5 and that they interact continually and in effect provide a system of "checks and balances" for behavior. He also described these personality parts as being affected in response to four distinct sources of tension encountered in the environment: physiological growth processes, frustrations, conflicts, and threats. For example, infants who are breast fed for several months after birth encounter tension when weaning occurs, and they may become frustrated if their mothers' breasts are unable to produce a sufficient amount of milk to satisfy increasing nutritional needs with growth. The conflicts between parent and child over learning to feed self, toilet training, bedtime, and dating point out the developmental and ongoing nature of children's needs for learning to cope with tension throughout their lives. Although Freud believed that by the age of 5 the child had experienced every type of conflict possible, the older the child becomes, the greater are the number of sources of tension encountered. Of course, these situations change as the child develops; nevertheless, children begin to learn to cope with them in early infancy. Freud called these coping strategies defense mechanisms.

The defense mechanisms that will be discussed in this chapter, fixation and regression, are identified directly with Freud's theorized stages of child development. The stages include the following: oral (0–1 year of age), anal (1–2 years of age), phallic (2–6 years of age), and genital (6 years – adolescence). If the sources of tension encountered in each stage by the child create excessive anxiety, the child may temporarily stop development or revert to less mature levels of behavior.

Fixation

Children who fail to move from one developmental stage to the next because of excessive anxiety would be fixated. For example, a child who clings excessively to mother or to teacher and demonstrates a need for constant reassurance with performance may be fixated at a dependent level and be prevented from learning independent behavior.

Regression

Children who encounter a traumatic experience revert to an earlier stage of development. For example, a school age-child may exhibit thumb-sucking, bed-wetting, or other infant behaviors when a new baby is introduced into the home. Other defense mechanisms include identification, displacement, repression, projection, and reaction formation (introduced in Chapter 3), and displacement, projection, and sublimation (discussed in Chapter 5).

Like Freud, Erik Erikson was schooled in psychoanalytic theory. This training is evidenced in his eight stages of man. As Table 1–1 shows, the first four stages correspond roughly in time of development with Freud's stages. For the purposes of this book on children, Erikson's last three stages—intimacy versus isolation, generativity versus stagnation and self-absorption, and integrity versus despair—have been omitted.

Erikson theorized that each developmental stage presents a "psychosocial crisis" which arises and must be resolved before the child can address a higher-level crisis. If sufficient resolution of the crisis does not occur, then the child will be forced to deal with the crisis time and again during subsequent stages until it is resolved. Erikson's first five "psychosocial stages," with potential positive and negative cognitive and affective learnings, are outlined in Table 1–1.

Abraham Maslow (1968) discussed survival in terms of the human organism's struggle toward "self-actualization". Maslow described a hierarchy of needs with lower-order needs being prepotent over higher-order needs. Once lower-order needs with greater potency were satisfactorily met, then children could press upward in the hierarchy to satisfy higher-level needs. Figure 1–1 provides a schematic diagram of the hierarchy of needs system. First-level and most potent needs are physiological needs such as hunger, thirst—and in adolescents who have reached puberty, sex. It is easy for most adults to realize that children who are not fed properly each day cannot absorb expected levels of information and develop understanding (learning) to maintain grade-level-achievement standards.

Second level needs of safety include the provision of adequate shelter in the home and security within the environment. Situations occur frequently where children can not sleep at night fearing a real physical danger from rats, break-ins (as in the case of Brad in Chapter 5), harm from other children (as with the 12-year-old girl in Chapter 5), or parental abuse. Less severe (nonphysical) threats to security are experienced by children who must readjust to new environments forced by relocation or

Table 1-1
ERIKSON'S DEVELOPMENTAL STAGES AND LEARNING OUTCOMES

Psychosocial Stage	*Cognitive and Affective Learning*	
	POSITIVE	NEGATIVE
Trust vs. mistrust (0–1$\frac{1}{2}$ years)	An infant who is well handled, caressed, loved, and cared for learns to trust the environment and becomes secure.	An infant whose needs are neglected becomes anxious, fearful, and learns to mistrust the environment.
Autonomy vs. shame (1$\frac{1}{2}$–3 years)	The child begins to learn control of self and environment which leads to sense of self-worth and pride in accomplishments.	The child learns to be dependent and controlled by others which leads to self-doubt.
Initiative vs. guilt (3–6 years)	Child learns how to learn and master environment. Uses imagination in self-initiated play. Cooperates in games and is both leader and follower. Receives praise and encouragement.	Child learns failure and is ridiculed and punished.
Industry vs. inferiority (6–13 years)	Child learns to master formal skills of life: to play by rules and teamwork. Child learns self-discipline, feels confident and competent.	Child repeatedly fails which leads to feeling inadequate and inferior.
Identity vs. role diffusion (13–20 yrs.)	Child experiments with values, interests, learns self-identity and feels powerful and in control.	Continued failure leads to role confusion and inept social behavior. Child feels rejected and unimportant.

those who have lost a parent by death or divorce and then live in fear of losing the remaining parent.

Once the physiological and security needs of children are adequately met, then their needs for belonging and love become prepotent. As Erikson also emphasizes in his developmental stages, children need the security of family and the feeling they are an integral, contributing part of the family unit. Children also need to be loved and be allowed to freely express their love to loved ones. As I write, I am experiencing these needs from my 3-year-old son, Jeff, who is struggling to find out where he belongs in our

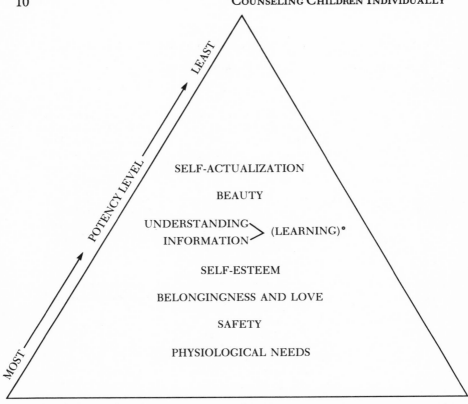

*Note: Learning is included by the author at the level of understanding. It is not a part of Maslow's paradigm.

Figure 1-1   Maslow's Hierarchy of Needs

family now that he has an infant brother. Last evening after mother and father each had shared the responsibility of feeding, changing, holding and cuddling the baby, he said, "It's my turn to hold Chris." When mother handed the baby to him as he sat on the couch, he said, "Mom, can I feed him tomorrow?" As children grow older, their needs for belongingness and love change. For reasons of security, belongingness, and love, kindergarten and first-grade children often identify strongly with their teachers. It is not unusual to hear teachers being addressed as "mom" in the classroom. A short time later, children will begin to transfer these needs to peers of the same sex, and when they reach adolescence or onset of puberty, they will begin to refocus them toward the opposite sex. Table 1-2 provides additional information regarding normal expectations for children's social and emotional development at various ages.

Self-esteem follows love and belongingness in Maslow's hierarchy. Self-esteem might be defined as the perception or opinion one develops of oneself in relation to the ability to cope within the environment. Children

Table 1-2

NORMAL EXPECTATIONS FOR CHILDREN'S SOCIAL
AND EMOTIONAL DEVELOPMENT

Developmental Stage	Social Development	Emotional Development
Infancy (0–2 years)	Dependent upon involvement with family members	Fear and anger may be indicated through crying. Happiness and contentment through smiling. Excitement through rapid movement of limbs
Early childhood (2–5 years)	Child is self-oriented. Beginning to develop friendships. No sexual or racial preferences in play. Bias not developed. Development of desire to play with others rather than alone	Further differentiation of affective responses. Understanding feelings at this stage crucial to later development. More secure in relationships outside family, but mother still most important person
Middle childhood (5–8 years)	Identification with same sex in friendships and as playmates. Peers influential. Need to belong and be liked. Play in cooperation with others. Beginning independence from family	Easily hurt by ridicule and criticism from important others. Adult reinforcement (approval) powerful motivator of behavior. A large need for love, belonging, and acceptance at home and school
Late childhood (8–11 years)	Peer group extremely influential. Bias and prejudice developed. Independence from family and adults developed. Team games and competition enjoyed. Opposite sex may be excluded in play. Interest in sex education and sexual differences developed	Need to receive reinforcement and approval from peers. Strong bond, attachment to same sex. May antagonize and be hostile toward opposite sex. More willing to accept constructive criticism. Accepts responsibility for behaviors and consequences of actions
Adolescence (11–14 years)	Status among peers predominates behavior. Dating begins. Personal appearance becomes important. Very interested in sex and body development. Sexual experimentation begins	Anxiety present related to acceptance by peers, status in group, personal appearance, dating, and body development. Growing need to express independence from parents. Antagonism in home may develop over "control"

learn about themselves, and develop a self-image and self-esteem, by what important adults say and do to them about their behavior in the environment. Children who achieve are those who learn to cope successfully in their environment and have their behavior reinforced through positive adult feedback, which in turn enhances their self-esteem. Children who do not recieve feedback on their achievement may question their ability to survive. Moreover, if they receive negative input from important others, they may feel inadequate, rejected, and unloved, and develop low self-esteem. Because behavior is determined by children's perceptions of the environment and their perceptions of the environment are influenced by their perceptions of self, children who possess high levels of self-esteem will behave in ways that will secure this positive self-image. On the other hand, children with low self-esteem may behave antagonistically toward an environment that is perceived as harmful.

Once the first four levels of Maslow's hierarchy are satisfactorily met, then children are ready for cognitive development: the acquisition of information and development of understanding. Maslow (1968) developed a formula for "healthy" child growth to contain the following elements:

1. Healthy children are spontaneous and reach out to interact with the environment and express whatever skills they have.
2. Healthy children, therefore, are nourished physically, not crippled by fear, and feel safe enough to venture forth.
3. These experiences with the environment are encountered either by chance, or with the aid of important adults.
4. Healthy children must then be secure enough and self-assured to risk these interactions and the outcomes, rather than be frightened by them.
5. If these experiences prove successful, then they will be repeated, and
6. Children will move forward in their growth toward more complex experiences.
7. Successful encounters with the environment enhance self-esteem and the feeling of capability, power and control.
8. Children will generally choose to move forward and to grow to the extent that they are not crippled. (pp. 57–59)

As Maslow and later Faust (1968) identified, when children's survival is seriously threatened, they tend to become crippled by excessive fear, anxiety, guilt, or defensive posturing.

I have only chosen to discuss the first six of Maslow's eight hierarchical levels because it has been my experience that these levels correspond closely to Erikson's developmental stages and are the ones that child therapists will use frequently in their work. Hershenson (1982) has described in detail how the theoretical structures of Erikson and Maslow coincide to yield "trends" in growth: Maslow's physiological and safety needs and Erikson's idea of trust are directed toward *survival;* Maslow's love and belonging and Erikson's intimacy are engaged in for *communica-*

tion; Maslow's self-esteem and Erikson's identity are focused on *recognition;* Maslow's information, understanding, and self-actualization and Erikson's industry, generativity, and ego integrity lead to cognitive and physical mastery of life's skills. Hershenson further developed his formulations by relating that the fundamental principle of counseling is to assist the survival and growth of the client.

> . . . counseling aims to facilitate personal survival and growth by maximizing communication and respect (recognition) between counselor and client in order to create an environment in which appropriate counseling procedures can be applied to help the client achieve mastery. . . . It is the counselor's responsibility to know how best to create the interpersonal environment that will maximize communication and respect, and to know and utilize those procedures that will best help the client gain mastery. . . . (pp. 408–409)

Of course, counseling children is not so simple, but the tenets of Freud, Erikson, and Maslow do provide a necessary framework from which therapists can: (1) conceptualize and diagnose the problems children are experiencing in relation to normal developmental growth patterns; (2) hypothesize as to primary foci for intervention; and (3) develop strategies for intervention and remediation. The counselor's task, then, is to diagnose the crippled position of the child, identify the developmental stage or level of needs at which the child is dysfunctional (not having needs met adequately), and provide the necessary process for intervention. A case illustration of this process will follow later in this chapter.

Previously we have discussed the prepotent nature of the physiological need to satisfy basic levels of hunger. Beyond starvation is the overall concept of nutrition and its impact on the survival and development of the organism. It is my opinion that the probability for healthy psychological development in children is increased proportionately with the degree to which their nutritional needs and physical development are met. There is substance to the ancient Greek saying "A sound mind exists in a sound body" and in the modern quip "You are what you eat."

Diet and Nutrition*

Physicians have recognized for years that nutritional deficiency can cause emotional distress and, in severe cases, mental illness. In a recent article, Pearson and Long (1982) reported on research that suggested ailments such as headaches or emotional and mental stress could be reduced through proper diet and nutrition. Fredericks (1976) in *Psycho-Nutrition* also discussed dietary control and vitamin therapy as a unique method of helping clients who suffered from day-to-day stress. Proper nutrition may

* The author gratefully acknowledges Mrs. Karen Anthony for researching the material in this section and in the following section, Children's Illnesses.

be a key factor in reducing mental disorder, but it is most certainly paramount in the normal growth and development of children. Therapists, therefore, need to know and understand the food intakes and adequate or inadequate diets of their clients and make recommendations for dietary interventions. The first step for counselors is to acquire some information on basic foods.

Pearson and Long (1982) identified sugar and salt as two of the most commonly misused foods in our society. Fredericks and Goodman (1974) estimated that 10 percent of our population suffered from adverse reactions to sugar. Hypoglycemia (low blood sugar) is a reaction to excessive amounts of sugar intake. The excessive sugar creates a metabolic malfunction because it stimulates the body to produce excessive amounts of insulin to metabolize it. The malfunction may then lead to hyperinsulinism, which drastically reduces the levels of sugar in the blood which in turn creates a chemical imbalance in the body. Physical symptoms of hypoglycemia include profuse sweating, heavy thirst, excessive urination, itching, anxiety, and depression. Hypoglycemia is easily diagnosed and controlled through a diet by reducing sugar, starch, carbohydrate, caffeine, and alcohol intakes while increasing protein consumption. Counselors need to be concerned with children who do not eat regularly scheduled meals, skip breakfast, and prefer "junk food" and snacks to more nutritious meals. Additional information on the effects of too much insulin to the body is provided later in this chapter in Table 1-3. Salt, when consumed in excess, can also be potentially harmful. It causes the body to retain fluids, and fluid retention is thought to be linked with hypertension. In addition to excessive use of sugar and salt, food allergies create problems for children.

Food allergies may be responsible for behavioral problems associated with "hyperactive" children. Symptom behaviors such as impulsiveness, aggressiveness, short attention span, and restlessness, which frequently lead to learning difficulties and hinder social–emotional development, have been attributed to hyperactivity. Typical treatment for this condition has called for the use of drug therapy, behavioral counseling or both. However, Feingold (1974) and Rapp (1977) have both suggested that the preferred mode of treatment for hyperactivity is the elimination of allergy-inducing foods and controlled dieting. Readers are referred to Table 1-3 for further information on hyperactivity and children's illnesses. As with hyperactivity, pediatricians will recommend diet therapy in conjunction with drug therapy for many cases of chronic illnesses in children.

Children's Illnesses: Drug and Diet Therapy

Any illness in children represents a serious and, in some cases, permanent disruption of the family system. Therefore, chronically or acutely ill children and family members will need additional understanding,

CHRONIC ILLNESSES*

Condition	Description and Symptoms	Medications	Diet Therapy	Other Considerations
Asthma (allergic rhinitis)	Pulmonary disorder caused by allergy. Sneezing, nasal congestion, wheezing, coughing, difficulty with breathing. May be caused by foods, inhalants, vigorous exercise, or emotional stress	Antihistamines: often on daily basis with allergic rhinitis. Should be discontinued during asthmatic attack. Bronchodilators: may also be used on daily basis, especially during an attack. These include epinephrine, ephedrine, and aminophylline. If these fail, a corticosteriod is appropriate. Expectorants: may also be used *Never* give cough suppressant during attack.	Avoid food substances to which child is allergic Encourage fluid intake	Attack may last few hours or *days*. Can lead to death. Never leave child alone. Seek medical help immediately Help child remain calm Avoid over-protection and undue attention Make sure child follows drug regimen
Diabetes	Body unable to metabolize carbohydrates owing to an insufficient production of insulin. Disease is inherited. Child likely to be overweight at onset Symptoms: increased thirst and appetite, weight loss, excessive urination (bed-wetting may occur), general weakness and dry skin.	Insulin injected on a daily basis. Dosage based on test of sugar. Other factors influencing dosage: diet, infections, exercise, and emotional stress	Regulated diet usually recommended. Avoid excesses, especially sweets foods high in carbohydrates	Constant care necessary. Two serious emergency situations: 1. insulin reaction, low blood sugar, too much sugar, too much insulin, not enough food, or excessive exercise Symptoms: excessive sweating, headache, hunger, trembling, irritability, or personality change *(continued)*

15

Table 1-3 (cont.)

Condition	Description and Symptoms	Medications	Diet Therapy	Other Considerations
				Action: give food with sugar immediately (candy bar); call doctor 2. coma—high blood sugar, too little insulin, failure to follow diet, infection, or stress Symptoms: increased thirst, urination, weakness, abdominal pain, loss of appetite, or nausea Action: Call doctor
Epilepsy: grand mal	Seizures with impaired consciousness or unconsciousness Tonic Spasm: (40 sec.) Child usually falls to ground, pupils dilate, and face is distorted. Muscles stiffen, child may bite tongue and urinate or defecate Clonic spasm: Alternate contraction and relaxation of muscles, lasts indefinitely. Followed by deep sleep and possible confusion on awakening	Anticonvulsants. Choice of drugs and dosage depends on individual child. Those commonly used: ethosuximide (Zarontin), phenytoin sodium (Dilantin), primidone (Mysoline), trimethadione (Tridione), and mephofarbital (Mebaral) (These drugs have many side effects)	May be prescribed	Child must be protected from injury during attack. Clothing should be loosened around neck. Child turned to side. Do not restrain body movement or force jaw open. Avoid stimulation. Observe and note occurrences before, during and after seizure. Notify family and doctor
Petit mal	Transient loss of con-			Help other child...

Disorder	Description	Medication/Treatment	Diet	Considerations
	of eyes, slight movements of lips or limbs. Staring in space			
Hyperactivity	Pattern of behavior includes poor concentration, increased motor activity, impulsivity, and short attention span. Child may demonstrate mood swings, temper tantrums, and be easily distracted	Dextroamphetamine sulfate (Dexedrine) and methylphenidate (Ritalin). Dosage depends on individual and severity of symptoms. Side effects present. Child must be monitored to assure optimum effectiveness in drug regimen	Salicylate-free diet recommended. Sugar-free diet recommended	No easy solutions. Careful observation and documentation of behavior necessary prior to diagnosis and drug therapy and continued thereafter to determine effectiveness. Behavioral counseling techniques are sometimes helpful
Sickle cell	Inherited dysfunction in the synthesis of hemoglobin. Only affects Black race. Symptoms: painful swelling in hands, feet, and joints; abdominal pain; fever; vomiting; blood in urine; convulsions; coma; paralysis, and anemia	None to prevent or treat. Codeine and aspirin to reduce pain	Large quantitites of liquids necessary. Well-balanced meals	Growth and development may be abnormal. Self-esteem may suffer as result. Fear of crises and death must be considered. Prevention from infection important and immediate treatment of infection imperative. Child usually hospitalized in crisis
Cystic fibrosis	Abnormality with mucous secreting glands of the body. Symptoms: respiratory difficulties and problems in maintenance of adequate nutritional state	Pancreas enzymes to aid digestion. Antibiotics may be prescribed routinely to prevent infection. Digitalis and diuretics are given if there is heart failure	Good nutrition essential. Protein intake 4 grams per kilogram of body weight, fat intake normal. Caloric intake high. Liberal amounts of salt should be given with food	Prevention of infection and maintenance of prescribed diet and drugs extremely important. Avoid overprotection. Family and child will need support

* Researched by Mrs. Karen Anthony

strength, stability, and support from professionals. Therapists can become more effective helpers of children who suffer from prolonged and severe disease states by becoming better informed. Information needed by counselors to assist these ill children and their family members includes the child's stage of development, psychosocial needs, child's and family member's perceptions of the illness, signs and symptoms of the illness, its treatment, prognosis for the child, and likely impact on the family. Steinhauer, Mushim, and Rae-Grant (1974) suggested that the nature and extent of cognitive and emotional disruption in children who are chronically ill will depend primarily on their stage of development when the illness occurs. For example, an independent and secure 7-year-old with asthma since the age of 3 would most likely cope better than an immature, insecure 12-year-old who recently developed seizures.

Today most children experiencing a chronic or acute illness are on medication. Along with positive benefits of the medication, there usually exist some unwanted side effects. Often the side effects of drugs have potential to interfere with children's growth and learning. For example, antihistamines which are routinely used for asthma often produce drowsiness. A teacher who is not aware of the side effect may assume the child is inattentive, bored, or not getting enough sleep. Through lack of information, the teacher may act inappropriately. On the other hand, a teacher who is aware and understands the illness and medication can be a resource in helping to regulate the medication regimen. Children often are taking drugs that have lost their effectiveness, are too strong or weak, and that are not being administered properly. Since teachers often spend approximately six hours a day with children, their observations of the ill child and reporting of these observations to parents and physicians are invaluable. To assist the reader in understanding some of the diseases of children, Table 1–3 contains descriptions of six chronic ailments children encounter (asthma, diabetes, epilepsy, hyperactivity, sickle-cell disease, and cystic fibrosis), the medications used in treatment, recommended diet therapy, and miscellaneous information. In a similar manner, Table 1–4 describes two acute conditions children often contract.

Drugs mentioned in Table 1–3 that are commonly prescribed for the chronic diseases (asthma, diabetes, epilepsy, and hyperactivity) include antihistamines, bronchodilators, insulin, anticonvulsants, dextroamphetamine sulfate (dexedrine), and methylphenidate (Ritalin).

Antihistamines are primarily used to treat nasal allergies and asthma when the child has allergic rhinitis. It is important to read the label, the package insert, and consult the *Physicians' Desk Reference (PDR)* to determine the specific side effects for each drug. Several undesirable side effects are common to most antihistamines, including drowsiness, dizziness, dryness in mouth and throat, nausea, diarrhea, disturbed coordination, blurred vision, urinary retention, increased heart rate, and low blood pressure.

Table 1-4
ACUTE CONDITIONS*

Condition	Description and Symptoms	Medications	Diet Therapy	Other Considerations
Ringworm (scalp)	Usually effects neglected children. Fungus which causes hair to break off at skin. Infection spreads in circular manner forming lesions. Scalp becomes red, scales appear. Child may complain of itching	Oral medication-grisefalvin. Griseofulvin (Grifulvin V) or any strong antifungal used locally	None	Diagnosis made by examining scalp under ultraviolet light Highly infectious
Head lice	Eggs are grayish, oval, translucent bodies which attack hair shaft. They hatch in 3 to 4 days Usually effects neglected children Severe itching Crusts will form and hair will become matted	Lindane (kwell shampoo) repeated in one to two weeks and rechecked Repeat treatment as often as necessary Antibiotic may be prescibed if pustules are present on neck and face	None	Eggs may be removed by combing hair with a fine-tooth metal comb dipped in hot vinegar Lice easily transferred from one child to next; therefore, anyone in close contact with infected child should be examined

* Researched by Mrs. Karen Anthony.

19

In some children, stimulation and excitation may occur such as nervousness, insomnia, and convulsions.

Bronchodilators are drugs which are also used in treatment of asthma. They relax the smooth muscles of the tracheobronchial tree, thereby decreasing resistance to air flow and congestion in the respiratory tract. Unpleasant side effects of bronchodilators include: stimulation or drowsiness, epigastric distress, palpitation, nausea, difficulty with urination, headaches, and low blood pressure.

There are many different types of *insulin*, and it is therefore necessary for the counselor to know what type of insulin the child is receiving and be aware of the time of onset, peak of effectiveness, and duration of effectiveness. Because space prohibits extensive discussion of the various types of insulin, interested readers are referred to the *PDR* for this information.

Anticonvulsants are drugs used to treat seizures. It is very important to administer the medications as prescribed and to watch for toxic side effects which may include skin rash, apathy, nervousness, dizziness, blurred vision, gastric upset, nausea, diarrhea, drowsiness, headaches, euphoria, irritability, hyperactivity, anorexia, and ataxia. Therapists are cautioned that it may take several months for the physician to properly regulate the drug level.

Dextroamphetamine Sulfate (Dexedrine) and methylphenidate (Ritalin) are two drugs used frequently to treat hyperactivity. Most hyperactive children will require medication for several years. Once the symptoms are controlled, it is possible to reduce the dosage and to interrupt drug therapy during summer months or when the child is experiencing extreme stress. Side effects of these drugs may include insomnia, initial irritability, inappropriate affect (crying without apparent reason), increased sensitivity, and fearfulness. These conditions are usually controlled by reducing the drug dosage, or eliminating the dosage in the afternoon or evening; sometimes the two methods are used together. The PDR recommends that, in children aged 6 and over, treatment begin with small doses (5 milligrams) with gradual increases of 5 to 10 milligrams weekly. Dosage above 60 milligrams per day is not recommended and, if improvement is not observed after one month, the drug should be discontinued.

As mentioned previously in this chapter when working with children who are under a physician's care, counselors should obtain a thorough understanding of the treatment, including drug and diet therapies. In addition to understanding the therapeutic regimen, teachers depend frequently on the therapist's knowledge and consulting skills to help integrate the hyperactive child into the classroom environment and to assist in peer acceptance of the child's behavior and problem. In addition to a working knowledge of medications prescribed by physicians and their potential side effects, it is also imperative for counselors to ensure that all medications are stored properly in the agency and administered according to instructions. Children who have medical problems, whether chronic or acute, will need these special counseling considerations to assist them with stabilizing the disease and helping them to develop as normal lives as possible.

INITIAL COUNSELING CONSIDERATIONS

Prior to entering into any helping relationship, it is important that counselors develop a set of prescribed procedures and processes for engaging their clients. In my work with individual children, I use a case approach to counseling which includes four elements: an intake interview with parent(s) (guardians) and the child, a child-centered counseling process, a client assessment including problem identification, and a plan of intervention.

The *intake interview* is arranged with parents and should include the child. It is important for children in counseling to learn that the therapist is primarily concerned with their welfare and not solely with parental interests. As parents discuss the presenting problem of their child, the child should be encouraged to interact at opportune times. Often it becomes necessary to interrupt parental discussion so that children can express their opinions. I have found this procedure to be useful in four ways. First, it enhances the child-centered image in the mind of the child and begins to build the bond for establishing the helping relationship. Children begin to view the therapist as a child advocate who is interested in them and their opinions. Secondly, the counselor is able to receive the child's perceptions of the situation as well as the parents'. A third reason is that both parents and child are involved initially in counseling together, which encourages family commitment and support for counseling and openness and honesty within the adult/child relationship regarding the problem presented. Lastly, parents and child hear jointly the professional and ethical boundaries applied in counseling. For example, the child hears the financial cost to parents of therapy and the parents must understand the concept of confidentiality. I often say to the parents, "What is discussed in counseling between your child and myself is privileged information, and it will not be discussed with you unless I first receive your child's permission." Next, I turn to the child and reiterate, "Our work together is confidential, which means what we say and do together is our secret and won't be shared with anyone else, including your parents, unless you give permission beforehand."

The consideration of children's rights as equal to adults' rights in counseling is the foundation upon which *child-centered counseling* is structured. Professional ethics should be applied equally no matter the age of the client. Children can and do understand these professional principles when they are explained in terms appropriate to the child's developmental level. In addition to children's rights, child-centered counseling will be discussed in detail in Chapter 2.

One of the primary purposes of the initial interview is *client assessment*. In the early stages of the interview, parents and child are encouraged to freely explore their perceptions of the presenting problem. Once the immediate anxiety of a new situation (counseling) diminishes and everyone begins to relax, specific questions relevant to the child's psychosocial development are asked. This developmental history, along with the presenting problem, provides the basic information to evaluate the client's condition. Appendix A contains a case study outline to be used as an aid for obtaining the developmental history on a child client. Although it is not inclusive, it provides the necessary structure for gathering most pertinent information, such as the presenting problem, circumstances of birth, medical history, food intake, social development and peer relationships, emotional development, family history and relationships, school/academic history, and any available test results. After receiving permission, audiotaping this part of the interview is more advantageous to taking notes. By taping, the therapist can concentrate entirely on what is said without begin distracted. In some instances where indicated, this preliminary information base can be supplemented by administering additional tests or inventories. The last business introduced in the intake interview is to schedule future counseling sessions and, in the case of private practice, set the fee and establish a payment schedule. The intake interview may last as long as 1½ hours because of the information-gathering process. In many instances where sufficient time is not available, parents and children might be asked to write autobiographical histories of their lives from their earliest recollections to the present.

Following the intake interview, the counselor is ready to make an initial hypothesis as to the primary cause for dysfunction in the child and develop a *plan for intervention*. This plan provides an outline for planning each individual counseling session and may be used as a continuous record of counseling progress. The plan contains the presenting problem and any special considerations that were discovered through the intake interview. Although the first hypothesis for intervention is formulated on minimal personal contact with the child, it is the counselor's best educated guess as to the primary cause of the child's problem. Often a personal brainstorming of probable causal factors to a child's problem and ranking these ideas in terms of potency of contribution to the problem are helpful. The most potent factor then provides the basis for developing the hypothesis and plan for intervention. The plan for intervention includes a primary goal which is directly related to the hypothesis and any secondary goals that might seem relevant. Specific objectives and strategies or activities to assist in reaching the goal are written. I would suggest a minimum of two objectives for each goal and two activities for each objective. This method takes into consideration the individual differences of clients. Should one activity be unattractive to the client, another is available and should two activities fail to meet the first objective, a second objective can provide alternative strategies for working with the child where the first approach failed. Finally, a personal evaluation of each session is necessary and should include brief written descriptions of thoughts as to the progress of therapy and direction for the next session. Now, let us examine a case example which illustrates the four elements discussed as initial counseling considerations.

CASE OF CHRIS

Name: Christopher West   Date: April 5, 19——
Age: 12

I. *Presenting Problem:*

Mother indicated recent academic deficiencies in school with an increase in unacceptable school behavior as primary concerns. Mother's goals for the child were to read on grade level, get along with peers, and respect rights of others. Chris described school as OK and indicated he would like to learn to stay out of trouble, but could not seem to control his temper.

II. *Circumstance of Birth:*

Chris was a premature baby who required a complete blood exchange. The mother reported no additional complications prior to or during pregnancy. Subsequent to the birth, she underwent a hysterectomy which she later found out to be unnecessary. As a result, she experienced severe emotional upset and mentioned she didn't function well as a mother for about one year.

III. *Motor Development:*

According to mother, Chris developed physically at a normal rate with no indications of visual or motor dysfunction. The mother could not recall exact ages at which he walked, talked, or controlled bladder and bowels; however, she asserted they were at normal ages without difficulties. Chris was characterized as athletic and enterprising in games of skill.

IV. *Medical History:*

In addition to the premature birth, as an infant, Chris had constant problems with poor health. He was allergic to milk and other foods; this in turn impaired his bone and teeth development. He formed no enamel on his baby teeth. Chris also experienced several hospitalizations in early childhood (ages 3, 5, and 7). The first time was for mild convulsions associated with a high fever. The second hospitalization was for influenza, high fever, and malnutrition. The third time he required surgery for a broken arm. During the last hospitalization, he was hysterical for about 24 hours prior to surgery. Currently, Chris is not under a physician's care, nor is he taking medications.

V. *Diet:*

Although Chris experienced infant allergies to some foods, his mother reported he now "eats like a horse." He likes all food groups and requires no encouragement to maintain a healthy diet.

VI. *Social Development and Peer Relationships:*

The mother reported Chris always interacted well with his peers until the fourth grade when the trouble with school began. Chris said he enjoys sports of all kinds with boys his own age. He concurred with his mother that he is both a leader and a follower. As an infant, both parents worked and a woman was hired to care for Chris during working hours. The mother felt this woman took good care of Chris's physical needs but not his social needs because she never talked or played with Chris. The past two years Chris has been in several serious fights at home and school. His mother said, "He flies off the handle."

VII. *Emotional Development:*

The mother described Chris as a "very good and affectionate child." She felt he was unhappy as a young child but happier now. Chris has severe temper tantrums at home when his mother or sister refuse to respond to his wishes. Although successful with athletics and friendships, Chris said he felt "dumb and different." Mother stated Chris had become "moody," difficult to control, and unmotivated. Chris has run away from home on three occasions and has threatened to kill himself.

VIII. *Family History and Relationships:*

A. Parents:

Both parents are living but were divorced two years ago. Father, who is 15 years older than mother, has remarried. He and his wife live in Washington, D.C. Mother has dated several men since the divorce. Both parents have college educations and mother is physically healthy. Father works for the government and mother is employed as a teacher in a local school system. Mother reported that father suffers from high blood pressure, cirrhosis of the liver, and other alcohol-related difficulties.

B. Siblings:

Chris has one sister, Sarah, who is 16 years of age. She, too, experienced many medical problems in early childhood. However, unlike Chris, she has not experienced difficulty with school or peers. Both children have responsibilities in the home. Chris takes out the trash, washes dishes, and vacuums. Sarah makes meals, dusts, and washes the clothes. Mother reported that she gets along better with her daughter. Mother indicated she tried to help Chris with his homework, but he became frustrated easily, sullen, and lost his temper. She then would yell back.

Both Chris and Sarah receive monetary rewards for grades, completion of chores, behaving, and a good attitude. The most effective method of discipline is to reduce privileges and rewards, and to talk about a disruptive situation.

IX. *School/Academic History:*

Chris hated kindergarten and did not like to participate in kindergarten activities. Otherwise, he generally likes school with the exception of two female teachers he had the last two years whom Chris described as "a lot like Mom." Chris indicated his favorite subject, and most difficult, was language arts. He disliked math and reading. Mother felt he needed a strict, consistent atmosphere to learn, but the school was committed to team teaching where children frequently change teachers for different subjects. Mother reported Chris had average to above-average standardized achievement scores.

INDIVIDUAL COUNSELING PLAN AND RECORD

Name: Christopher West
Age: 12

Presenting Problem:
Academic deficiencies and inappropriate school behavior.
Special Considerations:
Mother and father divorced in 1980 when presenting problem first appeared.
Child experienced many traumatic events in infancy.
Hypotheses of Causal Factors:
1. Appropriate levels of trust and security are apparently missing in Chris's life as a result of early illnesses, extended hospitalizations, an emo-

tionally distraught mother in his first year of life, working parents and care by another woman in infancy, parental arguments, separation, and divorce.

2. Chris seems to have lost control of his environment and self-discipline at home and school and feels inadequate to change.

3. No male image is present with which Chris can identify.

4. Chris feels he is no longer a part of his family. In addition, he may be assuming guilt for parents' divorce and feeling an excessive fear for (a) loss of his parental support system, and (b) his father's ill health.

Plan for Intervention: First Session
  A. Primary Goal
    1. To establish rapport with the client.
  B. Secondary Goal
    1. To explain the nature of a counseling relationship.
  C. Objectives
    1. Client and counselor will mutually self-disclose at a superficial level.
    2. Client and counselor will discuss things they would like to talk about in future sessions.
    3. Client will identify necessary conditions for a helping relationship.
    4. Client and counselor will discuss the necessary conditions of a helping relationship.
  D. Strategies/Activities
    1. Counselor and client talk about what they like to do after work and after school.
    2. Counselor and client write separate lists of things they want to talk about in the future. They take turns disclosing and briefly discussing items on their lists.
    3. Counselor asks client to think of a deep secret—something the client has not told anyone about himself. Counselor asks client, "What would it take for you to share your secret with me?"
    4. Necessary conditions—trust, acceptance, and confidentiality— are emphasized by writing them on a chalkboard. Other concepts that emerge are also included.
  E . Evaluation
    The client was eager to talk and take part in the counseling experience. He had a limited perspective of the role of a counselor and counseling relationship. He seemed pleased to realize I would listen to his thoughts and feelings although he experienced difficulty in identifying feelings. A typical response was, "I don't know. I guess so." As expected, Chris's list of items to talk about included his parents, divorce, one teacher, and school.
    Chris expressed concern regarding his relationship with adults.

He stated. "They make me nervous because they always judge me
and tell me what to do."

The case example of Chris will be continued in Chapter 2, Child-
Centered Counseling. The remainder of this chapter includes recommended
resources, a brief summary, references, and recommended readings.

RECOMMENDED RESOURCES

AMERICAN PSYCHIATRIC ASSOCIATION. *Diagnostic and Statistics Manual of Mental
Disorders.* (3rd ed.) Washington, DC: APA, 1980.

This manual is designed to assist professional counselors in clinical or
research work. The multiaxial system helps the user to make principal and
secondary diagnoses by providing diagnostic criteria and guides which indicate various levels of diagnostic certainty.

ILG, F. & AMES, L. *Child behavior.* New York: Harper & Row, 1955.

This book focuses on understanding the growth of children. It emphasizes the impact of a child's culture (home, school, and community) on
the development of personality. While exploring children's attitudes,
thoughts, and feelings, the book deals with the ages and stages of child
growth and behavior.

MAXIM, G. *The very young: Guiding children from infancy through the early
years.* Belmont, CA: Wadsworth, 1980.

This book covers the early childhood years from infancy through
kindergarten. Since the topic of infant care is a vital one, the information
and practical examples should help illustrate the developmental needs of
children as they progress through the age of 6.

Physicians' Desk Reference. (36th Ed.) Litton Industries, Inc., Medical
Economics Company, Oradell, NJ 07649, 1982.

The PDR is published annually with the cooperation of drug
manufacturers whose products are described in the product information
and diagnostic products information section. It is intended primarily for
physicians. The PDR's purpose is to make available essential prescription
information on major pharmaceutical products.

SUMMARY

This chapter on child development and counseling began with an introduction and rationale for counselors of children in today's society. The second section of the chapter described the key concepts of developmental

counseling, personality theory and child development, diet and nutrition, and children's illnesses, including discussion on drug and diet therapies. A third section focused on initial counseling considerations which included the four elements: intake interview, a child-centered counseling approach, client assessment, and the individual counseling plan for intervention. The fourth section contained a case example and the last part provided readers with recommended resources.

REFERENCE AND RECOMMENDED READINGS

BLOCHER, D. *Developmental counseling*. New York: Ronald Press, 1966.

DINKMEYER, D. Developmental counseling in the elementary school. *Personnel and Guidance Journal*, 1966, 45, 262–266.

ELEMENTARY SCHOOL GUIDANCE and COUNSELING INCENTIVE ACT HEARING. Ninety-seventh Congress, First Session on H.R. 1598, Washington, D.C., April 9. U.S. Government Printing Office, 1981.

ELKIND, D. Why children need time. *Parade*, January 10, 1982, 16–19.

———. *The hurried child*. New York: Addison-Wesley Publishing Co., 1982.

ERIKSON, E. *Childhood and society*. New York: W. W. Norton, 1950.

FAUST, V. *The counselor-consultant in the elementary school*. Boston: Houghton-Mifflin, 1968..

FEINGOLD, B. *Why your child is hyperactive*. New York: Random House, 1974.

FRANK, L., SIMONS, P., ABRAMSON, P. & ZABARSKY, M. The children of divorce. *Newsweek*, New York, February 11, 1980, 58.

FREDERICKS, C. *Psycho-nutrition*. New York: Grossett & Dunlap, 1976.

GOODWIN, D. Child abuse—our silent epidemic. *Parade*, September 16, 1979, 8–9.

HAVIGHURST, R. *Developmental tasks and education*. New York: David McKay, 1972.

HERSHENSON, D. A formulation of counseling based on the healthy personality. *Personnel and Guidance Journal*, 60, 1982, 406–409.

MASLOW, A. *Toward a psychology of being*. New York: Van Nostrand, 1968.

PEARSON, J. & LONG, T. Counselors, nutrition, and mental health. *Personnel and Guidance Journal*, 60, 1982, 389–392.

RAPP, D. *Allergies and the hyperactive child*. New York: Sovereign Books, 1979.

STEINHAUER, P., MUSHIN, D., & RAE-GRANT, Q. Psychological aspects of chronic illness. In Bain, H. (Ed.) *The pediatric clinics of North America*. Philadelphia: W. B. Saunders, 1974, 825–840.

TOFFLER, A. *Future shock*. New York: Bantam Books, 1970.

Chapter 2

Child-Centered Counseling

IN OUR LIFETIME most of us have experienced one of four different types of parents: the punitive parent, the do-nothing parent, the indifferent parent, and the person-centered parent. The punitive parent believes in an authoritarian approach for working with children, and prefers to use punishment as the primary method to achieve desired behavior change in children. This type of parent can be either physically or psychologically punishing. A physically punishing parent will never "spare the rod and spoil the child" but will readily administer a spanking for misbehavior. This adult behavior becomes understandable when you realize that we tend to mimic our parents' behaviors in our parenting behavior patterns and that approximately 90 percent of today's parents were raised by parents who believed in spanking, were therefore spanked, and now spank their children. An even more popular way for parents to punish is verbally. Words are easy to administer and, when spoken in anger or frustration such as sarcasm or to ridicule, they can be psychologically damaging over time. When faced with a choice, children prefer physical punishment over psychological. Physical pain for a short time is easier to accept and to endure than guilt.

The do-nothing parent has a permissive attitude and philosophizes that "everything will turn out all right." These parents believe that children learn to cope and become responsible citizens on their own. When confronted with evidence to the contrary, these parents will often respond by saying, "What can I do?" Then, when a suggestion is made by another person to help, do-nothing parents respond with, "Yes, but . . ." No matter how hard you work with them or how creative your ideas, they will always defend against becoming involved with their children. Do-nothing parents always seem to have excuses and rationalizations for not implementing a suggestion. Yet, do not be misled by the apparent apathy of these parents. They often love their children but feel helpless or are afraid to intervene on their behalf.

On the other hand, indifferent parents avoid interactions with their children because they do not care. These parents are cold individuals who provide no warmth, love, or other expression of interpersonal relationship with their children.

A person-centered parent is interested in the total child. This type parent communicates an interest in the child's thoughts and feelings to increase understanding of the child. Person-centered parents are therefore sensitive to their child's developing perceptions of self and they assume responsibility for helping to develop and shape the child's self-esteem. Person-centered parents are also humanistic and avoid physical and psychological punishment as methods of discipline. They avoid aggression (spanking children) because it teaches children that hitting is an appropriate manner to get what they want, and they eschew sarcasm and ridicule because children learn to mimic this kind of inappropriate verbal behavior in their interpersonal relationships. Rather, person-centered parents attempt to be democratic in disciplining children by respecting the child as a person, attending and listening to what the child is saying, and responding to the child's thoughts and feelings to indicate they have been heard. Yet, this type of parent is firm without dominating and consistent when disciplining children. Such a parent attempts to create an environment in which children will experience the natural and logical consequences of their actions. In Chapter 6 of their book *Children: The Challenge* Dreikurs and Soltz (1964) discuss the theory and application of natural and logical consequences.

Stated in simple terms, natural consequences are the unpleasant physiological processes children suffer as a direct result of a behavior. For example, a young boy I counseled recently decided to remain awake and watch Monday Night Football in its entirety. He overslept on Tuesday, missed his bus, and mother drove him to school. A natural consequence of a later bedtime is less sleep. Mother bought him an alarm clock and made sure it was set each Monday evening to provide plenty of time for her son to be ready for school on Tuesday morning. After two successive weeks of being awakened early and missing sleep, this boy returned to his previous 10 p.m. bedtime. Logical consequences will occur when adults cease to interfere following an undesired child behavior. My 3-year-old son, Jeff, used to dawdle at the breakfast table on weekends. He wanted to carry on a long conversation with mother and father without eating at a constant rate. As a result, we were finished with breakfast and he had barely begun.

Upon examining our behavior, my wife and I realized we were reinforcing his discussion by listening after we had finished eating and remaining seated until he was finished. Once we decided to begin our weekend activities, always in another room or outside the house, immediately upon completing our breakfast, the logical consequence of Jeff being alone with an unfinished meal began. His choices were to: (1) suffer the consequence and eat cold food alone, (2) eat more rapidly and finish with us, or (3) not eat, which would then initiate a natural consequence, hunger, later.

Over the last quarter of a century, person-centered parenting techniques have been popularized by other humanistic authors such as Haim Ginott (1965, 1969, 1972) and Thomas Gordon (1970, 1974) who developed their ideas from the self theory, client-centered, person-centered therapy of Carl Rogers. Rogers stated, "As it has moved into a wide variety of fields . . . marriage, family relationships, . . . it seems best to adopt as broad a term as possible: person-centered" (1977, p. 5). As the theory and principles of person-centered therapy are adapted and applied to children, child-centered counseling is practiced.

KEY CONCEPTS

Carl Rogers's theory of personality began to be formulated in his work as a therapist while on the staff at the Rochester Child Guidance Center, Minnesota, in the late 1930s. Rogers continued to develop and refine his theory through research at the University of Chicago and the University of Wisconsin from 1945 until 1964, when he moved to the Western Behavioral Sciences Institute in La Jolla, California. Although Rogers's self theory is heavily influenced by the writings of theorists Otto Rank (one of Freud's inner circle of psychoanlysists who later broke with Freud), Snygg and Combs' organismic theory including the phenomenal self, and Sullivan's interpersonal relations theory, most of Rogers's theoretical understanding evolved from his personal therapeutic experiences with clients. "But most of all it has meant a continual learning from my own experience and that of my colleagues at the Counseling Center as we have endeavored to discover for ourselves effective means of working with people in distress" (Rogers, 1961, p. 32). Three main components of personality are emphasized in Rogers' original theory: the organism, the phenomenal field, and the self.

The Organism

According to Rogers (1951), the organism is the whole person. The organism interacts at all times with the phenomenal field and is ". . .a total organized system in which alteration of any part may produce changes in any other part" (p. 487). The organism, therefore, consists of a person's self-perceptions including thoughts, feelings, and behaviors. The organism's primary goal is to act as a total entity to satisfy its needs, and its basic motivation is toward ". . .striving—to actualize, maintain, and enhance the experiencing organism" (p. 487).

Phenomenal Field

Phenomenal field consists of everything experienced by the organism. Experiences include everything happening within the organism at a given time, including perceptions, thoughts, feelings, and behaviors. As the organism reacts as a whole to the environment, it has the capacity to ignore these experiences or to symbolize them in the conscious or unconscious. Most experiences which are symbolized in the unconscious of the organism can be brought to the conscious if necessary. Emotions as a part of experiences accompany all behavior. The intensity of feelings generated relates directly to the perceived significance of the behavior toward maintaining and enhancing the organism. Behavior, then, is ". . .the goal-directed attempt of the organism to satisfy its needs as experienced, in the field as perceived" (p. 491). Whatever a person perceives in the phenomenal field then assumes primary importance and not the actual reality of events. Thus, reality is determined on a subjective, individual basis. However, Rogers believes individuals do tend to check their perceived experiences against how the world really exists so they can behave realistically. As a result of interaction with the environment, a part of the organisms' perceptions of the world are gradually separated into "the self."

The Self

The differentiated part of the phenomenal field known as self develops from the persons' ". . . evaluational interactions with others . . . ." (1951, p. 498). As a result of how others perceive a child's behavior and react to it a concept of "I" or "me" is formed. These experiences are assigned either positive or negative value. The self, then, is structured as an ". . . organized picture, existing in awareness either as figure (i.e., clear consciousness) or ground (i.e., hazy consciousness or unconsciousness), of the self and the self-in-relationship (to the environment), together with the positive or negative values which are associated with those qualities and relationships, as they are perceived as existing in the past, present, or future" (p. 501).

Rogers continues by defining "psychological adjustment" as the organism's ability to assimilate experiences symbolically into a consistent relationship with self-concept, and "psychological maladjustment" as the organism's denial of these experiences which then do not become a part of the self. One who accepts the three main tenets of Rogers' theory then to produce desired client behavioral change should require first that changes in the client's self-concept occur. This is exactly what Rogers' person-centered therapy attempts to do. It focuses first on the person, not on the person's problem. The aim of child-centered therapy is to help children perceive themselves accurately and positively in the growth process so that they can solve current problems, cope wtih past experiences, and face future life concerns.

Child and Therapist Relationship

According to Rogers (1961), it is significant learning in psychotherapy which influences the client's immediate behavior, future actions, attitudes, and personality. Person-centered counseling, therefore, promotes learning as follows:

- The person comes to see himself differently.
- He accepts himself and his feelings more fully.
- He becomes more self-confident and self-directing.
- He becomes more the person he would like to be.
- He becomes more flexible, less rigid, in his perceptions.
- He adopts more realistic goals for himself.
- He behaves in a more mature fashion.
- He changes his maladjustive behaviors, even such a long-established one as chronic alcoholism.
- He becomes more acceptant of others.
- He becomes more open to the evidence, both to what is going on outside of himself, and to what is going on inside of himself.
- He changes in his basic personality characteristics, in constructive ways. (pp. 280–281)

It is the child and therapist relationship, then, which facilitates learning in psychotherapy. For Rogers, a therapeutic relationship exists when five conditions are met:

- The client perceives himself as faced by a serious and meaningful problem
- The therapist is a congruent person in the relationship, able to be the person he is
- The therapist feels an unconditional positive regard for the client
- The therapist experiences an accurate empathic understanding of the client's private world and communicates this
- When the client to some degree experiences the therapist's congruence, acceptance, and empathy (p. 285)

According to Rogers, both the client and therapist are influenced by the relationship. As the relationship develops and the client experiences the therapist's congruence, unconditional positive regard, and accurate empathy, mutual growth and change occur. These three essential therapeutic conditions form the core of the therapeutic relationship.

Congruence

Congruence refers to the therapist's ability to be real or genuine. When congruent, therapist's behaviors, both nonverbal and verbal, are consistent with their feelings. If therapists project this authentic, honest characteristic without presenting a facade, then they will become free to openly express their feelings and attitudes with children. To facilitate an honest and open communication with a client, it is necessary for the therapist to model therapeutic behavior including the expression of both positive and negative feelings. When counseling with children, it may be necessary for the therapist not only to model the expression of feelings but also to teach children feeling words to expand their ability to describe emotions accurately.

Congruence does not mean that the therapist must always express all feelings openly. Therapists must weigh the impact of their disclosures on clients and, depending on the situation and the readiness of the client to accept the information, gauge the degree of genuineness necessary to move the relationship in a therapeutic direction. However, the reader is cautioned that counseling will not progress satisfactorily if the counselor acts one way with the client but feels another way. For example, I supervised recently a graduate student in counseling who was experiencing difficulty in establishing a therapeutic relationship with her client. She described her client and the presenting problem in the following way: "Other kids don't like her and I can understand why. She has the worst case of body odor I've encountered." My response was, "You find her odor unattractive, even disgusting." Following several more minutes of discussion and my graduate student's acceptance of her personal revulsion toward her client, she stated, "Now I know what Gloria meant when she said I was like all the rest."

Unconditional Positive Regard

This counselor characteristic implies a deep and genuine caring for the child as a person. It is a nonjudgmental acceptance of the child's feelings, thoughts, and behaviors. In child-centered counseling, there exists no "good" or "bad" feelings, thoughts, and behaviors, and children are neither good or bad. Children are valued as persons and provided equal status in the relationship, and are given rights equivalent to an adult in therapy in terms of the application of professional ethics in counseling. The conditions of congruence and unconditional positive regard encourage children to freely express themselves in the relationship without risk of ridicule or threat of a diminished relationship.

Acceptance at this level implies children have a right to feel as they do. It does not imply that the counselor condones all behavior. On the contrary, some of a child's behaviors may be accepted while others are rejected. Although child-centered counselors may reject behavior as socially inappropriate or harmful to learning, they *never* reject the child. Unconditional positive regard also implies respect for the child's right to have a problem and respect for the child's capacity to deal successfully with it. Nothing hurts a child more than to have an adult regard a problem as unworthy of attention. A rule of thumb I follow in my counseling with children is that no problem is too small for consideration; expressed concerns deserve understanding.

Empathy

Empathy might be described as the counselor's ability to understand the client from the client's point of view, as if the counselor were in the "client's shoes." Empathic understanding of children requires therapists to relate with children at their developmental ability level. In many instances, the therapist demonstrates empathy by "getting down" physically to the child's level. This means the counselor does not maintain the traditional verbal patterns of interaction with the child but becomes involved in the child's world through play, art, music, books, and other similar sources of children's communication. Frequently, the therapist will interact with the child in counseling "on the floor."

In addition to nonverbal demonstrations of empathy, counselors demonstrate empathic understanding by consciously restructuring language used in communicating with children so as not to "talk over a child's head" or beyond a child's capacity to reason. Accurate empathic understanding requires the counselor to be with the child and to identify and to accurately respond to a child's feelings. However, it involves more than merely responding to the obvious, or surface level, emotions of children. It implies that the therapist can sense the underlying feelings of a child's innermost experiences. Then, as a result of this knowledge, the counselor can help the child to develop additional insight and understanding of self by reflecting these deep feelings.

Related Research on Rogerian Theory

One of the most admirable qualities of Carl Rogers was his insistence that his theory be exposed to rigorous and continuous tests of research so that it might be refined and improved. One of the major problems researchers had with Rogers's theory was that the essential conditions of the helping relationship (congruence, unconditional positive regard, and empathy) were not quantifiable, nor could they be isolated for study. However, two of Rogers's students, Robert Carkhuff and Charles Truax, in the early 1960s undertook an extensive review of research reporting results of therapeutic relationships. After analyzing the data, they discovered about one-third of the clients in therapy improved, approximately one-third remained the same with no improvement, and approximately one-third became less well mentally. In an attempt to define those factors present in the relationship that contributed to improved mental health, they then examined extensively only those cases in which improvement occurred. Truax and Carkhuff (1967) concluded that the conditions of genuineness, nonpossessive warmth, and accurate empathy could be measured both in terms of presence and degree and that persons who demonstrated these in the helping relationship were more effective in facilitating positive mental changes in clients.

BASIC TECHNIQUES

The Carkhuff Model

In his later works, Carkhuff (1969, 1980) described and refined a model for helping based upon the necessary conditions for establishing a therapeutic relationship first described by Rogers. He extended the original three conditions to four helper skills which could be taught: attending, responding, personalizing, and initiating. These skills are used by the therapist to assist the client to obtain the self goals of exploration, understanding, and action.

According to Carkhuff, the first goal of helping is *self-exploration*. The client must explore self in relation to self, important others, and the environment. Clients must identify and specify their problems before positive change can occur. It is the counselor's responsibility to create the conditions in therapy which facilitate the client's self-exploration and exploration of identified problems in detail. The skills of attending and responding assist the client to reach the goal of self-exploration. *Attending* as a skill includes subskills identified by Carkhuff as attending physically, observing, and listening. *Responding* also is subdivided in the more specific skill components of responding to content, responding to feeling, and responding to feelings and content. Carkhuff describes his helper skills as additive; that is, as each helper skill is used, it "builds upon the last skill" (1980, p. 21).

Carkhuff's second goal of helping is *self-understanding*. This goal involves clients' ability to integrate information about self so that they understand who and where they are as persons in the present and who and what they would like to be in the future. As a result, self-understanding involves a thorough examination of client's problems and feelings associated with each problem. This process assists the client and counselor to pinpoint the causal factors of the problem. The helper skills used to achieve this level of self-understanding are what makes personalizing possible. *Personalizing* is the activity in which the helper seeks to ". . . go beyond the helpee and understand the meaning of the situation and the helpee's personal deficits. . . . Content only becomes meaningful when it is personalized for the helpee. . . . When we personalize, the helpee will come to experience [self] more accurately in the area of [personal] concern" (1980, p. 123). According to Carkhuff, personalizing consists of five subskills: building a base for personalizing, personalizing the meaning, personalizing the problem, personalizing the feeling, and personalizing the goal.

Action is the final helpee goal in the Carkhuff Model and is accomplished by the client with the assistance of initiating skills of the helper. The counselor assists the client by initiating: an operationalized goal, steps toward goal accomplishment, a schedule, and reinforcements for goal attainment.

In addition to the skills of attending, responding, personalizing, and initiating described in Carkhuff's model, other specific skills for training counselors in a systematic, person-centered fashion have been identified and described by Carkhuff (1969), Gazda (1973), Ivey and Authier (1978), and Egan (1982). These experts extend Rogers's theory to include core counseling dimensions of basic empathy with additive and advanced levels of empathy, respect, concreteness, counselor self-disclosure, confrontation, and immediacy. Carkhuff (1969) in his original model and later Gazda (1973) assigned these dimensions to each of three helper phases: facilitation, transition, and action. The facilitation phase included empathy and respect; the transition phase contained concreteness and counselor self-disclosure; and the action phase embodied confrontation and immediacy. Although I do not subscribe totally to all of Rogers's theory or recent modifications to his theory, I have found the structure of these experts' thinking helpful in planning for child-centered counseling with children, monitoring their progress, and evaluating my work with them.

Child-Centered Counseling Model

There is only one therapeutic procedure in the person-centered therapy of Rogers, the establishment of a facilitative relationship which provides an atmosphere that encourages personal growth in the client. Therapeutic techniques are also constant throughout counseling. They consist of the communication of the essential conditions mentioned previously by the therapist: genuineness, unconditional positive regard, and empathy. Once therapists provide these essential conditions and clients allow themselves to experience them, a natural therapeutic process ensues which leads to client growth. However, when counseling children in the schools, counselors are not provided the luxury of unlimited time with clients. Counselors can not afford to wait for children to experience therapy naturally or allow therapy to take its course. An overwhelming caseload and the need to speed up the personal growth process in children, so they can begin to cope in class more readily and to learn in this environment, forces counselors to adapt the person-centered counseling process to a child-centered approach in which they become active/directive participants, who provide more structure and direction for therapy. As a result, counselors must assume greater responsibility for facilitating the relationship, overcoming resistance, identifying basic problems, and encouraging specific courses of client action.

Facilitation Phase

Although an increasing number of child clients are self-referred, experience has demonstrated that most children are "other" referred for counseling. Parents, teachers, judges, social workers, probation officers, and physicians represent only a few of the adult populations who have responsibility for the lives of children and who refer children for mental health counseling services. In the referral process, these adults are saying, "This child has a problem." Therefore, it is not unusual to discover in the intake interview that many children do not perceive themselves to have a problem they need help with. It becomes crucial in child-centered counseling, then, that the therapist model initially a "oneness" with the child and a sense of comfort, relaxation, and well-being in the office. If a referring adult is present, the therapist must focus first on the child by asking for the child's perceptions of counseling and the reason for referral before seeking the adult's opinion. In many instances with very young children, after taking a few minutes to make "contact," I encourage them to explore the room and play with available media while I discuss the situation with the adult present.

Following the intake interview, I never grant the referring adult equal status to the child in counseling. The child is allowed total access to me and my time during therapy. No one is more important than the child, and I tolerate no interruptions of my attending to the child from adults. In schools and many homes, adults feel they have a right to interrupt children in their activities while refusing to reciprocate this behavior with children, no matter the concern. A child-centered attitude helps a potentially reluctant child who is unaware of personal life problems to accept and want to attend therapy if for no other reason than, and I quote a former client of mine, "In here I'm number one. No one bugs me or tells me what to do." The differences in the attitudes of the child-centered therapist and in the atmosphere of a child-centered counseling office instill a feeling of temporary relief and reduce the everyday pressures of the child's world. Once the child accepts refuge with the therapist in the counseling office, therapy has begun.

To encourage and maintain "oneness" with the child, it is necessary for the child-centered counselor to consciously demonstrate the core conditions of empathy, respect, and warmth in the first session and throughout the time the child remains in counseling. These conditions become apparent to the client through the attitudes of the counselor and the nonverbal and verbal interactions between the child and the therapist. The attitudes and nonverbal behavior of the counselor have been emphasized in this chapter. Nonverbal interactions are discussed further in Chapter 5, "Developmental Play." Therefore, the remainder of this chapter will emphasize child-centered responding skills. Table 2–1 depicts the child-centered phases of counseling, including goals for the counselor and the client, while focusing on the responding skills to be demonstrated in each phase by the therapist.

While facilitating the development of the therapeutic relationship by attending and listening to the child in counseling, the counselor recognizes that initially a strong defensive posture by the child prevents exposure of deep feelings too soon. In the early stages of therapy, children disclose their "public" self or that role which they exhibit every day with most people. An intellectual, social, or conversational air exists which appears superficial in nature. As a result, the counselor must begin to demonstrate empathy by *responding to feelings* that are expressed overtly.

To attempt to move a child to a deeper level of self-disclosure in the facilitation phase may increase client anxiety to the point that the child may fear to move further. Self-disclosures that typify children in this phase deal with "things" in their lives, or hobbies and interests they may have. For example, many children will discuss their school activities, both academic and extracurricular (such as sports or dance). Younger children will talk about favorite television series or characters, and some children may not talk at all. In any case, an accurate response to feeling conveys to children that you are attending and listening to their feelings and understanding their situation as it appears to them. Once a response to feeling has been made, pause a moment and allow the impact of the response to be assimilated by the child. My experience has been that many children in need have not experienced this level of caring and interest by adults. They will find a feeling response unique and, at first, be suspicious, but in a short time, they will value highly this sensitive, caring com-

Table 2-1
PHASES, GOALS, AND RESPONDING SKILLS IN THE COUNSELING PROCESS

Phases	Facilitation	Transition	Action
Counselor goals	Build therapeutic relationship Overcome resistance to counseling	Monitor client anxiety experienced in self-exploration and self-development Encourage further open exploration of client's life and problems Assist client to identify several personal areas of concern	Assist client to identify and act on specific personal problem or area of personal growth
Client goals	Develop self-awareness of counseling need Begin self-exploration Self-disclose (at public level)	Continue self exploration Self-disclose (at intermediate and deep levels) Develop self-understanding Develop commitment to change	Implement a specific course of action to help self
Basic counselor responding skills	Respond to expressed feeling Be silent Clarify content in session Use open questions Support/encourage client behavior that enhances therapy Summarize significant content and feelings of session	Respond to intermediate-level and deep-level feelings Provide interpretation of content and feelings to aid client insight into self Provide counselor self-disclosure to support client; move client from an intermediate, affective level to deep level; or move client into action stage Use closed questions to assist client in probing a specific problem Personalize content and feelings to assist client self-understanding and ownership of problems	Respond to "immediacy" or "here and now" of counseling Share personal feelings with client about self in the relationship Confront client behavior Initiate client action by encouraging problem identification, discussing alternatives and consequences to courses of action, selecting "best" plan of action, and planning action Provide appropriate advice

Note: Once begun, all goals and responding skills are continued through each phase of counseling.

40

munication by the counselor. Often early in training, students ask, "But, what if I'm wrong? What if I pick the wrong adjective to describe the feeling?" I have often missed a feeling. However, children usually say to me, "No, that's not it!" and go on talking about a situation in an attempt to help me better understand. At the very least, children accept my response attempt because they know that by my response I am *trying* to understand them.

Being silent can also be an effective way for a therapist to respond while attending to the child. Silence can mean to the child that the therapist is listening and is desiring to hear more. It also indicates to children the child-centered patient attitude of the therapist who is willing to wait and allow children the necessary time to collect their thoughts and put them into their own words. Remember, children are not used to these considerations. Silence can also be used to motivate children in counseling to deeper levels of thought and feeling. I have found that sometimes a child uses verbal skills to escape self-examination. Such a child is most comfortable when conversing with the counselor in an ongoing fashion. When I interrupt this direction with silence, I discontinue my reinforcing behavior and imply to the child that I do not approve of the discussion and direction of counseling. A mild anxiety is then created in the therapeutic situation which may motivate the child to change courses and often moves the child to deeper levels of thinking, feeling, and self-disclosure.

Preventing children from defending through intellectualizations can be difficult while attempting to demonstrate empathic understanding. Yet, equally problematic is encouraging nonverbal or reluctant children to disclose more of themselves. *Clarification* is a responding skill that demonstrates the counselor's desire to understand the child's situation. It can also be used to assist children to make sense out of their world by providing them with a new picture or different view of what is happening to them from the therapist's perspective. Clarification is not mere restatement of content or mechanical, rote "parroting" of children's words. It involves the therapist's listening beyond the child's statement. A clarification statement involves paraphrasing of what the child has said and, in the case of play therapy or art therapy, what the child is doing. It requires that the counselor rework the significant material that has been heard or seen, and, using fresh words, present a statement to the child in an effort to simplify and to make sense out of a confusing situation. Like clarification, open questions can also help the counselor to overcome client resistance and assist the client to begin to self-explore.

Open questions are used to direct the client to provide more information about a particular area of concern or interest to the counselor. An open question implies to the child that the material being discussed or worked on is important and conveys the counselor's respect for the child's thoughts and behaviors. It may also indicate to the child that if a particular area being discussed is delved into more deeply, the child will benefit from the self-exploration. Open questions, unlike closed questions, encourage children to provide more than a one-word (yes or no) response. These questions begin with the words *what, how, when, where,* and *who* and are typically used by investigative reporters and detectives in their work when they are trying to obtain information from an unknowing, frequently unwilling, person.

A word of caution to the reader. Although open questions can provide a valuable responding skill, when used repeatedly, they can create defensive posturing in the client. No one appreciates being "grilled" by another person. In fact, children who tire of the questioning process may begin to pick up on the direction of what the "overuser" wants to hear and begin to merely provide the counselor with inaccurate information to satisfy the counselor's need.

All of us can relate to the stage children encounter between the ages 2 and 4 when they ask the questions "Why do we need to keep milk cold?" "Why does the refrigerator keep food cold?" "Why do we have to warm up cold food?" At this stage, children ask these why questions repeatedly and no answer is sufficient to satisfy the child's need for information and curiosity. Eventually, after responding to several why questions, Mom or Dad will say angrily, "It's just because I said so." "I don't know why." Well, in the case of children, very often they do not understand why they behave the way they do. If counselors ask why questions, they imply children have the ability and understanding to provide reasons for their behavior and that they can make cause and effect mental associations. The information that can be obtained is not worth the risk. As in the case with Mom and Dad above, why questions can create negative affect and defensive posturing in clients, and, when used by counselors repeatedly, can lead to partial truths and even totally false statements by children under stress. In effect, when using why questions, therapists practice self-defeating behavior by encouraging movement in children toward a fictitious world and away from reality. It is my opinion that why questions should be eliminated from counselors' vocabulary. It is much better to simply change the why question to an open question to get the desired results.

Encouragement is the fifth responding skill introduced in the facilitation phase. Encouragement is intended to support and reinforce positively children's behavior in therapy. It can instill feelings of worth, power, and control in children and can imply to them that they are behaving successfully. All children need to experience success in some parts of their lives. However, counselors must avoid using encouragement inappropriately and, therefore, reinforce behavior that is antithetical to therapy. For example, children often "storytell" when stressed. The frequency and duration of storytelling by child clients is often increased by therapists' inappropriate reinforcement.

Near the end of every counseling session, I *summarize* what has occurred. To summarize, I must organize, analyze, and synthesize the significant points of therapy. This summary statement includes a skillful presentation of the highlights of the session and is an attempt to help the child hear, one last time before getting ready to exit, those salient points of content and feelings expressed. To be most effective, the summary needs to be brief, provide pertinent feedback to the client, be encouraging, and indicate what the child might expect in the next session.

Transition Phase

When entering the transition phase, the counselor makes the assumption that the therapeutic relationship has begun, the child is amenable to counseling (no longer resistant), and rapport between therapist and client has reached a level whereby the child can tolerate greater levels of anxiety. The counselor gently guides the child toward recognizing the need to continue self-exploration at deeper levels. After thoroughly discussing the presenting problem, the counselor may suggest it is only symptomatic of greater underlying concerns. The therapist's role is to assist clients to consider and discuss as many personal problems in depth as they perceive and introduce areas of concern not evident to the client. A result of thorough self-exploration is that children become self-aware and gain self-understanding which is preparatory to a commitment to change. Child-centered counselors become more directive and evaluative in the transition phase as they help children define their problems and accept responsibility for their lives. Activities may be initiated which assist children to self-disclose at intermediate and deep levels.

Intermediate level self-disclosure occurs when the client ceases to discuss superficial (public) matters and begins to share information in therapy related to important other persons in life (parents, siblings, friends, teachers, other family members like grandparents, aunts, and uncles). With children, I also include discussion of pets in this category. Many children develop a close bond with their pet, and this tie may be equal to or even stronger than those established with friends or family. When counselors respond to feelings children experience in relation to important others in their lives, they are responding to *intermediate-level feelings*.

Deep-level self-disclosure occurs when children expose underlying feelings related directly to the self and examine openly the impact of these feelings on themselves and other people. An example might be a child who says, "I get angry anytime I get accused of things I didn't do." The therapist might respond to this *deep-level feeling* by saying, "You become furious with those who blame you unjustly." Deep-level self-disclosure often includes feelings associated with personal inadequacy or phobic reactions. More often than not, children experience difficulty disclosing at this level and counselors must assist them to recognize defensive statements (like "Dad doesn't love me. All he cares about is work, work, work!") by *interpreting content and feeling* to help children develop insight in a situation. For example, "You love your father a great deal. It hurts deeply when he's away so much."

Interpretation can be a significant response in the skilled counselor's repertoire. Therapists use interpretive responses to assist children to develop insight into themselves, their feelings and behaviors, and their problems. Interpretive statements can help children make connections between past events and feelings and present thoughts and behaviors. These responses are one way to assist the child to go beyond the mere words of what is said and explain or shed light on events in the child's life as they have occurred. It is extremely important that children develop self-understanding in the transition phase so that they can make a commitment to positive personal change in their lives. Interpretive statements imply to children issues that they ought to consider carefully for self-exploration and self-understanding. One very positive use of interpretation in therapy occurs when the counselor points out the impact of children's feelings on their behavior and how their behavior then impacts upon the lives of important other persons in their world. For example, A 13-year-old girl was failing all but one of her subjects in spite of the fact she had been identified to have superior ability. After several counseling sessions, it was interpreted that she felt rejected by her father and afraid of failing when compared by her father to her older brother and sister who were in college (his alma mater) performing very successfully. Her father had pressured her to achieve so she, too, might enjoy the benefits of this college education. It was suggested to the client that she felt pushed by her father to do something she was not ready to do or did not want to do and that her father was really satisfying his own needs, not hers. Let us continue to follow this interpretation through the client and counselor dialogue.

> *Cl:* Yes, it makes me so mad. I try to tell him how I feel but he won't listen.
> *Co:* You have many unpleasant feelings associated with Dad right now. You may want to get even just to show him once and for all you are not like your brother and sister.
> *Cl:* What do you mean? Get even!
> *Co:* Oh! I wondered if you had thought of the possibility that you might be failing in school so you wouldn't have to go to Dad's college. He has to listen to poor grades.
> *Cl:* (Silent. Pensive look on her face.)
> *Co:* You must understand that, if what I'm saying is true, you are hurting Dad but you are hurting yourself more.
> *Cl:* I know I could do better but what's the use.

Fortunately in this case, counseling continued to the point whereby this young girl initiated a conference between herself, her father, and the counselor. With the therapist's help, she was able to convince her father that she was an individual who wanted to lead a different life than her older siblings and that she was capable of making her own decisions about college when the time came.

Although interpretive statements can be very helpful to the child-centered counselor, they can also be used inappropriately. Some suggestions I would make to avoid inappropriate use are:

1. Before interpreting, make sure you have established the therapeutic relationship.
2. Never interpret too soon. Be sure you have enough information on the client and the problem situation so that the interpretation is not guesswork but an educated act intended to help.
3. When interpreting, avoid projecting your own values, attitudes, and feelings onto the child.

Like interpretation, *counselor self-disclosure* can move therapy in a positive direction by opening therapeutic channels of communication. In a reciprocal learning experience like child-centered counseling, the level of counselor self-disclosure is as important as that of client self-disclosure. Appropriate counselor self-disclosures are responses which provide factual information about the counselor's past experiences. Counselor self-disclosure must relate directly to the client's self or problems and be intended to enhance therapy.

Some of the positive aspects of counselor self-disclosure used appropriately are: (a) serve as a model for the client and increase the amount of client self-disclosure; (b) encourage the client to self-disclose at deeper personal levels; (c) reinforce the client to remain in and continue working at a deep personal level; and (d) cement the therapeutic relationship and the client's commitment to change. Therapist self-disclosure can be tremendously enlightening for children to learn that adults have experienced similar concerns and encouraging for children to know that problems like their own have been solved by other persons. Counselor self-disclosure therefore can help children associate their life experiences with those experiences of a valued adult and learn indirectly from it. However, as with interpretation, I feel it is necessary to make some suggestions on how to use this skill:

1. Avoid using counselor self-disclosure in the facilitation phase. This response may increase anxiety in the client thus increasing resistance.

2. Use the response sparingly. If used to excess, it can shift the focus of therapy from the client to the counselor and create excessive concern and anxiety in the child.
3. Remember also that the more time spent by the therapist on self-disclosure decreases time for the child to respond. Keep it brief.
4. Avoid implying to children through self-disclosure how they should or ought to behave because it worked for you. Be sure to allow the child to decide.

In the facilitation phase, I discussed the open question as a response used to encourage the client to elaborate on an area of concern. The *closed question* can also be an effective counselor response when used in the transition phase to concretize or "hone in" on a specific problem. While the open question facilitates development of the client's problem in any direction the child wishes, the closed question implies that the counselor needs immediate, specific information to be helpful or to continue a specific direction in therapy. For example, many states require by law that counselors report all suspected incidents of child abuse. Aside from the ethical issues inherent in this situation, therapists often need simple yes or no replies from children to make these critical decisions. Closed questions such as "Did your father hit you with the belt buckle?" "Are there any welts and bruises where he hit you?" get the job done efficiently. The reason this responding skill is not introduced earlier in therapy is that material which would require probing in this way is usually not exposed until after a therapeutic relationship has been established.

Because the skill of *personalizing* involves being able to respond to intermediate and deep feelings and interpretation, it is necessary for counselors to be competent in their use first. Personalizing often occurs in conjunction with responses to feeling and interpretation. It requires that the therapist relate the meaning of what children say or do in therapy to their lives outside the counseling room. When personalizing, the counselor is helping the child explore and understand the problem from the perspectives of all persons' who are involved in the situation while assisting the child to take ownership of the problem. As the counselor and the child search for and explore feelings and behaviors of other participants in a problem, the counselor associates these to the child's own world and makes explicit the impact of the child's feelings and actions on these other people. As a result, the therapist is helping the child to recognize his or her role in the problem. Once the child understands what that role is, he or she will gain control over the problem. Oftentimes, a child's commitment to change directly follows this level of awareness and understanding. In the previous dialogue describing interpretation, the counselor was also personalizing with the client in relation to her father.

Many responding skills of the facilitation phase and the transition phase are demonstrated in the following audiotaped excerpt of the fourth counseling session with a 12-year-old girl experiencing separation anxiety resulting from a recent family relocation.

Responses	*Dialogue*
	Cl: (Intermediate level self-disclosure) I wish I could see my old friends. Sometimes it seems like I've never been there and I feel I'd never be back again.
SUPPORTING	Co: Un huh!
	Cl: I always thought we might move back one day. I don't think we will, but I wish we would.
CLARIFYING RESPONDING TO SURFACE FEELING	Co: Friends are important to you. Yet, it seems futile, even hopeless, to you to hang onto the thought of returning.
	Cl: Yeah! But you know I really wish I could move back to Florida cause I feel like Florida is my home. I just like it there. I just feel good when I'm there. My best friend is in Florida.
SUPPORTING ENCOURAGING USING OPEN QUESTION	Co: Un huh! Go on. I'm interested in what you have to say about Florida. How is it different from here?
	Cl: (Rapidly) Florida has always been a secure place for me. I don't feel safe in Richmond.
BEING SILENT	Co: (About 10 seconds pass.)
	Cl: I live in a very safe neighborhood, but I'm afraid to go outdoors. Especially at night, I can't see things. In Florida I couldn't see things, but it didn't bother me. I didn't look on the bad side of things.
BEING SILENT	Co: (Several seconds pass.)
	Cl: I was very happy. My grandmother is there and things were in place.
RESPONDING TO SURFACE FEELINGS CLARIFYING	Co: You're uncomfortable in Richmond. It's confusing here and nothing seems to be in place. You really want to be settled and feel like you're a part of something.
	Cl: Yeah! Some people feel they are superior here. One of my new friends was invited to a party and I didn't get invited. Some people just look down on new folks.

Responses	*Dialogue*	
USING OPEN QUESTION	Co:	What do you mean by looking down on you?
	Cl:	You know. They just look down on you because they don't think you're good enough. They think they're better than you.
BEING SILENT	Co:	(About 20 seconds pass.)
	Cl:	It's like I'm a new kid and everybody is checking me out. I'm ignored. Once my new friend Tammy came over to me and Sherry. We were at the lunch table. She says, Hello Sherry! and starts talking to Sherry just saying things; then, as she leaves she says, Oh, Hi Angela.
RESPONDING TO INTERMEDIATE AND DEEP-LEVEL FEELINGS	Co:	It's difficult to be accepted on equal terms in a new place. The experience with the girls sort of made you feel inadequate or rejected.
	Cl:	I've got mixed feelings now. I'm not totally unhappy now, but life could be better.
INTERPRETING CONTENT AND FEELINGS	Co:	Angela, it seems to me you are searching for a close friend in Richmond. Someone you could depend upon when things are going bad. Someone who will understand you when you need them. Moving from one place to another is painful. It destroys many close relationships, and it isn't easy to rebuild your life in a new place.
PERSONALIZING		
	Cl:	(Silence)
PERSONALIZING	Co:	You may even be afraid to try to make a close friend fearing you may move again.
	Cl:	(Silence, head down, playing with necklace)
USING CLOSED QUESTION	Co:	Are you afraid to allow yourself to initiate a deep friendship here?

Action Phase

Once the child has owned the problem and made a commitment to change, the counselor can enter the action phase by assisting the child to identify and to act on a *specific* personal problem. The responding skills of immediacy, confrontation, and initiation are all integral components of the therapist's verbal ability to assist children to implement a plan to help themselves. Gazda (1973) has defined immediacy as the counselor's ability to describe the relationship between the therapist and the client as it exists in the "here and now". A *response to immediacy* requires a straightforward, honest reply in which the counselor expresses his or her feeling for the client and the counseling issue at that moment in the relationship. It can also be a conscious, objective attempt by the therapist to help the client perceive and examine material which may be repressed in the unconscious. The following guidelines to help counselors respond more accurately to immediacy are summarized from those generated by Carkhuff (1969).

1. Counselors must examine objectively their experiences in the therapeutic interaction and voice these interpretations to overcome client resistance and defensive behavior.
2. Counselors must search beneath and beyond the content of clients' messages and focus on messages which are not available to the consciousness of the child.
3. Counselors must be able to judge whether or not an interaction that is "going nowhere" is the client's need for a momentary emotional reprieve or an effort by the client to sabotage therapy.
4. Counselors must make ongoing evaluations of the strength and movement of the therapeutic relationship.

It is possible that a response to immediacy may be perceived by the client and reacted to as if it were a confrontation. *Confrontation,* however, is a direct attempt by the therapist to point out discrepancies noticed in the therapeutic experience and not to describe it. Confrontation is helpful when the client: (1) contradicts something stated previously; (2) acts (nonverbally) in a way that contradicts what he or she is saying; or (3) discusses an experience falsely which the counselor knows to be untrue from personal experience. Students in training often resist learning how to give confrontation and frequently describe it as a negative learning experience. Because of the potential for confrontation to be perceived by the client as harmful, the reader is encouraged to remember that this response skill is recommended only for the action phase after the therapeutic relationship has been firmly established.

Gazda et al. (1977) suggested guidelines for understanding the intensity of confrontation and for giving confrontation. To make confrontation less intense and, therefore, less threatening for the client, the guidelines recommend that the counselor:

1. Establish a strong therapeutic relationship.
2. Precede the confrontation by responding to the client's feelings.

3. Generalize. Talk about people in general rather than the client specifically. This allows the client an opportunity to own the behavior first.
4. Provide "wiggleroom" by using such statements as: "I may be mistaken but didn't you say . . . ." and "It could be we misunderstood each other, but I thought you had agreed to . . . ."
5. Confront to be helpful. Counselors cannot justify confrontation to punish or to harm.
6. Model the behaviors you want the client to learn.

To increase the intensity of confrontation, Gazda et al. (1977) advises the counselor to:

1. Personalize. Make certain children understand you are talking about them and their specific behavior.
2. Specify. Be accurate and concrete in your description of what has occurred. This forces the child to either own the behavior or reject the confrontation.
3. Use confrontation with immediacy. Confronting a current behavior is more powerful than past behaviors.

In addition to Gazda's suggestions, I offer the following recommendations for counselors to consider when using confrontation:

1. Earn the right to confront by demonstrating the necessary conditions of the therapeutic relationship before you confront.
2. Confront to demonstrate you care, want to be involved, and that you desire to help.
3. Confront yourself first. Be aware of your bias and prejudice.
4. Proportion the strength of the confrontation to the needs, sensitivities, and abilities of the child.
5. Confront only behavior that the child has the ability to change.
6. Be prepared for defensive behavior from the child who is confronted.
7. Be open to confrontation in return from the child who has been confronted.

Initiating has been described by Carkhuff (1980) as finding direction in life and bringing meaning to life through productive behavior. It is the counselor's responsibility to influence the child toward acting on his or her behalf. It is important for children to learn sound decision-making skills. As a result, when I initiate action with children, I often use the following steps:

1. Encourage children to identify as many problems as they can. As problems are reviewed, I write them on paper or a chalkboard.
2. Ask the child to rank all problems from most important to least important.
3. Select the most important problem for detailed discussion. Select the problem which is most likely to be changed easily. It is important with some children to build in success experiences.
4. Discuss alternative strategies for change to act on the concern.
5. Discuss all consequences to each alternative strategy.
6. Pick the "best" alternative and plan a course of action. The plan should include specific behavioral objectives. A step-by-step process from simple tasks to more complex will help children operationalize and succeed at initiating the plan.
7. Encourage the child's progress.
8. Reevaluate the plan and adapt it when necessary.

Once children have learned the problem-solving technique and have demonstrated their ability to put this new behavior into practice, both in therapy and in their everyday lives, readiness for termination of therapy is imminent. Terminating each counseling session and therapy as a whole requires the responding skill discussed previously—summarization. In addition, counselors will need to *provide appropriate advice*. Advice implies to children how they should or ought to behave. It often becomes necessary for the counselor of children to prepare children for the closure of each session by informing them in advance that, "We have only 10 minutes left in our session. Our time together today is about over and we need to prepare to stop." Advice statements are especially important when children are involved in play therapy and art therapy that requires enough lead time to clean up the room. Advice might also include the therapist's telling children that they have demonstrated the capacity to cope with life on their own and that they no longer need therapy or the counselor to function effectively. Termination of therapy is not so obviously easy for the counselor as to merely provide advice. Additional skills for closing are identified in Appendix B, "Individual Counseling Competencies Checklist," which I use with students in training.

Now let's return to the case of Christopher West introduced in the first chapter. Because Chris indicated a preference for play and art activities, these were incorporated in the third session.

PLAN FOR INTERVENTION: THIRD SESSION

A. Primary Goal: To continue to establish rapport.
B. Secondary Goal: To introduce the therapeutic nature of the counseling relationship.

C. Objectives
  1. Client will self-disclose at the intermediate level.
  2. Client will self-explore in relation to friends and family.
D. Strategies/Activities
  1. Client will draw a picture of an animal he is most like.
  2. Client will draw a family.
  3. Client will play with a puppet family.
E. Evaluation

Chris first drew a fish facing a fish hook on a line. He wrote the words "no way" in a cartoon cloud. He stated the reasons he chose a fish were that (1) "When I got big I could pick on little fish," and (2) "I could make people mad by stealing their bait." Both these statements appear indicative of his desire for revenge or to have others feel the hurt he has been exposed to. The picture itself might indicate his nontrusting feeling for the counselor and the counseling relationship at this point.

When asked to draw a family, Chris asked, "How many people?" The counselor said, "You decide." He then proceeded to draw a family with three persons, father, mother and young boy, as if there had been no divorce. Chris refused to interact with the puppet family.

The evaluation of Chris's pictures and play was purposely brief because Chapter 3, "Play Therapy"; Chapter 4, "Developmental Play"; and Chapter 5, "Art Therapy and Serial Drawing," discuss this material in detail.

RECOMMENDED RESOURCES

EGAN, G. *The skilled helper.* (2nd ed.) Monterey, CA: Brooks/Cole, 1982.

An excellent text which integrates counseling skills into practice. Egan presents a problem-management model for helping step by step in detail. The entire model is directed toward assisting clients in pursuing and accomplishing behavioral goals, which helps them to manage problems of their lives more effectively.

MARTIN, D. *Counseling and therapy skills.* Monterey, CA: Brooks/Cole, 1983.

This book is designed for the beginning counselor or therapist. It consists of four parts. The first three focus on the following: developing basic skills, putting skills into practice, and moving beyond basic skills. The fourth part is an interesting and informative section on research evidence.

SUMMARY

This chapter on child-centered counseling included an introduction of the self theory and person-centered counseling of Carl Rogers. It focused on six key components of Rogers's work: the organism, phenomenal field, self, congruence, unconditional positive regard, and empathy. The second section of this chapter introduced the Carkhuff model and discussed the skills of attending, responding, personalizing, and initiating. The third focused on the child-centered counseling model including the three phases—facilitation, transition, and action. Counselor verbal skills were highlighted for each phase using counselor/client interaction to provide examples. The last section included a continuation of the case example introduced in Chapter 1.

REFERENCES AND RECOMMENDED READINGS

CARKHUFF, R. *Helping and human relations: A primer for lay and professional helpers.* (Vol. 1) New York: Holt, Rinehart & Winston, 1969.

———. *The art of helping IV.* Amherst, MA: Human Resource Development Press, 1980.

DREIKURS, R. & SOLTZ, V. *Children: The challenge.* New York; Hawthorne Books, 1964

EGAN, G. *The skilled helper* (2nd ed.) Monterey, CA: Brooks/Cole, 1982.

GAZDA, G., ASBURY., F., BALZAR, F., CHILDERS, W., & WALTERS, R. *Human relations development: A manual for educators.* (2nd ed.). Boston: Allyn & Bacon, 1973, 1977.

GINOTT, H. *Between parent and child.* New York: Avon Books, 1965.

———. *Between parent and child.* New York: Avon Books, 1969.

———. *Between parent and teenager.* New York: Avon Books, 1969.

———. *Teacher and child.* New York: Avon Books, 1972.

GORDON, T. *P.E.T.: Parent effectiveness training.* New York: Peter H. Wyden, 1970.

———. *T.E.T.: Teacher effectiveness training.* New York: David McKay, 1974.

IVEY, A., & AUTHIER, J. *Microcounseling: Innovations in interviewing, counseling, psychotherapy, and psychoeducation.* (2nd ed.) Springfield, IL: Charles C. Thomas, 1978.

MEADOR, B. & ROGERS, C. Person-centered therapy. In R. Corsini (Ed.) *Current psychotherapies.* (2nd ed.) Itasca, IL: F. E. Peacock, 1979.

PATTERSON. C. *Theories of counseling and psychotherapy.* (3rd ed.) New York: Harper & Row, 1980.

ROGERS, C. *Client-centered therapy: Its current practice, implications, and theory.* Boston: Houghton Mifflin, 1951.

———. *On becoming a person.* Boston: Houghton Mifflin, 1961.

———. The conditions of change from a client-centered viewpoint. In B. Berenson & R. Carkhuff (Eds.) *Sources of gain in counseling and psychotherapy.* New York: Holt, Rinehart & Winston, 1967.

———. *Carl Rogers on personal power: Inner strength and its revoluntionary impact.* New York: Delacorte, 1977.

———. *A way of being.* Boston: Houghton Mifflin, 1980.

TRAUX, C. & CARKHUFF, R. *Toward effective counseling and psychotherapy: Training and practices.* Chicago: Aldine, 1967.

Chapter 3

Play Therapy and Play Process

THE INTRODUCTION OF PLAY into child counseling has been attributed to Hug-Hellmuth when she first reported in 1921 that play was essential in child analysis and therapy with children 7 years of age or younger (Lebo, 1955). As with most adult therapy during this period of time, her method was heavily laden with observation and psychoanalytic interpretation. Although an educative emphasis in Hug-Hellmuth's therapy was important, most early child analysts failed to realize that child analysis and therapy was distinct and different from adult analysis.

Lebo(1955) also cites Anna Freud and Melanie Klein as making significant contributions to play therapy in the late 1920s. Anna Freud developed the classical Freudian theory into a system for child analysis. In her theory, play was used for observational and diagnostic purposes only. Play was perceived as best used to obtain knowledge of children's reactions, aggressive tendencies, and need for sympathy. Play was also used by Anna Freud to get acquainted and establish rapport. However, she felt that much of play lacked symbolic meaning and was mere repetition of current experience of the child and she de-emphasized interpretation. Unlike Anna Freud, Melanie Klein regarded the superego as already developed and emphasized immediate interpretation to the child. Play therapy was, therefore, used as a means to the unconscious and spontaneous play was a substitute for free association.

In the late 1930s, two distinctly different approaches to play therapy were advocated: active play therapy, in which children were given a few selected toys by the therapists who then directed them to act out certain traumatic scenes (Cohn, 1939; Levy, 1939), and passive play therapy, in which therapists did not restrict children's play (Gitelson, 1938).

Active play therapy emphasized concrete problems which had arisen at a specific time in the child's life. The therapist decided prior to therapy the nature of the problem and orchestrated the play scene. Levy (1939) introduced a form of active play therapy he termed "release therapy." The fundamental goal of this therapy was the release of difficult emotions (e.g., fear and aggression, infantile pleasure, and sibling rivalry). Passive play therapy, on the other hand, emphasized the acceptance of emotional expression through "free play." The therapist allowed children in therapy to play at their own speed and to develop the direction and the limits of the play situation. The children decided whether or not and when to include the therapist in play. When included in play, the therapist might offer simple interpretations and encouragement.

Passive play therapy was later modified slightly and termed relationship therapy to accommodate the theory of Otto Rank. Relationship therapy differs from the psychoanalytic play therapies discussed previously in that it focused primarily in the curative power of the emotional attachment developed between the therapist and the child (Moustakas, 1953). The curative power of insight gained through interpretation of past experiences, dreams, fantasy, or memory was de-emphasized. The intent of this existential approach to play therapy was to develop a strong therapist/ client relationship and to focus on the present feelings and actions of children in play. This therapy allowed children complete freedom in play. The therapist waited to be involved in play by children, but discussed freely with them any experiences encountered in play.

As a result of Carl Rogers' work in the 1940s, a nondirective therapy emerged in which the therapist made no attempt to control, to direct, or to provide interpretation and meaning to the client. The focus of nondirective therapy was on creating therapeutic relationships which provided the clients an opportunity to solve their emotional problems. The client controlled the direction of therapy and the therapist believed in the client's capacity to motivate self-help.

Rogers' therapeutic philosophy was integrated into play therapy by Virginia Axline (1947). Axline theorized that children's attitudes developed from past experiences with others and that these attitudes influenced their self-perceptions either positively or negatively. These self-perceptions in turn determined behavior, which was then interpreted as effort to maintain psychological identity or to ward off psychological harm. Axline also subscribed to implementing limitations in play therapy to prevent children from harming themselves, harming the therapist, or destroying property. She felt that limitations established boundaries which provided a feeling of security and stability necessary for a therapeutic relationship. Once limits were set, children could experience therapy freely and learn to understand feelings objectively without additional guilt, fear, or anxiety. The therapist emphasized children's frame of reference in play and responded to their nonverbal and verbal play behavior.

More recently, changes in play therapy that provide additional techniques include the works of Ginott (1961), which provided a rationale for toy selection; Dreikurs and Soltz (1964), which emphasized logical and natural consequences for behavior; Moustakas (1971), which emphasized the experiencing of the existential relationships of therapy; and Brody, Fenderson, and Stephenson (1976), which focused on physical contact between therapist and child through developmental play. The physical contact concepts of developmental play will be discussed in depth in Chapter 4.

The Value of Play Therapy

Play therapy is unique in that it is characterized by the use of toys, games, puppets, and other play media which children naturally and universally find attractive and want to be involved with. As children initiate play, the tension that often exists between therapist and client is reduced. Once the therapeutic relationship is established, children are encouraged to use their imagination in play, and express feelings and behaviors which lead to the reduction of anxiety and eventual problem resolution.

Caplan and Caplan (1974) cited several unique features of play that children find attractive:

1. Play is a voluntary activity by nature. In a world full of requirements and rules, play is refreshing and provides a respite from everyday tension.
2. Play is free from evaluation and judgment by adults. Children are safe to make mistakes without fear of failure and adult ridicule.
3. Play encourages fantasy and the use of imagination. In a make-believe world, children can exercise the need for control without competition.
4. Play increases interest and involvement. Children often experience short attention spans and are reluctant to participate in a lower interest, less attractive activity.
5. Play encourages the development of the physical and the mental self.

Children who engage in play are, therefore, *active* learners. As children grow, much of the information they receive and the skills they learn are obtained in social play activities. According to Piaget (1962), it is through play that children transcend the sensory motor experience of infancy to the symbolic (fantasy) experiences of early childhood. At the age of 4 or 5, symbolic play is replaced gradually by social play. In social play, children learn to function within rules systems, to cooperate, to share, to lead, and to follow.

Amster (1943) has also provided several reasons suggesting the value and use of play in therapy.

1. Play is a useful tool in establishing the therapeutic relationship.
2. Play assists the therapist as a diagnostic tool for understanding children.
3. Play helps relax children, and it reduces anxiety, and defensive posturing, which enhances therapy.
4. Play encourages reluctant or nonverbal clients to become involved with therapy.
5. Play helps children to get out feelings about significant traumatic life experiences in a safe environment.
6. Play provides children opportunities to develop social skills which may be generalized to everyday behavior.

To summarize the value of play, it is an activity in which children feel comfortable. Play is a natural way for children to communicate and to act out sensitive material related to frightening situations. Through play, children gain the security and self-confidence necessary to express underlying emotions and to try out new ways of thinking and behaving.

KEY CONCEPTS

As noted previously, play therapy developed primarily from the psychoanalytic theory of Freud and the person-centered theory of Rogers. To implement the child-centered counseling approach discussed in Chapter 2, it is necessary to consider several basic principles of both theories. Freud felt that children developed personality composed of id, ego, and superego, and that it was formed basically by age 5. He also professed that the three parts of personality interacted continuously and developed in response to four sources of tension: physiological growth processes, frustrations, conflicts, and threats. As tension increased in the child from these sources, the personality formed using defense mechanisms to deal with the anxiety. In understanding children as they encounter anxiety-producing play situations in counseling, it is important to have a basic knowledge of often used defense mechanisms.

Defense Mechanisms

1. Identification. In order to enhance their position in the world and their self-esteem, children will often "take over" features or behaviors of persons perceived to be important in their lives as part of their own personality. For example, young children often emulate the characteristics of parents, or pretend to be powerful figures such as the Incredible Hulk[M]. Older children may turn to hero worship and identify with athletic heroes or movie stars. I've noticed recently that some boys are assuming the exact, unusual, batting stance of George Brett. I also counseled an adolescent girl who dressed and made up like Marie Osmond and wrote one fan letter each day to her heroine. The counselor must use caution not to overlook the possibility that some children may attempt to regain or replace a lost object of affection such as a parent or pet through identification. It is also possible for children who have been rejected by divorced parents to form strong identifications with their lost parent in the hope of regaining lost love.

2. Displacement. Children who are unable to satisfactorily obtain an original object of choice, such as personal attention through academic success, may refocus their energy on a different object or goal such as personal attention through misbehavior. The direction of displacement is determined by several factors: (a) the resemblance of the substitute object to the first choice, (b) the ease of accessibility of the second object, and (c) the limits imposed by the environment or society.

3. Repression. Children who encounter in play situations objects that arouse excessive anxiety may force the threat out of their conscious thoughts into the unconscious. The more children use repression to cope with tensions, the less they are able to deal with reality. The degree of severity of the trauma produced by the situation or object is directly related with the degree of repression of the material into the unconscious. This is to imply that a situation which causes severe anxiety will be deeply repressed. Once material is repressed, it is extremely difficult for children to recover it.

4. Projection. Children who feel excessive anxiety resulting from a neurotic fear or moral guilt may convert this anxiety into an objective fear. This conversion is readily accomplished because of fear of punishment from an external agent. For example, a child may say "She hates me" instead of "I hate the teacher," or "She always blames me," rather than "I feel guilty about hitting my little sister."

5. Reaction Formation. Children may replace in their consciousness an anxiety-producing stimuli by its opposite. For example, a child who has

difficulty expressing love toward another may say, "I hate you" during a tense moment. Reaction formations are characterized by compulsiveness and extravagant behavior. Extreme forms of behavior typically denote reaction formation.

Other key concepts in play therapy derived from psychoanalytic theory include the unconscious, resistance, transference, and counter-transference.

Unconscious

The unconscious contains all memories of children's experiences in life of which they are unaware at any given moment. As the therapist attempts to derive meaning from children's play, it is important to recognize the role of the unconscious. Freud perceived the unconscious as the primary motivator for most behaviors. Children who have encountered severe anxiety-producing situations repress the experiences and the emotions associated with them into the unconscious. To face these memories or to bring them to consciousness would create incapacitating anxiety. The goal of play therapy, therefore, is to create a safe and comfortable climate so that the children will gradually relieve the unconscious of repressed material, and bring it into consciousness. The therapist can better understand unconscious by being aware of children's defensive posturing in play.

Resistance

This concept is basic to the psychoanalytic interpretation of child's play. It involves any defensive behavior that prevents children from dealing with unconscious material. For example, to avoid involvement with the therapist in play, a verbal child may choose to talk incessantly about mundane topics not related to self such as comics or TV shows, while a nonverbal child may merely sit avoiding any involvement in therapy. Some resistance is a natural part of building the therapeutic relationship. Other resistances may involve hurtful experiences in previous counseling sessions, a lack of personal knowledge of what is to happen, a lack of faith in counseling as a helping process or a fear of adult ridicule and reprisal. To overcome initial resistance in play therapy, the counselor might best be referred to Axline's (1947) eight basic principles of counseling:

1. The therapist develops a warm, caring relationship with children; establishes rapport as quickly as possible to gain their confidence.
2. The counselor accepts children unconditionally.
3. An atmosphere of permissiveness is encouraged so that the children feel free to explore feelings.

4. The therapist follows children's lead in play.
5. The counselor reflects feelings and play behaviors back to children in an attempt to assist them to gain insight into their behavior.
6. At all times the counselor respects children and their ability to solve problems and to make decisions for themselves.
7. The therapy process is gradual. The counselor moves with children and makes no attempt to hurry the process.
8. The counselor establishes the necessary limitations to prevent personal harm and property damage.

Resistances are important points in the progression of the counseling relationship and should be recognized as such by the counselor. Once children accept the nature of counseling while playing, the therapist might simply point out certain instances of reluctant behavior. After a period of time in therapy and with the establishment of high levels of trust and rapport, the counselor may decide to confront behavior directly in an effort to overcome the resistance.

Transference

Transference involves the process by which a child projects feelings generating from past relationships onto the therapist. It most often involves the release of unconscious material and should be perceived as healthy movement in counseling. As resistances are overcome, transference is encouraged in the nonthreatening therapeutic environment of play therapy. As the child projects anxiety-related feelings onto the counselor, the counselor accepts and reflects these feelings back to the client in an attempt to aid the client's understanding of them. In later stages of counseling, the therapist may choose to assume the role of a parent so that the child might "talk to the parent" without fear. Or, the client and counselor might use role reversal, whereby the child acts out an adult role and the counselor behaves as the child. Yet, in another instance, the client might play his or her own part as child and that of the adult. All three of these activities mentioned involve an active therapeutic intervention which is more appropriate for use with children ages 9 through 12 than with very young children.

Countertransference

Countertransference involves the therapist projecting unresolved conflicts and unmet needs into the therapeutic relationship. Under no circumstances should a counselor undertake to help children when both the counselor and the potential client are experiencing anxiety from similar concerns. For example, a therapist who is experiencing marital difficulties and separation from the family unit ought to avoid counseling children of divorce. Frances G. Wickes (1968) summarized the issue of countertransference quite well in the following passage.

> "No one would embark upon a journey without a vision of the destination, and one ought not to attempt to meet the problems of child development without a knowledge of that development. There is no way in which we can understand the problems of the child's unconscious except to have met and faced those problems in ourselves. The first requisite for one who wishes to work with ill-adapted children is a searching personal analysis. Only the free individual who has found his own way of life can help others to freedom.
>
> In the meeting of any two persons, the smallest point of contact is the conscious or known part; all the rest is in the unconscious unknown. Unless we understand the thing which the difficult, neurotic child may stir in our own unconscious, we cannot deal with him justly . . . . (p. 34)

Because Axline adapted the self-theory of Carl Rogers to play therapy, it is important to review briefly the key concepts of this person-centered approach. For an in-depth discussion of these key concepts, the reader is referred to Chapter 2, "Child-Centered Counseling." Axline's eight principles mentioned earlier in this chapter also provide excellent examples of how she used Rogerian theory in play therapy.

The Relationship

Rogers believed strongly that the relationship developed between counselor and client was the foundation for therapeutic success. He hypothesized that all persons possessed the innate capacity within themselves to use the counseling relationship for personal growth and development. It, therefore, became the counselor's responsibility to orchestrate this unique relationship. This person-centered relationship contains three essential elements that are necessary for the therapist to model with the client: genuineness, warmth, and empathy.

> *Genuineness.* Genuineness refers to the counselor's ability to be aware of his or her own feelings, values, and attitudes; and, as much as possible, to express these aspects of self in the relationship. Rogers felt that by being genuine, the counselor provided reality in the relationship, which was necessary for the client to find reality and function realistically.
>
> *Warmth.* Warmth involves the amount of liking and acceptance that the therapist feels genuinely for the client. The greater the degree of warmth provided in the relationship by the counselor, the greater the opportunity for the client to grow and develop.

Empathy. Empathy refers to the counselor's genuine desire to understand the content and the feelings of the client. Empathy involves the therapist's ability to perceive the world from the client's perspective.

BASIC TECHNIQUES

Once theory is understood, it is essential to the counselor that there be methodology through which theory is implemented in practice. The methodologies that are described by professionals in counseling are often referred to as basic techniques. In play therapy, two main techniques are required to bridge the gap between theory and practice: play media and responding.

Play Media

Children in treatment are different from adolescents and adults in that they often do not possess the capacity to express their feelings verbally. Children ages 5 to 8 who are immature and who have experienced social or emotional deprivations may have diminished or undeveloped language skills. When these children find it difficult to accurately express their feelings in words, they often are able to express emotions through play media. Play media also provide a natural environment for the child in counseling, which reduces tension and apprehension for both client and counselor. As a result, the technique of play media encourages the development of the therapeutic relationship and encourages the creative use of imagination and fantasy, which in turn elicits the self-expression of feelings. Play media, therefore, are used as a therapeutic catalyst which provides the counselor with a means to obtain information useful in diagnosing client difficulties, in prescribing procedures for remediation, and in gaining access to the inner world of children.

Play media that are durable, inexpensive, and safe should receive primary consideration for purchase. Nelson (1968) suggested three additional criteria for selecting play media in counseling: (1) materials that might be used in many ways, such as clay, paints, and pipe cleaners; (2) materials that encourage communication, like toy telephones; and (3) materials that elicit expression of aggression, such as a toy gun or Bobo. Ginott (1961) also recommended that a toy selected for therapy should: (1) assist in the establishment of rapport with the child, (2) encourage catharsis, (3) enhance opportunity for insight, (4) allow for reality testing, and (5) provide for sublimation.

Toys that are unstructured and lead to creative imaginative play are generally preferred. For example, a piece of paper can be colored, wadded into a ball and thrown, made into an airplane or hat, and cut into dolls. In all cases, children should have available to their use a variety of play media consistent with their developmental level, such as primary pencils, crayons, and a large nerf ball for young children. Older children might prefer chess, checkers, card games, or water colors. Toys that are attractive and useable across developmental levels are more cost efficient. These toys might include: puzzles, coloring books, blocks, dolls, puppets, stuffed animals, or Legos^M. There exists practically no limit to the counseling potential of toys or media when used in play therapy. Any toy that is attractive to children and encourages the child to express emotions is valuable to the counselor. The environment in which play media are used in therapy is also important.

Axline (1947) suggested that a large playroom and many toys were not necessities to effective counseling in play therapy. She felt an adequate play environment could be generated in the counselor's office if it included a small rug, an easel, and a toy box located in the corner. The toy box should contain a doll family, nursing bottle, telephone, puppets, crayons, paints, toy gun, and cars or trucks.

The playroom should include a few comfortable pieces of furniture and contain shelves that are easily accessible so children can move freely, see play media easily, and choose readily those materials that are desirable. The floor and walls should be easily cleaned. The room should be painted in bright, cheerful colors, well lighted, and ventilated. If not in the playroom, a sink with running water for cleaning up should be accessible in the immediate area. A sandbox and wooden workbench are also desirable. Prior to each counseling session, the room should be clean. Children should also have access to old shirts or a smock to protect school clothing. An alternative would be to have parents dress children in "old" clothes on the day of therapy. Children who are not worried about keeping clean will be less inhibited in self-expression in their play. The counselor should also be dressed comfortably in clothing which allows freedom of movement and involvement.

Responding

As the permissive relationship is initiated and develops, children learn that they can use any of the play media available in the room. While children are involved with play media, the therapist gains information necessary to understand the client such as developmental level of maturity and feelings toward self and others. The counselor then accepts and responds to the client's behavior expressed in play. These responses include the reflection and clarification of feelings, thoughts, and behaviors that were discussed in depth in Chapter 2.

The following excerpt was extracted from the popular book *Dibs In Search of Self*. It provides the reader an example of how responding techniques are used in play therapy and includes the firmness necessary to establish limits in a counseling session.

> He twisted his hands together and turned around toward me, looking very miserable and unhappy. "Miss A say it paint one picture of a house and then it leave you," he said huskily. I noted how confused his language had become. Here was a child capable of great intellectual achievement, whose abilities were dominated by his emotional disturbance.
>
> "That is what I said, Dibs," I replied quietly. "And you have finished painting the picture and it is time to go."
>
> "I'll need some more grass here and some flowers," he said suddenly.
>
> "There is no more time for that," I said. "Our time is up for today."
>
> "Dibs walked over to the doll house. "I'll have to fix the house. I'll have to close it up," he said.
>
> "You can think of several things to do so you won't have to go home, can't you? But your time is up now, Dibs, and you will have to go home now."
>
> "No. Wait. Wait," Dibs cried out.
>
> "I know you don't want to go, Dibs. But our time is up for today."
>
> "No go now," he sobbed. "No go now. No go ever."
>
> "It makes you unhappy when I say you have to leave, doesn't it, Dibs? But you may come back again next week. Next Thursday."
>
> I picked up his hat, coat, and books. Dibs sat down on the little chair by the table. He eyed me tearfully as I put his cap on his head. (Axline, 1964, p. 56–57)

PLAY PROCESS

As evidenced by the excerpt involving Dibs and Dr. Axline, the playroom and play media help provide an atmosphere and the necessary vehicles for free self-expression. However, it is the counseling process, rather than the play materials, that assists children toward healthful change. Without purposeful counselor interaction, the use of play media is hardly more than random play. The term *play process* focuses on communication between the client and therapist and the developmental learning process. Children express self in play and the counselor responds to their feelings and behaviors in such a way as to convey the necessary conditions of a child-centered relationship. As children experience this relationship, they tend to express conscious feelings openly and to explore and to create situations in play which allow for the expression of unconscious emotions. The counselor is then able to assist in the understanding of feelings and behaviors and their relationship to life.

While the Axlinian approach to processing children in play therapy is extensively used in mental health clinics and child guidance centers, counselors in some settings such as schools have found this approach difficult to implement. Play therapy sessions, in which the therapist follows the child's lead, often require an hour a week for as long as one year. With increasing caseloads, many counselors find it difficult to justify spending large amounts of time with small numbers of children. To meet the therapeutic needs of more children in a shorter time span, it is necessary for the counselor to be more actively involved in directing therapy for children. Myrick and Haldin (1971) introduced and outlined a more active, directive approach for counselors to use when processing children in play therapy and termed this procedure "play process."

Play process actually combines much of the theory discussed previously in passive play therapy and active play therapy. As a result, play process is both child-centered and counselor-directed. Because it is counselor-directed, the counselor dictates the speed and the direction of therapy. In agencies and educational settings where time in counseling is often controlled by others and may range from 15 to 45 minutes, play process provides an acceptable alternative to play therapy.

Play process is defined in three progressive developmental stages. Progression from one stage to the next is counselor-controlled and is related essentailly to the following factors:

1. The counselor's ability to establish the therapeutic relationship
2. The goals of counseling, including the counselor's ability to identify accurately the children's problems
3. The planning skills of the counselor, including the creative use of play media
4. The facilitative responding skills of the counselor
5. The time available to be spent in therapy with children

The first stage of play process is characterized by an open, permissive atmosphere and involves the therapist's attempt to create the conditions necessary for a child-centered relationship. The counselor is building an unconditional relationship by creating an atmosphere in which children are free to explore their feelings and behaviors. As children play, the counselor first focuses on feelings generated by play behavior and responds to these feelings. When necessary or appropriate, the therapist may clarify play behavior or ask open questions in an attempt to get children to elaborate verbally about the play. It is absolutely essential that the counselor avoid giving advice, making judgmental statements, or introducing information that would tend to teach children how to feel or to behave. During this stage, the therapist is also developing several possible hypotheses regarding the nature of the client's problem or developmental needs.

The second stage is introduced when the counselor feels that a positive, trusting relationship has been established and she or he can be more assertive in directing play process without harming the relationship. The therapist reviews and prioritizes the initial hypotheses regarding the client's concerns and selects the one for work that seems most crucial to the client's welfare. This initial hypothesis is then introduced into play process as the counselor encourages the child to play with certain toys that have a high probability of eliciting feelings and behaviors related to the hypothesis. The counselor also initiates additional exploration of feelings and behaviors as they are demonstrated by the client when playing with these particular toys. Should the therapist decide at any time that the initial hypothesis was incorrect or not the primary problem, then the decision is made to redirect the play toward another hypothesis.

The third stage is characterized by more counselor activity. The counselor is reasonably certain of the child's presenting problem and, therefore, engages the child in a systematically structured series of play sequences that encourage the client to face an area of conflict. The play sequences should proceed along a continuum of nonthreatening activity to threatening so that the child gradually becomes desensitized to the problem area. In all three stages, the therapist responds to feelings, clarifies play behaviors, and uses open questions in an attempt to encourage the child to verbally elaborate on the play. The following case demonstrates the three stages of play process.

Patricia is an immature 12-year-old black girl in the sixth grade, who referred herself to counseling. Although not formally identified as retarded, she might be characterized as exceptionally slow. In the initial session, the counselor, a female graduate student, indicated to Patricia that she could play with anything in the room as long as she didn't hurt herself or destroy any toys. Patricia examined the room for a few minutes, went to the toy box, and picked out a doll. She then sat next to the box and began to straighten the doll's clothes and fix her hair. The counselor responded, "You are helping the doll look pretty." As Patricia continued to play with the doll, she began talking about her grandmother. The following excerpts were taken from the counselor's interaction with Patricia as she played with the doll and talked about her grandmother and a trip to Washington, D.C.

Stage 1

P: Grandma paid to have her hair fixed, but she fixed mine. I went somewhere special on Easter. I went to church in Washington.

C: You and Grandma got dressed up for a special occasion.

P: Yeah! We get dressed up every Sunday for church.

C: Going to church on Sunday is special.

P: (Smiling) Uh huh, Grandma gets ready first, then she helps me. I do my own clothes, but she fixes my hair.

C: It's important to look nice in church, but it's hard to do it all yourself.

P: Yes, Grandma helps, the church was so big and pretty. Everyone was dressed up. So were we.

C: Grandma is very special and important to you.

P: There were lots of people there. We sang songs and played games, too.

C: Church can be fun.

P: Sometimes (with a perplexed expression on her face).

Following this statement, Patricia put the doll aside and continued to discuss her pleasant activities at church in detail. The session concluded when the counselor indicated it was time to go.

After consulting the child's teachers and grandmother, the counselor hypothesized that three issues introduced and discussed in the first session by the child ought to be explored further. These issues were: (1) Patricia's relationship with her grandmother, (2) Patricia's concept of church, and (3) Patricia's concept of family. With these tentative thoughts in mind, the counselor met Patricia in the second session.

C: Well, Patricia, what would you like to play with today? (Patricia hesitated, went to the toy box, and again selected the doll. She examined it briefly and replaced it.)

P: Can I draw today?

C: Yes, the paper and crayons are on the shelf. (Patricia busied herself drawing a picture of a person. Next to the person was a building with a steeple. After finishing the picture, she began to color and talk.)

P: Grandma has white hair. She's old.

C: As people get old they change.

P: I don't want to die.

C: You're afraid to die.

P: Yeah, you might have a heart attack.

C: Heart attacks can kill.

P: Yep, you get heart attacks when you're old.

C: You don't want to grow old. You want to stay 12 and not worry.

P: I wish nobody wouldn't die in this world.

C: It's sad when people die. (Patricia nods affirmatively.)

P: Sometimes I wonder how did God make everything. Like make buildings and stuff and create.

C: Uh huh! Create things.

P: Yep, create the world. I don't understand that part. I don't know how he can do it.

C: It is confusing.

P: He's got power. (Patricia seemed to say this as a statement of fact.)

C: We don't understand everything about God.

P: Like up there? (Pointing toward ceiling.)

C: In heaven?

P: (Nods affirmatively.)

C: Uh huh!

P: When we go up to heaven, we can see what he does, right?

C: You're curious about heaven and God. It's hard to understand.

P: How can we see when we're dead?

This session drew to a close as Patricia finished coloring her picture which she took home to show her grandmother. Patricia had helped the counselor tremendously. She selected an art activity and with the counselor's assistance elaborated on the first two of the three preliminary hypotheses made regarding her needs. Most often the relationship between therapist and client is not so easily obtained. Patricia might, therefore, be classified as an ideal client. First, she was self-referred, which indicated a readiness and willingness to be involved in therapy. Secondly, she demonstrated through her words and actions that her concerns involved conscious thinking and understanding abstract concepts.

Following this session, the counselor decided to become more assertive. The counselor now hypothesized that Patricia believed strongly in God and heaven, yet was confused and unable to understand these concepts. In addition, she seemed to experience a fear that her grandmother might die soon which threatened her security. Patricia's grandmother was her family. It appeared to the counselor that Patricia's lack of understanding about religion and her dependence on her grandmother as an only means of family support had created in her excessive anxiety and underlying fear of death and dying. Because Patricia was interested in drawing and enjoyed it in the previous meeting, the counselor asked her to draw a picture of a family in the third session.

Stage 2

As expected, Patricia again drew an old lady (her grandmother), but also drew a smaller person (herself) in the picture. Patricia talked animatedly about her grandmother and shared many exciting experiences they had had together. The counselor responded to Patricia's feelings of excitement and love for her grandmother.

C: It's frightening to love someone as much as you love your grandmother.

P: If she dies, who will love me?

C: Knowing you are loved and cared for by someone is important. Everyone needs to love and be loved.

P: (Nods affirmatively.)

C: It's also important that you have someone to take care of you.

P: (Tearing) I don't know what I'll do if Grandma dies!

Discussion continued with the counselor supporting Patricia by continuing to respond to her feelings and clarifying her situation at home. When Patricia had settled down, the counselor asked if she knew what the movie "Roots" was all about. She indicated she had watched it on TV and knew that it meant tracing your family history. The counselor then introduced the idea of drawing Patricia's family tree and identifying members of her family on the tree.

> *P:* My father is in jail and mom took off.
> *C:* Uh huh.
> *P:* (Eyes shining) But my sister could go on it . . . She's married and lives in an apartment with her husband and children.
> *C:* Oh! Yes, she is part of your family.

It seemed that Patricia had suddenly realized she wouldn't be helpless or alone should her grandmother die. Following this session, the counselor felt that Patricia was ready to explore her beliefs about religion and fear of death through more-specific, sequentially planned play sessions.

Stage 3

Stage Three began in the fourth meeting with the counselor introducing a blank chart titled "Things People Believe." The counselor led Patricia through a brief discussion on beliefs people possess to distinguish among the concepts of what a few people believe, what some people believe, what most people believe, and what everyone believes.

> *C:* What's this? (Holding an apple.)
> *P:* Apple.
> *C:* How do you know?
> *P:* It's real.
> *C:* It's real. What do you mean?
> *P:* I can eat it.
> *C:* Oh, as you eat the apple you taste it and tasting something tells you if it's really an apple. What else helps let you know it's an apple?
> *P:* You can look at it and touch it and smell it.
> *C:* Ah ha! The taste, touch, and smell of the apple makes you believe it's an apple.
> *P:* Yes.
> *C:* OK. Here it is. See if it's real. (Patricia holds apple momentarily, then takes a bite.) What do you think?
> *P:* It's real.
> *C:* Uh huh! Then you believe it's real because you can hold it, smell it, and taste it. Would everyone who saw this apple believe it's a real apple?
> *P:* No, some are fake.
> *C:* Uh huh! Would most people believe it's a real apple?
> *P:* Yes.

The counselor then asked Patricia to draw an apple on her chart, color it, and write the words taste, touch, smell, and see next to it. To reinforce the concept and to conclude the session, the counselor led Patricia through a similar process substituting an orange for the apple. The fifth session began with the counselor reviewing the fourth session.

C: (Holding an apple in one hand and an orange in the other.) What are these?

P: Fruit.

C: Anything else?

P: Real.

C: Yes, they are real and we know that if we asked most people what they believed they would also say the apple and the orange are real. Are you afraid of the apple and the orange?

P: No

C: Uh huh! Things that you can taste, touch, smell and see aren't frightening. If these real things were in your house, you would feel safe.

At this point in therapy, the client had been introduced to the concepts of beliefs and reality. In addition, the client had been helped to associate the idea that real things that we can see, smell, touch, and feel are not fear-inducing. In subsequent sessions, the counselor planned to help the child understand that: (1) some persons can and do want us to believe the way they do; (2) we develop beliefs early in life, but they often change as we get older; (3) we learn to fear the unknown; and (4) we will tend to believe persons whom we trust even though we are fearful. The following taped excerpts were transcribed from these sessions, starting with the sixth:

C: Now this is your chart, and these are the things that most people believe because you can taste, touch, smell, and feel it is real. You can understand it and you aren't afraid of it.

P: It seems like I'm on TV doing a commercial.

C: (Laughing) OK, it seems as if we are doing a commercial. What are people who do commercials trying to do?

P: Get us to buy something.

C: Uh huh! They want us to believe in their product, that it is good.

P: So we will go out and buy it.

C: Yes, most young people believe things that adults say to them if they trust the older persons. (A prolonged silence.)

C: All right now, sometimes we believe things when we are young, but as we get older, those beliefs change. What are some things you believed in when you were younger that you don't believe now?

P: I don't know.

C: O.K. When you were little, were you afraid of anything that you aren't afraid of now?

P: Dogs and cats.

C: Your belief has changed?

P: I'm bigger now and I go and pet them.

C: Now they are pleasant to touch. You no longer think they will hurt you.

P: Right.

C: The reason you went from being scared to liking them is because you got more information. You first thought they would hurt you, but you learned more about them and realized they were friendly and you could enjoy them.

P: Yeah.

C: When we believe in something, it is as if it's real. We can hold it, touch it, and feel it. Before you had a cat and dog, you couldn't hold it or touch it and you were afraid of it. Now that you can hold it, you are no longer afraid because you learned not to be afraid.

C: What about Santa Claus?

P: (Puzzled look.)

C: Do all people believe in Santa Claus?

P: No

C: Not all people do so we have some things that some people believe. This brings us to another part of our work. Some people believe in certain things and some don't.

P: That's right.

The counselor concluded the sixth session by encouraging Patricia to draw a dog and cat on her chart and writing the words scared and friendly next to them. The seventh session began with the counselor introducing a plain, brown-paper bag.

C: What do you believe this is?

P: A bag.

C: What do you hear?

P: Nothing.

C: Do you believe there is something in the bag?

P: No.

C: Will you close your eyes and put your hand in the bag?

P: Yes.

C: You're not afraid. You believe nothing is in the bag that can hurt you. What if there were a mouse trap in the bag?

P: I wouldn't put my hand in.

C: How do you feel about the bag now?

P: Good.

C: You still feel there is no reason to fear the bag. Who is holding the bag?

P: You are.

C: Who do you think put something in the bag?

P: You.

C: You trust me and know me. You believe in me and believe that I wouldn't hurt you. All right, close your eyes and reach in.

P: (Laughs, doesn't reach.)

C: (Laughing) Come on, you've got to reach in.

P: (Giggling) (A squeaky noise is heard as she reaches in the bag.) (Pulls hand away.)

C: You are scared. It was furry.

P: It doesn't make sense.

C: You're not sure now. Uncertain.

P: I'm not going to put my hand back in there.

C: You can't see what is in the bag so you don't know and you are scared. You don't trust me now. What if I show what is in the bag?

P: OK.

C: (Opens bag.)

P: It's just a toy animal!

C: What scared you? You thought something might hurt you that wasn't really there. You didn't know because you couldn't see it.

As with the other activities in the previous sessions, the counselor encouraged Patricia to draw a picture of the bag and a toy animal on the chart, color it, and write her feelings next to it. The chart now contained a picture of an apple, orange, dog and cat, Santa Claus, a brown paper bag, and a toy mouse.

The next to last session began with Patricia saying, "Guess what? We're going to move to Washington next week." After a brief discussion and explanation of this new information, the counselor decided to accelerate the play process and introduce the concept of death.

C: Patricia come sit and play puppets with me.

P: (Joins the counselor on the carpet.)

C: (Manipulating the puppets) some time back you told me you were afraid your grandmother might die. You were afraid of death. You didn't know about it or understand it. (Silence) Remember the brown bag and toy mouse. When you touched that furry thing in the brown bag, you didn't know what was going to happen to you.

P: Yeah.

C: All right, you can't touch death and don't know what will happen to you.

P: I'd be lonesome in the casket.

C: You'll be lonely if your grandmother dies—and when you die you will be all alone in the casket.

P: (Reaches for the puppets and lays them on a pillow, folds their arms and straightens legs.) Uh huh.

C: Right now talking about death and dying scares you. Remember the dog and cat? What made you less afraid of them?

P: I could get to know them.

C: The only way to understand death is to talk about it. We can't experience it. I can't help you taste it, like the apple and orange, or touch it. When you don't know about something and can't taste it, touch it, hold it, experience it, then you become afraid of it. You become afraid of what might happen like in the bag and what you don't know.

P: Yes.

C: You're also afraid of a casket.

P: I'd be lonesome.

C: They will put you in a casket and you will be lonesome.

P: They put fluid in you.

C: That's right, they do. Some people do that, but not everyone. Most people in our country have embalming fluid put in dead bodies in place of blood. It helps keep the body until it is buried.

P: Oh!

C: Yes, and some people aren't as afraid of death as other people because they believe different things. Some adults are afraid of death, too. Some people get so afraid of death that it keeps them from living.

P: They're unhappy like me.

In the last session, the counselor continued to explore the child's beliefs about death and introduced the concepts of funeral and going to heaven. These concepts were discussed from the child's belief system as she played funeral and going to heaven with puppets. The counselor urged her to understand that not everyone believes the same way. One of Patricia's final statements was, "It doesn't matter. Everyone dies. So even if Grandma dies and goes to heaven, I'll only be lonesome for a little while. Then, when I die, I'll go there, too." Patricia moved shortly after the last session.

RECOMMENDED RESOURCES

Books

LANDRETH, G. (Ed.) *Play therapy: Dynamics of the process of counseling with children.* Springfield, IL: Charles C. Thomas, 1982.

In this book, the contributors discuss how play reflects children's perceptions of their world and the significance of play in child development, present major approaches to play therapy, recommend materials, outline stages of emotional adjustment in the play therapy process, cover assessment of the child's progress, and describe how to train parents and teachers to be play therapists.

SHARP, E. *Thinking is child's play.* New York: Avon, 1969.

This book provides a guide to developing learning and teaching games for young children. It describes how to make games from cardboard cartons, tape, jar tops, playing cards, paper plates, napkins, and other items.

WISEMAN, A. *Making things.* Boston: Little Brown, 1972.

This book describes improvisation and how to create activities and games from everyday materials.

Journal

Journal of Play Therapy. Association for Play Therapy, 540 Scarsdale Road, Yonkers, N.Y. 10707.

Kits

Davis, D. *My Friends and Me.* American Guidance Service, Inc., Circle Pines, MN, 1979.

This kit contains a sequenced program of activities to encourage young children's (ages 3 to 6) personal, social, physical, intellectual, and emotional growth. The kit contains activities which use dramatic stories, dolls, blocks, magnetic shapes, sponge, felt-tipped pens, pictures, and cassettes or records.

Dinkmeyer, D. *Developing Understanding of Self and Others* (DUSO Kit D–1). American Guidance Service, Inc., Circle Pines, MN, 1970.

This kit was designed for use with children in the primary-age group (5 to 7 years). It makes extensive use of an inquiry, experiential, and discussion approach to learning. The kit contains sequentially planned activities which utilize role playing, puppetry, stories, readings, music, and art to help children understand their social and emotional development.

———. *Developing Understanding of Self and Others* (DUSO Kit D–2). American Guidance Service, Inc., Circle Pines, MN, 1973.

This kit was developed along the same format as DUSO D–1, with the major exception being that it is directed toward children in the intermediate-age group (8 to 12 years). DUSO D–2 also contains songs, stories, posters, role-playing activities, puppet activities, and career awareness activity cards.

Dunn, L., Chun, L., Crowell, D., Dunn, L., Halevi, L., & Yackel, E. *Peabody Early Experiences Kit.* American Guidance Service, Inc., Circle Pines, MN, 1976.

This kit contains a program of sequenced lessons designed to build cognitive and social growth in young children (early childhood, preprimary, and primary ages). The kit contains puppets, blocks, beads and strings, picture cards, story pictures, story cards, sound cards, and records.

Dupont, H., Gardner, S., & Brody, D. *Toward Affective Development.* American Guidance Service, Inc., Circle Pines, MN, 1974.

This kit contains discussion pictures to stimulate creative thinking and discussion, cassette tapes which act as stimulus recordings, posters, duplicating masters for student activity sheets, feeling wheels, and career folders. The purpose of the kit is to promote psychological and emotional maturity in children grades three to six by focusing on children's feelings, interests, aspirations, and conflicts.

SUMMARY

This chapter on play therapy and play process was divided into five major sections. The first section provided an introduction and brief overview of the historical development of play therapy. The overview related the influence of psychoanalytic theory and self-theory on play therapy, including discussion of the contributions of Anna Freud, Melanie Klein, and Virginina Axline. It also described in detail the value of play as a therapeutic tool. The second section defined and described the following key concepts: defense mechanisms, unconscious, resistance, transference, countertransference, and the relationship. The third section contained an explanation of play media and responding techniques. The fourth section described play process and provided an extensive example of the use of play process in counseling. The last section contained a list of recommended resources.

REFERENCES AND RECOMMENDED READINGS

Alexander, E. School centered play-therapy program. *Personnel and Guidance Journal*, 1964, 43, 256–261.

Amster, F. Differential uses of play in treatment of young children. *American Journal of Orthopsychiatry*, 1943, 13, 62–68.

Axline, V. *Play therapy.* New York: Ballantine Books, 1947.

——. *Dibs: In search of self.* New York: Ballantine Books, 1964.

Bender, L. Therapeutic play technique symposium. *American Journal of Orthopsychiatry*, 1955, 25, 784–787.

Brody, V., Fenderson, C., & Stephenson, S. *Sourcebook for finding your way to helping young children through developmental play.* Tallahassee: State of Florida, Department of State, 1976. (Distributed by Pupil Personnel Services Demonstration Project, All Children's Hospital, St. Petersburg, FL).

Caplan, F. & Caplan, T. *The power of play.* New York: Anchor Books, 1974.

Cohn, J. Child reveals himself through play-method of the play interview. *Mental Hygiene*, 1939, 23, 49–70.

Dreikurs, R. & Soltz, V. *Children: The challenge.* New York: Hawthorne Books, Inc., 1964.

Erickson, E. Studies in the interpretations of play. *Genetic Psychology Monographs*, 1940, 22, 561.

——. Toys and reasons, In M. R. Haworth (Ed.) *Child Psychotherapy.* New York: Basic Books, 1964.

Furness, P. *Role-play in the elementary school.* New York: Hart Publishers, 1976.

Ginott, H. G. *Group psychotherapy with children.* New York: McGraw-Hill, 1961.

GITELSON, D. Clinical experience with play therapy. *American Journal of Orthopsychiatry*, 1938, 8, 466–478.

HAMRIDGE, G. Structured play therapy. *American Journal of Orthopsychiatry*, 1955, 25, 601–617.

HOSFORD, P. & ACHESON, E. Child drama for group guidance and counseling. In G. Gazda (Ed.) *Theories and methods of group counseling.* Springfield, IL: Charles C. Thomas, 1976, 90–143.

LEBO, D. Development of play as a form of therapy from Rousseau to Rogers. *American Journal of Psychiatry*, 1955, 112, 418–427.

LEVY, D. Release therapy. *American Journal of Orthopsychiatry*, 1939, IX, 4.

LYONS, V. M. Psychodrama as a counseling technique with children. *Elementary School Guidance and Counseling*, 1977, 11(4), 252–258.

MOUSTAKAS, C. Situational play therapy with normal children. *Journal of Consulting Psychology*, 1951, 15, 225–230.

———. *Children in play therapy.* New York: McGraw-Hill, 1953.

———. *Psychotherapy with children.* New York: Harper & Row, 1971

MURPHY, G. Play as a counselor's tool. *School Counselor*, 1960, 2, 52–58.

MYRICK, R. & HALDIN, W. A study of play process in counseling. *Elementary School Guidance and Counseling*, 1971, 5(4), 256–263.

NELSON, R. Elementary school counseling with unstructured play media. *Personnel and Guidance Journal*, 1966, 1, 24–27.

Chapter 4

Developmental Play

THE PREVIOUS CHAPTER emphasized the value of play in therapy and cited several reasons why children find play attractive. This chapter provides an overview of a recent modification of play therapy, developmental play (DP) (Brody, Fenderson & Stephenson, 1976), which is a highly structured play program. In DP, children experiencing emotional, social, or learning deficiencies are paired with trained adult partners who assist the children through play activities to develop intense interpersonal relationships with them that involve deep levels of commitment, caring, and acceptance.

The DP program is therefore designed to assist children to overcome personal difficulties through the development of positive, loving interactions, and attachments with significant adults who are then used by the children as models for relating to others (Brody et al., 1976). As these relationships between children and adults grow, and the attachment bonds are strengthened, the children are encouraged to develop awareness of themselves and others and to express their feelings. It is through the highly structured, interpersonal, therapeutic process of developing attachments with significant adults that children learn about themselves, learn to express repressed emotions, and learn appropriate methods of communication (Bowlby, 1969). Most child counselors and therapists would agree that play is necessary to a child's healthy social, physical, intellectual, and emotional development.

Brody et al. (1976) established the structure for the DP program following their study of the interpersonal interactions among effective parents and young children. These parents and children were observed

78

getting acquainted with each other through play activities which involved body contact that were mutually enjoyable. The authors of the program emphasize that through the planned play activities involving physical contact, children develop socially and emotionally by learning to: (1) experience their bodies and sense physical feelings (pain and pleasure), (2) generate psychological feelings (anxiety and love), (3) communicate (nonverbally and verbally), and (4) organize their inner worlds through play media and relate it to the outer world (p. 9).

The Value of the Developmental Play Program

Developmental play is of value to both the child in therapy and the adult helper. Children in DP experience an affective personal and interpersonal education which helps remediate social–emotional deficiencies. That remediation in turn leads to increased achievement and intellectual functioning. Brody et al. (1976) report that children who participated in the DP program for about five months averaged an increase of seven points on the full scale intelligence score of the Wechsler Intelligence Scale for Children. However, because DP is a relatively new concept in therapy, little empirical evidence exists describing the therapeutic benefits for children. Burt and Myrick (1980) report a survey of 19 children six months after they completed a DP program. Children were interviewed and administered a questionnaire consisting of 17 self-report items including open-ended questions and yes/no questions. To assure that the children were recalling the DP experience, the interviewer asked them informally if they remembered any of their experiences in the program. Comments reported on the open-ended questions by the children were essentially positive toward the DP experience. Results obtained on yes/no questions included unanimous agreement by the children that their friends would enjoy a DP group. In addition, 89 percent of the children reported they had obtained new friends. Many children (79 percent) thought about their adult partner after the DP program. A majority (61 percent) stated they continued to play DP games with friends, experienced school more positively (56 percent), and noted a difference between their adult partner and other adults (56 percent).

In society today, children often learn to repress feelings, or when given the opportunity to reveal themselves, learn that adults do not really listen. To have the opportunity to self-express and to feel that adults have listened and understood can be a therapeutic experience for a child. When children feel they are heard, they feel important and useful. Children who play as equals with an adult in a DP program learn to contribute, to cooperate, and to control in various aspects of the relationship. These children gain a feeling of belonging to the adult world and develop a sense of well-being or security. As relationships and attachments with adult helpers grow, children are also able to partially meet their love needs in that they are able to give and receive positive feelings with a significant other.

In addition to receiving many of the same benefits as children in the DP program, adult helpers also gain self-fulfillment through helping children in need to become more fully functioning individuals. Persons who provide help to others feel useful. Adult helpers who develop attachments to children feel important and needed. These adults are often rewarded by sharing children's love and enthusiasm for life and learning what may be missing or unmet in their personal lives. Brody et al. (1976) and Burt and Myrick (1980) also included in their reports several positive statements of personal growth made by participating parents, teachers, and other adult partners of children in DP programs. Examples of these are: "I was able to relax more. I can play with a child spontaneously now. I really want to care and be cared for." "The DP experience helped me get in touch with myself. In most of life relationships, people don't really care. In DP, they do care."

KEY CONCEPTS

The Developmental Play Program

The DP program has been used successfully with groups of children from ages 5 to 7. Each DP group typically consists of six to eight children and an identical number of adult helpers. One child and one adult are paired as partners for the duration of the treatment program. The children and adults meet together with the group leader (therapist) in the same setting at the same time of day for about 75 minutes each week for approximately 15 weeks. The group leader is typically a counselor who has had experience and training in the DP program.* Each DP session is divided into three parts: (1) "one-to-one" play between child and adult helper (30 minutes); (2) "circle time" with all group participants (30 minutes); and (3) "juice time" for reduced activity levels, and transition to closing (15 minutes). The adult helpers also meet with the therapist in a 30-minute warm-up session before working with children and in a one-hour post-session supervisory conference.

Although each of the three segments of the DP program has specific objectives with structured play activities to meet program goals which have been tried and proven, professionals who are becoming involved in DP are encouraged to develop different activities or adapt those provided

*Professionals interested in DP training workshops should write to Pupil Personnel Services Demonstration Project, Euclid Student Services Building, 1015 10 Avenue North, St. Petersburg, Florida.

in the program to individual need systems. Brody emphasizes that the most successful play activities are those that remain flexible in their nature and allow for creative play between adult and child. The DP program goals and objectives were established to assist the adult helpers and children move through four developmental process stages in one-to-one play and three process stages in circle time.

The Developmental Stages of One-to-One Play

Table 4–1 provides an overview of the four developmental process stages, goals, and sample activities for the first part of the DP program, one-to-one play. The first stage, the *honeymoon stage*, emphasizes the development of the child/adult partnership. The dyads get acquainted and learn to enjoy the comfort of each other's company. In the beginning, the adult responds to child-initiated play and attempts to encourage the child's creativity. In the second or *painful stage*, both participants recognize and assimilate the reality of their relationship, such as schedule changes, and the limits of their relationship. For example, no child is allowed to physically hurt self or others, destroy furnishings, or completely distance self from the adult helper. Children are never punished. No matter what behavior children exhibit, they must understand that they will neither lose nor be able to rid themselves of their adult partners. In the third stage, the *separation and love stage*, children make personal growth by recognizing the adult helper as separate or apart from themselves. Children may ask sensitive questions about the adult's personal life such as, Are you married? Do you have any children? and Do you love your children? Children in this stage are able to communicate more effectively and actively demonstrate affection for the adult helper.

Preparation for termination is the final stage of one-to-one play. This stage is characterized by ambivalent feelings by both child and adult helper. Some children may regress to earlier behavior patterns by attempting to not be involved with their adult partners, by crying, or by becoming excessively dependent and clinging. Adult helpers, although prepared to understand and expect these behaviors, may feel rejected, unwanted, hurtful, and want to "father" or "mother" the child. As the feelings of separation and loss are internalized by children and adults in the dyads, a sense of accomplishment and respect for the other emerges which facilitates successful closure.

The Developmental Group Stages of Circle Time

Table 4–2 provides an overview of the three developmental process stages, goals, and sample activities in the second part of the DP program, circle

Table 4-1
Developmental Play Process Stages, Goals, and Sample Activities
for One-to-One Play

Stages	Goal(s)	Sample Activities
Honeymoon	Develop positive emotional attachment between adult and child Learn that it's OK to enjoy one another	Simple touching: Adults describe each of child's body parts as they touch Washing: Using a small pan of water, and washcloth, adults and children take turns washing each others hands, arms, and faces
Painful	Develop realization of relationship and limits in play Begin to express positive and negative feelings freely	Hide and seek: Children hide in room, without disturbing it, and adults try to find them. Adults may respond while seeking, "Where did Joe go? I miss him. It's awful being alone"
Separation/love	Develop awareness that partner is an individual separate from self Continue to express emotions freely	Playing baby: Adults hold children as if they were babies, and rock or sing to them Playing hurt: Adults fantasize a hurt and act it out. Children often say, "Let me help you make it better," then clean and bandage the hurt area. Reverse roles
Preparation for termination	Prepare children for termination of relationship several weeks in advance Express feelings of anxiety and loss Recognize growth and accomplishments	Countdown: Toward the end of the session, adults begin a countdown, "We have six more sessions until our last day together. It hurts to stop seeing you. I will miss you" Favorite game: Children choose to repeat favorite play activities they have experienced. "We had a great time playing together. I love you"

time. The first, or *touching or getting-acquainted* stage, is characterized by warm-up activities and icebreakers such as "follow-the-leader" and "pass-it-on." The second, the *aggressive, motoric, and physical* stage, enhances appropriate play behavior among children, and allows children to vent their energy in constructive ways. This increased awareness of self

Table 4-2
DEVELOPMENTAL GROUP PLAY PROCESS STAGES, GOALS, AND SAMPLE
ACTIVITIES FOR CIRCLE TIME

Stages	Goal(s)	Sample Activities
Touching/getting acquainted	Get acquainted with others in program Encourage children to begin to become aware of self in relation to others	Pass it on: Leader touches person next to self and says, "Pass it on." That person then touches next person on same part of body. Activity continues until the circle is completed. A new leader is chosen and encouraged to be original
Aggressive/ motoric/ physical	Stimulate children to interact with peers using physical contact and body awareness activities Encourage children to self-explore and develop self-understanding in relations to others	Modified Simon Says: The leader says something and pantomimes. Everyone else copies. No one drops out Wheelbarrow: Children pair up. One child grasps the ankles of partner and walks wheelbarrow around room. Reverse roles Leapfrog: Children are arranged in two lines (teams). On signal go, the last child in each line leapfrogs teammates to front. Activity continues until all children have performed and are back in original place
Fantasy	Encourage children to develop and express fantasies Encourage children to organize their behavior around peers in the group	Group sculpturing: Children are paired and one child is selected to "sculpt" the other. The children (sculptors) mold their partners by moving their hands, arms, and legs. The partner must try to hold position. Reverse roles Body-drawing and coloring. Children are paired. A piece of paper larger than the child is placed on the floor. One child traces body of the other. Reverse roles. Children then draw in details and color in their figures

and others builds self-confidence and self-esteem in the children. The last, the *fantasy* stage, encourages the development and creative expression of feelings and thoughts with age mates. In this stage, children often act out repressed emotions.

Group Leader (counselor)

The group leader's responsibility is to (a) supervise adult interaction with children in DP and intervene when necessary, (b) help orient the adults to the play activities prior to each session, (c) educate adults to anticipate and understand emotions and behaviors the play activities might generate in children, and (d) provide supervision for the adult helpers after each DP session. The supervisory sessions provide the adults with the guidance and support necessary to be effective helpers. In these sessions, the counselor encourages the adult helpers to discuss their feelings related to their child partners, the play activities, and the DP program. As a result, group supervision sessions often create an atmosphere in which adult helpers make personal growth. Additional supervisory assistance may be provided by the therapist who instructs the adult helpers regarding the value of nonverbal communication or body language.

Body Language

Body language or nonverbal communication is the "heart" of developmental play. The meaning and value of body language in developing relationships and communication has been explored extensively (Argyle, 1975; Goffman, 1969; Mehrabian, 1971; Scheflen, 1972; and Scheflen, 1973). Of particular importance to DP are the nonverbal communication concepts of *touching, space,* and *facial language.*

An amazing number of children have retarded social–emotional growth as a result of being deprived of an adequate amount of physical contact with adults. Maternal deprivation or the lack of touching in infancy and early childhood such as patting, stroking, and fondling has been well-documented in studies involving children who were separated from their mothers and institutionalized (Spitz, 1945; 1946). In these studies, the children's immediate reaction to separation was crying, followed by withdrawal from people, and, later, despair and apathy. Spitz reported that these children were unable to form emotional attachments to adults which led to depression and permanently reduced intellectual and emotional functioning. Although criticized extensively by other investigators for lack of controls, Spitz's results are supported by animal research (McCandless, 1967).

Activities encouraging *physical contact* are planned for every DP session. Physical contact encourages children to experience self through others and is the most potent way to develop attachments. Touching also provides reluctant participants sensory experiences through which they can communicate their thoughts and emotions which might otherwise be denied or repressed. It follows naturally that for the adult helper and child to engage in touching they must spend much of their time together in close proximity.

Nonverbal communication also involves the study of proxemics, which describes personal space and how it is used. Four distinct zones are present in all human groups: intimate space (0 to 18 inches), personal space (18 inces to 4 feet), social space (4 to 12 feet), and public space (12 to 25 feet) (Hall, 1966). The use of intimate space encourages close physical contact between persons. It is usually reserved by individuals for loved ones or very close friends (Hall, 1964; Scheflen, 1973). The use of personal space enhances privacy in verbal communication. At this distance, persons do not usually touch but may do so if the need arises or situation warrants it. Most therapeutic encounters occur in the personal space. DP activities require the adult helpers and children to function effectively in both intimate and personal space. It is the adult helpers' responsibility to decrease the distance between themselves and the children to increase attachments. Social distance is the space reserved for acquaintances but not close friends. This is the distance maintained by the therapist with the adults in supervision. It encourages socialization and businesslike relationships. Social space is also reserved for juice time when a reduced activity level is sought between adult and child and a transition from the intense attachment of DP to the real world is occurring in closure.

Facial language is a third important aspect of nonverbal communication in developmental play. Adults are encouraged to make and maintain eye contact with their child partners as frequently as possible. This assumes the adult is "getting down" to the child's level which often requires sitting on the floor. Eye contact indicates a readiness and willingness to be involved in interpersonal communication. It also suggests attentiveness and listening behavior by the adult. A lack of eye contact on the other hand may be interpreted by the child as avoidance or lack of interest. In addition to eye contact, smiling is considered important in developing positive feelings between the adult helper and child. Smiling reduces interpersonal anxiety and increases security and trust between partners. Smiling expresses pleasure, happiness, and a desire to continue being with the child.

Fantasy

The use of relaxation and fantasy in counseling is discussed thoroughly in Chapter 9. Briefly, it is important to emphasize that the concept of fantasy maximizes the child's use of creativity and imagery. Fantasy is a powerful therapeutic aid that requires the counselor to carefully plan for its use, constantly monitor the ongoing activity, and provide thorough processing of the experience. Fantasy provides a reduced state of resistance in children and encourages the release of repressed thoughts, feelings, and experiences kept in the unconscious.

BASIC TECHNIQUES

As mentioned previously, basic techniques are those methods by which counselors implement theory into practice. Developmental play, as an outgrowth of play therapy, utilizes many of the same concepts and techniques. The description of the DP program and other key concepts emphasized the use of play media and responding techniques as the primary catalysts for psychological growth in children. The reader is encouraged to review the material on responding and play media in Chapters 2 and 3. The reader is also referred to Chapter 12, which contains a detailed description of the organization and use of DP activities in group counseling with children experiencing behavioral and emotional disorders. Because the DP therapist's responding behavior and use of play media are similar to that described in play process in Chapter 3, the following example of counselor behavior in DP focuses on the organization of play activities and the child's response to DP.

This case example demonstrates the progressive movement of the therapist and child through the first two stages of one-to-one play: honeymoon and painful. Because the counselor is still working with this client, the lase two stages, separation/love and termination, will not be described in detail but are outlined briefly as planned.

Rick is an emotionally deprived, 7-year-8-month-old Caucasian boy in the third grade, who was referred to me for counseling by his mother and school counselor. Rick was identified by the school system as a "disturbed" youngster and placed in a self-contained classroom for disruptive children. He remained in this educational setting for 1 ½ years before his mother insisted on his removal.

Rick is an only child from a broken home. His parents were divorced when he was 5, which was about the same time he began to exhibit disturbed behavior in school. Rick's mother disclosed that she has experienced several personal problems since the divorce, including alcoholism and other drug abuse. She indicated that she was in therapy and that when her son was born, she could not relate to him. The mother said, " . . . about all I did was to feed him and make sure he was clean." She mentioned that on several occasions when he was an infant the only way she could prevent herself from abusing Rick physically was to leave his room, avoid him, and shut out the crying. At the present time, Rick lives with his mother and her male friend in a small apartment. While mother is a full-time graduate student at a local university, Rick attends the neighborhood school, which is his fifth different school in four years.

Rick's current educational and psychological assessment includes the following scores: Wechsler Intelligence Scale for Children–revised (WISC–R), full-scale I.Q. 126; verbal scale I.Q. 133; performance scale I.Q. 112; Wide Range Achievement Test (WRAT) reading scale 6.5 (99th percentile); spelling 4.3 (88th percentile); and arithmetic 2.9 (55th percentile). On the Bender Visual-Motor Gestalt Test, Rick's developmental age equivalent was 7 to 7.5.

Analysis of the WISC-R scores placed Rick in the superior range of intellectual functioning with a significant difference between overall verbal and performance scale scores favoring the former. Individual subtest scores ranged from average to very superior with the majority being superior or above. Rick did least well on the subtest arithmetic. According to his scores on the WRAT, Rick was found to be functioning like the average sixth grade student in the fifth month of school in reading, like the average fourth grade student in the third month of school in spelling, and similar to the average second grade child in the ninth month of school in arithmetic. These scores were in keeping with his level of measured intelligence except for arithmetic where he was clearly underachieving. Rick's visual motor coordination was average for his age.

Based on Rick's family and school history, his present family and school status, and testing information, he might be characterized as an impulsive, aggressive child whose behavior in school is unstable. He seemed to need more structure and limits in his environment. In addition, his demonstrated behavior indicated intense feelings of inadequacy and large needs for affection and attention which appeared largely unmet. With these thoughts and information, it appeared Rick would benefit most in counseling by initially experiencing a one-to-one developmental play approach.

The first assumption was that Rick had not developed a sufficient love or attachment relationship with a significant adult in his life and had not had the opportunity to identify with a male, father image. His experiences in infancy and in the first years of school with adults had created a basic mistrust of them and insecurity toward life in general. As a result, Rick had never learned how to ask for attention and love in socially appropriate ways, nor was he allowed to give love to loved ones. It was hypothesized that Rick's acting-out behavior in school was symptomatic of these unfulfilled emotional needs.

Initial contact with Rick, and all subsequent counseling sessions, was at his school. Rick was prepared to meet the counselor by his mother who had been interviewed for an hour the previous day. Rick and the therapist were introduced by the school counselor and directed to an assigned room. We familiarized ourselves with the room and began to get acquainted. Rick wanted to know who the counselor was and what they were going to do. It was explained that the counselor was a university professor and in private practice and that they were going to spend a half hour together twice each week on Wednesday and Friday from 1:15 to 1:45 p.m. The explanation also indicated that we would get to know one another, play together, talk about ourselves, and enjoy each other's company. "Each time we meet, I will suggest a play activity for us. If time remains in our session following the activity, then we will play at anything you like." No other limits were established. Rick introduced Fred, his stuffed toy penguin that accompanied him everywhere. Rick then escorted me around the school and we finished at his classroom. While walking, the counselor held his hand for as long as he would allow and touched his shoulder and back several times to begin establishing contact. He was animated in his description of the school, its classrooms, teachers, and children. The session concluded with a visit to his class where he introduced his teacher. Initial impressions of Rick were that he was not an attractive child; in fact, he was unkempt, dirty, and disheveled. But he could be characterized also as an energetic, very intelligent, loving child with a zest for life. Throughout the counseling sessions, Rick always met the therapist at the school's entrance with a smile on his face.

Honeymoon Stage

Sessions 2 through 5 focused on DP activities designed to build the attachment relationship with Rick. Activities were planned that were nonthreatening and involved light physical contact—which were enjoyable. In the second session, Rick was instructed to sit in a small chair facing the counselor and to name parts of my body that he could see. As he named each he smiled, giggled, and then said, "OK." This entire interaction took less than five minutes.

> R: This is your hand. It's rough, the knuckles are hard. But that means they are good for fighting. You have fingers and a thumb and fingernails.
> C: My hand is calloused and rough.
> R: (Touching elbow) Your elbow is sharp, pointed, and very hard. It could hurt, too. (Touching knee) It's like your elbow, but not as pointed; kind of smooth.
> C: (Silence) (Rick pushes chair back and away.)
> C: You appear uncomfortable. What other parts can you touch? (No response, Rick looks away toward ceiling, then floor.)
> C: Would you mind if I touched you and named some of your body parts?
> R: O.K. Just don't touch my private parts.

C: (Moving chair toward Rick) This is your hair, it's soft and fluffy. (Rick giggles) These are your ears, they are small, rather round on the outside, with small lobes beneath. The lobes have very few nerve endings. When we pinch them lightly, it doesn't hurt; there isn't much feeling. (Rick, with a surprised expression, grasps his earlobes and pinches hard.)

R: I must have more nerves in my ears than you. It hurts when I pinch them hard.

C: The nerves in our bodies help us to feel pain and hurt. Sometimes I feel hurt without being pinched. (Rick looks puzzled and again moves away.) How do you feel right now Rick?

R: Weird! Let's do something else. (Rick picked up his stuffed toy penguin and described how his nose, wings, and feet felt.)

The third session began with the fantasy-related activities: "washing" and "X marks the spot." We again faced each other in chairs.

C: Rick, would you enjoy using your imagination today?

R: (Smiling) Yes.

C: O.K. We are going to pretend that we have a bowl of warm, sudsy water and a wash cloth, a bowl of cool water to rinse, and a large fluffy towel to dry ourselves. First, I will wash your hands, arms, and face and then you can do mine.

R: (Grins, moves chair close.)

C: (Begins washing activity, no words spoken until we are almost finished, Rick suddenly pulls back, puts his thumb in his mouth, and grabs Fred.)

R: Goo goo! Gah gah!

C: You're feeling small like a baby who gets cared for and cleaned.

R: (Nods head affirmatively.)

C: It's OK for babies to need help and attention. How do you feel?

R: Funny, I got chills.

C: Some of the things we do will give us goose bumps. It's your turn to wash me.

R: (Jumps up smiling, moves so he stands directly between my legs and actively washes my hands and face, then aggressively dries me with his cloth jacket giggling the entire time.)

C: It's a little silly but fun to do this to me.

R: Yeah! Let's do some more.

C: OK, turn around and close your eyes. I am going to lightly touch your back (using my index finger, I begin to make a large X, across Rick's back, three dots down his spine, pinch his ribs on right side and squeeze ribs on left while saying) X marks the spot and three dots, a pinch, a squeeze, and an ocean breeze. (I then blow lighly on his neck.)

R: (Smiling) That's fun. Do it again.

R: OK Let me do you. (The activity is repeated several times.)
(Roles are reversed. He remembers the exact sequence and wording of the activity.)

C: How would you like to teach that to your mom?

R: Maybe. (Grabs Fred) Let's draw.

The entire fourth session was devoted to the activity "body drawing." Two pieces of large, plain paper were cut from a roll to lengths longer than the child and the counselor.

> C: Let's spend today tracing each other on these papers. First, you lie down here and I will trace you.
> R: (Gets on paper and assumes a rigid posture.)
> C: (Touching Rick's arms and hands.) Try to relax, spread your fingers and keep your arms away from your body. (A grin appears on his face.) It feels funny to have me draw around you.
> R: Yeah! It tickles. But I like it.
>   (The tracing continued through completion.)
> R: Is that really how I look?
> C: It is the outline of your body. Many times we aren't aware of how we look on the outside to others or how we feel inside.
> R: Can I fill the inside in? I'm naked. But, I haven't traced you.
> C: You may either trace me now or draw features on your picture. It's your decision.
> R: I'll trace you, then we can draw together. OK?
> C: Fine. (Rick smiles and picks up his pencil.)

This activity continued through the fifth session because Rick desired to draw in detailed features on the two outlines, color them, and hang them in the room.

Painful Stage

Although Rick was allowed to make decisions in the previous sessions and exert some control in the play relationship, activities designed specifically to elicit the realization of the attachment relation and limits in play were not initiated until the sixth session. An additional goal was also instituted at this time to encourage the child to explore and express his feelings about the counselor, himself, his father, and his mother respectively. The seventh session involved the activities "piggy-back-ride" and "tickle."

> C: Today, I'll give you a piggy-back ride. Get on the chair so I can get you on my back.
> R: (Laughing) Are you sure? I'm pretty heavy.
> C: You're big all right, but I think I can carry you for awhile.
>   (Rick gets on, puts arms around my neck and legs around waist, we gallop around the room, back to the chair, Rick says nothing and remains expressionless.) That wasn't too bad! How would you like to try my shoulders? It will be less stressful for my back.
> R: OK, but go slow, I'm not too sure.
> C: Get on the table and I'll bend down.
>   (Rick puts his legs over my shoulders and arms around my head and neck. I grasp Rick's legs firmly.) Ready? Here we go.

R: Wow! (The ride nears the door.)

I don't want to go in the hall. Bet you don't dare!

C: What do you mean? You don't want to go in the hall, yet you dared me to go.

R: Oh! I really do want to go. Other kids can see me. It's great.

I wish we could cover your head and people could see me here. I'm big.

C: You're strong, powerful, in control.

R: Yeah! Invulnerable.

C: No one could hurt you. You wouldn't be afraid of anything.

R: I really wish we could go out in the hall.

C: No, our play and what we do together must remain in this room. When we leave we have to abide by the school rules.

R: Rules can be a pain.

C: I'm tired. I need to sit down. (Counselor and Rick sit in chairs facing each other.)

Whew! That was harder to do than I thought, but it was fun. Let's play tickle.

R: What's that?

C: (Moves toward Rick until knees are touching his.)

Put your hands on my shoulders and I'll show you how. (Rick follows instructions. His ribs are counted and tickled.

Rick tries to maintain his composure but begins laughing.)

R: OK Stop. I want to do you. (Roles were reversed and the session concluded.)

The eighth session involved the counselor and client in an activity called "wrestle." The client was instructed by the therapist in several high school wrestling techniques including: take downs, escapes from the controlled position, and maintaining control in the "top" position. Practice of each wrestling technique followed the instructions. The ninth and tenth sessions continued the wrestling activity and the client experienced being in control, being controlled, and winning and losing points. Throughout these sessions, the counselor responded to the client's feelings of power, control, self-respect, and self-esteem. Temporary plans have been made to initiate the separation-and-love stage through bibliotherapy activities where the therapist will initially read some nursery rhymes and other fun stories to Rick as he sits on his lap. Following these stories, "reading-in-lap" will continue but focus on children's books about divorce. Readers are referred to Chapter 7 for an extensive discussion of bibliotherapy and the list of recommended resources. Termination plans are tentatively made to include: (a) enrolling Rick in the local Boy's Club, (b) getting him a big brother from the local community, (c) increasing his contacts with the male, school principal, (d) beginning counseling sessions with the female school counselor, and (e) decreasing therapy sessions with the private counselor to once each week. The two counselors, school and private, will consult with each other to assist in the transition and continuation of service. Once these activities are accomplished, closure will be finalized with the private counselor assuming the role of consultant. The counselor's role as consultant is discussed in detail in Chapter 14.

RECOMMENDED RESOURCES

BRODY, V., Fenderson, C., STEPHENSON, S. *Sourcebook for finding your way to helping young children through developmental play.* Tallahassee, FL: Department of State, 1976. (Distributed by Pupil Personnel Services Demonstration Project, All Children's Hospital, St. Petersburg, FL.)

This handbook contains a description of the DP program including rationale, research, goals, and activities. The activities are designed for use on one-to-one adult–child interactions and children's group interactions. These activities utilize physical contact, fantasy, and creativity. The handbook also contains a section on the selection, training, and development of adults who will work in DP. Of particular help are the appendixes, which provide sample forms, rating scales, and other handouts.

JERNBERG, A. *Theraplay.* San Francisco, California: Jossey-Bass, 1979.

This book focuses on a special form of play therapy for children experiencing low self-confidence and lack of trust. The author describes it as an intimate, physical, and fun intervention therapy. Theraplay requires the therapist to develop a sequence of highly structured activities to challenge and add structure to the child's life. Techniques, practical examples, case studies, recommended activities, and "do's and don'ts" are provided throughout the book. Also included are chapters on family therapy and techniques for use with exceptional children.

SUMMARY

This chapter on developmental play was divided into four sections. The first section provided an overall description of the DP program including theory, rationale, goals, and sample activities. The second section described the key concepts: developmental play program, developmental play process stages of one-to-one play, developmental group process stages for circle time, physical contact, body language, and fantasy. The final section mentioned basic techniques, provided an example of DP activity, and contained a list of recommended resources.

REFERENCES AND RECOMMENDED READINGS

ARGYLE, M. *Bodily communication.* New York: International Universities, 1975.

BARUCH, D. *One little boy.* New York: Random House, 1954.

BOWLBY, J. *Attachment and loss.* Volume I, Separation. New York: Basic Books, 1969.

——. *Attachment and loss.* Volume II, Separation. New York: Basic Books, 1973.

BRODY, V., FENDERSON, C., & STEPHENSON, S. *Sourcebook for finding your way to helping young children through developmental play.* Tallahassee, FL: Department of State, 1976.

BURT, M. & MYRICK, R. Developmental play: What's it all about? *Elementary School Guidance and Counseling,* 15(1), 1980, 14–19.

CALL, J. Games babies play. *Psychology Today,* January, 1970.

GOFFMAN, E. *Behavior in public places.* New York: Free Press, 1969.

HALL, E. Silent assumptions in social communication. *Disorders of Communication,* 1964, 42, 41–55.

——. *The hidden dimension.* New York: Doubleday, 1966.

LOWENFELD, M. *Play in childhood.* New York: Wiley & Sons, 1967.

MCCANDLESS, B. *Children behavior and development.* New York: Holt, Rinehart, & Winston, 1967.

MEHRABIAN, A. *Silent messages.* Belmont, CA: Wadsworth, 1971.

MONTAGUE, A. *Touching.* New York: Harper & Row, 1971.

PIERS, M. (Ed.) *Play and development.* New York: W. W. Norton, 1972.

SCHEFLEN, A. *Body language and social order.* Englewood Cliffs, NJ: Prentice Hall, 1972.

——. *How behavior means.* New York: Gordon Breach, 1973.

SPITZ, R. Hospitalism: An inquiry into the genesis of psychiatric conditions in early childhood. In O. Fenichal et al. (Eds.) *The psychoanalytic study of the child,* Vol. I. New York: International Universities Press, 1945, 53–74.

——. Hospitalism: A follow-up report on investigation described in Vol. I, 1945. In O. Fenichal et al. (Eds.) *The psychoanalytic study of the child,* Vol. II. New York: International Universitites Press, 1846, 113–117.

Chapter 5

Art Therapy
and Serial Drawing

No SINGLE COUNSELOR or therapist can be credited with the introduction of "art therapy" in the mental health professions. In fact, even today arguments among counselors, educators, therapists, and psychotherapists continue vehemently as to what is art therapy. The term *art therapy* is currently used to describe widely varying practices of all these professionals. In an attempt to define art therapy, Elinor Ulman (1977) has pointed out that certain professionals and volunteers are referred to as art therapists "... even though no similar educational preparation, no set of qualifications, nor even any voluntary association binds these people together. Possibly the only thing common to all their activities is that the materials of the visual arts are used in some attempt to assist integration or reintegration of personality" (p. 3). Because of the current state of confusion regarding definition of the professional status and practices of art therapy, I choose to limit my introductory remarks to the last 40 years and to those professionals clearly designated as art therapists, and not to professionals identified merely as doing art therapy.

In the early 1940s, Margaret Naumberg first introduced art as a tool in a form of psychotherapy that she termed "analytically" and "dynamically" oriented. Naumberg's art therapy has its origins tied closely to psychotherapy and key concepts are derived from psychoanalytic theory. Her art therapy has evolved to emphasize the "therapy" and to focus on the patient's release of unconscious material through spontaneous art expression. Treatment depends on the development of the transference relationship between patient and therapist, and the patient's ability to "free associate" through art media and interpret these images which constitute "symbolic speech" between patient and therapist. The use of art in this way is an extension of psychoanalytic interpreting and is the central focus of an intensive one-to-one relationship with the patient. Art was, therefore, considered as the primary therapeutic method and not as an ancillary treatment to other methodologies. However, Naumberg felt that any well-trained psychotherapist interested in the creative application of art media in treatment of patients could use art therapy. In addition, she limited the use of art media to those materials that were easily obtained and managed (Naumberg, 1958; 1966).

In the 1950s, Edith Kramer established a contradictory theoretical opinion. Although Kramer also relied heavily on psychoanalytic concepts, she centered her theory and treatment on the inherent healing qualities of the creative, artistic process: "In the creative act, conflict is reexperienced, resolved, and integrated . . . In the artistic product, conflict is formed and contained but only partly neutralized. . . . " (Kramer, 1958). Art therapy then complemented psychotherapy by assisting the release and expression of unconscious material without eliminating necessary patient defenses. As a result of these symbolic experiences, clients are able to "try out" behavior changes in a safe environment and in a relatively protected way. Kramer also differed from Naumberg in that she advocated patients be seen in groups in which the art activities and products became a part of the overall therapeutic milieu. In the group environment, Kramer's art therapist portrayed three roles, including artist, teacher, and therapist (Kramer, 1958). Kramer's influence on art therapy remained in force throughout the 1960s and 1970s.

The decade of the 1970s witnessed several additional changes in art therapy. Kwiatkowska expanded upon Kramer's group therapeutic milieu to include family groups in which the psychodynamics of relationships among and between family members was primarily stressed (Ulman, Kramer, & Kwiatkowska, 1978). Rhyne (1973) also introduced art in groups of "normal" persons to expand and enrich their lives. She used art activities as a method to encourage self-expression, self-perception, and group interactions. Art therapy, therefore, was viewed as a method to assist healthy changes in personality or life-style that could be transferred to the real world outside of therapy.

Art therapy is currently considered as a generic term that includes a broad range of activities which include both art and therapy. Communication and insight may take precedence over artistic creation or vice versa. Art therapists, in general, agree that in order to proceed successfully in therapy, the therapeutic and the artistic processes proceed hand in hand. In the last 10 years, art therapy has experienced an increase in professional status with the establishment of the American Art Therapy Association and the publication of the *American Journal of Art Therapy* (formerly the Bulletin of Art Therapy).

The Value of Art Therapy

Art has been historically associated with unique, gifted, and creative persons who used their talents to produce satisfaction for a limited wealthy few. However, today art is considered for everybody not only in the sense of being made accessible for the aesthetic appreciation of the general public, but also from the perspective that all persons can profit from self-expression through art and that they possess the ability to be artistic. Self-expression through art must be perceived by the counselor as an extension of the client and treated as such. The art therapist, therefore, does not interfere with the client's art activity but allows and encourages "free expression" with explanation by the client.

As with play therapy and the use of toys, art therapy provides children with an active therapeutic milieu that is attractive and fun. Although participating in art activities may be initially threatening to some children, once children learn that their work is appreciated and not evaluated, and that they have total control and are responsible for its disposition, they eagerly become involved. Generally, art in therapy is beneficial to children and the counselor in the following ways:

1. Art involves children in using their minds and their senses. It fulfills a cognitive function in that it requires children to think before they act and to utilize their knowledge of environmental influences by synthesizing various sensual inputs into an integrated product, such as a picture or a sculpture.
2. Children can express their thoughts and emotions related to past events, the present, and even project them into future activities. As a result, the counselor has access to clients' perceptions of their behavior that are often directly unobservable.
3. Art allows for the catharsis of angry, hostile feelings of children in a socially accepted and harmless fashion. Children who are violent towards others often act out aggressively and physically because they feel they have no alternative strategies through which they can release these negative tensions.
4. Art is self-initiated and self-controlled. It is the product of the child and as such is ego-enhancing.
5. Art media, the artistic process, and the finished product provide children with a sense of growth and accomplishment, personal satisfaction, and self-worth.
6. Art is useful to the therapist in that it provides a means of establish-

ing rapport and building the therapeutic relationship with reluctant or non-verbal children.

7. Art provides the therapist with access to unconscious material of children without disturbing fragile or necessary defense mechanisms.

8. Art also may be used as a diagnostic indicator to supplement other sources of information on the client. It allows children to express the truth of the moment, that which is real for them at that time. For example, children who are defending at high levels may tend to create monotonous reproductions or may want to trace rather than draw.

I recently experienced one client who would draw nothing but Superman and another who in the first stages of counseling persisted in drawing only the cartoon characters from the Peanuts™ comic strip.

Art produced by children, therefore, has the capacity to indicate their talent, physical and mental developmental levels, personality, and their relationships to the real world or everyday environment.

Most children like art because it is an expression of themselves and an emotionally satisfying experience. Art can be of particular value to those children whose disturbance restricts their capacities to participate in play. In addition, art therapy allows children the freedom of choice and expression and is closely linked to fantasy and imaginative play. Through art, children can symbolically express forbidden wishes, painful experiences can be assimilated and integrated, and hostile and aggressive feelings can be safely emoted. Children need to be able to express and experience their positive and negative impulses without fear of reprisal or everyday consequences. Art therapy provides this freedom of expression, yet also provides the necessary external structure and organization which helps children to trust and feel in some control of themselves and their relationship with the counselor.

KEY CONCEPTS

Art therapy, like play therapy, was heavily influenced by psychoanalytic theory. The unconscious and the defense mechanisms (displacement and projection) were discussed in Chapter 3. However, it is necessary to briefly review and embellish these key concepts as they relate to art therapy.

Unconscious, Displacement, and Projection

In art therapy, one goal of the therapist is to use art media as a source for gradually uncovering the client's unconscious. However, the universal appeal of toys for children is not necessarily present with art media. Children's preferences for using specific art media such as finger painting and sculpting with clay are readily apparent. Just as obvious is their avoidance of involvement with other art activities. For example, many children will resist or refuse to draw; especially human figures required in drawing a person or drawing a family. Some children say "I can't"; others "I won't"; still others will only sit and stare at the pencil, crayons, and paper. These children experience the common fear of being inadequate in their performance and ridiculed by an adult. It is a fear of failure that is imbedded in youngsters by our achievement-oriented society in which children and their work are compared and contrasted from birth. It becomes imperative in using art therapy to uncover the unconscious that the technique and media selected be ego-supportive and enhancing and not anxiety-producing. A helpful suggestion would be to initially provide a variety of media from which the client might choose to work. I have found that a limited "art media menu" is effective in the beginning of counseling. It is also important to remember that no two children experience the world in the same way. Both the selection and use of art media by a child is characteristic of only that child and his or her problems, no other. In art therapy, counselors must maintain a sense of individualization of the child. As trust for the therapist and a sense of security and control in the therapeutic relationship are experienced and developed, the counselor may decide to attempt to involve the child in a more-structured art activity to uncover specific repressed material in the unconscious as described in the "Play Process" section of Chapter 3.

Use of the defense mechanisms displacement and projection in art therapy serve to reduce client anxiety and provide excellent sources of information for the counselor. When hurt, angered, or frustrated, children who are experiencing emotional problems often exhibit socially inappropriate behavior such as fighting or withdrawal. Often the use of art in therapy allows children to displace these pent-up emotions in ways that relieve their personal pain without damaging themselves or others physically, mentally, or educationally. Figure 5–1 provides an example of how one client used displacement successfully in her counseling. The client, a 12-year-old white female had previously described threats from a black female child and her eventual confrontations and fights. She was intimidated to the point of experiencing psychosomatic illnesses before school each day in the form of stomach aches, headaches, and vomiting, and eventually had become school phobic. In a later session, while discussing this incapacitating fear, the therapist suggested that she draw a picture of her tormentor. She began immediately and became totally involved in the drawing. The therapist observed her as she drew and remained silent. When she had completed the picture, she sat back in her chair and sighed. When asked, "What would you like to do to this person?" She replied,

Figure 5-1

"destroy her, eliminate her." As she said these words, she marked across the picture several times. Following this spontaneous, cathartic discharge of anger, the client was able to initiate rational discussion of her situation for the remainder of the meeting. The displacement of her emotions was continued through her drawings in later sessions.

I personally find projection in art therapy most helpful as a representation of my clients' perceptions of their relationships to important others in life such as family or friends and to their environments such as home and school. More often than not, these projections are a combination of fact and fantasy, and the therapist's efforts to understand children and their worlds are complicated indeed. As a result, I will typically use draw-a-person and draw-a-family activities as methods for obtaining supplementary or corroborating information on a client. For example, George, an

8-year-old child of divorced parents, was referred by his mother for therapy because she felt he did not relate well with others and repressed his emotions. Most of George's initial drawings involved conflict and fighting between spaceships. He would discuss *Star Wars*ᵐ and the *Empire Strikes Back*ᵐ as he drew. These stories focused on the concepts of hostility, aggression, and "firepower" (I interpret this as potency) as being important in controlling the universe. When asked to "draw a person about his age" in a subsequent session, he selected a pencil and began by drawing a straight line the length of the paper as ground. He then drew rectangular feet to which he attached legs and body. At the lower portion of the body, he drew a distorted oblong shape—"the penis." He then drew a head on the body and horizontal lines across the body. As he began to color the person, he recognized his omission of arms and drew them in to complete his person. A sun and two birds were also included as he colored. It is noteworthy that his sun and largest bird included smiling faces while his human appears emotionless. I asked George what the penis was by pointing to it and saying, "What is this?" He looked perturbed, hesitated, then said, "I forget." George's drawing supported his mother's concern regarding unexpressed emotions. It also indicated his confusion with his maleness and possible fantasies about his role as a male.

Art is a media through which fantasies can be expressed. Bob was a 13-year-old who was small for his age and weak from repeated illnesses. He drew a basketball player with a large and strong upper body, fists clenched, and a determined, strong face, and no lower body.

No doubt his fantasy about being strong and competitive with others motivated the drawing. What interested me was his omission of the lower body. My conjecture was that he was not only fantasizing his desire for strength, but that he was also experiencing ego and sexual-identity concerns. This conjecture was corroborated somewhat in his drawing of his family in which he placed himself next to his mother on a raised platform which indicated his indentification with the opposite sex, need for "raised" status in the family, and/or competition with father for mother. None of the family members are touching and mother's breasts are a predominant feature in his drawing of her.

Sublimation

Sublimation is a form of displacement in which psychic energy or anxiety is transferred from one goal or object choice which is lower order to a higher order goal. To help distinguish lower-order from higher-order, goal-directed behavior, readers are referred to Chapter 1 and the discussion on Maslow's hierarchy of needs. Sublimation in art therapy occurs when children move forward in their psychological growth processes (progress up Maslow's hierarchy) through creative art activity. For sublimation to be in effect, counselors must expect a change in client's objects of interest, goal directedness, and intensity of involvement in activities used to achieve their goals. Other critical factors for sublimation are that activities be highly pleasurable and ego enhancing. Art therapy, therefore, is directed toward achieving sublimation. Sublimation increases children's ability to be creative and learn to cope with life stresses.

Creativity

Children's general growth is related to their creative development. Lowenfeld (1957) has defined creative development as the development of awareness, originality, and self-identification. In addition, he postulated eight basic sub-concepts of creativity:

1. *sensitivity*—the child's awareness and understanding of problems (thoughts and feelings) related to self and others.
2. *fluency*—the child's abilty to think and act rapidly and freely.
3. *flexibility*—the child's ability to adjust to new situations.
4. *originality*—the child's ability to think of and develop novel ideas.
5. *reorganize*—the child's capacity to redefine problems.
6. *abstract*—the child's skill for analyzing parts of problems and seeing relationships among those parts.
7. *synthesize*—the child's ability to combine in thought several elements of an activity into a potential product.
8. *organize*—the child's ability to implement elements of an activity into a product.

The art therapist's task is to structure conditions which provide for maximal individual creative expression with sufficient boundaries to prevent unnecessary anxiety and isolation. To do this, the therapist must be aware of and understand the emotional growth processes of children's work, which includes their age appropriate and developmental stage appropriate performance. Naumberg (1966) described four steps of self-identification in drawing that can be recognized as part of the emotional growth process.

1. *Stereotyped repetitions*, which are usually observed in children's drawings who are inflexible and experience adjustment problems.
2. *Objective reports* or *generalizations*, which are escapes into a pattern and seem to be a projection generated by environmental stress. These reports or generalizations are representative of children who are detached from their emotions and who do not include anything personal in their work.

3. The *occasional inclusion of self*, which represents children who have achieved some emotional growth and feel free enough to express it in their work.
4. The *inclusion of self*, which represents children who are emotionally free and unhibited in their creative expression.

Developmental Growth Stages in Children's Drawing

In an effort to relate children's art to developmental growth stages, Lowenfeld (1957) adapted the developmental stages of Erikson to pencil drawings of children. He established five stages: the scribbling stage (2 to 4 years), the preschematic stage (4 to 7 years), the schematic stage (7 to 9 years), the gang stage (9 to 11 years), and the pseudonaturalistic stage (11 to 13 years). Table–1 summarizes these stages.

Scribbling Stage

The beginning of scribbling on the child's part is important because it represents first attempts at self-expression. This stage is divided into three parts. *Disordered scribbling* is characterized by random marks with the absence of visual-motor control. Since the child lacks fine motor skills, the only shapes repeated are large sweeps. Satisfaction for the child is achieved through experiencing kinesthetic motion. *Controlled* scribbling occurs about six months after disordered scribbling when children realize they can control motions and there is a connection between their motions and marks on a paper. This scribbling contains horizontal and vertical lines and circles. *Naming* of scribbling is the level in which children connect their motions to their environment. Children begin to think imaginatively and form mental images which lead to their first pictures of environment. No conscious use of color is made. The role of the counselor is to develop trust, to accept children's work, to attempt to understand what is drawn, and to encourage and support.

Preschematic Stage

In this stage, children consciously begin to reorganize scribblings in symbols. Man is usually the first symbol achieved because of the importance of people in the child's world. Man is typically drawn with a large circle for a head and two vertical lines for the body or legs. However, there exists a constant change of symbols used. Flexibility in drawing is characteristic of this stage, and so a child who has stereotyped repetitions or repeated drawings may be experiencing emotional blocks. Different colors are used to designate meaning based on their emotional appeal. The role of

Table 5-1
DEVELOPMENTAL STAGES IN CHILDREN'S DRAWING

Stage	Age	Characteristics	Human Figure	Space Representation	Color
Scribbling	2–4	Little motor control, circular motions, beginning self-expression	None or only imaginatively	None or only imaginatively	No conscious use
Preschematic	4–7	Discovery of relationships between objects, large muscle control, some fine motor skills, beginning self-awareness, first representational efforts	Search for concept, changing symbols	No order, relationships according to emotional significance	Emotional use, according to appeal
Schematic	7–9	Discovery of concepts through repetitive drawing, motor skills accomplished, achievement of form concept	Definite concept, use of geometric shapes	Baseline discovered and used, discovery of self in environment	Definite relationship between color and objects in environment, visually oriented
Gang	9–11	Increased self-awareness, developing position with peers, drawing realism	Removal of geometric lines, greater stiffness, emphasis of clothes and sexual differences	Removal of baseline concept, overlapping in objects, two dimensional	Movement away from visual, objective use of color, some subjective coloring based on emotional significance of object
Pseudo-naturalistic	11–13	Developed intelligence, verbally oriented, preadolescent emotions, realistic views, reasoning	Visual interpretation of body movements, body parts in proportion	Two- and three-dimensional	Definite relationship between color and emotions, haptically oriented

the therapist is to stimulate the child's thinking, feeling, and perceiving capacities. The child is encouraged to develop autonomy by making choices and assuming the responsibility and the consequences for these choices.

Schematic Stage

Lowenfeld defines schema as the concept "at which a child has arrived and which he repeats again and again whenever no intentional experience influences him to change this concept." For example, the concept human schema would be achieved when a child repeats the symbol for man several times. By the age of seven, this human symbol should contain a head, arms, legs, and a body. The mouth, nose, and eyes should be distinctly different; there should be hair and an awareness of the neck. Hands, fingers, and feet should also be included as separate symbols. Clothes may take the place of the body. The human schema is an individualized concept which reflects the psychosocial growth of the child. At this time, children's awareness of their thoughts and feelings and their perceptions of environment are projected in and around the human schema. As a result, drawings of family become valuable resources for counselors when this stage is reached.

Children will usually draw objects on a ground line which runs horizontally across the paper. Objects drawn will exist in logical relationships with other objects on the paper. The selection of color is no longer subjective and emotional but has a definite relationship with the object such as green grass, blue sky, or a yellow sun. Notable deviations from human and environmental schema would include body parts that are exaggerated in terms of size, omitted body parts, and illogical or unrealistic placement of body parts and objects. The therapist's role is to encourage the child to self-initiate in art activities; that is, to plan, organize, and implement creative ideas and work toward sublimation. Children need to feel independent, in control, accepted for what they do, and valued for their accomplishments by the counselor.

Gang Stage

Children recognize the importance of their associations and relationships with society and peers. A greater social independence from adult direction is developed and there exists a greater awareness and understanding of environment. Children's art includes more naturalistic representations. For example, the sky and ground are integrated into an entire design. Greater effort is expended on providing details to the human figure. Color is used according to the subjective experiences of children with the significant objects. Any discussion of color between therapist and child should focus on the child's experience with the object and not the color. The counselor should focus on motivating the child toward developing personal potential. Children are encouraged to examine values and to make value judgments in relation to society and important others. Self-criticism and competition with peers is to be expected and should be channeled in ways that will enhance success experiences and personal growth rather than self-depreciation.

Pseudonaturalistic Stage

Children are experiencing preadolescence. They have developed intellectually to the point of being able to communicate as adults verbally; yet, they are not emotionally or physically mature. Children in this stage experience confusion related to the transition taking place between a child's thinking and feeling to that of an adult level. Drawings of the human include a knowledge of detail previously unachieved and a sense of proportion among body parts. Color may be used either as an expression of visual impressions or as an expression of subjective, emotional experiences. The counselor should focus on helping children develop individuality and socially acceptable ways to release confused emotions or excessive anxiety.

BASIC TECHNIQUES

Basic art techniques that I have found useful with children include selection and use of art media, perceiving, and responding. Although Chapters 2 and 3 included discussion on responding to feelings and behaviors, I am including reponding here also to introduce the additional verbal skills of support, self-disclosure, and interpretation, which are necessary for the successful art therapist. The responding skills discussed in this text are valuable in all modes of counseling at all times. However, I also recognize that some verbal responses are identified more with certain modes of therapy.

Art Media: Selection and Use

Art therapists may select and use a wide range of materials. As in the case of play process and developmental play, art media should be selected purposely. Some important considerations in the selection of media are the developmental levels of children in counseling, and the potential of the media to facilitate the client's growth and control. As pointed out in Table 5-1, children develop different motor skills and cognitive abilities in drawing as they grow older. These skills and capabilities are generalized to all facets of art therapy. Very young children lack fine motor coordination and will experience frustration with drawing or painting with brushes. Yet, they can enjoy and be creative with primary crayons and finger paints. Clay and easel painting may also be used successfully with very young children. In any case, very young children and handicapped children need materials that are easily manipulated. A good rule of thumb in selecting media for young children is the simpler the medium the better.

Older children provide more flexibility in selection of art media. Art supplies might be arranged so the client can choose from many. A preferred method is to present a menu of art activities from which the client can "order" the activity. A sufficient variety of paints, colors, sizes of paper, clay, felt-tip pens, and pencils should be provided to encourage spontaneity and creativity in the child. Other media that have been beneficial, depending on the child's interest and abilities, are sculpture (wire, pipe cleaner, sponge, and papier mâché), collages, mobiles, tie dye, macramé, pottery, ceramics, photography, and poetry.

To facilitate client growth, it is important for the counselor to remember that too many materials can be overwhelming to some children. The therapist must respect the individuality of each client and be sensitive not to use those materials that will increase anxiety. For example, I once worked with a young lady who welcomed the opportunity to smear with finger paints. However, at the conclusion of our session, she became distant and her face expressed extreme worry. Following a brief discussion, I learned she had soiled some of her clothing and was afraid to go home to reproachful parents. In addition, different media are likely to evoke different emotions in clients. For some children, clay might be an excellent outlet for aggression. It can be molded into shapes resembling objects of anger, thrown, pounded, and cut. However, other children might use clay to reconstruct images of love such as a heart. The counselor's job is to become familiar with different media and knowledgeable regarding the types of behaviors and feelings each tends to elicit from children. The therapist can then weigh the advantages and disadvantages of materials prior to their use and select accordingly.

Kramer (1971) discussed five ways that art activities might be used in art therapy:

1. *Precursory activities:* Scribbling, smearing, exploring physical properties of the material in ways that do not lead to creation of symbolic configuration but are experienced as positive and egosyntonic.
2. *Chaotic discharge:* Spilling, splashing, pounding, and other destructive behaviors leading to loss of control.
3. *Art in the service of defense:* Copying, tracing, banal conventional production, and stereotyped repetition.
4. *Pictographs:* Pictorial communications which replace or supple-

ment words. Such communications occur as the therapeutic relationship grows.

5. *Formed expression:* Art in the full sense of the word: the production of symbolic configurations that successfully serve both self-expression and communication.

With children, it is also important to have materials stored securely so they do not invite distractions or improper use. Other considerations in selection and controlling the use of art media are room size and preparation and clean-up time. A studio with tile floors and sink is ideal. The art therapist should avoid potentially messy activities in carpeted areas or other hard-to-clean surfaces. Time is an important factor to most everyone involved in the treatment of children. It is foolish to select activities that require as much or more preparation and clean-up time as is allowed for processing of the activity. My rule of thumb is a one-third, two-thirds formula. I do not allow any more than 20 minutes of a therapeutic hour for preparation and clean-up; this ensures a minimum of 40 minutes for performing and processing the art activity. As a result, I prefer quick, easy access, easy-to-use and easy-to-clean medias. Drawing is the single most productive resource.

Perceiving

The technique of perceiving includes establishing the therapeutic relationship. First, it is necessary to view (perceive) the world as it appears to the child. What are the important issues for the client? How does the child think and feel about significant others and environment? The attempt to perceive the child's world is important, but even more important is the accuracy with which the therapist perceives it and responds to it. The speed with which therapy progresses is directly proportional to the accuracy of the counselor's perceptions and responses. In establishing the therapeutic relationship, I attempt to put myself into the child's world, view it from his or her perspective (be aware), understand it, and empathize with the experience by responding to the child's feelings and thoughts. The reader is referred to Chapter 3 for a more detailed discussion and example of responding to feelings. Thus, the ability to perceive accurately includes being empathic and responding.

Responding

The supportive milieu provided by an empathic, understanding, accepting, nonjudgmental therapist who responds to feelings is important in establishing the therapeutic relationship and maintaining the curative process. In addition to this support system, counselors can provide verbal *support* by encouraging clients to experiment with new ideas and skills. I may reinforce a child who self-initiates a new activity readily by saying, "John, you are always ready to work and waste little time getting started. It is fun working with you. You keep me on my toes." Or, in another instance, I might support a child who has reached an impasse in a drawing activity by saying, "Drawing details does not always come easy or naturally. Sometimes it helps just to stop and think it over." Children need the support of the therapist to learn to trust themselves and their judgments. Verbal support provided at appropriate times can help facilitate client movement by increasing self-confidence and self-esteem.

Children may also feel supported by the therapist's *self-disclosure*. I may demonstrate or verbalize to the child that, "I, too, have difficulty drawing or making certain objects the way I want." In these instances, self-disclosure is intended to reassure children that frustration in learning is a part of success. Therapist self-disclosure can foster a child's self-acceptance. Self-disclosure can also advance therapy if used as a form of interpretation. For example, when working with a child who was being repetitive in his drawing, I have said, "When I was in second grade, I drew only tigers. I was the best at tigers in the school and everyone wanted me to draw them a tiger. But you know the real reason I drew tigers was that I felt I couldn't do other things very well." My interpretation and reason for using this self-disclosure is, of course, that the child may be afraid of failing or fearful of reaching out and experiencing the environment. It is hoped the child will understand that it is acceptable to make mistakes and that failure at certain tasks are a part of learning in life.

Interpretation

Interpretation is a skill which is invaluable to the art therapist. *First,* the therapist must attempt to perceive accurately what the client is projecting when using art media. Several studies (Burns & Kaufman, 1970; Di Leo, 1970; and Koppitz, 1968) have provided empirical evidence which suggests that certain items appear more frequently in drawings of disturbed children than those of healthy children. In the draw-a-person activity, disturbed children consistently draw: 1) distorted, grotesque, monster figures; 2) stiff, rigid figures suggesting high degrees of anxiety; 3) unintegrated, nonconnected figures; and 4) bodies with excessive shading or coloring, which also suggests high anxiety.

Machover (1949) made the following suggestions for interpretation of the human figure:

1. Head: A child will offer a head as a completed person but never a trunk, neck, or arms. A disproportionately large head may indicate an inflicted ego, paranoid, or narcissistic individual. If the

head is drawn last, it may indicate disturbance in interpersonal relationships.

2. Face: The face might be interpreted as the social feature of the drawing. Children who deliberately omit facial features in drawing while showing delineation in other parts of the body may be indicating difficulties with interpersonal relationships.

3. Mouth: The mouth when overemphasized may indicate excessive anxiety associated with eating habits and control such as that experienced by the obese or anorectic child. The mouth drawn as a straight line indicates tension.

4. Eyes: The eyes have been characterized as the focal point of the self. Large, rounded, dark, or menacing eyes which create an image of hostility and suspicion are projected by paranoid children. Small, beady eyes may also indicate the nontrusting child.

5. Hair: The location and emphasis placed on hair by the individual child may indicate striving toward virility or sexual identity. Sexually delinquent girls often combine wavy, long hair and specific body detail of the breasts in their drawings.

6. Neck: The omission of the neck might be interpreted as a sign of immaturity.

7. Arms and hands: Vague or missing arms and hands may indicate a lack of confidence in social interactions. Hands behind backs or in pockets might be interpreted as avoidance or evasiveness. Excessive size in hands and arms may be a desire for strength from a weak child or a reaction to guilt over use of the hands in socially "taboo" behaviors such as masturbation or stealing.

8. Legs and feet: Legs and feet are indicators of social conflicts. Crippled children often omit these features or draw a seated figure. As shown in Bob's drawing of the basketball player, children who experience sexual problems are also less likely to draw the human figure below the waistline.

In the draw-a-family activity, the therapist is most likely to obtain pertinent information related to the client's perceptions about important others and the family environment. Di Leo (1973) discusses the following factors for consideration of family drawing:

1. Size of family members: The most influential or dominant member of the family is usually drawn the largest and first.

2. Position: Children will tend to draw themselves next to the preferred parent, as described where Bob drew himself elevated next to his mother.

3. Similarity: Children often will draw themselves to appear like the person they prefer to be. Children's desire for similarity often appears in the drawing of details such as clothing and jewelry.

4. Omission of family member or self: Children who omit family members may be projecting anger toward that member and a desire to remove the source of tension. An omission of self from the drawing might indicate a sense of insecurity in the family or a lack of the sense of belonging.

5. Isolation and interaction: Children who feel ignored or not a part of the family often draw themselves away from other family members and last.

It is helpful to remember that children who are well adjusted usually draw family members holding hands—father and mother are together, and all members are drawn in proportion.

Following the intuitive interpretation of art, the counselor should develop a hypothesis related to the client's personality and personal problems. A word of caution is appropriate here. These perceptions, intuitions, and hypotheses are most beneficial when used in conjunction with all other available psychosocial data on the client. Once the hypothesis is developed, the therapist structures and shares the intuitive interpretation with the client through a verbal statement to assist the child in developing insight into self and the problem. Interpretation requires the therapist to have a strong theoretical background.

My personal bias regarding the counselor's involvement with the child in art therapy has been indirectly expressed in the discussion of the three techniques: art media, perceiving, and responding. However, I would like to emphasize several points. I feel it is important that the counselor not participate with children in art activity in most instances. Too often children compete and compare their works with the adult counselor. This comparison may intimidate children or diminish their work in their eyes and reduce self-esteem rather than be ego-enhancing. There also exists the danger of the counselor's forgetting the therapeutic role and becoming ego-involved in the artwork rather than focusing on the child. A time that I might be involved occurs when I help a child to overcome an impasse or a reluctance to initiate an activity as mentioned previously in the discussion on self-disclosure. The counselor's time is best spent observing the child's work as it develops, attending to the child's nonverbal expressions, and listening to the child's comments. By doing these things, the therapist will be able to perceive, respond accurately, and ask questions about the art object for purposes of clarification or more information. When following the child's lead in this manner, the counselor is making a maximum effort to be with the child and be involved in the child's world.

SERIAL DRAWING

In an unpublished paper, Allan (1979) described serial drawing as an interesting technique for involving disturbed children who enjoy drawing in therapy. The author cited two basic purposes for the technique: (1) to rework or reinforce the attachment relationship between adult (counselor) and child, and (2) to encourage the expression of the child's unconscious in symbolic form and assist the curative powers of the psyche.

Serial drawing is a therapeutic technique which involves meeting for 20 to 30 minutes per session on a regularly scheduled basis. The themes presented in the drawings of children usually depict three stages of therapy: initial, middle, and termination. These stages are described as they occurred with an eight-year-old boy, Brad, that I worked with in counseling using serial drawing. Brad was referred by his mother (single parent) and school teacher for aggressive, acting-out behavior—both at home and at school. All of Brad's drawings were done in pencil on 8½-by-11-inch plain paper. In the first session, he was instructed that he would meet with me twice a week indefinitely and that he could "draw any pictures he wanted to do."

Initial Stage

In this case, the initial stage lasted longer than the two to three sessions expected. Three main themes are typically presented in beginning drawings:

1. *A view of the child's internal world.* Brad's initial drawings depicted boats defended by thick, heavy armor plates, guns, and sophisticated radar and radio equipment. The boats were drawn in the upper portion of the paper with a horizontal line leaving a wide expanse of empty water beneath. Figure 5–2 is an example of an early drawing. The themes in all Brad's early drawings depict an insecurity and need to protect himself with a vast emptiness beneath.

2. *An impasse or blocked position.* Early drawings also indicated the overwhelming impact of Brad's problem. Another of Brad's early drawings, Figure 5–3, indicated the internal turbulence he was feeling within

Figure 5–2

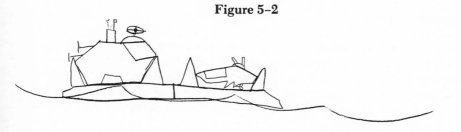

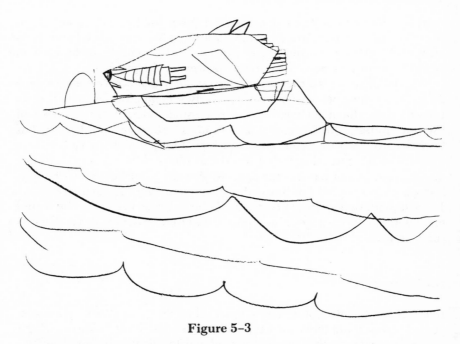

Figure 5–3

himself. The armored boat was drawn again on top of the water but the water beneath was wavy and choppy.

3. *A means of establishing communication with counselor.* Children often use their drawings to express feelings about themselves with the counselor. In Figure 5–4, Brad began to allow a look beneath the water but not without protection from potential danger (form of a shark). He said, "Do you know what I'm drawing?" When I answered no, he continued, "It's a bathysphere. We can go down in it together." This comment was interpreted to be an invitation to proceed in therapy, and the beginning of attachment.

Middle Stage

1. *Separation of ambivalence.* According to Allan (1979), this stage usually begins around the fourth through seventh session. In this phase, painful feelings are recognized and expressed. For example, Brad continued to draw boats with armor and weapons, but the boats now contained the labels "good" and "bad." In addition, he was becoming more verbal and readily discussed his pictures as he drew. Figure 5–5 provides an example of the two boats. The bad boat is a submarine which "roves about beneath the sea," and the good boat remains on the surface of the water. The bad boat is engaged in active warfare with unidentified objects. When

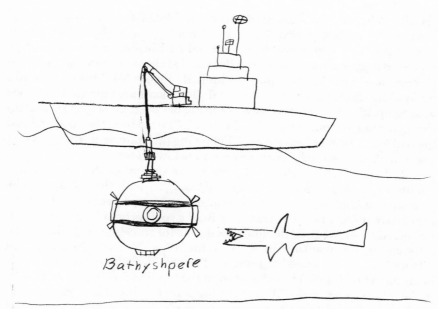

Bathyshpere

Figure 5–4

Figure 5–5

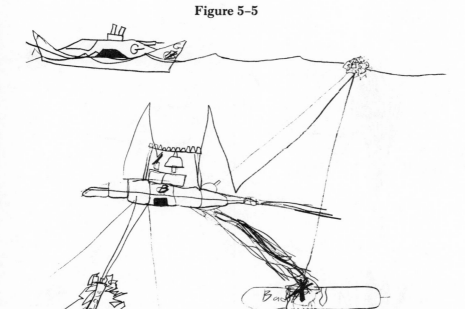

asked, "What are the dark spots in the middle of the two boats?" Brad replied, "Vulnerable spots! But only the good boat is really vulnerable, it can't tell what's happening below." Brad had begun to self-disclose his repressed aggression and hostile feelings and at the same time indicated his awareness of two different parts of himself. Figure 5–6 illustrates Brad's internal struggle between good and evil. Both boats are now on the surface waring openly. A line was drawn vertically between the ships to maintain the separation of concepts. In Brad's words, "I need both the good one and the bad one. I'm not always good." Following this statement, the good ship was attacked repeatedly from above and below water.

  2. *Deeper relationship.* With the establishment of the relationship, children will share deeper feelings and thoughts with the therapist. The counselor should begin to provide intuitive interpretation as discussed previously. Figure 5–7 was drawn by Brad two days before a visit with his father. As he drew, Brad disclosed his dislike for traveling on the bus alone (40-mile trip one way) and his anger at his father. "He says I'm stupid and hits me when I do something wrong. Do you fart? Everybody farts! He beats me when I do." The exhaust from the bus became angry swirls as he spoke. My response was, "Riding the bus is lonely, but it is even more difficult to be forced to visit someone you don't like. It really hurts to feel unloved." In Figure 5–8, a picture of his room, Brad began to express his mixed and angry feelings about living with his mom in their apartment. As

Figure 5–6

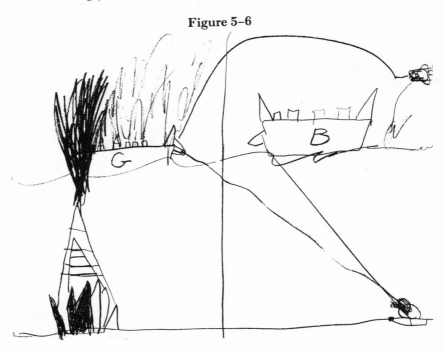

Figure 5-7

Figure 5-8

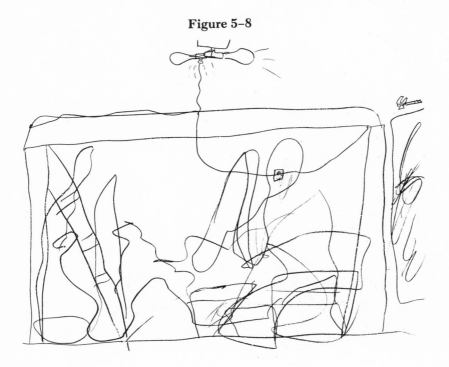

he drew he made the following comments, "Our apartment is a mess. My room is a mess. I can't find a thing. You know what this is? (pointing to object in upper right part of picture). It's a hammer. I keep it over my window for protection in case somebody tries to break in. There's a lot of kooks out there, you know." My response: "Keeping things straight in your life and organized is important. It helps you understand, feel safe, and in control."

Termination Stage

As deep feelings are expressed symbolically and shared verbally, the drawings begin to contain images of self-control and self-worth. Figure 5–9 indicates Brad's progression in therapy. This picture of his room was drawn one month following the picture presented in Figure 5–8. The room is clean and organized. No hammer exists above the window. When I asked, "Where is the hammer?" Brad's reply was, "I don't need it anymore." A few weeks later, Brad drew his last picture in counseling. Figure 5–10 was drawn just before the Thanksgiving holiday at school. The boat (Mayflower) covers most of the paper. It has no armor or guns for defense. The water line is lower and the water clear. Although the dorsal fin of a shark (danger) is visible, the fish in the foreground is much smaller and smiling. All persons on the ship are smiling, saying, "Land ho!" When asked about

Figure 5–9

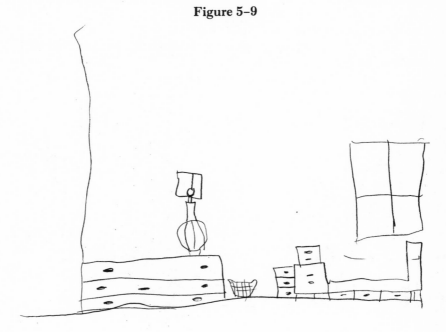

Figure 5-10

the picture, Brad replied, "They've had a long trip and everyone is glad to see land." My reply was, "You've come a long way and reached your destination just like the pilgrims." A smile crossed his face as he said, "Yeah!" After Thanksgiving, Brad said he didn't want to draw anymore. Closure was reached when he indicated he would rather work on the computer in the library than be with me. Brad's aggressive behavior at home and in school has diminished drastically almost to the point of extinction. However, the behavior reappeared at times before his legally required monthly visits to his father's home.

RECOMMENDED RESOURCES

Books

GARDNER, H. *Artful scribbles: The significance of children's drawings.* New York Basic Books, 1980.

The author describes observations of his children's art throughout their childhood development. The book challenges many of the more-traditional developmental thoughts on art and focuses on aesthetic processes as well as art products.

LOUGHRAN, B. *Art experiences: An experimental approach.* New York: Harcourt, Brace, & World, 1962.

This book lists a multitude of activities using various kinds of art media with children. Many of these activities could be easily adapted to counseling.

MAYNARD, F. *Guiding your child to a more creative life.* New York: Doubleday & Co., 1973.

A book written primarily for parents. However, many of the suggestions for using art media, including the recipes, are easily adapted to counseling use. It also contains an excellent bibliography on "how-to" books for using art media with children.

OAKLANDER, V. *Windows to our children.* Moab, UT: Real People Press, 1978.

This book contains descriptions of gestalt techniques and activities to be used in counseling children, such as storytelling, poetry, drama, fantasy, and many other artistic and play activities.

PARAS KEVAS, C. *A structural approach to art therapy methods.* Collegium, 1979.

This book is written for anyone wishing an introduction to art therapy. It defines art therapy and differentiates four schools of thought in art therapy and responds to questions regarding art therapy and other professions such as art education. In the last part of the book, the author discusses art therapy groups, provides several drawings from group art therapy sessions, and suggests exercises for group sessions.

SHAW, A. & STEVENS, C. (Eds.) *Drama, theatre, and the handicapped.* American Theatre Association, 1979.

This book provides a collection of articles by authorities who are involved in the direct application of drama and theatre for handicapped persons. The book also contains reviews of specific programs that have been successful with the handicapped and an annotated bibliography.

SILVER, R. *Developing cognitive and creative skills through art.* Baltimore, MD: University Park Press, 1978.

Various programs and techniques used with handicapped children are outlined by the author. These techniques focus on communicative disorders, learning disabilities, and hearing impairment. The book describes the role of art in cognition, adjustment, and assessment and explains the development of cognitive and creative skills through practical art procedures, such as drawing, painting, and using clay.

Journals

American Journal of Art Therapy. American Art Therapy Association, 428 E. Preston Street, Baltimore, MD. 21202

The official journal of the American Art Therapy Association is published on a quarterly basis. It usually contains several full-length feature articles relating to art theory, practice, or related issues. In addition, the journal provides the following contents: reader's forum, job-information exchange, news, recent periodical literature, and reviews of current books.

Art Education. *Journal of the National Art Education Association*, 1916 Association Drive, Reston, VA 22091

The official journal for the National Art Education Association is published six times a year. It contains general and feature articles relating to art education.

The Arts in Psychotherapy: An International Journal. Ankho International, Inc., 7374 Highbridge, Terr., P.O. Box 426, Payetteville, NY 13066

A quarterly international journal for professionals in fields of mental health and education. The journal publishes art, dance, music, poetry, and drama articles, which reflect the theory and practice of therapists and counselors.

SUMMARY

This chapter on art therapy and serial drawing contained five major sections. The first section was an introduction and historical overview of the development of art therapy. It contained discussion of the major contributions of Margaret Naumberg and Edith Kramer. Also included in this section was a detailed analysis of the value of art activity as a therapeutic technique. The second section further discussed three key concepts, unconscious, displacement, and projection, as they applied specifically to art therapy. Additional key concepts, sublimation, creativity, and developmental growth stages in children's drawings, were also introduced and defined. The third section contained an explanation of the basic techniques of art media: selection and use, perceiving, and responding. The verbal responses of support, self-disclosure, and interpretation were emphasized. The fourth section described serial drawing and an example of it being implemented in counseling. The last section was a list of recommended resources.

REFERENCES AND RECOMMENDED READINGS

ALLAN, J. Serial drawing: A therapeutic approach with young children. Unpublished paper, 1979.

ALLIGER, B. Painting with clay. *Instructor*, 79(46), April 1970.

ALSCHULER, R. & HATTWICK, L. *Personality and painting: A study of young children.* Chicago: University of Chicago Press, 1947.

ANDERSON, H. & ANDERSON, G. *An introduction to projective techniques.* Englewood Cliffs, NJ: Prentice-Hall, 1951.

BENDER, L. *Child psychiatric techniques.* Springfield, IL: Charles C Thomas, 1952.

BHATT, M. Art and the socially maladjusted. *School Arts,* 54, 1955, 23–25.

BLOOM, L. Aspects of the use of art in the treatment of maladjusted children. *Mental Hygiene,* 1957, 378–385.

BURNS, R. & KAUFMAN, S. *Kinetic family drawings.* New York: Brunner/Mazel, 1970.

CHILD, I. Esthetics. *Annual Review of Psychology,* 23, 1972, 669–694.

COLE, N. *Children's art from deep down inside.* New York: John Day Co., 1966.

DENNIS, W. *Group values through children's drawings.* New York: John Wiley & Sons, 1966.

DI LEO, J. *Young children and their drawings.* New York; Brunner/Mazel, 1970.

——. J. *Children's drawings and diagnostic aids.* New York: Brunner/Mazel, 1973.

FREEMAN, R. & FRIEDMAN, I. Art therapy in mental illness. *School Arts,* 54, 1955, 17–20.

GONDOR, E. *Art and play therapy.* New York: Random House, 1954.

GOODENOUGH, F. *Measurement of intelligence by drawings.* New York: World, 1926.

GORDON, J. Art helps free a troubled mind. *School Arts,* 58, 1959, 13–14.

HARRIS, D. *Children's drawings as measures of intellectual maturity.* New York: Harcourt, Brace, & World, Inc., 1963.

KASLOW, F. A therapeutic creative arts unit for children with learning disabilities. *Academic Therapy,* 3, 1972, 297–306.

KELLOGG, R. *The psychology of children's art.* New York: CRM-Random House, 1967.

KOPPITZ, E. *Psychological evaluation of children's human figure drawings.* New York: Grune & Stratton, 1968.

KRAMER, E. *Art therapy in a children's community.* Springfield, IL: Charles C Thomas, 1958.

——. *Art as therapy with children.* New York: Schocken Books, 1971.

——. *Childhood and art therapy.* New York: Schocken Books, 1979.

LANGER, S. *Problems of art.* New York: Charles Scribner's & Sons, 1957.

LOWENFELD, V. *Your child and his art: A guide for parents.* New York: Macmillan, 1954.

——. *Creative and mental growth.* (3rd ed.) New York: Macmillan, 1957.

——. & Brittain, W. *Creative and mental growth,* (6th ed.) New York: Macmillan, 1975.

MACHOVER, K. *Personality projection in the drawing of the human figure.* Springfield, IL: Charles C Thomas, 1949.

NAUMBERG, M. Art therapy: Its scope and function. In E. F. Hammer (Ed.)

The clinical application of projective drawings, Springfield, IL: Charles C Thomas, 1958.

———. *Dynamically oriented art therapy: Its principles and practice*. New York: Grune & Stratton, 1966.

PROTINSKY, H. Children's drawings as emotional indicators. *Elementary School Guidance and Counseling*, April 1978, 249–255.

RHYNE, J. *The gestalt art experience*. Monterey, CA: Brooks/Cole, 1973.

ROBBINS, A. & SIBLEY, L. *Creative art therapy*. New York: Bruner/Mazel, 1976.

RUBIN, J. *Child art therapy*. New York: Van Nostrand Reinhold Co., 1978.

ULMAN, E., KRAMER, E., & KWIATKOWSKA, H. *Art therapy in the United States*. Craftsbury Common, VT: Art Therapy Publications, 1978.

WADESON, H. Conjoint marital art therapy techniques. *Psychiatry*, 31, 1972, 89–98.

———. *Art psychotherapy*. New York: John Wiley & Sons, 1980.

Chapter 6

Music Therapy:
Implications for Counseling

George Giacobbe, Richard Graham,
and Frederick Patrick

E. Thayer Gaston (1968), the recognized "father of music therapy," stated that:

> Music and therapy have been close companions, often inseparable, throughout most of man's history. Each culture has determined the nature and use of its music in the treatment of illness. Mystic, therapeutic powers have often been attributed to music, even in cultures that took pride in their rationality. (p. 1)

Gaston continued to describe music as a therapeutic tool:

> Music, a form of human behavior, is unique and powerful in its influence. It can benefit handicapped and ill persons by helping them to change their behavior by acquiring new or better behavior. At times, music itself elicits these behavior changes. However, most often there is the purposeful persuasion, either directly or indirectly, of the therapist. By means of music and persuasion, then, the ultimate goal—to bring about desirable changes in human behavior—is attempted." (p. 7)

Because the history of music therapy has been discussed thoroughly in detail elsewhere (Gaston, 1968; Maas, 1982), the remainder of this chapter will be to embellish the concept of music as a therapeutic technique in counseling.

The Value of Music in Counseling

Counselors who undertake work with children through the medium of music should understand the value of music to all humankind, and particularly to children. Starting from this perspective, the counselor makes use of the direct appeal of music to children in forming and sustaining music counseling groups. The very nature of music makes working in groups a more-effective helping procedure than would be the case if music were used in the traditional one-to-one counseling situation. Actually, the one-to-one relationship allows for a kind of group experience, but the history of humankind has taught us that music is experienced best in larger numbers; for the counselor a group of from 3 to about 15 might be indicated. For such a group, music enhances group interaction. When the therapist wants children who are shy or uncomfortable in groups to learn to interact in a socially acceptable manner, music can be called upon to provide a means of interaction and cooperation which is not dependent upon words, which might not come easily to such children. E. T. Gaston describes this characteristic of music groups in the following statement: "Music enhances verbal and nonverbal social interaction and communication . . . Music may speak where words fail." (Gaston, 1968, p. 43).

The therapist who works with a music group quickly discovers that singing, playing, and listening together leads to a kind of "group cohesiveness" characterized by close personal interchanges and sharing. The group music experience is characterized by a group aesthetic response the likes of which can be evoked only through music activity.

Aesthetic and Expressive Values

One hears a great deal of talk about the need for affective education of today's youth. The aesthetic experiences which are easily obtainable from the counselor-directed music group represent one excellent example of affective education. Music's reason for being is expression of beauty. The singing or playing group may represent the only time in the lives of the individuals involved when they work together for the sole purpose of creating something of beauty.

The same singing or playing experiences may provide a means for release of the tensions which normally build up during the course of the school day. The cathartic values of music expression have been long known and often documented in practically every culture of humankind.

Avocational and Vocational Possibilities in Music

Nearer to the traditional role of the counselor is the development and nurturing of vocational interests. There are numerous possibilities for artistic and business occupations in music in the future of today's children. The therapist will not form a music group for the purposes of creating vocational interests in music, but should such interests arise in talented and highly motivated children, these interests should not be ignored.

There will never be more than a small few who will pursue music as a vocation, but it is highly likely and very desirable that most children will pursue music as an avocation to greater or lesser extent. To help the child in preparing for what may be a favorite avocation may well be one of the counselor's most important tasks.

The Counselor and Music Therapy

The term *music therapy* refers to the use of music and music-related activities to bring about positive changes in impaired individuals. A more detailed definition and description of the nature and principles of music therapy can be found in the literature of the discipline (Gaston, 1968; Forsythe & Jellison, 1977; Graham, 1982). The counselor can apply the principles and techniques of music therapy in a variety of ways. Ordinarily the children receiving music therapy would have been assessed and classified as handicapped. The counselor, in collaboration with a music therapist when possible, would structure music activities to remediate problems in learning, for example. Other types of activities would be designed to assist behaviorally disordered children to learn appropriate social behavior. Still other activities might be directed toward helping children with perceptual problems of any of several developmental disabilities. The children undergoing music therapy are typically those who qualify for individualized education programs (I.E.P.'s) and do require specially designed experiences which permit them to practice those skills in which they excel but also to improve those areas where there is deficiency.

When it is a question of handicapped children, the goals of the discipline of music therapy blend well with those of other helping professions. Flick (1975) lists goals for music programs with exceptional children which, according to her, should be given "first consideration."

1. Each child will enjoy successful musical experiences in an atmosphere of contentment and acceptance.
2. Each child will grow socially, in his respect for himself and others, through pleasurable interaction with peers and adults in numerous musical experiences, thus developing positive human relationships.
3. Each child will develop in self-realization by contributing ideas or creating new learning experiences with familiar musical songs and experience games as a track.
4. Each child will develop an increasing awareness and understanding of music concepts in an orderly sequence through musical experiences. (p. 48)

The goals offered by Flick are general ones and to them should be added the specific changes in behavior or attitude desired by the counselor. Music therapy activities in which the musical goals are met tend to be particularly conducive for attaining the social, academic, or behavioral goals which may have eluded the student prior to music therapy.

Kinds of Music

The kinds of music to be sung, played, heard, or created may be numerous and varied. Although the music employed in music therapy should without exception be "good music," the kind or type (classical, pop, rock, country, blues, etc.) will vary depending to great degree upon the tastes of the children and the counselor. The reference to good music means that, whatever the style, there should be an effort to seek out the best artists and selections for listening and that every effort is made to sing or play as well as possible when the students, themselves, are the music makers.

The uses of music in the counseling setting are limited only by the therapist's imagination and available resources. Just as in the traditional counseling setting, each child and each group will offer a new challenge. Each group will have a unique music personality which will change when a child joins or leaves the group.

Each involvement with music and the music group will have an effect upon the child. These effects can be seen and even measured in terms of physiological changes. The literature of music therapy is rife with reports of the influence of music on behavior. Growing numbers of these reports are of reliable scientific studies revealing the irresistible nature of the music stimulus in certain carefully structured settings.

Skills Needed to Use Music in Counseling

The counselor who would use music in therapy should have certain basic music abilities. Ideally the counselor will have sung or played a musical instrument for a number of years. At least the counselor will have actively used the singing voice in church or elsewhere and have a definite fondness for music. Other minimum requirements include:

1. Valuing music as an important human endeavor
2. Understanding that music can be used for a functional purpose
3. Understanding that, with respect to quality, taste, or beauty, no one type of music is better or worse than any other type.

Furthermore, the counselor should have the ability to:

4. Sing familiar songs "on pitch"
5. Sing, clap, dance, and step to simple musical rhythms
6. Recognize "off-pitch" singing or playing
7. Recognize "out-of-rhythm" clapping, stepping, and moving to simple musical rhythms of others

8. Identify personal music behaviors, such as skills and preferences, and their interaction with daily, weekly, and yearly activities

9. Interview others and discern their musical skills, preferences, their "musical environment," and the times when they interact with music

10. Sing songs effectively and with style, that is, in the United States, various subcultures have songs with which members of these groups strongly identify. Therefore, it is important to know how to sing a close approximation of the "proper" style, as dictated by that culture.

MUSIC THERAPY ACTIVITIES

Music therapy can take place when a counselor and one child or a small group of children combine their efforts in a structured, goal-directed therapy session, using music to some extent as a supplement for words. A summary of music therapy activities is presented in Table 6–1.

Setting

The music counseling setting should be located or scheduled both to isolate it from external sounds and to isolate others from the sounds coming from it.

The room should be attractive, but decorative objects should be kept to a minimum to allow for concentration on movement and sound. The room should be of reasonable size so that the child or children can sit or stand comfortably without crowding. If the room is too small, movement is hindered. If it is too big, the sound gets dispersed and it becomes more difficult to make and keep contact with the therapist. When available, it is ideal to include a piano in a larger setting.

Background Music

Background music is often provided in various settings, including waiting rooms. Background music should not exceed five decibels above the threshold of sound for any given room. Carefully selected music at critical periods during the treatment day is much more effective than any program of music that is played without interruption because continuous music creates its own monotony. Selection of the proper music to be programmed as background music requires knowledge of the therapeutic goals of the child or children and involves deciding which musical selections lend themselves best to reaching these goals.

Table 6-1
MUSIC THERAPY ACTIVITIES

Listen	Sing	Move	Play Instruments	Create
Background music	Informal singing	Play	Play	Play
Recorded music—listening alone or in a group	Community "sings"	Eurhythmics	Rhythm instruments	Free improvisation on instruments
Attending live musical performances	Singing games	Rhythms (e.g. Orff)	Simple melody instruments	Writing lyrics or music (e.g. songs)
	Choruses	Action songs	Simple harmony instruments	Psychodrama with music (psycho-opera)
	Glee clubs	Folk, square, and other types of dances	Fretted instruments	Group improvisation ("jam sessions")
	Quartets and other ensembles		Bands, orchestras, chamber groups, and other combinations	Making and playing improvised musical instruments
	Solos		Solos	Using the tape recorder to create music

127

Evaluation

After a music counseling activity has been completed, the counselor should try to analyze the session.

Typical questions to be answered regarding the session are:

Were therapeutic goals met?
What music and musical activities were used, and how successful were they?
Was there enjoyment?
Did the child or children show interest?
Did the child or children willingly participate?
Did the child or children allow the counselor to assist?
Was each child accepted by the group?
Did a certain child function as a leader or a follower?

These observations are of great value in reporting results as well as in planning subsequent activities.

Building Listening Skills and Interest in Music

Interest may be created by having the child read about music, from such sources as information on record covers, biographies about composers and performers, and music anecdotes. In addition to reading, listening skills and interest can also be developed through repeated hearings of the same compositions. Important considerations for counselors to remember is that children (a) have their own ideas about music, (b) like to listen in groups, and (c) do not like their listening interrupted.

After listening, some children may enjoy comparing different arrangements of the same musical selection in regard to interpretations, artists, accompaniments, etc. Other children may enjoy "weaving" various musical selections together around a given story.

Because some music and songs have stories or other programmatic ideas, generating discussions can be helpful. The following are some suggested musical selections (classical only) which may be utilized because they tell a story, describe a setting, or set a mood.

Music that tells a story

Berlioz, Hector   *Symphonie fantastique*
Dukas, Paul   *Sorcerer's Apprentice*
Kodaly, Zoltan   *Hary Janos Suite*
Mussorgsky, Modest   *Night on Bald Mountain*
Prokofief, Serge   *Lieutenant Kije Suite*
                           Peter and the Wolf

Rimsky-Korsakov, Nikolai	*Scheherazade*
Sanit-Saens, Camille	*Danse Macabre*
Stravinsky, Igor	*Firebird Suite*
Tchaikovsky, Peter	*Nutcracker Suite*

Music that describes a setting

Britten, Benjamin:	*Young Person's Guide to the Orchestra*
Debussy, Claude	*La Mer*
Gershwin, George	*An American in Paris*
Grofe, Ferde	*Grand Canyon Suite*
Mussorgsky, Modest	*Pictures at an Exhibition*
Ravel, Maurice	*Daphnis et Chloé* (Suite No. 2)
Respighi, Ottorino	*Feste Romane*
	Fountains of Rome
	Pines of Rome
Saint-Saens, Camille	*Carnival of the Animals*
Smetana, Bedrich	*"Moldau"* (from *My Fatherland*)
Stravinsky, Igor	*Le Sacre du printemps*
Tchaikovsky, Peter	*Francesca da Rimini*
Villa-Lobos, Heitor	*"Little Train of the Caipira"* (from *Bachianas,* No. 2)
Wagner, Richard	*Die Walküre* (Ride of the Valkyries)

Music that sets a mood

Albinoni, Tomasso	Adagio for Strings and Organ (attributed)
Bach, Johann Sebastian	Toccata and Fugue in D Minor for Organ
Barber, Samuel	Adagio for Strings (from Quartet, Opus 11)
Bloch, Ernest	Schelomo-Rhapsody for Cello and Orchestra
Ravel, Maurice	*Boléro*
	Pavanne pour une Infante Défunte

Although these compositions are likely to engage children's interest, the music of other traditions and contexts work as well. When making the selections, the counselor must consider the individual receptivity of each child. " . . . it should be noted that there has been no suggestion that a client be led to 'appreciate' music. Rather the emphasis has been upon using music that appeals in various ways to individuals depending on their previous background, experience, and exposure to music." (Giacobbe & Graham, 1979, p. 148)

Music Therapy Through Singing

Singing creates a situation where individual singers interact with one another while focusing on the mechanics of music (pitch, loudness, phrasing, expression, etc.) in order to reasonably accomplish the singing activity. Thus group singing unifies a group of otherwise disparate individuals, gives them a joint task and promotes fellowship through the sharing of an aesthetic experience, a common goal. Group singing can be an excellent way to open therapy.

The singing group offers individual children the opportunity to strengthen their self-image in a group context and to develop social relationship skills. The singing group may also serve as an experimental setting in which creative risk taking is possible. In addition, the group singing provides children the opportunity to explore their bodies as instruments of sound.

Preparation of Materials

If the singing activity is to be a therapeutic one, the selection of the songs is very important. The lyrics of the selected songs should offend no one, especially racial, religious, or national groups.

The range of pitches of the songs must correspond to the range of voices of the singers. Figure 6–1 illustrates that the mean range and midpoint tone of educable mentally retarded children is different from those of nonhandicapped children (Larson, 1977, p. 141).

The age of the singers must also be considered in song selection. Songs particularly liked by young children include children's religious songs, lullabies, and action songs. Older children and young adolescents tend to enjoy popular music and love songs. In any case, the therapist must know the songs well.

Figure 6–1 Mean Range and Midpoint of "Normal" and Educable Mentally Retarded Boys and Girls

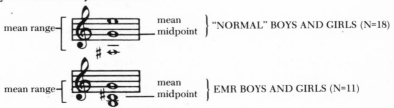

Singing Suggestions

Participation of all the group members should be developed as soon as possible. This is best accomplished by beginning the music counseling session with songs that are familiar to all the members of the group. Familiar songs offer words, melody, and interpretation which the children know. The counselor, therefore, avoids embarrassing children through their lack of knowledge.

Starting the group can best be done by simply saying the words "ready, sing" in the rhythm of the beginning words of the song. Before starting these songs, hum the starting pitch, make certain that all are ready, then say "ready, sing" in the pattern of the first two words or syllables of the song.

An example of how to begin the song "Brother John" (Frere Jacques), would be:

Counselor: "Now let us sing 'Brother John.'" (Hum the pitch of the first note, see that all are ready to begin) "Ready-sing!" (Spoken in the rhythm of "Are you . . .)

Group: "Are you sleep--ing, ..."

Directing Skills

Directing, in its simplest form, takes place when counselors move their hands in the air to the basic beat of the music being sung. This includes starting the group together with a preparatory beat (after humming the pitch and giving them a "ready, sing") and keeping this basic beat going in the characteristic mood of the song being led. The end of the song is indicated by bringing hand and arm down firmly with a flourish to indicate that all singers should stop together. Figure 6–2 illustrates the typical beat patterns.

Novelty is added to the music therapy session by introducing new songs to the children. Teaching new songs, particularly to nonmusicians, is best accomplished by ear or rote. To teach a song "by ear" means to teach the entire song (words and music) by demonstration with no access to the printed song materials. Thus, the children learn new songs from hearing the counselor sing these songs during therapy. The three most effective methods of teaching a song by ear are:

1. The part or "chime-in" method
2. The whole method
3. The phrase method

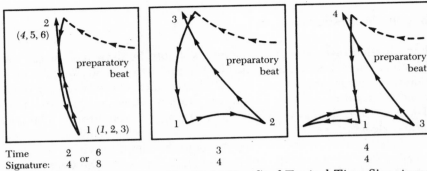

Figure 6-2   Beat Patterns (for Right Hand) of Typical Time Signatures, as seen by the director. The group sees the mirror image of these beat patterns.

With the *part method*, the singing group is told to "chime-in" on the section of the song that is repeated at regular intervals. "Old MacDonald Had a Farm" is an example of a song with repeated sections that can be taught easily using the part method. After rehearsing in this manner several times, the singers join in on any additional parts that they can remember. Eventually the group can sing the entire song without help.

The *whole method* has the counselor sing the complete song through several times (perhaps over two or more sessions) before the children attempt to sing it. After the children have been well exposed to the song, they try to sing it. If there are weak places, the therapist gives assistance in those places. Once this method is in operation, any music counseling session will have new songs that are being introduced, songs being sung by the children for the first few times, and songs that have been sung many times.

The *phrase method* begins with the therapist singing the entire song. Then the first phrase (or phrases if they are very short) is sung and the children sing this phrase of the song. Each phrase is sung back until learned. This process is repeated until all phrases are learned, and then the phrases are put together in a final singing of the completely learned song.

MUSIC THERAPY AND MOVEMENT ACTIVITIES

Nash (1974) states that "Movement is not only essential to man, it is also one of his most powerful means of self-expression, communication and outlet [sic] for well-being . . . . Rhythm and melody express movement, and movement is the natural human response to music. Therefore, the direct and natural path for the child's understanding of music and musical form, and his development of musicality, muscular coordination and freedom of self-expression, lies in movement." (p. 80)

Many activities, such as marching, skipping, hopping, galloping, clapping hands, snapping fingers, stomping feet, tapping, etc., can be performed to music. Movement to music can include the entire body or some portion (such as the arm and hand). Examples of movements that can be done to music include:

1. Pretending you are walking, skipping, marching, crawling, or pantomiming in various settings—on the moon, underwater, on the ceiling, on the beach, in a sports arena (playing a sport), etc.
2. Pretending you are an elephant, a duck, a crab, a fish, a martian, etc.
3. Doing a "playback"—that is trying all actions (such as the above) in reverse.

The child or children select, learn, and participate in patterned dances, such as folk, square, rock, modern, ballroom, and body movement sequences. The counselor sequences the movement activities in terms of complexity of patterns, formations, and the ability to perform the body movements.

Rhythm Band Activities

In organizing the rhythm band, one instrument at a time is introduced. This allows children the chance to experiment with the instrument so that they can become familiar with the rhythmical responses.

It is important to choose carefully the instruments for the first sessions. It is advisable not to put more instruments than children in the group. More instruments than children makes integration difficult and imposes an immediate competitive situation.

The task is to keep time and play with precision. In some instances, the therapist may introduce the rhythm to the child and then follow and observe the child to discover where the child will go with this rhythm. Or the counselor may direct the rhythm and discern how well the child can imitate.

When given the opportunity to freely handle sound-producing instruments, the child often passes through a period of irrational and indiscriminate manipulation of the instrument. This sensory exploration of unorganized sound is not yet music. When moving beyond this stage and making a conscious effort to find and repeat certain "organized" sounds, the child is making music.

Music Therapy Through Playing Musical Instruments

All types of musical instruments, including the latest electronic musical instruments, can be used in the music counseling setting. Unless the therapist comes to the music counseling setting with considerable training and background, the greatest success in dealing with musical instruments will probably be with "informal" instruments. "Informal" instruments are those that are relatively easy to learn to play. This makes them particularly suitable for the counselor who has less than extensive musical skills. These instruments include the kalimba, melodian, recorder, tonette (song flute, ocarina), melody bells, xylophone, harmonica and autoharp. (Many music stores and institutions of higher learning offer instruction on these instruments which can quickly lead to, at least, limited skills.)

Music Therapy Through Creating

The child may spontaneously modify music behaviors without direction from the counselor or peers. Preconceived plans for developing unique musical activities include making up new words for songs, developing new melodies, selecting new harmonies, producing unique sounds and musical instruments, or creating signs and symbols for unique musical communication with others. The therapist's role in child creativity is to faciliate the ongoing process or, when necessary, to suggest alternatives or modifications.

Composing Activities

Sometimes a "right" song for a child cannot be found or does not even exist. Songwriting skills can be used to prepare original compositions. The composing experience can be shared between counselor and child with the child gradually assuming more and more of the initiative and responsibility.

The composer deals with the following: melody, harmony, rhythm, timbre (the type of sound produced by voice or instrument(s) which can be either "traditional," unique, or both), dynamics (the loudness and softness which lends to the mood of the composition), the length of time of performance, the composition's meaning or task, and the anticipated response of the audience for which is it intended. (The anticipated response of the audience is whether the composition moves them in the desired way—for example, a sad song should convey the quality of sadness to the audience.)

The knowledge of the range of pitches that the children can sing will also be useful when composing for them.

Lyric-Writing Activities

Anyone who can use words can write lyrics. The words do not need to rhyme, but rhyming offers a challenge that most children find hard to resist.

Making Improvised Instruments

Improvised instruments are sound-producing instruments devised and created by the child with or without the aid of the therapist. These instruments are important in the counseling sense because they are intimately related to the child and his or her situation which, of course, includes the problem(s) being treated.

Using the Tape Recorder

Many creative activities can include the use of the tape recorder. Besides live performances of the group being recorded for future listening, the tape recorder offers the creative child or group the chance to design and produce unique musical compositions which are easily repeated. "Traditional" or unique sounds, recorded on tape, can be used as background for musical performance or for movement.

Splicing the tape can produce unique and creative sounds. Splicing small amounts of tape and then attaching the ends together and playing the resultant "tape loop" can present unique repetitive sounds or rhythms. In addition, playback at speeds other than the recorded speed, the use of sound on sound, the use of several tape recorders to create music or a number of these combined are just a few of the possible ways the tape recorder can be utilized.

Integration of Musical Activities

Although musical activities have been described in an isolated fashion, that is, only one activity at a time, the interactional effect of several activities not only is logical, but enhances and improves the overall effect of the music. For example, marching to music does not have the same effect as marching, playing rhythm instruments, and singing (at the same time) does. Possible advantages of doing the latter include combining social adaptation, muscular control, and increased attention span.

THE INTEGRATION OF COUNSELING AND MUSIC THERAPY

If the counseling process is broadly conceived as three parts—a beginning, a middle, and an ending, therapeutic music concepts can be integrated into these parts in the following manner:

The Beginning

Initially, a precounseling assessment is often made to determine the child's interests, self-concept, attitudes, etc. Rapport, through warm, accepting, understanding, uncritical attitudes, is established to surmount initial fears and doubts related to the seeking of help and involvement with music. The child's goals for counseling are identified, and counseling is begun.

Sears (1968) has observed that music enhances verbal and nonverbal social interaction and communication. "Most social occasions are accompanied by music, which generally increases sociability. With music in the background, many individuals find it easier to talk with others. In psychotherapy, patients often talk more freely in the presence of music. They may express in music or through musical preferences feelings not otherwise expressible. *Music may speak where words fail.*" (p. 43) Nonverbal expressions are often much more honest than words, and often there is a large discrepancy between the two. In most instances, incongruent verbal messages are cancelled and disqualified by nonverbal messages.

During the first few sessions, mistrust or idealization of the counselor and resistances of various kinds will be encountered. Benezon (1981) notes that music can deal with each issue " . . . more quickly and handle it with great clarity in the nonverbal context because the task is soon experienced as gratifying both by the patient and by the music therapist as a result of the pleasure of sound and bodily expression and of the channels of communication that appear because of them." (p. 74)

"Some people resist by being either completely imitative or totally unable to communicate. Since creative improvisation can be best communicated nonverbally, examples of instrument exploration by the therapist can begin to show the client that it is both safe and appropriate to express one's own ideas." (Silverman, 1982, p. 101) Children and adolescents may fear that they are incapable of worthwhile spontaneous expression. Some children may express embarrassment or discomfort during or after a joint interaction with the counselor because of the intimacy involved. As a result, it is oftentimes easier to communicate intimately in a nonverbal, musical manner than to do so on a verbal level.

Sometimes the integration of a new member into the group makes the group strongly competitive. Sabotage activities such as playing loudly or retaining one's own rhythm without listening to the group can occur. As the therapist points out these overt musical activities, a beginning insight into these jealous and competitive actions often occurs in children and resistances are gradually overcome.

The Middle

An atmosphere of trust, acceptance, and reduced resistance promotes the child's feelings of security so that the more basic issues may be clarified. As problems are explored and tentative solutions put into practice, the child maintains security and flexibility regardless of the success or lack of success of the solutions. Implementation of music therapy activities aids in problem exploration and in developing solutions leading to desired changes which can enhance the child's self-actualization. For example, Segal (1981) cited an activity used in family counseling:

> [When] some family members were unable to express angry feelings that had been aroused because of family conflicts, they were encouraged to beat out these feelings on a drum. Some simply stroked the drum lightly, indicating their hesitancy to express their anger, even symbolically. Others pounded on the drum violently. The family then discussed their reactions to this experience and verbalized the meaning of these behaviors. This experience freed them to discuss the specific events that provoked their anger in the family. They were again encouraged to express these feelings of anger on various percussive instruments. The meaningfulness and depth of these symbolically expressed emotions were clearly evident. The opportunities to ventilate these feelings, first on a symbolic level, then on a verbal level, proved very therapeutic. (p. 223)

In the middle stage of therapy, it is often observed that children who serve as leaders tend to choose instruments which typically become leader instruments. These instruments are usually easy to handle, large, and have a powerful, rhythmical sound. With the assistance of their chosen instruments, these children quickly become the facilitators around whom the rest of the group gathers.

The Ending

In music counseling, the decision to terminate therapy is usually recognized and shared by the counselor and the child. Children's verbalizations tend to increase and intensify as the last sessions come closer. These verbalizations may be about the therapeutic process, the changes produced, the sensations experienced or all three aspects of the counseling situation. The incorporation of songs that contain messages of separation, mourning, and sadness occurs more frequently at this time and should be encouraged. After terminating, follow-up at appropriate intervals is recommended.

RECOMMENDED RESOURCES

Information Sources

American Association for Music Therapy (AAMT)
Department of Music and Music Therapy of New York University
35 West Fourth Street—777 Education Building
New York, NY 10003

American Orff Schulwerk Association (AOSA)
Post Office Box 18495
Cleveland Heights, OH 44118

American Society of Group Psychotherapy and Psychodrama
39 East Twentieth Street
New York, NY 10003

British Society for Music Therapy
48 Lancaster Road
London, N. 6, England

Canadian Association for Music Therapy (CAMT)
6 Drayton Road
Point Claire, Quebec H9S 4V2, Canada

Kodaly Musical Training Institute, Inc.
525 Worcester Street
Wellesley, MA 02181

Music Educators National Conference (MENC)
1202 Sixteenth Street, N.W.
Washington, DC 20036

National Association for Music Therapy, Inc. (NAMT)
Post Office Box 610
Lawrence, KS 66044

Films*

Are You Ready?

Part of this film presents the music therapy activities of a group of children with Down's syndrome in a prescriptive teaching program at the Orchard School for Special Education in Skokie, Illinois.

*All films are available through: National Association for Music Therapy, Inc. P.O. Box 610 Lawrence, KS 66044

Music and Your Mind: A Key to Creative Potential

Two adult subjects are presented in this documentary describing the Guided Imagery and Music technique. The procedure, done by an experienced guide, is briefly explained. The film uses live performance as well as taped music to explore consciousness from the psychodynamic point of view of creativity.

The Music Child

Narrators of this film include, among others, noted music therapists Paul Nordoff and Clive Robbins. They appear in demonstrations as they explain their own personal techniques and strategies using improvised music as a treatment technique for handicapped (autistic, emotionally disturbed, mentally retarded, and cerebral palsied) children.

A Song for Michael

This film presents one session between Michael and his music therapist at the Music Therapy Center in New York City. By age 14, Michael has been in treatment for 10 years and has been diagnosed as autistic, schizophrenic, mentally retarded, and brain-damaged. He has no spontaneous speech, has frequent outbursts of motor activity and a very short attention span. (This film is intended for professional audiences and is not appropriate for general public showings.)

Songs and Music

HARTWELL-WALKER, M. & FRIEDEN, W. *Songs for Elementary Emotional Development.* Amherst, MA: Education Research Associates, Box 767—PGA, 1982.

A unique program which includes songs in both audio-cassette and sheet-music forms, a Leader's Guide, and follow-up activities. The songs are catchy, easy to learn, and about feelings and situations with which children readily identify.

SUMMARY

The work that a counselor does with children can be enhanced by using music as a tool to help in the exploring, understanding, and working through of problems. Music is a nonverbal medium through which security and acceptance can be provided as well as a nonthreatening medium through which feelings can be experienced and expressed. This chapter began by providing an introduction to the use of music with children in counseling. A subsequent section focused on skills necessary for a counselor to successfully use music. The authors then provided descriptions of several music therapy activities, and closed with an outline of the counseling process.

REFERENCES AND RECOMMENDED READINGS

Benezon, R. *Music therapy manual*. Springfield, IL: Charles C Thomas, 1981.

Flick, M. Educating exceptional children through music. In Graham, R. M. (Ed.) *Music for the exceptional child*. Reston, VA: Music Educators' National Conference, 1975, 148–171.

Forsythe, J. & Jellison, J. It's the law. *Music Educators Journal*, 1977, 64, 30–36.

Gaston, E. *Music in therapy*. New York: Macmillan, 1968.

Giacobbe, G. & Graham, R. Music therapy: Implications for recreational programming. In Wehman, P. (Ed.) *Recreational programming for developmentally disabled persons*. Baltimore, MD: University Park Press, 1979, 145–161.

Graham, R. Music therapy. In Karasu, T. B. (Ed.) *Report of the American Psychiatric Association Commission on Psychiatric Therapy*. Washington, DC: American Psychiatric Association, 1982.

Larson, B. A comparison of singing ranges of mentally retarded and normal children with published songbooks used in singing activities. *Journal of Music Therapy*, 1977, 14, 139–143.

Maas, J. An introduction to music therapy. In Nickerson, E. & O'Laughlin, K. (Eds.) *Helping through action: Action oriented therapies*. Amherst, MA: Human Resource Development Press, 1982, 87–100.

Nash, G. *Creative approaches to child development with music, language and movement*. New York: Alfred Publishing Company, Inc., 1974.

Sears, W. Processes in music therapy. In Gaston, E. (Ed.) *Music in therapy*. New York: Macmillan, 1968, 30–44.

Segal, R. Integrating art form therapies and family therapy. *Social Casework: The Journal of Contemporary Social Work*, 1981, 62, 218–226.

Silverman, D. Creative development through musical improvisation. In Nickerson, E. & O'Laughlin, K. (Eds.) *Helping through action: Action-oriented therapies*. Amherst, MA: Human Resource Development Press, 1982, 110–113.

Chapter 7

Bibliotherapy

Since the time of the early Greek philosophers, authors of books, poetry, and other dramatic forms have influenced their readers' feelings, values, and behaviors. The following statement from Plato illustrates this point: . . . for the part can never be well unless the whole is well. . . . If the head and body are to be well, you must begin by curing the soul; that is the first thing. And the cure, my dear youth, has to be effected by the use of certain charms, and these charms are fair words." The term *bibliotherapy* originated from two Greek words. The first is *biblion*, meaning "book," and the second is *therapeio* meaning "healing" (Moses & Zaccaria, 1978). Thus, bibliotherapy, in general, is healing through books, and it is reasonable to assume that it had its historical beginning in ancient times. In fact, an inscription over the library of Thebes read "The Healing Place of the Soul." The Thebans valued books for their ability to add quality to one's life through communication, through education, and through therapy (Schrank & Engles, 1981).

Bibliotherapy received its modern impetus as a therapeutic technique from psychotherapists and analysts who viewed books as art and used books as an access to their patient's innermost feelings. As a result of uses of bibliotherapy in psychiatric hospitals in the 1930s and 1940s, bibliotherapy was defined early as a program of treatment involving reading activities to be controlled by a physician and administered by a professional librarian, the two of which then worked as a mental health team in treating the patient (Tews, 1962). In the 1960s, definitions of bibliotherapy attempted to differentiate between its clinical use in psychotherapy

(Alston, 1962) and its educational use in schools by teachers and counselors (Lejeune, 1969; Moses & Zaccaria, 1969). Recently, Berry (1978) distinguished between clinical and educational uses of bibliotherapy in three ways:

   a. the different facilitator roles and functions (i.e., therapist vs. group leader/ manager/discussant);
   b. the different characteristics of the participants ("sick" vs. "well" or patients or clients vs. students or volunteers);
   c. the different goals of the bibliotherapeutic process ("getting well" vs. self-actualization or attainment of some educational goal). (p. 186)

As a result of these distinctions, Berry (1978) arrived at the following general operational definition of bibliotherapy:

> Bibliotherapy is a family of techniques for structuring an interaction between a facilitator and a participant, an interaction which is in some way based on their mutual sharing of literature in the broadest sense possible. . . . encompasses all possible literary forms, from poems to short stories to autobiographical novels and to personal diaries, life histories and so on. (p. 186)

As Berry has so ably illustrated in his definition, I see no reason to limit the use of bibliotherapy to a clinical or educational setting; nor, for the purposes of this book, do I wish to imply that one must be a trained therapist or counselor to use bibliotherapy successfully. As Spache (1977) emphasized, the reactions from professionals on who should be involved with bibliotherapy differs tremendously. One of the major reasons for ambivalence regarding who, how, and when bibliotherapy should be used is the lack of research activity using the technique (Schrank & Engels, 1981).

Although these important questions of who should use bibliotherapy, how should it be used, and when should it be introduced remain unanswered without adequate research, I believe the value and the potential of bibliotherapy as a positive force in the therapeutic process far outweighs possible negative outcomes. However, before discussing the value of bibliotherapy, I feel it is important to present the reader with the following four precautionary principles for using bibliotherapy that were adapted from Moses and Zaccaria (1969):

   1. Examine the nature, dynamics, key concepts, and basic techniques of bibliotherapy and develop an understanding of how they fit into your counseling theory. Be prepared to provide a rationale for its use.
   2. Possess familiarity with the literature which the client will use.

Important considerations for the bibliotherapist include both client characteristics (age, sex, problem area, reading ability, and reading interests) and literature characteristics (length, plot, and reading level). Bibliotherapy is most effective with children who have average and above-average reading ability. Never suggest to children that they read something you haven't read.

3. Be aware of the timely use of the technique.

Bibliotherapy, as a technique, depends upon the counselor's knowledge and understanding of the client's problem(s), which is a natural outgrowth of the development of the therapeutic relationship over time. Bibliotherapy is an adjunctive technique and should be used to supplement other techniques, not to replace them.

4. All bibliotherapy should be processed between the client and the counselor.

Discussion and meaningful feedback from counselor to client following the use of literature in therapy are essential ingredients to successful therapy. Without this dynamic interaction, there exists little opportunity for children to benefit from their identifications, experience sufficient catharsis, or to develop the necessary insights to make attitudinal or behavior changes. Reading without this critical interaction can hardly be expected to make a significant impact in the life of the child.

The Value of Bibliotherapy

As indicated in the introductory statement to this chapter, the use of words have served in methods of treatment in the field of mental health for centuries. Quite naturally the oral communication process between counselor and child is the primary and most-important link in therapy. However, as discussed in the chapters on play therapy, art therapy, and music therapy, children often lack the necessary verbal skills to express their thoughts and feelings accurately or they are so traumatized they are unwilling to discuss their problems directly. As a result, the therapist must find access to the child's inner world through somewhat less demanding and less direct approaches. The written word has recorded almost every conceivable aspect of human life. Children need not rely on their own experiences to gain greater self-awareness and self-understanding. They have access to a world of children's literature which is easily available at little cost and a widely accepted way to spend leisure time. By and large, written words are less offensive, less intrusive, and not as demanding as spoken words. As with play, art, and music, children can approach sensitive life areas and express themselves with a minimum of defensive posturing through literature.

Today, children are more sophisticated and more knowledgeable than any other generation has been. They have been exposed to war, crime, substance abuse, political scandals, and prejudice. Through mass media and a greater openness and willingness by parents to allow children access to taboo topics, they have developed greater depth of understanding and insight into the aforementioned topics and concepts of death, divorce, sex, abortion, drugs, and violence. Information in all these areas has gradually become a part of the world of children's literature. Several factors influence the content of children's literature but none more strongly than the mores of the culture in which we live. Because children identify strongly with the literature they read, their values and attitudes are influenced and even changed by reading at each developmental stage. In order that readers might have a better opportunity to have positive impact on client's adjustment, you should consult the developmental stages of Maslow and Erikson discussed in Chapter 1 as guidelines for selecting literature for children when using bibliotherapy. However, it is important to remember that each child will respond to literature differently and in a very personal and individual manner.

Alston (1962), Lejeune (1969), Shrodes (1949) and Spache (1978) have recommended bibliotherapy to be of value in the following ways by:

1. Providing information and instruction necessary to help solve problems.
2. Providing instruction and guidelines for developing new skills.
3. Identifying and satisfying personal interests.
4. Assisting to bring repressed problems to consciousness.
5. Aiding in the examination of more personal, threatening topics by providing ideas and ways to communicate them.
6. Assisting with self-awareness and awareness of self in relation to others.
7. Assisting in the socialization process by stimulating a sense of belonging with others.
8. Providing a sense of universalization, well-being, and security by helping children to understand that others feel as they do and have lived similar experiences. It reduces the aloneness and isolation typically felt by troubled children.
9. Helping to relax the child by reducing anxiety through emotional release.
10. Assisting in the reexamination of attitudes and values.
11. Helping to provide enjoyment and entertainment through an aesthetic experience.
12. Developing a critical and aesthetic appreciation for the value of books and other forms of literature.

Naturally all clients will not experience the 12 values of bibliotherapy identified previously. The amount and degree of benefit of bibliotherapy to the client depends on the client's ability to help self and on the therapist's experience, skills, theoretical approach, assessment of client's needs, and counselor's goals in therapy. Some fundamental counseling goals for which bibliotherapy may be an appropriate approach are: (1) long-term client maintenance and enrichment, (2) short-term support in situational crises and reality testing of critical decisions, (3) problem prevention by improving self-perceptions and learning to cope creatively with developmental situations which cannot be controlled or changed, and (4) problem resolution through reeducation and the development of insight. The use of literature as a maintaining and supportive mechanism is legitimate. However, the most significant value of bibliotherapy is that it enhances problem prevention and problem resolution by facilitating the therapeutic interaction between counselor and child through several key concepts of identification, transference, suggestion, insight, and catharsis.

KEY CONCEPTS

Although the concepts identification and transference were discussed in Chapter 3, "Play Therapy and Play Process," it is necessary to examine them in detail as they relate to bibliotherapy.

Identification

When counselors select appropriate literature for children, it is possible for any child to paradoxically be emotionally involved with the characters and their experiences (thus providing counselors a means to get closer to children) yet also be afforded the necessary psychological distance to function effectively in therapy. Identification occurs when children imagine themselves to behave like or to possess the personality and characteristics of other individuals with whom they have associated emotionally. Children identify through literature when they associate with the story's characters and experience vicariously the lives of the characters, their emotions, ideas, decisions, and behaviors. From a Freudian perspective, identification helps the client to have access to unconscious material which when brought to the conscious through literature allows for self-recognition and understanding. Shrodes (1949) has quoted Hans Sachs (1942) who describes the process of identification in literature the following way:

> The readers of a work of art are taken out of their ordinary surroundings and put into the realm of illusion. This illusion enriches the individual life with experience beyond the personal horizon, but never imposes on it to such an extent that the critical function which distinguishes between reality and fantasy is suspended. The writer shapes the characters and their emotional life so they seem to have their own individual existence and yet represents the universal.

He appeals to the unconscious of the reader without bringing it into conflict with his censor. The emotional reaction which he produces in him means an involuntary admission that his own repressed wishes are the same as those of the writer. In this way he is brought out of his isolation. (p. 99)

Bernstein (1977) suggests that identification through literature serves several therapeutic purposes with children, which are:

1. Readers have the opportunity to realize their own problems when they perceive the problems of others.
2. Reading is a private activity and self-awareness often occurs in solitude.
3. Embarrassment is minimized. When children experience problems such as sexual abuse, they can first examine the problem within themselves and secondly realize they are not alone in the situation.
4. Readers can rehearse resolutions to their problems without being observed or interfered with.
5. Readers may be encouraged to discuss their problems associated with a character. (p. 25)

When using bibliotherapy, the single greatest value of the identification process to the counselor may be that it sets the stage for the occurrence of other therapeutic mechanisms, transference, suggestion, insight, and catharsis.

Transference

As Shrodes (1949) points out, transference in therapy may provide significant contributions or the direst consequences. The function of transference in bibliotherapy is to recreate a traumatizing incident in the child's past, and by assisting the child, to project unconscious material and innermost feelings onto the characters in the literature. The key for the therapist is to help the child understand that these projections in "here" and "now" of therapy with the counselor are really the products of the earlier incident. Projections are, therefore, expressions of the unconscious and, as such, the initial step toward psychological integration and self-recognition. However, until children are able psychologically to realize the connection between projections on characters in stories and personal real-life experiences and assimilate these feelings into their conscious selves, the problem has not been resolved.

This expression of the transference in reaction to characters in a book can give the patient insight into the manner in which he is re-living early experiences and feeling the same ambivalence that he did as a child without due regard for the fact that the situation is now changed. . . . (Shrodes, 1949, p. 106)

The implication for transference here is that what might have been a necessary and appropriate emotional reaction and action for a child to survive mentally at one point in time is no longer appropriate for mental well-being. In my experience, an example would be the child coping with the loss of a parent through death, who must pass through stages of adjustment including denial, anger, bargaining, depression, and acceptance. In this instance, projections are apparent in the first three stages. Once self-awareness and self-understanding begin to surface, then depression occurs. In the case of a client's experience with death, literature can be suggested which is appropriate for each stage of the bereavement process.

Suggestion

Although suggestion is a basic technique, I choose to introduce it here to aid in the comprehension of other key therapeutic concepts. Suggestion not only involves the recommendation of specific literary assignments but also the interpretation of repressed feelings and thoughts which have been projected in transference. Suggestion as interpretation assists the child to assimilate the newly experienced unconscious affect in the conscious or present reality. It is based on the counselor's overall knowledge of the client within the counselor's relationship and is subject to the counselor's biases regarding the child. Because interpretation was discussed at length in Chapter 2, "Child-Centered Counseling," little more will be said here. However, I feel the need to emphasize that it is through suggestion and skilled interpretation that client defenses and resistances are overcome and that insights into self are awakened. It is also paramount to monitor carefully the levels of anxiety generated through suggestion and interpretation. Suggestions that are too anxiety-provoking can damage the therapeutic relationship and either encourage regression in the child or deeper repression. The strength of the suggestion and of its presentation is very important for the counselor—who may either create excessive anxiety or motivate the client to deeper levels of self-understanding through increased insight.

Insight

The development of personal insight in children involves the self-awareness and self-understanding of their emotions, thoughts, and actions, as well as the motivations and behaviors of others toward them. As mentioned previously, insight also includes the reeducation of emotions in children. For example, I worked recently with an 11-year-old girl, Patty, who continued to love blindly and devotedly a father who had divorced mother and family for several years without communication. This child was immobilized emotionally and was incapable of loving and being loved by a stepfather. She had to recognize her father for what he was and realize the futility of her misdirected efforts so that she could redirect her emotional energy and identification to someone who would reciprocate in the present and future. A part of this self-recognition involved first hating her father for abandoning her and the mother, second being angry for the father's refusal to communicate and recognize important events such as birthdays and Christmas, and finally acceptance of the reality that she probably would never see or hear from her father again, but that she would survive without him and she could give and receive love from others, including her stepfather. This particular girl was helped to develop insight by reading Gardner's *The Boys and Girls Book About Divorce* (1971) and *The Boys and Girls Book About Stepfamilies*(1982). Counseling excerpts from this case are presented later in the chapter to elucidate basic skills.

Shrodes (1949) wrote:

> [E]ach child . . . brings to bear on the situation in a novel his own predispositions, the congeries of circumstances in his own life, his unique perspective, and he must add them up in relation to what is given in the book. He must search for meaning and order, . . . and hypotheses to account for both his own experiences and those portrayed in the book. This is productive thinking. (p. 111)

Productive thinking encourages analysis of self and self in relation to others, which leads to greater self-awareness and self-understanding. Through productive thinking, a change in perceptions of reality can occur which enhances the reeducation of emotions, values, and attitudes. This entire process contributes to the achievement of insight. Once insight has been achieved, children are capable of new, more-productive behavior. If for any reason, insight is not achieved, bibliotherapy would likely provide minimal therapeutic value through catharsis.

Catharsis

If children can identify with characters in literature, then they should be able to experience catharsis. Catharsis allows children to experience repressed emotions through the characters in the literature. It also allows an outlet for the expression of socially inappropriate emotions and actions such as aggression and sexual desires. In a sense, the catharsis that literature encourages is a freeing experience which allows the child the opportunity to momentarily unlock personal emotional constraints and societal barriers to self-expression by feeling with the characters in the literature.

BASIC TECHNIQUES

Essentially bibliotherapy involves three distinct techniques: (1) the task of selecting appropriate types of literature, and suggesting its use to children at appropriate times; (2) the therapeutic process or interaction between child and therapist related to the literary experience; and (3) the activities used by counselors to stimulate this interaction.

Selection of Literature

Some experts feel that it is best to allow children to select what they shall read from a variety of alternative titles chosen by the bibliotherapist (Moses & Zaccaria, 1978). However, satisfactory results can be experienced by selecting specific material for children to read. Some children avoid their problems and often choose not to read about situations like their own unless encouraged to do so. In addition, no two pieces of literature are equal in what they contribute to the reader. Some are definitely superior to others and it behooves the therapist to take the responsibility for knowing the child's needs, knowing the available literature, and matching the two to make optimal gains.

The first part of making a "best fit" between client and literature, *knowing the child*, involves being sensitive to such factors as age, sex, type of problem, reading ability, and reading interests or other literary interests. Regardless of ability, what children read or do with literature will be related to age and sex. For example, children who are 11 years old, whether below average, average, or above average in ability, will be interested in similar content: naturally, 11-year-old boys will typically prefer male-oriented material, whereas girls prefer stories with female protagonists.

In selecting literature, the therapist must also consider the type of problem a child has and the counseling goals for that particular child. Four principles for using bibliotherapy were discussed earlier in this chapter. However, in terms of selection of literature, I agree with Moses and Zaccaria (1978) that problems can be categorized as either situational or developmental. *Situational problems* are unique to each child and may involve such difficulties as handicaps, phobias, and child abuse. *Developmental problems* are those problems that most children must face and overcome at a given age level. For younger children, these problems may include learning how to get along in the family, learning to play effectively, and learning to lead and follow. For older children, these tasks may include developing appropriate same-sex and opposite-sex relationships, developing personal values and attitudes, and developing independence from parents.

Reading interests are also important in knowing the child and in the selection process of bibliotherapy. Children will readily read books related closely to their interests and reject books that are boring. As a classroom teacher and counselor, I found children aged 5 to 8 to be primarily interested in short stories, nursery rhymes, stories about animals, families, and heroes. By ages 9 to 12, children become interested in literature involving adventure, mystery, biographies, animals, sports, and family and school life. In adolescence, children are interested in advanced literature about animals, adventure, mystery, sports, biographies, history, romance, and value-laden topics related to developing man and womanhood.

The second part of applying literature in therapy is *knowing the literature*. Moses and Zaccaria (1978) emphasize the bibliotherapist be familiar with the literature's level of difficulty, plot, length, readability, format, style, and overall appropriateness, including realistic approach with focus on the identified problem. Hoagland (1972) stresses lifelike characters and accurate social-group presentation. In addition, Bernstein (1977) suggests several questions which should be answered to help select books:

> What is the book's scope and nature?
>
> Are all the statements within the book accurate?
>
> If not, is the misinformation or objectionable attitude one that an adult might wish to clarify or correct?
>
> What is the book's emotional impact?
>
> What is the religious persuasion of the book?
>
> Is the book worthwhile from a literary viewpoint, satisfying readers on the verbal and emotional levels and, possibly, on the spiritual level?
>
> Does the book appear to be straight fiction or based on fact—or is it propaganda? (p. 4)

No matter the criteria of selection of utmost concern is that the literature serve the purpose for which it was selected. A bibliotherapy reference list is available to the reader in Appendix C. This list is not exhaustive and represents only topics in which I have had personal experience. All references listed are recent, from 1970 to present. Although I recognize that there are many excellent books and literary sources published prior to this date, I have not included them in the bibliotherapy reference list because of space limitations. For comprehensive listings on topics other than death, divorce, stepfamilies, and accepting relocations, readers are referred to the recommended resources section of this chapter.

Counseling Process in Bibliotherapy

In discussing the helping process of bibliotherapy, it is important to conceptualize that the child undergoes a self-help process first and an interactive process with the therapist second. Hynes (1981) discusses four process steps that can be applied to help define clients' self-processing of literature: recognition, examination, juxtaposition, and self-application. *Recognition* involves the reader's perception of what the literature has to say. The participant must be able to identify something about the message of the literature that is personally relevant. *Examination* involves a dissecting of the relevant material, which means investigating the immediate value and interest by asking such questions as "What is it about this book that interests me?" "How are my values similar or different from those of the characters?" *Juxtaposition* is described as resulting from self-recognition and self-examination of two or more impressions of what has been read. Juxtaposition should involve a self-dialogue in which the characters' values, attitudes, feelings, and actions are placed on a dichotomous continuum so that the reader can then examine the extremes and the grey areas between. This process helps the child to develop the realization and the insight that one often has ambivalent feelings about issues; this is OK. For example, in the previous case, Patty learned that part of loving someone deeply is that it creates potential to hate just as deeply, and the truth of her real feeling for father following these insights could be placed somewhere in between. *Self-application* is the manner in which the child integrates the insights developed from the literature and makes personal life adjustments to accomodate these insights. It is the action the child takes or would like to take to change behavior to improve personal living. Again, in our case example, once Patty realized her father was rejecting her love, she stopped writing her weekly letters that were not reciprocated. When she discontinued this frustrating and self-punishing behavior, she began to feel more positively toward herself.

When using literature with children, I have found the following processing steps to be helpful.

1. *Focus on the Literature*

a. Review the literature. Ask the child to reconstruct what was read from his or her perceptions. Who were the major characters? What happened during the story? Who did what to whom? Emphasize major events from the child's perspective. Help the child be specific in describing the events.

b. Clarify children's perceptions of each character's behaviors and feelings in the literature. Be ready to identify possible projections in this step, but do not focus on them in discussion.

c. Elicit and clarify children's perceptions of character's alternative actions and possible consequences of each behavior. This step should be futuristically oriented and involves children's imagination. Again, stimulus questions can be used. What would happen to—— if . . . ? How many other ways could—— handle the problem?

The entire first step is directed toward maximizing the child's identifications and projections. In addition, it takes advantage of the child's own recognition and examination process.

2. Focus on the Child's Reality

This step should be planned carefully in that children must be ready to own and to define their problem as it exists for them. The child is encouraged to personalize and relate himself or herself to the appropriate themes in the literature—in view of *past* personal experiences. Have you experienced anything like the characters in the literature? How was your experience the same, different? How did you feel? What did you do? Once past experiences have been examined, the focus is changed to current reality. Are you experiencing anything like this story at the present time? As the child's problem is registered in the "here" and "now" of the counseling session, the counselor encourages the child to analyze the situation by examining thoroughly crucial ideas and feelings. The therapist will elicit and clarify the juxtapositions the child had made or is making at this time.

Hynes (1981) states:

> The skilled and trained bibliotherapist will seize the opportunity to help . . . bring to consciousness what is significant for . . . self-understanding without endangering self-preservation. The facilitator may also help uncover unconscious material by responding with empathy to the individual and adroitly challenging previously held ideas or feelings while helping to form more effective adaptation. (p. 240)

Therefore, as children self-disclose, the therapist responds in a child-centered manner by reflecting and clarifying feelings, assisting in the development of insight through interpreting, and then eliciting and suggesting alternative behaviors. These action strategies should first take advantage of the child's self-application process. Often all that is necessary for some children to act effectively is for the counselor to encourage and support decisions which have already been made but lie dormant because of the child's fear or insecurity.

3. Evaluate

Evaluation is necessary to determine the effectiveness of the child's actions. Children often need assistance to determine the extent of helpfulness of their new behaviors. We, as adults, have a tendency to belittle our efforts and overlook small positive gains we make by our assuming, erroneously, that we should be able to accomplish everything at once, including a drastic behavior change, peace of mind, and happiness. Children are no different in this attitude than adults and will need the help and understanding of the therapist through evaluation to reinforce their efforts and progress.

Examples of the therapeutic process stages can be identified in the following audiotaped excerpts with Patty, which were made after she read *The Boys and Girls Book About Stepfamilies* (Gardner, 1982). Prior to this book, Patty had been in counseling for five months, one hour, once per week. She had successfully worked through her parents' divorce and accepted living with her mother and not seeing her father, Jack, who had remarried. For a year, her mother had been dating several men but decided recently to limit her efforts to one special person. This decision by mother disrupted seriously the dynamics of the one-parent home and Patty's security and position in it. Patty began to resist her mother's decision in several ways but her behavior is characterized by her saying to mother, "If you loved me, you wouldn't date Ben." It is noteworthy that the book was used only to begin the counseling process in this case.

Process/Responses	Dialogue
OPEN QUESTION	Co: How did you do in your reading?
FOCUSING ON LITERATURE	Patty: I read most of it. The beginning is an explanation of stepfamilies.
SELF-EXAMINATION	It's stupid, like: What is a step-family? What is a stepfather?
CLARIFICATION	Co: It defines all the terms.
SELF-RECOGNITION	Patty: I read what you should call your
SELF-EXAMINATION	stepmother. I don't even care about that. I call her what I want to: Betty. At first my dad wanted me to call her Mom, but I couldn't call her Mom.
	Co: You decided Betty was best for you.
	Patty: Yeah, I called my father by his first name, too, Jack. I never called him Father.
OPEN QUESTION	Co: What about the chapter (on)

Process/Responses	*Dialogue*
CONCRETENESS FOCUSING ON LITERATURE SELF-RECOGNITION	Things you should know about feelings in stepfamilies? Patty: Last night Ben came over. He asked if he could spend the night and I said yes. What was I supposed to say? (angrily) No!
RESPONSE TO FEELING FOCUSING ON CHILD'S REALITY	Co: You felt neglected, left out.
SELF-RECOGNITION	Patty: I always feel neglected and jealous when he comes over. All they do is talk and do things together and unless I stick my nose into it, I'm not welcome and don't understand.
CLARIFICATION	Co: You aren't included and don't understand why. Patty: Yeah.
CLARIFICATION	Co: You're experiencing difficulty in working things out between you and Mom, and when Ben gets in the conversation, there is more confusion.
SELF-EXAMINATION	Patty: That leaves me on the outside.
RESPONSE TO FEELING	Co: As if you are unwelcome, unwanted.
SELF-EXAMINATION	Patty: And I don't know why.
OPEN QUESTION	Co: When your mother explains some of this, how do you feel?
JUXAPOSITION	Patty: Good. I don't like when Mom hides things from me. She has a tendency to do that. I like it when she talks to me.
CLARIFICATION	Co: You feel as though you would understand your mom if you had more information.
SELF-RECOGNITION	Patty: If I knew what was going on.
CLARIFICATION	Co: Mom isn't as open and honest with you as you want her to be.
SELF-EXAMINATION	Patty: I don't know where Mom's relationship is going with Ben. I'm scared. He's always in a good mood, and I think that's unrealistic. It makes me so mad. It's like an act.
INTERPRETATION	Co: He knows that his access to Mom depends on you. Patty: Right! He plays it real cool with me. He gives me a lot of things.
INTERPRETATION SELF-EXAMINATION SELF-APPLICATION	Co: You feel he's buying you. Patty: Yeah! Sometimes I do. I don't mind getting free stuff. I think that's real nice, but it's like he's trying to win me over to get to Mom. I don't know. I just can't ex-

Process/Responses	Dialogue

Process/Responses

Dialogue

plain it. It's like he's acting, on stage. I'm so scared.

RESPONSE TO FEELING
SELF-APPLICATION

Co: It's frightening.

Patty: When he's over, Mom's great. When he's away, she's terrible. I think it would be better to have someone else around. He lives out of town.

CLARIFICATION
CONCRETENESS

Co: Apparently, your mother's and Ben's relationship is at a crossroads for you and your life. You've made some decisions. Where does it leave you?

SELF-EXAMINATION
SELF-APPLICATION

Patty: Left out. For some reason, I don't know . . . even when I understand, I just feel like I'm getting pushed away, farther and farther. I don't know why. Every time I think about Ben, I just feel like I'm pushed away, and I'll be forced to do something I don't want to do.

INTERPRETATION

Co: It seems to me some is physical closeness but some is mental. Mom spends a lot of time thinking about Ben. She either gets upset with you or becomes aloof and distant. Pushes you away by yelling or pushes you out of her mind.

SELF-APPLICATION

Patty: Sometimes, but when I ask to be included, she says real mean, "No, we want to be by ourselves." That's what I mean about being pushed away for one thing.

Co: Uh, huh! Sarcasm is painful.

Patty: It's like a war with words when we are yelling and fighting.

INTERPRETATION

Co: Listen and tell me what you think about this. Mom is under a lot of stress in her relationship with Ben, but feels she can't direct her anger toward him so she yells at you. You love Mom, but are angry at her at the same time. You decide to get mad at Mom and at Ben, who appears to be upsetting Mom.

Materials and Activities

Contrary to the popular notion most counselors have that bibliotherapy involves only books, bibliotherapists can and do use a variety of materials, including books (fiction, nonfiction, biographies, autobiographies, etc.), films, filmstrips, audiotapes and videotapes, poetry, journals, magazines, and diaries. This brief series of examples is by no means exhaustive. In general, using children's literature in counseling may entail any material or activity that applies written (in some cases, spoken) words to enhance the therapeutic process. These written words may be provided by the therapist or the child. For example, several literary activities that I have found useful early in counseling are:

1. *Autobiography.* Often in the initial stages of counseling, it is difficult to get a young child to self-disclose. However, children who are skilled with language usage may, with encouragement, write an autobiography highlighting important events in their lives. Other children who cannot write effectively can tell their story into a tape recorder and then play it back. Or, the therapist may choose to type the taped story so that the child can hear it played as he or she reads along. In any of the three activities mentioned, children usually begin to self-disclose and interact with the counselor. They are creative in their efforts and involved in a highly personal interesting activity, and the therapist is provided a source of information with documentation on the client. I always ask children whether they would like to keep what they have created or have me keep it for them. In most instances, children want me to safekeep their work. However, during those times when children wanted to take work home, all have allowed me to make copies for my files.

2. *Lifeline.* Another activity designed to elicit information from children is the lifeline. In this activity, children are asked to first draw a long, straight line on a piece of 8½-by-11 inch paper. Then, to help get them started, I draw a baby on one end of the line and place a zero over its head, while telling the child, "This picture of an infant indicates your birth. Now, as you think of the best (happiest) and the worst (saddest) times in your life, draw a symbol on the line at about the time in your life you think it happened. You may want to write words rather than draw, which is all right." As children develop the lifeline, they are encouraged to discuss each incident briefly. Again, I would recommend recording the activity and following those procedures discussed in the child's autobiography.

Activities that I have initiated at intermediate stages of counseling are:

3. *Unfinished Stories or Poems.* In these situations, I develop brief statements (no longer than a paragraph or few lines) based on a particular resistance or impasse the child is experiencing in therapy. The child is then encouraged to read what has been written and add the next part to the story or poem. We can interact in this fashion as long as the child is able and willing to participate. Of course, when the resistance is too strong, children will write "The End" early.

4. *Last Words, Obituaries, or Epitaphs.* To develop greater insight into problems and resistances, children can use their imaginations and

respond in writing to the statement: "If you were to die today, what would your last words be to each member of your family and friends?" Children might also be helped to focus on themselves by writing an obituary or drawing a gravestone to include an epitaph accurately describing who they were, how they would like to be remembered, or both.

Although the concept closure has not been discussed in detail, it is essential that therapists be prepared for this highly emotional event both for themselves and their clients. I have found that terminating a long-term relationship is the most difficult part of counseling for me. Most children are also reluctant to let go. In preparation for our last session together, I often begin to systematically reduce the frequency and the intensity of our meetings. In the case of Patty, we began to meet every other week for one hour and then every other week for one half hour. Finally, we agreed that to meet only once a month was sufficient. To fill the "gaps" or off weeks in therapy, I have found two activities, letter-writing and diaries, especially valuable to begin to get children involved in self-thinking and self-helping and to keep our lines of communication open even though we are not meeting.

5. *Letter Writing.* Letter writing is a natural, fun, and educational activity for children to communicate with friends. Most children will write only one or two brief pages but are afforded the opportunity to continue to invest themselves with an important other. Children usually write about their interests and what they are doing that is exciting, but almost always sign their closings "I love you." Initially, in termination, the need to continue to give and receive love from the therapist is primary. In my letters of response, I reinforce the children for their positive life actions and let them know that I, too, miss them and love them. Gradually, toward the end of therapy, their closings and mine change to "your friend, . . . "

6. *Diaries.* For me, personal journals or diaries have been the most effective way of discontinuing the face-to-face relationships, yet maintaining privacy of communication. I often am able to get older children to express their innermost thoughts and feelings in a diary when they will not in letter form. Children sometimes make free associations by writing in the diary in random style or as events occur rather than sitting down and collecting their thoughts for a letter. Often they will also share their dreams. Diaries can be mailed or dropped off at the counselor's office. It only takes a moment to read the material and respond to the child in the margins about what was written. An edited excerpt regarding closure with Patty follows. Some dates are included for the reader's edification.

Date	Diary	My Response
February 10	I am going to keep this for my last meetings with Jim. Time will be	You have given me a great deal. For example, pride in your growth

Date	*Diary*	*My Response*
	running short and I don't want to waste any of it. Sometimes all I'm going to talk about are feelings or things that happen. Right now I'm more sad than angry. What you don't know is that I feel like I do all the taking. I hope I've given you something.	gives me a sense of personal accomplishment and self-satisfaction.
	I'm tired of getting angry at Mom. We only talk about our bad parts. How do I stop?	Remember, you are in control. When anger sets in, give yourself at least 20 minutes alone before talking with your mother.
March 10	I'm not different, but I've changed. I still get angry but act different. It feels good.	Unpleasant feelings are as much a part of our lives as pleasant. We need to accept, integrate, and learn to act on both types of feelings successfully.
	Sometimes I feel Mom cuts me out completely. I can't get her to see my side. I love her and need her so much.	When you feel lonely, you have a tendency to get scared and want to cling to Mom for security. Loving someone and being dependent are two different issues. Your mother loves you but wants to be independent and also love another. You, too, can love others than Mom.
April 7	I told Mom it's hard to give you up. She agreed. I guess much of our problem is we are a lot alike. When you love someone, it's difficult to give any part to someone else. Letting go is very	Recognizing you can take care of yourself is a large responsibility. One of my biggest gifts from you has been the privilege of helping you accomplish this independence.

Date	Diary	My Response
	hard for me. It makes me sad. I almost don't want to be OK. Being OK means I have to be responsible and that's scary. Sometimes I feel even guilty about feeling good, for just being me. I feel everything will fall apart without you, and Mom will want to get rid of me again. I want to cry right now. "Please don't leave me by my-self." Leaving you is one of the hardest things I've had to do.	I would like to correct you. You are not leaving me nor I you. True, soon we will no longer work together, but we are friends and very close.
April 8	Today I'm OK without you. It's like when I see you reminds me I won't see you some day, but the sad feelings pass the day after. I'll miss you again in two weeks.	It seems that you realize I am both a source of comfort and support and pain for you. I, too, am experiencing hurt as we begin to part.
April 13	I really do miss you, Jim. Guess what, I've made two new friends. I'll tell you all about it next time we meet. Now I have Amy, Susan, Mom and you.	Congratulations. I'm pleased for you. It's ex-citing to get to know new persons with whom you can share your life.
April 20	I feel content with Mom. It's like we have grown up together. She said she loved me today and I really felt she meant it.	There are times when your doubt of your mother's love for you has seemed to me a refusal on your part to accept and to return it.
April 30	Only a month to go, so short. I'm going to miss you, Jim. You are part of my support system. What am I going to do when you aren't around? This writing helps but it's just not the	I will miss you, too. It is

Date	Diary	My Response
	same. Ha! I know what you'll say. I know I've talked a lot about my friends lately, but it's like you are pushing me away too fast. I'm mad at you. Now I wish I hadn't said anything. I hate my diary.	frightening to stand on your own two feet.
May 25	Although tomorrow is our last day, I want to see you again. Jim, thank you for all your help. You have helped me travel far. I love you.	Everyone is on a life journey that begins at birth and ends with death. Along the way we learn, live, and love other people. Thank you for allowing me to share a part of your travels and your love. I love you.

RECOMMENDED RESOURCES

Time and space prevents the creation of an exhaustive list of children's literature. What follows are several sources I have found most valuable in helping select children's literature.

BERNSTEIN, J. *Books to help children cope with separation and loss.* New York: R. R. Bowker Co., 1977.

This book contains a listing of books by age level and reading level related to a multitude of areas associated with children's personal loss, including moving to a new school, coping with death and divorce, losing pets, losing friends, facing foster care, and understanding adoption.

HARRIS, C. & GARDENHOUR, N. *Developmental tasks resource guide for elementary school children.* Metuchen, NJ: Scarecrow Press, Inc., 1976.

An annotated guide to books, filmstrips, films, records, transparencies, audiotapes and videotapes, focusing on the major developmental tasks of childhood, including tasks for self-development such as developing personal independence, personal values, and physical skills and accepting and valuing oneself; and tasks for social development such as developing symbol systems, peer relations, and one's social role.

MURO, J. & DINKMEYER, D. *Counseling in the elementary and middle schools: A pragmatic approach.* Dubuque, IA: William Brown Co., 1977.

Chapter 10, titled "Bibliocounseling," contains an extensive reference list including book selections dealing with adoption, appearance, behavior, birthdays, children without a form, family problems and changes, handicapped, on being Jewish, moving, on being Black, overcoming obstacles, peer groups and friendships, poverty, self-concept, and sports.

ZACCARIA, J. & MOSES, H. *Principles and practices of bibliotherapy: A resource book for teachers and counselors.* Champaign, IL: Stripes Publishing Co., 1968.

This book provides a comprehensive listing of books for most problems experienced by children of all ages and backgrounds.

SUMMARY

Bibliotherapy, the use of literature to enhance mental health, had its historical origins in ancient Greece. As a therapeutic tool, bibliotherapy has evolved in the 20th century from a cooperative team concept in psychiatric hospitals, involving physician prescribing and professional librarians implementing book therapy, to an adjunctive counseling technique in which a variety of literary activities are used. A recent thorough examination of the research literature revealed that bibliotherapeutic results in general appear to be ambivalent (Schrank & Engels, 1982). Bibliotherapy with children appears to be most effective in changing personal attitudes and somewhat effective at increasing self-concept and academic achievement and reducing fear (Schrank, 1982).

In addition to the above introductory remarks, the first part of this chapter included a section on the value of bibliotherapy with children. Part two discussed the key concepts: identification, transference, suggestion, insight, and catharsis. The third section focused on basic techniques including the skills of (1) selecting appropriate literature which involved two basic components: know the child and knowing the literature, (2) the counseling process, and (3) materials and activities. Counselor and client dialogue were used to provide examples of the therapeutic process and diary activity. The last part of the chapter contained a list of recommended resources and references and recommended readings. A bibliotherapy reference list on the topics: coping with human death, coping with divorce, accepting stepparents and stepfamilies, and accepting relocation was also included in Appendix C.

REFERENCES AND RECOMMENDED READINGS

ALSTON, E. Bibliotherapy and psychotherapy. *Library Trends,* 1962, (11), 159–176.

Baruth, L. & Phillips, M. Bibliotherapy and the school counselor. *School Counselor*, 1976, 23, 191–199.

Bernstein, J. *Books to help children cope with separation and loss.* New York: R. R. Bowker Co., 1977.

Berry, F Contemporary bibliotherapy: Systematizing the field. In R. Rubin (Ed.) *Bibliotherapy sourcebook.* Phoenix, AZ: Oryz Press, 1978, 185–189.

Brown, E. *Bibliotherapy and its widening applications.* Metuchen, NJ: Scarecrow Press, 1975.

Carlsen, R. *Books and the teenage reader.* New York: Bantam, 1971.

Chambers, A. *Introducing books to children.* London: Heinemann Educational Books, 1975.

Cianciolo, P. Children's literature can affect coping behavior. *Personnel and Guidance Journal*, 1965, 897–901.

Cohoe, E. Bibliotherapy for handicapped children. *NEA Journal*, 1960, 49, 34–36.

Coody, B. *Using literature with children.* Dubuque, IA: William Brown Co., 1973.

Crosby, M. (Ed.) *Reading ladders for human relations.* (4th ed) Washington, DC: American Council on Education, 1963.

Cross, G. & Cross, L. Bibliotherapy for young children. *Journal of Clinical Child Psychology*, 1976, Fall, 35–38.

Cullinan, B. & Carmichael, C. *Literature and young children.* Chicago: University of Chicago Press, 1977.

Fassler, J. *Helping children cope.* New York: Free Press, 1977.

Gardner, R. *The boys and girls book about divorce.* New York: Science House, 1971.

Gardner, R. *The boys and girls book about stepfamilies.* New York: Bantam, 1972.

Garner, H. The therapy of books. *Journal of Counseling Services*, 1976, 1, 37–42.

Gottschalk, L. Bibliotherapy as an adjunct in psychotherapy. *American Journal of Psychiatry*, 1948, CIV, 632–637.

Hoagland, J. Bibliotherapy: Aiding children in personality development. *Elementary English*, 1972, 390–394.

Huck, C. *Children's literature in the elementary school.* New York: Holt, Rinehart & Winston, 1976.

Hynes, A. The goals of bibliotherapy. *The Arts in Psychotherapy*, 1980, 7, 35–41.

———. Some observations on process in biblio/poetry therapy. *The Arts in Psychotherapy*, 1981, 8, 237–241.

Jaskoski, H. Poetry, poetics and the poetry therapist. *The Arts in Psychotherapy*, 1980, 7, 275–279.

Larrick, N. *A parent's guide to children's literature.* New York: Bantam Books, 1975.

Lejeune, A. Bibliocounseling as a guidance technique. *Catholic Library World*, 1969, 41, 156–164.

Lewis, C. *Writing for young children.* New York: Anchor Press, 1981.

McKinney, F. Exploration in bibliotherapy. *Personnel and Guidance Journal*, 1977, 550–552.

MORGAN, S. Bibliotherapy: A broader concept. *Journal of Clinical Child Psychology*, 1976, 39–42.

MOSES, H. & ZACCARIA, J. Bibliotherapy in an educational context: Rationale and principles. *High School Journal*, 1969, 52, 401–411.

———. *Bibliotherapy in rehabilitation, educational, and mental health settings.* Champaign, IL: Stripes Publishing Co., 1978.

MURO, J. & DINKMEYER, D. Bibliocounseling. In *Counseling in the elementary and middle schools.* Dubuque, IA: William C. Brown Co., 1977, 251–273.

RUBIN, R. (Ed.) *Bibliotherapy sourcebook.* Phoenix, AZ: Oryz Press, 1978.

———. *Using bibliotherapy: A guide to theory and practice.* Phoenix, AZ: Oryz Press, 1978.

RUDMAN, M. *Children's literature: An issues approach.* Lexington, KY: D. C. Heath and Co., 1976.

SACHS, H. *The creative unconscious.* Cambridge, MA: Sci-Art Publishers, 1942.

SCHRANK, F. Bibliotherapy as an elementary school counseling tool. *Elementary School Guidance and Counseling*, 1982, 16, 218–227.

——— & ENGLES, D. Bibliotherapy as a counseling adjunct: Research findings. *Personnel and Guidance Journal*, 1981, November, 143–147.

SHEPARD, T. & ILES, L. What is bibliotherapy? *Language Arts*, 1976, May, 569–571.

SHRODES, C. Implications for psychotherapy. Chapter VIII. Bibliotherapy: A theoretical and clinical experimental study. Ph.D. dissertation, University of California, 1949. In Rubin, R. (Ed.) *Bibliotherapy sourcebook.* Phoenix, AZ: Oryz Press, 1978, 96–119.

SPACHE, G. Using books to help solve children's problems. In Rubin, R. (Ed.) *Bibliotherapy sourcebook.* Phoenix, AZ: Oryz Press, 1978, 241–250.

SUTHERLAND, Z. & ARBUTHNOT, M. *Children and books.* (6th ed.) Chicago: Scott, Foresman, & Co., 1981.

TARTAGNI, D. Using bibliotherapy with adolescents. *School Counselor*, 1976, 24, 28–35.

TEWS, R. Bibliotherapy. *Library Trends*, XI, 1962, 97.

WATSON, J. Bibliotherapy for abused children. *School Counselor*, 1980, 27, 204–209.

ZACCARIA, J. & MOSES, H. *Principles and practices of bibliotherapy: A resource book for teachers and counselors.* Champaign, IL: Stripes Publishing Co., 1968.

Chapter 8

Behavioral Counseling

BEHAVIORISTICS, the study of behavior as an integral part of psychology, originated in Russia in the last half of the 19th century with the research and publications on reflexes by Sechenov. This work was continued in the early 20th century by Bekhterev, who described his work as objective psychology and later reflexology, and Pavlov, who is credited with the discovery of the conditioned reflex. E. L. Thorndike's work at Columbia also at the turn of the century provided a model which accommodated the everyday activities of humans that Pavlov's could not. He proposed the "Law of Effect" that "instrumental" behaviors would be repeated when followed by desirable consequences.

In 1913, J. B. Watson, at Johns Hopkins University, led a movement which successfully converted objective psychology to behaviorism, which became in effect the psychology of stimulus and response. By the 1920s, behaviorism was solidly entrenched in American psychology and, in 1938, B. F. Skinner helped formalize the distinction between the methods of Pavlov and Thorndike by naming the former "respondent" conditioning and the latter "operant" conditioning (Boring, 1950). As a result of Skinner's influence, behavioral laboratory and applied research increased tremendously in schools, clinics, and other mental health institutions throughout the United States.

In 1965 the Cubberly Conference was held at Stanford University to explore methods for increasing counselor effectiveness in various settings. The theme of the conference was "Revolution in Counseling." Programs consisted of four major addresses as well as numerous demonstrations, and both organized and informal discussions were directed at examining the status and development of the field and to generating innovations in counseling techniques. The majority of these programs emphasized use of operant learning strategies in counseling practice. Approximately 500 individuals attended the conference now recognized as the beginning of the behavioral counseling movement (Krumboltz, 1966). Recently, Krumboltz (1980) accentuated the progress behavioral counseling has made in the last 15 years and identified prevention, self-control, and the integration of thinking, feeling, and acting as future directions for growth.

Prior to the Cubberly Conference in the 1950s and 1960s, an overwhelming majority of counselor education programs and counselors in the field had adopted a Rogerian focus in training and practice. This approach stressed the client's innate capacity to solve problems and move toward a self-actualized life. However, my own experience in working with children has indicated that they do not necessarily possess the capacities or abilities to progress in positive directions by themselves at all developmental levels. Some children cannot verbalize extensively; others have relatively immature decision-making skills, lack adequate levels of responsibility for self, and have inadequately developed cognitive ability. I have found behavioral counseling to be the therapy of choice when first working with children who lack many of these social, emotional, and intellectual skills. What, then, is behavioral counseling?

According to Krumboltz (1966), behavioral counseling entails that:

> the counselor focuses attention on the goals and behaviors of each client and sets as his task the planning of an experience that can yield satisfaction to the client and at the same time move him in the direction of the goal he has set . . . . In behavioral counseling much more attention is paid to what one does, to the specific reinforcement of a specific act rather than just the provision of an all-enveloping warmth. (p. 82)

Krumboltz continued to express that behavioral counseling had yet to effectively integrate human problems with theory and practice. However, in the short span of time from 1966 to the present, results of extensive research investigations have proven that behavior principles have been used successfully by counseling practitioners in a variety of settings (Krumboltz, Becker-Haven, & Burnett, 1979).

For clarification of the term behavioral counseling in this book, I offer the following definition: *Behavioral counseling* is the systematic application of behavioral concepts and techniques in therapy with the intent to alter children's behavior by either maintaining and increasing desirable behavior or decreasing undesirable behavior for the purposes of improving clients' ability to cope with everyday developmental problems. In these instances, behavioral concepts and techniques are implemented to help establish a work environment and prepare children mentally to be ready to function in a child-centered counseling atmosphere. This definition implies that, although behavioral counselors focus initially on setting behavioral goals and manipulating the child's environment and reinforcing properties, the therapist is always concerned with the relationship and maintaining its therapeutic nature. In most instances, when the primary goals of controlling maladaptive behaviors have been realized, therapists can concentrate on goals of self-awareness, self-understanding, and attitude development while using child-centered techniques.

The Value of Behavioral Counseling

As alluded to in the previous paragraph, the major value of behavioral counseling to children and therapists is found in the systematic organization and planning of the behavioral counseling program. Organization and planning will be discussed later in relation to the key concept operant conditioning. Second, although most behaviors for change are identified by adults, children must be involved in the decision-making process. Children in counseling must agree that particular behavioral goals are advantageous to their welfare and they must indicate a willingness and a commitment to work toward these ends. Therefore, children should be aware and should have agreed to the behavioral goals. As a result, they are active participants in a self-development process. Third, when specifying behavioral objectives in operational fashion, children have the opportunity to learn to break large, complex behavioral processes into smaller components. Thus, as a part of analyzing their behavior, they learn to think critically and learn that a whole is the sum of its parts. It is hoped that children are also able to synthesize and integrate these desired behaviors into their overall behavioral repertoire. At a very minimum, children learn that complex behaviors (or tasks) are accomplished by building a sound foundation on simpler ones. When generalized, this concept is true for most life skills. Fourth, a baseline count of behavior and any subsequent count daily, weekly, or longer, provides children a realistic, accurate description of what they are in fact doing. In essence, each child controls his or her own development. Once goals and objectives are agreed upon, children know that if they perform a task they will be reinforced, and if they do not perform, they will not be reinforced and may be punished. It is their choice. Lastly, whether behavioral goals and objectives are realized or not, children are involved in a therapeutic relationship and have opportunities to discuss themselves and their growth or lack of it with an adult interested in their welfare.

   In this section, I have referred to several behavioral terms without explanation. There exists several key concepts, some already mentioned, that provide a basis for understanding behavioral counseling. These include respondent and operant conditioning, reinforcement, reinforcement schedules, reinforcers, reinforcement menu, extinction, and satiation.

KEY CONCEPTS

As mentioned in the introductory paragraphs to this chapter, the terms *respondent conditioning* and *operant conditioning* are credited to Skinner when he described the two conditioning models of Pavlov and Thorndike. Before discussing the differences in the two conditioning processes, it is important to differentiate between respondent and operant behavior.

Respondent behavior is reflexive in that it occurs independent of conscious thought in response to a stimulus. Examples of respondent behavior would include the curling of infants toes when scratched gently on the soles of their feet or the dilation of pupils in the eyes when entering a dark room. *Operant behavior* is learned and is influenced by past learning which preceded it and the consequences that follow it.

Respondent Conditioning

The respondent (classical) conditioning process requires two types of stimuli: a neutral stimulus which is not sufficient by itself to elicit an involuntary response and an unconditioned stimulus which elicits the response automatically. Figure 8–1 describes Pavlov's respondent conditioning of dogs. Conditioning begins after pairing the neutral stimulus, bell ringing, with the unconditioned stimulus, food, for a period of time to get the unconditioned reflex response, salivation. When the bell ringing elicits the response, salivation, without food, respondent conditioning has occurred.

Figure 8–1 Pavlov's Respondent Conditioning

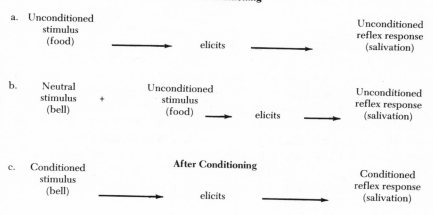

Before Conditioning

a. Unconditioned stimulus (food) ⟶ elicits ⟶ Unconditioned reflex response (salivation)

b. Neutral stimulus (bell) + Unconditioned stimulus (food) ⟶ elicits ⟶ Unconditioned reflex response (salivation)

After Conditioning

c. Conditioned stimulus (bell) ⟶ elicits ⟶ Conditioned reflex response (salivation)

Respondent conditioning is important in therapy because of the generalization effect that occurs with the conditioned stimulus. For example, let us assume that teachers are neutral stimuli for most incoming kindergarten children. Unexpected loud noises (unconditioned stimuli) elicit a startled reaction and possibly fear (unconditioned reflex responses). If a kindergarten teacher yells and scolds children repeatedly, it is possible that the neutral stimulus (teacher) can become a conditioned stimulus which produces the conditioned reflex response (fear). Children can develop a conditioned phobic reaction to a teacher. Of greater concern is that generalization will eventually occur and the phobic reaction will not be to an individual teacher but to all teachers and even school. I became personally aware of this power of generalization effect in respondent conditioning when I was asked to work with a first grader who experienced nausea, some vomiting, and headaches each day prior to school and cried frequently when in school. Following several sessions, she disclosed that she was most afraid of her teacher who yelled constantly. When asked how many times the teacher had yelled at her, she replied, "Oh! never, but I know my turn will come." This child was experiencing a conditioned fear of her teacher that was in the process of generalizing to a fear of school.

Operant Conditioning

A behavioral counseling program is typically planned using the following seven fundamental steps:

1. Identify Behavioral Goals

To state it simply, counselors through the socialization, training, and education of children are attempting to (a) help facilitate children's acquisition of desirable behavior that is not present in their behavioral repertoire, and (b) change nonadaptive behavior that is already acquired and socially undesirable or self-defeating. In the second instance, two basic rules apply, the unwanted behavior must be unlearned and new learning must occur that allows the child to function effectively. Blackham and Silberman (1975) have set three criteria for deciding whether behavior is considered maladaptive or not. First, the suspected maladaptive behavior must occur with sufficient frequency. For example, most children engage in occasional fights, but few children fight daily. This atypical behavior is maladaptive. Second, it must be a behavior pattern which, if continued over time, will be harmful to the child or the child's environment. If intervention and remediation are not planned for a learning-disabled child, the child's disability will impair his or her ability to learn certain developmental tasks. In addition, a frustrated learner is often disruptive in the classroom, which may be detrimental to the learning of other students. Third, the behavior must hinder future healthy development. To illustrate, children who constantly need reassurance that they are properly doing what is expected of them by working for brief periods of time and then seeking parental or teacher approval may be developing an excessive dependency. This dependency will likely create future problems in decision making and self-image. To assist the reader in deciding what desirable behaviors should be learned, I would recommend reviewing the material on child development in Chapter 1.

2. Specify Behavioral Goals

Once behavioral goals are identified in general terms, they must be specified objectively in operational language to ensure they can be assessed. For instance, a general desirable goal may be for a parent or teacher to get a child to complete and turn in a homework assignment in one week. However, to accomplish this task, several discrete steps are required which lead up to it, such as writing down the assignment, taking home the required books, sitting down at home and working to completion, returning to school with the completed assignment, and handing it in. Five behavioral goals/objectives can therefore be specified for the overall goal of completing and handing in homework: (a) John will write in his notebook the mathematics assignment within five minutes of its being given by the teacher, (b) five minutes before dismissal, John will collect the necessary math books to carry home, (c) when arriving at home, John will go to his room and complete all math homework before play, (d) John will collect all his books and completed homework just before leaving home for school, and (e) John will hand in completed homework. The first two objectives and the last one can be easily monitored by the teacher at school, whereas the third and fourth can be assessed at home by the parent. The important factor to remember when attempting to evoke desirable behavior is that a complete analysis of the general goal is necessary to break it down into sequential, successive behavioral steps. The old saying "first things first and one at a time" applies here.

3. Obtain a Baseline Level

"Care enough to count." The therapist must observe the client's behavior personally or train another person to observe the targeted behavior before treatment begins to determine its frequency. This step might be accomplished when determining whether or not a behavior is maladaptive (see step 1, item [b]). Baseline is the key to assessment of treatment effect as it provides a basis of comparison of behavior before, during, and after intervention strategies are implemented.

4. Prepare the Treatment Environment

Once it has been ascertained that the child has the ability to perform the desired behavior, the counselor can decide what reinforcement schedule to implement and which reinforcers will be most effective with a particular client. The environment in which the desired behavior is to be demonstrated must then be arranged so that there is a high probability of occurrence. In the previous homework example, the teacher must make the assignment each day for reinforcement to be possible daily.

5. Select the Reinforcement Schedule and Identify Reinforcers

The client, client's problem, and the environment are all factors to be considered when selecting a reinforcement schedule. For example, I have found that with groups larger than five, a fixed-interval schedule is easier to handle (Gumaer & Myrick, 1974; Gumaer & Simon, 1979; Hiltzheimer & Gumaer, 1979), and when counseling with disturbed and disruptive children, a fixed-ratio schedule works well initially to reduce the disruptive behavior to a manageable level and to get their attention. Reinforcement schedules can and should be adjusted to accommodate client learning and growth. In fact, many children have verbalized to me in counseling that it was no longer necessary for me to use a certain reinforcement schedule or reinforcer like candy because they could perform the behavior without it. Reinforcement schedules are defined later in the chapter.

In order for a stimulus to act as a positive reinforcer, it must strengthen the behavior it follows. By strengthening the behavior, the therapist is increasing the likelihood that the child will repeat the desirable behavior. As a result, it is important that stimuli are identified that have reinforcing properties for particular clients. One way to identify reinforcers is to observe children's play and free-time activity. During these times, children are often self-reinforcing in their selection of activities. Another way is to present a reinforcement menu to the child and have the child select the reinforcers. The reinforcement menu will also be discussed later in this chapter.

6. Implement the Treatment Program

Once the desirable behavior is demonstrated, it is necessary to reinforce it immediately and continuously until it reaches a satisfactory strength level. After performance of the behavior reaches this higher frequency level, the reinforcement schedule may be changed so that the emphasis of reinforcement is changed from primary reinforcers to secondary reinforcers and therefore from extrinsic reward to intrinsic reward systems. The frequency of reinforcement can be reduced as well as the kind and the amount. I have found that moving from a fixed-interval schedule to a variable-interval schedule or from a fixed-ratio to a variable-ratio schedule an effective first change in scheduling. In any case, the reinforcement program is continued until the desired behavior is accomplished at a suitable rate.

7. Maintain Records of the Behavior

It is important to document client progress or lack of progress. Some behaviors require extensive shaping and it is difficult to realize behavioral growth in small steps. Children need to be aware of their growth, which is reinforcing in itself. Adults also need to have performance-based information to encourage their efforts in obtaining transfer of the behavior from the counseling office to the classroom or home. Operant conditioning programs fail when parents and teachers expect too much too soon and discard the program before it has had a chance to work. For instance, in the previous example, it would not be unusual for John's teacher or mother to expect him to complete our five objectives in the first day. John, for some reason, may not be ready and only accomplishes satisfactorily the first two objectives in his first day. He has not failed and the program has not failed. In fact, progress is being made. One must remember that the original goal was to complete and turn in one homework assignment in one week. This schedule may appear too lax to some readers. However, I have worked with several children who needed to begin at this level to experience success. Visual aids such as charts, bar graphs (histograms), or line graphs of behavior improvements are reinforcing to children and involved adults.

Reinforcement

Reinforcement is an important part of the operant conditioning process. Any consequence following a behavior that increases the likelihood of that behavior's being repeated is reinforcement. Reinforcement can be either positive or negative in nature. As mentioned previously, *positive reinforcement* involves using a stimulus which acts to strengthen the occurrence of the behavior it follows. In the example on homework, positive reinforcement could be used by rewarding John with a quarter after completing each objective. *Negative reinforcement* results when a stimulus is removed which strengthens the behavior by its removal. This is often a difficult concept to understand; and so I will present two examples to help add clarity.

Objective (c), in the second step of the operant conditioning plan, stated that John would go to his room and complete math homework before playing. Once John completes the homework he is allowed to leave his room. Naturally, John prefers to play outside with his friends. Working in his room, therefore, becomes an aversive condition (stimulus) which is removed immediately upon completion of work. John can then decide to work rapidly and remain only a brief time in his room; thus, the thought of removing the negative stimulus increases work productivity. With this one objective, it is possible to use two types of positive reinforcement and negative reinforcement at the same time. Let us consider that John receives a quarter (positive reinforcement) for finishing the assignment. Next, by finishing quickly, he leaves his room (negative reinforcement) and has more time to play with friends (positive reinforcement) before dinner. A second example that I often use to explain negative reinforcement involves two friends in a classroom setting who gossip rather than work on task. Both children are stimulating each other not to work. By moving one child to another seat in the room (removal of negative stimulus), both children remain on task and get more work done (strengthening desired behavior). A word of caution. The introduction of negative reinforcement should be used only when positive reinforcement proves ineffective alone.

When introducing reinforcement, counselors can select one of two basic schedules, either ratio or interval. A *ratio reinforcement schedule* establishes the number of desired behaviors or responses that must be demonstrated before positive reinforcement is given. In a fixed-ratio schedule the therapist specifies with the client exactly how many behaviors are required before reinforcement. A variable-ratio schedule, on the other hand, allows the counselor the flexibility of introducing reinforcement in an unpredictable manner after any desired behavior. As mentioned earlier, disturbed children function best initially with the consistency of a fixed-ratio schedule. An *interval reinforcement schedule* may also be either fixed or variable but differs from a ratio schedule in that it is concerned with the passage of time, rather than a number of responses, that takes place before reinforcement is introduced. A fixed-interval schedule, therefore, requires that a specific amount of time must pass before reinforcement can occur, no matter how many desired behaviors have been demonstrated (a minimum of one behavior is necessary in the required time frame there is no maximum). For instance, the therapist may decide to reinforce children in a group who have demonstrated desirable behavior after every 10 minutes the group is in operation. No mention has been made of undesirable behavior, but counselors can choose to ignore it while reinforcing desired behavior or use various forms of punishment, which will be discussed more in the techniques section of this chapter. Of note, however, is that *punishment* can be either the withdrawal of positive reinforcement or the introduction of negative reinforcement. A variable-interval schedule, like a variable-ratio schedule, can be implemented at the therapist's convenience such as after every third, seventh, or tenth minute.

Reinforcers

Stimuli which act as reinforcement because they satisfy biological needs are categorized as *primary reinforcers*. Food items like unsalted nuts, raisins, popcorn, cookies, and small candies are examples. Candy has been criticized because of its high sugar content and lack of nutritional value. Drinks such as fruit juices and unsweetened Kool Aid are also useful. Of practical importance is that the primary reinforcer be inexpensive, easy to administer, and to store. Because most adults feel that children should perform certain behaviors without external rewards, it is also critical to the behavioral counselor that secondary reinforcers are used so that primary reinforcers can be gradually phased out of the program as children learn to value intrinsic satisfiers. *Secondary reinforcers* are stimuli that also act as reinforcement because they are paired originally with primary reinforcers. In Chapter 4, "Developmental Play," the concept of touching as well as eating and drinking was emphasized as a biological necessity for infant survival. As children grow from infancy to childhood, their basic need for adult love is gradually diminished so that adult touching and cuddling becomes less socially desired, whereas verbal recognition or praise for accomplishments becomes more important. In time, praise (secondary reinforcer) usually replaces touching (primary reinforcer) as the most potent means for parents and teachers to demonstrate their appreciation and approval.

Changes resulting from normal growth and development in children influence heavily the reinforcement properties of various objects. What is reinforcing at one age is rejected at another. Objects that are attractive to females may be unattractive to males and therapists must keep in mind ethnic and cultural group differences when presenting reinforcers. One method that I prefer to use to determine high probability reinforcement is to have the client select from a *reinforcement menu*.

Blackham and Silberman (1975) have defined the reinforcing events menu as "a list of activities that have reinforcement properties from which a child may choose when a desired behavior has been performed" (p. 313). Because no two children are the same, the reinforcement menu must contain a wide variety of reinforcers that are age- and sex-appropriate. The following list contains some reinforcers that have been found to be effective with children of both sexes from ages 5 to 12. The reinforcers are inexpensive, easily delivered, and quiet when being used. For reinforcers to be of most value, they should possess a general appeal to children at most times. With the activity reinforcers, I recommend that children spend only a few minutes at any one activity to avoid satiation.

Foods	Articles	Activities
unsalted nuts	combs	listening to records or tapes
raisins	pencils	with earphones
popcorn	paper	playing short, simple puzzles
cookies	erasers	run off a duplicator: search
crackers	balloons	and find; connecting dots
unsweetened gum	crayons	cutting paper dolls
unsweetened lollipops	notebooks	dressing up
small candies	pipe cleaners	painting
apples	ribbons	reading comic books
peaches	sweat bands	interest stories
pears	T-shirts	making puppets
		drawing and coloring

Satiation, receiving too much of one reinforcer at one time so that the reinforcer loses its reinforcement value, occurs rapidly in children. With all children's reinforcers, I recommend doing a little bit at a time. For larger items, I would suggest using a credit system whereby children bank and save tokens toward purchasing the item. Readers should also not overlook the value and strength of reinforcement received by a child when spending time with and touching important adults like parents, teacher, or counselor. One child I worked with not long ago selected to be held and rocked. For extensive additional lists of reinforcers for children, I would recommend Blackham and Silberman (1975), Appendix B; Madsen and Madsen (1972); or Sulzer and Mayer (1972).

BASIC TECHNIQUES

Shaping and Chaining

When organizing and implementing an operant conditioning process, the therapist must analyze the behavioral elements necessary to enhance the demonstration of the desired behavior. In *shaping*, if the counselor wishes to evoke a desired goal behavior, then each successive approximation of that behavior is reinforced immediately upon execution. Through reinforcement, the therapist attempts to strengthen and increase the frequency of behaviors that are closer approximations of the final behavioral goal. The specific behavioral objectives discussed in John's case with the concept of operant conditioning provide examples of successive approximations and the shaping technique to get John to complete and hand in homework.

Another technique similar to shaping is chaining. *Chaining* involves taking simple behaviors already existing in the behavioral repertoire, and demonstrated by the child, and combining them into complex behaviors. An example would be children who, having learned to write single letters of the alphabet, are now writing two letters together to make simple words, and who will be writing greater numbers of letters for more complex words next. This chaining process continues as children learn to write words together in simple sentences to complex sentences and paragraphs. Other behavioral counseling techniques used to enhance desirable behavior are modeling, behavior rehearsal, and contingency contracting.

Modeling

Modeling is the tendency of children to imitate behaviors similar to those of other persons, usually peers or valued adults. Children will copy the unique mannerisms of professional athletes as quickly as they are demonstrated. For example, on any Saturday whether watching a professional baseball game or little league, you will see teammates congratulating each other with "high fives." Modeling can be helpful to therapists by (1) assisting children to acquire new desirable behaviors, (2) suppressing behavior that is not desirable, (3) freeing the expression of acquired behavior that is no longer expressed, and (4) initiating greater expression of behavior that is used infrequently. In accomplishing three of the four advantages cited above, to model effectively to evoke desirable behavior, Blackham and Silberman (1975) state that the counselor must (1) specify the behavior that is desirable for the child to learn, (2) identify an appropriate model to perform the behavior, (3) reinforce the model for performance of the behavior, and (4) reinforce the child when an appropriate imitation of the behavior is demonstrated.

Several factors have been identified that influence children to imitate modeled behavior. Bandura (1971) described models who were warm and caring and who had prestige, power, modeling skill and were of the same sex as more likely to be copied. In addition to the characteristics of models, Goldstein, Heller, and Sechrist (1966); and Bandura (1971b) found that imitation of models increased when children had a history of accepting rewards for imitating behavior, considered the behavior to be exemplary, and were considered dependent and incompetent learners.

Modeling can be useful in therapy to assist children to self-disclose about specific situations that may be aversive to them. In addition, models can be used successfully in group counseling to help shy children learn assertion skills (Leone & Gumaer, 1979; Gumaer & Leone, 1982). The use of modeling as a behavioral technique to increase desirable behavior has been researched thoroughly by Bandura (1965, 1967, 1969, 1971). For a more complete description of this technique, readers are referred to these references.

Behavior Rehearsal

Behavior rehearsal involves teaching children new behaviors in therapy that are then practiced under the supervision of the counselor. As children practice, they receive critical feedback on performance and experience appropriate support and reinforcement from the counselor for their efforts. Next, children are encouraged to gradually try out these newly acquired behaviors in the "real" world outside the therapist's office. Behavior rehearsal in the counselor's office provides children with an optimum learning environment. Children can make mistakes without encountering adult disapproval, being criticized, or feeling a fear of failure.

Behavior rehearsal is most effective when it involves children learning behavior necessary to act productively in anxiety-laden situations such as speaking out in class, approaching and asking an adult for help, joining in play activity, or handling the school bully. Children who experience debilitating levels of anxiety are usually expecting the worst to happen: to be laughed at, ridiculed, rejected, and humiliated.

Once the child's problem is identified, the counselor may ask the child to demonstrate (role play) and discuss how he or she would handle the situation. Avoidance behavior and immobility are characteristics of this stage. It is then the therapist's responsibility to introduce alternative behaviors to the situation and the possible consequences of these behaviors to the child. In so doing, it is best the counselor create in a mental hierarchy (least desirable to most desirable) the anticipated reactions of the person(s) the child is encountering. These alternative behaviors and projected reactions can then be rehearsed with the child playing himself or herself and the therapist the antagonist. In some instances, it may be effective to reverse these roles so children can begin to feel what it is like to be in the position of their adversaries. The following dialogue between John and the counselor illustrates the technique of behavior rehearsal.

Counselor: I understand both your mother and teacher say you aren't doing your homework.
John: Yeah, that's right.
Counselor: What's the problem?
John: No matter, even when I do it, all I get is yelled at and problems to do over.
Counselor: You mean they aren't satisfied with your work.
John: Yep! They want it perfect—no mistakes.
Counselor: Uh huh! Kind of impossible for you.
John: Sure is. No way can I do that.
Counselor: I know you feel there is no way out, but let's role play your prob-

lem and see what might happen if your mom and the teacher changed their expectations and you changed your attitude.

John: OK, but it is hopeless.

Counselor: You be yourself and I'll be your teacher. You pretend you have finished your assignment and hand it to me.

John: All right. Mrs. B——, here's my math homework.

Counselor: Ah! I see you have completed all your work John, but they are all wrong. You will have to do them over until you get them right.

John: That's it. Just the way it is. No way can I do it.

Counselor: OK. Let's try again and see what happens.

John: Mrs. B——, here's my math homework.

Counselor: Ah! I see you have completed all your work John, but they are all wrong. Do the first problem again to see if you can get it correct. If not, I'll sit down with you and we will go over it to see where your mistake is. Then, if you understand, I'll accept five completed, correct problems for today.

John: Unreal. It would never happen. My teacher always says she doesn't have time. Next to that she treats everyone the same no matter what. But, I would try it. At least I'd have a chance.

Counselor: Maybe if I talk with your teacher I can get her to go along. How about it? If we can negotiate a contract between you and the teacher, it might work.

John: You mean like a baseball player's contract.

Counselor: Something like that. You agree to do some things, the teacher agrees to do some things, and I agree to do some, too.

John: Sounds fair. OK.

Behavior Contracting

Behavior contracting is a technique in which the counselor makes a written agreement with the client specifying the behavioral goals of the client and positive reinforcement procedures to be implemented upon completion of the agreed-upon client behavior. Behavior contracting, also known as contingency contracting, is based upon the principle that children will be more inclined to work, and to work with more enthusiasm, if they are involved with adults mutually in structuring their own learning. As with operant conditioning, contingency contracting should emphasize performance of goal behavior that can be split into successively approximated observable behavior steps from simple behavior to complex. Thus, the learning of a series of smaller behaviors may lead to the accomplishment of the desired goal. Blackham and Silberman (1975) identified five basic steps for implementing a behavior contract as follows:

1. Identify exactly the behavior to be eliminated and the behavior to be promoted.
2. Hold initial conference with those involved in child's problems.
3. Devise behavior contract for presentation to all involved people.

       a. Contract specifies behavior to be eliminated and desirable behavior to be reinforced.

       b. Begin with the reinforcement of successive approximations of desired behavior . . . .

    4. Supervise roles and administration of procedures.

    5. Modify reinforcement schedule as appropriate.(p. 128)

Figure 8–2 illustrates John's behavior contract.

Because the behavior contract defines specifically the role and expected behaviors of all persons involved, it leaves little doubt when default occurs as to who is responsible for not fulfilling obligations. My experience has been that adults (teachers and parents) are just as likely to break the contract as a child. To avoid this embarrassment and enhance the probability of success with the technique, readers might adhere to the following ten rules for contingency contracting suggested by Homme, Csany, Gonzales, and Rechs (1969).

Rule 1.   The contract reward should be immediate.

Rule 2.   Initial contracts should reward small approximations of behavior.

Rule 3.   Behavior should be rewarded frequently in small amounts.

Rule 4.   The contract should reward behavioral accomplishment rather than obedience.

Rule 5.   Behavior must be rewarded after it occurs, never before.

Rule 6.   The contract must be fair.

Rule 7.   The contract promise must be clear and explicitly stated. The child must always know what behaviors are expected, how often, and what can be expected as a consequence.

Rule 8.   The contract must be honest; that is, carried out to the letter of the agreement. There exists no room for excuses for noncompliance.

Rule 9.   The contract must be positive. It should contribute to the child's learning and enhance pleasant feelings.

Rule 10.   Use behavior contracting systematically.

Time Out

When using operant learning principles in behavioral counseling, we are concerned not only with enhancing the acquisition of desirable behavior but also with weakening undesirable behavior. Two behavioral techniques

Figure 8-2   John's Contract

Persons Involved: John, Dr. G., Mrs. B. (Teacher), Mrs. W. (parent)

Approximated Goals:

1. Write math assignment in notebook within five minutes.
2. Collect necessary math books to carry home five minutes before dismissal.
3. Upon arriving home, go to room immediately and complete all homework.
4. Collect all books and completed homework before leaving home for school.
5. Hand in completed homework to teacher.

Responsibilities:

John: work toward accomplishing all goals

Dr. G.:   a) meet once each week with John to discuss progress
             b) administer reinforcement (praise and tokens)
             c) supervise adult roles and reinforcement procedures

Mrs. B.:   a) provide additional help to John when asked at first opportunity
             b) monitor goals one, two, and five
             c) administer reinforcement (praise and checkmarks)

Mrs. W.:   a) provide additional help to John when asked at first opportunity
             b) monitor goals three and four
             c) administer reinforcement (praise and menu)

Reward Statement:

John will receive one checkmark on his card from either teacher or mother each day a goal is accomplished. Each week John meets with Dr. G., he will receive one token for every checkmark on the card. Tokens may be saved by John or exchanged with mother to buy any item on the reinforcement menu.*

I agree to fulfill my responsibilities to this contract. This contract may be renegotiated only at the agreement of all parties involved.

Signed _____

_____

_____

_____

* Tokens are worth $.05 (five cents) each.

that are used frequently with children to reduce unwanted behavior are time out and extinction. *Time out from positive reinforcement*, or removing children from access to all positive events for a brief period of time, must be carefully implemented and monitored to prevent unwarranted stress to a child. Time out simply means that the child who exhibits unacceptable behavior is isolated. Wehman (1980) outlines several guidelines for implementing time out in classrooms. It will be advantageous for counselors to consider these guidelines.

1. The teacher should be able to identify the reinforcing events that are maintaining the child's inappropriate behavior.
2. All behaviors that result in time out must be stated clearly and posted before time out is begun.
3. The teacher should attempt other behavioral change techniques first.
4. The teacher should document use of these milder techniques.
5. The teacher should develop a written procedural plan to systematically follow when placing a child in time out. It should:
   a. avoid lengthy explanations to the child being placed in time out;
   b. identify all behaviors, if any, that will receive a warning before time out is used;
   c. allow children an opportunity to implement their own time out;
   d. minimize the duration of time out, no more than five minutes; and
   e. indicate release from time out is contingent upon the child's behavior while in time out.
6. The time out area should be at least six feet by six feet, well-lighted and ventilated, unlocked, and free of items with which children could harm themselves.
7. For each time out, documentation should be kept including child's name, a description of the incident, the exact time the child entered and exited time out, and the child's behavior in time out.
8. Positive reinforcement of appropriate behavior while in time out should follow implementation. (pp. 342–343)

Extinction

Extinction is closely associated to time out in that it is a process by which behavior is reduced by withdrawing stimuli that are reinforcing it. This technique is particularly useful for terminating behavior that is maintained by environmental reinforcement. In John's case, his mother and teacher provided constant attention for his undesirable work habits. Yet, before the problem appeared, neither adult attended to John when he performed his work. This pattern of adult reinforcement had to be reversed, that is, get the adults to attend to desirable behavior performance while ignoring the undesirable. Extinction is often most effective when used in conjunction with the operant learning process.

Systematic Desensitization

As with undesirable behavior, undesirable emotional response can be changed. Changing fears and phobias involves counterconditioning or the learning of a new response to an aversive stimulus. In my own practice I have used systematic desensitization frequently. *Systematic desensitization* was developed by Joseph Wolpe (1973) to reduce fear and anxiety which occur in some situations because they are associated with similar situations in the client's past. Wolpe hypothesized that anxiety could be eliminated by the gradual presentation, in a systematic fashion, of anxiety-eliciting stimuli while the client was relaxed.

Initially, the therapist teaches the child how to relax. Relaxation techniques are presented and discussed thoroughly in Chapter 9. Once the child has learned to relax, the counselor develops a hierarchy, including the anxiety-producing event at one end and a related event which is least anxiety producing at the opposite end. A ladder of anxiety-provoking events is constructed and the client begins by imagining the least-stressful event until anxiety is no longer provoked. Each event on the hierarchy is encountered systematically in a like manner until no anxiety is produced by any event. Finally, the child will be able to imagine the feared event without excessive anxiety. Once the child is able to cope successfully with imagined events in the counselor's office, it is best to structure practice sessions on the outside to ensure the client's readiness to function independently.

The case of Danny, an 11-year-old sixth grader, illustrates systematic desensitization. Danny referred himself to the counselor at the beginning of the school year. The first time Danny came into the office he was distraught and close to tears. When queried about his apparent discomfort, he replied, "I don't know how to tell you this. I know you'll laugh and think I'm stupid." With a few minutes of reassurance and support, Danny disclosed that he was deeply afraid of snakes, his classmates knew about his fear, and some of the boys and girls caught snakes and then chased him around the schoolyard with them. After discussing Danny's embarrassment, harassment, anger, and fear, he was asked if he would like to overcome his fear. His reply: "I'd do anything." The concepts of systematic desensitization were then discussed and future counseling sessions scheduled to learn relaxation techniques.

Danny learned quickly to discriminate feelings of tension and relaxation in the large and small muscles of different parts of his anatomy. With practice, he was able to relax in about five minutes. He commented, "It feels good to relax when I'm worried so much of the time. You know I get real upset just thinking about those kids chasing me with a snake."

While Danny was learning relaxation, he explored the history of his phobia and other considerations involving his status at home and school. As the information unfolded, it became apparent that Danny was a victim of his mother's fear of snakes and that she had probably unwittingly conditioned him to it. For example, she refused to go into the yard, or allow her children into the yard, unless it was mowed recently and inspected for snakes by Danny's father each day. She also cried hysterically when she did encounter a snake and was immobolized until someone removed it from her presence. Although not fearful himself, Danny's father accommodated his mother's wishes and avoided discussion about the topic.

In three sessions, Danny had learned to relax sufficiently to develop his desensitization hierarchy. The experiences listed in the hierarchy were developed cooperatively by Danny and the counselor. No situations were included that could not be practiced in the office or at home.

Danny's Hierarchy

1. Discussing snakes in the counselor's office.
2. Going to the library and selecting books to read on the life and habits of snakes.
3. Discussing the idea of going to a pet store to look at snakes.
4. Meeting the counselor after school to visit the pet store.
5. Discussing the idea of buying a snake as a pet to be housed in the counselor's office.
6. Going to the pet store, selecting and purchasing a snake as a pet. Buying a cage.
7. Visiting the counselor's office daily to check on the pet snake.
8. Talking about holding the pet snake while the snake is in the cage on a shelf in the counselor's office.
9. Talking about holding the snake while the snake is in the cage next to him.
10. Talking about holding the snake while the cage is on his lap.
11. Removing the snake and holding it for a short time (a minute, then longer).
12. Removing the snake and holding and playing with it for half a session (15 minutes).
13. Taking the pet snake to his classroom and making a presentation on snakes including a demonstration on how to handle snakes properly.
14. Asking his father and mother for permission to bring his snake home and keep it in his room.
15. Taking the pet snake home.

In each session, once Danny was relaxed he was instructed to imagine performing the tasks on his hierarchy. When the image was set in his mind, he was asked to continue thinking about it for approximately 15 seconds. Relaxation and repetition of the scene occurred until Danny experienced no anxiety. He then moved on to the next scene. Danny's eagerness to change allowed rapid progress through the first eight experiences. Each of the first 12 tasks were modeled by the therapist for Danny before he physically performed them. Because tasks 13 through 15 involved his teacher and parents, it was necessary to consult with them on several occasions to inform them of Danny's progress in therapy and need for their involvement and support. The most difficult single incident in this case was to convince the mother of Danny's need to bring his snake home. With the father's support, mother finally agreed as long as the snake was limited to Danny's room. Danny had conquered his fear in eight weeks.

I have purposely omitted the presentation and discussion of several additional behavioral counseling techniques—relaxation, guided imagery, covert conditioning, cognitive behavior training, and assertion training—so they might be included in the next chapter on relaxation and guided fantasy.

RECOMMENDED RESOURCES

Books

BLACKHAM, G. & SILBERMAN, A. *Modification of child and adolescent behavior.* (2nd ed.) Belmont, CA: Wadsworth, 1975.

This book provides a detailed discussion of behavior modification theory and procedures as they are applied to children and adolescents in the classroom, a clinical setting, and the home. It contains clear explanations of most behavioral techniques and includes several examples of therapeutic interventions with such problems as phobias, stuttering, silent children, timid children, excessive crying, truancy, nervous habits, and self-abusing behavior.

McAULEY, R. & McAULEY, P. *Child behavior problems.* New York: The Free Press, 1982.

A detailed empirical assessment of Applied Behavioral Analysis including methodology, planning, and implementation. It is particularly useful to clinicians in deciding on treatment techniques.

SLOANE, H. *Five practical behavior guides.* Champaign, IL: Research Press Catalog, 1982.

Each short booklet features simple behavior activities to help children overcome troublesome behaviors with regard to the following: whining, coming to dinner, acting on instructions, fighting, and cleaning the room.

Films

B. F. Skinner and behavior change. Champaign, IL: Research Press, 1982.

Outstanding professionals in various disciplines discuss issues of behavioral psychology—with Skinner. Viewers visit a home where parents work with their mentally retarded child, a hospital for treatment of an epileptic child, and a youth center where children with social problems are learning effective social skills. Useful for introductory psychology or counseling courses and behavior therapy practitioners.

Hosford, R. *Behavioral counseling: A package of eight films.* Falls Church, VA: American Personnel and Guidance Association.

    a. *Identifying the problem*—demonstrates how a behavioral counselor translates a problem into behavioral terms and into expressing feelings.
    b. *Formulating the counseling goal*—demonstrates how a behavioral counselor helps a client consider a variety of counseling goals before selecting a specific goal.
    c. *Observing and recording behavior.*
    d. *Counseling techniques: Reinforcement procedures*—demonstrates how to use verbal and nonverbal reinforcement with client and how to use self-modification techniques.
    e. *Counseling techniques: Social modeling*—demonstrates how a counselor models behavior for client learning.
    f. *Counseling techniques: Assertive training.*
    g. *Counseling techniques: Desensitization*—demonstrates how a counselor uses desensitization to dispel a client's phobia.
    h. *Counseling techniques: Self-as-a-model.*

Journals

Behavioral Counseling Quarterly. New York: Human Sciences Press.

This journal provides an interdisciplinary forum to a broadly conceived social learning orientation for counseling and community level interventions. It stresses the importance of scientific method, empirical testing, and clearly stated concepts and procedures.

Behavior Modification. Beverly Hills, CA: Sage Publications, Inc.

An interdisciplinary journal designed to publish research and clinical papers in the area of applied behavior modification. Readers will be able to understand the what, how, and why of a particular strategy that was selected in each case. The journal is published four times annually.

Behavior Research and Therapy. Maxwell House, Fairview Park, Elmsford, NY 10523: Pergamon Press.

An international interdisciplinary journal focused toward crossing the boundaries which separate psychiatry, education, clinical psychology, remedial teaching, psychotherapy, and social work. The journal stresses the application of existing knowledge to psychiatric and social problems and the publication of experimental and observational studies. It is published bimonthly.

Behavior Therapy. Association for the Advancement of Behavior Therapy, 420 Lexington Avenue, New York, NY 10170.

An interdisciplinary journal primarily for publication of original research of an experimental and clinical nature which contributes to the theories, practices, and evaluation of behavior therapy modification. The journal includes articles, brief reports, book reviews, and case reports.

SUMMARY

This chapter began with a brief description of the evolution from behavioristics and objective psychology to behavioral counseling. This section also described the value of behavioral counseling to children. The second part discussed the key concepts: respondent and operant behavior, respondent and operant conditioning, reinforcement, positive reinforcement, negative reinforcement, reinforcement schedules, reinforcers, reinforcement menu, and satiation. Basic techniques provided the focus to the fourth section, which included a discussion of shaping, chaining, modeling, behavior rehearsal, behavior contracting, time out, extinction, and systematic desensitization. The case example of John was used to highlight some of the key concepts and techniques. A second example, Danny, was used to illustrate systematic desensitization in practice. The last section of this chapter included recommended resources from books, films, and journals.

REFERENCES AND RECOMMENDED READINGS

BANDURA, A. Behavior modification through modeling procedures. In L. Ullman & L. Krasner (Eds.) *Research in behavior modification*. New York: Holt, Rinehart, & Winston, 1965, 310–340.

———. Behavior psychotherapy. *Scientific American*, March, 1967, 78–86.

———. Principles of behavior modification. New York: Holt, Rinehart, & Winston, 1969.

———. Psychotherapy based on modeling principles. In A. Bergin & S. Garfield (Eds.) *Handbook of psychotherapy and behavior change*. New York: John Wiley, 1971, 653–708.

———. *Social learning theory*. Morristown, NJ: General Learning Press, 1971.

BLACKHAM, G. & SILBERMAN, A. *Modification of child and adolescent behavior.* (2nd ed.) Belmont, CA: Wadsworth, 1975.

BORING, E. *A history of experimental psychology.* New York: Appleton-Century-Crofts, 1950.

GOLDSTEIN, A., HELLER, K., & SECHRIST, L. *Psychotherapy and the psychology of behavior change.* New York: John Wiley, 1966.

GRODEN, G. & CAUTELA, J. Behavior therapy: A survey of procedures for counselors. *Personnel and Guidance Journal,* November, 1981, 10(3), 175–180.

GUMAER, J. & MYRICK, R. Behavioral group counseling with disruptive children. *School Counselor,* 1974, 4, 313–317.

————. & SIMON, R. Behavioral group counseling and schoolwide reinforcement program with obese trainable mentally retarded students. *Education and Training of the Mentally Retarded,* April, 1979, 106–111.

————. & LEONE, S. Assertion training in group counseling for shy children revisited: A follow-up report. *Virginia Counselors Journal,* Spring, 1982, 10, 12–20.

HILTZHEIMER, N. & GUMAER, J. Behavior management and classroom guidance in an inner city school. *Elementary School Guidance and Counseling,* 1979, 13(4), 272–278.

HOMME, L., CSANY, A., GONZALES, M., & RECHS, J. *How to use contingency contracting in the classroom.* Champaign, IL: Research Press, 1969.

KEAT, D. *Fundamentals of child counseling.* Boston: Houghton Mifflin Co., 1974.

KRUMBOLTZ, J. (Ed.) *Revolution in counseling.* Boston: Houghton Mifflin Co., 1966.

————. A second look at the revolution in counseling. *American Personnel and Guidance Journal,* March 1980, 58(7), 463–466.

————. BECKER-HAVEN, J., & BURNETT, K. Counseling psychology. *Annual Review of Psychology,* 1979, 30, 555–602.

————. & KRUMBOLTZ, H. *Changing children's behavior.* Englewood Cliffs, New Jersey: Prentice-Hall, 1972.

LEONE, S. & GUMAER, J. Group assertiveness training of shy children. *School Counselor,* 1979, 27, 134–141.

MADSEN, C. & MADSEN, C. *Parents/children/discipline.* Boston: Allyn & Bacon, 1972.

SULZER, B. & MAYER, G. *Behavior modification procedures for school personnel.* Hinsdale, IL: Dryden Press, 1972.

WEHMAN, P. Group work for children with special needs. In J. Duncan & J. Gumaer (Eds.) *Developmental groups for children.* Springfield, IL: Charles Thomas, 1980, 321–351.

WOLPE, J. *The practice of behavior therapy.* (2nd ed.) Elmsford, NY: Pergamon, 1973.

Chapter 9

Relaxation
and Guided Fantasy

IN THE PREVIOUS CHAPTER, relaxation training was introduced in the discussion about systematic desensitization. When used in conjunction with systematic desensitization, relaxation training as a therapeutic technique to reduce adult anxiety is well documented (Woody, 1971). However, the use of relaxation training as a therapeutic technique for children is more recent and for this reason has not received extensive research attention. As in the case of adult therapy, most of the available literature indicates that relaxation training with children is successful when used in conjunction with either behavioral techniques, such as systematic desensitization and covert conditioning, or guided fantasy. In general, these therapeutic combinations have achieved positive results with both primary-grade children (McBrien, 1978) and with intermediate-grade children (Rossman & Kahnweiler, 1977). Specifically, relaxation training with other behavioral counseling techniques has proven beneficial for children by helping to reduce anger (Boswell, 1982); reduce test anxiety (Deffenbucher & Kemper, 1974); overcome shyness and learn assertion skills (Gumaer & Leone, 1982; Leone & Gumaer, 1979); improve self-esteem and class social status (Gumaer & Voorneveld, 1975); overcome phobic reactions (Lazarus & Abramovitz, 1962; Wolpe, 1973); reduce hyperactivity (McBrien, 1978); reduce disruptive behavior (Schneider & Robin, 1974); and to treat insomnia (Weil & Goldfried, 1973).

In the introduction to Chapter 1 of this book a rationale was provided to explain the need for child counselors. Part of this statement was directed toward the increased pressure and anxiety children are experiencing in today's fast-paced, competitive society. Other child concerns which generated additional anxiety for children, such as their increasing experiences with disrupted homes, were also discussed. Certainly, relaxation training, which has proven successful in reducing anxiety in children, needs to be considered highly as a therapeutic technique of choice by counselors who are working with children experiencing anxiety as a primary or secondary source of dysfunction.

The Value of Relaxation

The primary benefit of relaxation training for children is the temporary relief they experience from the stress and pressure in their lives. In many instances, the expression of relief has been as dramatic as that experienced by children when a splinter is removed from a hand or a cut is treated with a Band-Aid. It is as if for the time being everything is OK in the child's world. Some comments children in counseling have made regarding relaxation include: "I've waited for this all week. It's the only time my headaches go away." "I couldn't sleep at night worrying about school . . . . It helped." "I use it when I'm angry at Mom to calm down and when I can't sleep at night. It works." Aside from the more obvious relief from tension, children benefit from relaxation training by:

1. Learning skills for self control
2. Learning how to cope with physical and mental fatigue
3. Learning to adjust and make the transition from physical activity (play) to mental activity (schoolwork)
4. Increasing body awareness and sensory awareness
5. Increasing motivation and enjoyment of the therapeutic experience

Counselors also benefit from utilizing relaxation training in that the exercises help (1) prepare children for the counseling process, (2) reduce client anxiety, defensiveness, and resistance, (3) establish rapport quickly, and (4) encourage self-disclosure. Children seek naturally relief from pressure and pain. When they can anticipate relief, they look forward to their therapy and learn to prepare themselves mentally before arriving at the office. Oftentimes, I have seen children arrive at my office, go immediately to the floor, and assume the prescribed posture for relaxation training without saying a word to me. This level of readiness is difficult to obtain with other techniques.

KEY CONCEPTS

What is relaxation training? *Relaxation training* can occur during individual or group counseling sessions or in larger classroom-sized groups.

However, children will resist practicing their skills before peers. A general rule of thumb is the smaller the group for training the better. Training begins typically with the therapist instructing children on the need to relax, the value of learning to relax, and tensing and relaxing the muscles of the body. For primary-age children, I recommend only discussion and training with the large muscle groups. Following instruction, children are ready for training. First, children are instructed to lay on the floor (carpeted) with their heads on pillows and their eyes closed. This posture seems to create the most comfortable environment. Training can be accomplished with children seated in chairs and eyes opened. However, open eyes create resistance to training. Once children are readied for training, begin by making a few brief suggestions before introducing the tensing and relaxing exercises. These suggestions to the children include the following: (1) put all thoughts from your mind; (2) try to follow all my instructions, even though some might seem ridiculous; (3) concentrate on your muscles (you must be able to feel the muscles tense and relax); and (4) continue to practice relaxing outside my office at home. I recommend to children that the practice occur 10 minutes before going to bed.

Tensing and Relaxing

Tensing and *relaxing* of muscles is programmed from head to feet. It is best to allow 5 to 10 seconds for the tensing of muscles with 15 to 30 seconds for relaxing. This sequence provides sufficient tension and also allows time for deep breathing to relax. Therapists might begin tensing with the following statement, "When you tense each muscle, tense it as much as you can for as long as you can or until I say relax. Remember, keep your eyes closed. Now, wrinkle your forehead, and shut your eyes tight as you can . . . hold it . . . and relax. When you relax, allow your entire body to relax and breathe deeply." Tensing and relaxing are continued through the muscle groups until all major muscles have tensed and relaxed from head to feet. The following training sequence is recommended for readers to follow.

1. *Head and neck.* (In addition to the forehead exercise): (a) Press your lips tightly together. (b) Smile as hard as you can. (c) Push your head back as hard and far as you can against your pillow. (d) Turn your head first left as far as you can, then right.
2. *Shoulders, arms, and hands.* (Once finished with the head and neck, the counselor should attend immediately to the shoulders and arms): (a) Lift your shoulders to your head. (b) Stretch your shoulders as far back as they will go. (c) Lift your arms in front of you, now over your head. (d) Clasp your hands together, push hard one against the other. (e) Clasp your fingers together and squeeze. (f) Make a tight fist.
3. *Back, stomach, and hips.* (Continuing relaxation training down

the body, the therapist next focuses on the back, stomach, and hips.): (a) Curl into a ball and hold your legs with your arms. (b) Cross your right arm and leg over your left side, touch the floor. (c) Cross your left arm and leg over your right side, touch the floor. (d) Lift both legs over your head and touch the floor. (e) Push your stomach as far out as possible. (f) Pull your stomach as far in as possible. (g) Make your stomach as tight as you can. (h) Keep your back and legs on the floor, and raise your hips. (i) While on your stomach, raise your shoulders, chest, and legs off the floor.

4. *Legs and feet.* (The last part of tensing and relaxing of muscles.): (a) Lift your legs off the floor a few inches, spread them apart, then bring them back together and down. (b) Cross your legs at the ankles, and press hard, one leg against the other. (c) Lift your toes up as far as you can. (d) Curl your toes tightly.

In instructing children in relaxation, no more than 20 minutes or one-half the counseling session should be designated for tensing and relaxing. In fact, it may be worthwhile to plan a shorter period of training time and devote this time to learning how to practice relaxing one body area per session. By implementing training in this way, children's shorter attention spans would be considered and overall task, body relaxation, would be broken into smaller parts which are easier to learn. This method would necessitate the repetition of previously learned material each session until children had internalized the skills. This review of practice should not be construed negatively. Children often need reminding of process and practice until the skills are learned. Readers are also urged to remember that children are easily led into relaxing experiences and they will need sufficient time to readjust to therapy when tensing and relaxing are finished. A minute of standing, stretching, and moving about before moving on to other considerations is all that most children require. Oftentimes I will say, "We have finished our relaxation exercises. At the count of three, I want you to open your eyes, stand up and stretch, and get ready to continue our counseling session. One, open your eyes. (Pause) Two, stand up and clear your head. (Pause) Three, stretch your body and get ready to proceed. (Pause) Now, return to your pillow on the floor and sit ready to work."

Relaxation Through Imagery

Another helpful method in training children to relax is through imagery. Wittmer and Myrick (1974) suggested the following guidelines to enhance imagery experiences for children:

1. Use imaginary examples to set the mood. Ask students to get into the ex-

perience, to be there. Let them know that if they go along with the experience, they will enjoy it.
2. Talk about the importance of keeping eyes closed.
3. Help children relax before beginning an activity.
4. Use a soft, soothing voice.
5. Tape or write out the experience beforehand.
6. Use soft music as background, if possible, but don't let it detract from the experience.
7. Use words in the imaginary experiences that connote texture and that utilize all the senses.
8. Allow ample time for discussion . . . .(p. 91)

Similar preparatory procedures are recommended for imagery experiences that are used for relaxation training exercises. Once children are reclining comfortably on the floor with their eyes closed and the lights out, the imagery begins. The following example of an imagery experience to induce relaxation in children was designed by the author from an example provided by Wittmer and Myrick (1974). It was included as part of a group counseling program to help gifted children learn to relax (Gumaer & Voorneveld, 1975).

Close your eyes and fold your hands lightly on your stomach. (Pause) Take a deep breath and let the air out very slowly. Slowly take another deep breath and again let the air pass gradually from your body. As you begin to breathe more deeply, more smoothly, and more slowly, you feel the tension in your body flow downward from your head toward your feet. (Pause) Let the tension move down through your body. Let it move from your head through your neck. Feel yourself relax as the tension passes from your head, shoulders, and hands through your chest. (Pause) You are becoming more and more relaxed as the tension flows from your chest through your legs and feet. (Pause) Slowly take another deep breath. It's as if all your worries are steadily flowing down and out of your body. You feel calm. (Pause) It's as if you are riding on a large, soft, white cloud that is slowly drifting in the sky. Enjoy the lazy, dreamy feeling . . . .(Pause) It is getting late and we must return to the room. At the count of three you will open your eyes and return to the room. One, you have left your cloud. Two, your eyes are open. Three, you are back in the counselor's office. (p. 89)

As children learn to relax, both relaxation training exercises and imagery exercises can be shortened. If you have ample time with a child in therapy, I would recommend training in relaxation skills as a first step followed by the use of imagery experiences.

Guided Fantasy

Historically, the use of guided fantasy in therapy can be traced back to the work of Breuer and Freud in 1895 and their description of a directed mental imagery technique (Owen & Wilson, 1980). However, the use of fantasy was not popularized as a counseling technique until the last two decades. Since 1970, several journal articles have reported successful use of fantasy techniques to help children to overcome emotional disorders (Kelly, 1972), eliminate phobias (Lazarus, 1971), reduce test anxiety (Deffenbucher & Kemper, 1974), control aggressiveness (Anderson, 1975), and help highly anxious children learn to relax (Davis, 1969; Gumaer & Voorneveld, 1975; Koeppen, 1974).

Anderson (1980) emphasized that researchers are "only now" beginning to explore and understand the importance of the imagery system and the almost daily need for humans to fantasize and use their imaginations. Anderson (1980) also pointed out that through the work of researchers and practitioners, such as Leuner (1969) and Wolpe (1973), we now know that when clients are relaxed they tend to have greater access to unconscious material and are able to deal more effectively with that which is expressed. What then is guided fantasy? *Guided fantasy* is a structured therapeutic technique involving the child's imagery abilities, designed for a specific purpose, which involves extensive preparation and planning by the therapist. In addition to organizing the experience, the counselor's skills in setting the stage for the guided fantasy activity, introducing the fantasy, concluding it, and discussing it with children all influence how therapeutic the technique will be. Anderson (1980) offered the following suggestions for using guided fantasy:

1. Before using a guided fantasy experience, "try it out" yourself.
2. Explain the guided fantasy experience to children and emphasize that they are in control. For example, "when you close your eyes you will see only those images you want to appear."
3. Use relaxation exercises prior to the fantasy.
4. Begin the fantasy experience with simple exercises to practice and to prepare children for the experience.
5. If necessary, remind children to keep their eyes closed.
6. Introduce the structured fantasy.
7. Each time an image is introduced, allow time for reflection.
8. Create situations in each guided fantasy exercise for children to independently develop images.
9. Prepare children to return from the fantasy experience by structuring in reality factors toward the conclusion.
10. Allow ample time for children to discuss the experience. (pp. 41–42)

BASIC TECHNIQUES

Relaxation training and guided fantasy were presented as key concepts in this chapter because they are frequently included as preliminary or readiness techniques with covert conditioning, cognitive behavior therapy, and assertion training—all of which utilize multiple behavioral counseling techniques in their methodology.

Covert Conditioning

Covert conditioning is a set of imagery-based procedures designed to effect behavior changes in clients by having them imagine specific behaviors and the consequences to those behaviors (Cautela & Baron, 1977; Groden & Cautela, 1981). Cautela postulates as a basic premise of covert conditioning that covert thoughts, feelings, actions, and images are responsive to the same laws of behavior, such as learning, as overt behaviors. In addition, he further emphasizes that overt and covert behaviors are mutually reinforcing and predictable. In Chapter 8, the overt procedures for enhancing desirable behavior, positive reinforcement, negative reinforcement, and modeling were discussed. Cautela describes covert positive reinforcement, covert negative reinforcement, and covert modeling as corresponding covert procedures. Likewise, covert sensitization is a procedure used to decrease undesirable behavior and emotional response. When using covert procedures, I recommend that all the precautions and preparations described for relaxation training and guided fantasy be followed.

Cognitive Behavior Therapy

Cognitive behavior therapy involves several procedures that are not based in learning theory as other behavioral techniques. These procedures include Albert Ellis's (1977) rational emotive therapy and Donald Meichenbaum's (1977) self-instructional technique. Because rational emotive therapy has been used primarily with older adolescents and adults and not recommended for use with children (Boyd & Grieger, 1980), the focus in this section on cognitive behavior therapy will be on self-instructional training.

Meichenbaum and Goodman (1969) evaluated a cognitive self-instructional model developed for impulsive children and found that children who experienced training performed significantly better than controls. They also examined the effectiveness of modeling versus modeling with self-instruction on the impulsive behavior of kindergarten and first-grade children. Results of this study demonstrated that modeling with self-instructional training altered significantly, in a positive direction, the attending skills of impulsive children (Meichenbaum & Goodman, 1971). In other clinical work with impulsive children, Meichenbaum (1977) reported that the self-instructional training model could be paired successfully with imagery. Based on these findings, it seems reasonable to assume that the self-instructional training model might be joined with a variety of behavioral counseling techniques to help remediate several problems of children in therapy.

Meichenbaum's cognitive self-instructional training model consists of the child's:

1. Observing a self-verbalizing model perform the task
2. Performing the same task while listening to verbal instructions from the model
3. Copying the model's talk while completing the task
4. Whispering the instructions to self while completing the task
5. Observing the model perform the task using covert self-instruction with pauses demonstrating thinking
6. Performing the task using covert self-instruction.

Verbalizations to be modeled included questioning the nature of the task, planning and cognitive rehearsal of alternative behaviors, self-reinforcing (e.g., "good work," "I'm doing well"), self-evaluating, and correcting errors (e.g., "It's OK to make a mistake" and "If I err, I can go more slowly").

Some children may require many cognitive modeling trials with overt self-rehearsal, while others can proceed directly to covert rehearsal, covert modeling, and covert sensitization after observing and listening to the model. In all instances, the strength of this technique remains closely tied to the therapist's ability to adapt behavioral counseling techniques to self-instructional training and the individual needs and abilities of the child. As discussed previously by the author in operant conditioning, Meichenbaum has also suggested the learning progression of children's tasks be from simpler tasks to more complex tasks and that shaping be used as a general strategy in planning.

Assertion Training

Assertion training with children has received increased attention the last few years to assist them to overcome their problem behaviors involving inappropriate communications skills (Bower, Amatea, & Anderson, 1976; Rashbaum-Selig, 1976). A basic tenet of assertion training is that two incompatible responses cannot exist at the same time. For example, if a child is experiencing anxiety regarding interpersonal communications and cannot express self appropriately, then the anxiety is inhibiting free and appropriate expression of feelings. Theoretically, once the child learns to express self through assertion training, the anxiety will decrease.

What is assertion training? *Assertion training* is defined by Holmes and Horan (1976) as, "A generic behavioral counseling procedure involving a number of specific techniques, such as behavioral rehearsal or forms of modeling, to help people engage in appropriate behavior previously blocked by the presence of maladaptive anxiety." (p. 108) Assertive behavior allows children to actively involve themselves with others in their environment. For example, assertive behavior includes the ability to initiate discussion with others, ask for help, initiate play with others, engage in cooperative play, and participate in class and family discussions.

Because my experience with assertion training of children has been in group counseling, and because I feel that assertion training is most successful as a technique in a group counseling format, I choose to share with readers, as an example, a group assertion training (AT) program for shy children developed and implemented by myself and a colleague. This problem-centered group example will also serve as an introduction to Part II of the book, "Counseling Children in Groups."

GROUP ASSERTIVE TRAINING WITH SHY CHILDREN*

Initiating the Program

Teachers were asked by the counselor to identify children who interacted nonassertively with peers or adult authority figures. Specifically, teachers were asked to identify children who failed to initiate discussion with others, ask for help, initiate play, or participate in class discussion. The counselor then administered a sociogram to determine the degree of class social status for each student whose name was submitted by a teacher.

The sociogram contained three positively worded parts: (a) classmates I would most like to work with on a class assignment, (b) classmates I would most like to play with, and (c) classmates I would most like to invite to my birthday party. For each part, children responded by writing the names of classmates who would be their first, second, and third choice. The choices were scored 3, 2, and 1, respectively.

On the basis of teacher observations, sociometric data, and counselor and teacher consultation, a group of 28 shy children were identified. From these 28 children, two counseling groups were formed by a random stratified procedure. Initially, each counseling group was composed of 3 boys and 3 girls. One child moved after the first session, reducing the total number of children involved to 11.

Before beginning the group sessions, the counselor interviewed each prospective group member and discussed the proposed program. All children interviewed agreed to participate. Next, parents of the children were informed by letter about the AT group program and encouraged to

*Leone, S. & Gumaer, J. *The School Counselor*, 1979, 27(2), 131–141. Reprinted in part with permission of the American Personnel and Guidance Association.

contact the counselor, should they have any questions or concerns. Two parents phoned the counselor for additional information. No parents objected to their child's participation in an AT group . . . .

Planning the Group Sessions

The AT sessions were held in two phases because of the intervening Christmas holiday. Phase 1 consisted of twelve 40-minute sessions, which were conducted before the holiday. Phase 2 consisted of six 40-minute sessions conducted after the holiday. For both phases, general goals were established: to help group members to (1) become more self-confident, (2) become less anxious in groups, (3) increase social status in the classroom, (4) identify situations in which children behave assertively, nonassertively, and aggressively, (5) discriminate among assertive, nonassertive, and aggressive behavior, (6) understand how personal feelings affect behavior, (7) decrease nonassertive behavior and increase assertive behavior, and (8) understand personal rights and responsibilities in relation to adults and peers. Specific plans were then developed for each group session, consisting of objectives, structured activities, and recommended counselor responses. Activities were planned to be sequential so that children's learning developed from simple to complex and concrete to abstract.

An outline of Phase 1 counseling sessions' objectives and activities follows in Table 9–1. Objectives and activities from Phase 2 are not included because they were basically a continuation of Phase 1 of the program. For recommended group-leader responses, readers are referred to Chapter 12.

Phase 1

The first session began with the children's getting acquainted and reviewing the purposes for the group meetings. Group members were asked to draw a picture of their favorite animal on construction paper and print their first name on the front of the animal. The children became readily involved in this activity. The counselor then encouraged children to introduce themselves to the group, identify their animal, and discuss their reasons for selecting that particular animal. Children were encouraged to use the following simple sentence format: My name is . . . . I chose a . . . . because . . . .

As expected, nearly all the children were reluctant to contribute verbally. One or two introduced themselves, but several children remained silent. Almost all verbal responses were elicited through the encouragement and support of the counselor. The counselor then collected the

Table 9-1

Session	Objectives	Activities
1	a. Get to know one another. b. Review group purpose. c. Begin group discussion.	Favorite animal. Students draw picture of favorite animal on construction paper, print first name on front of animal, cut it out. On back of animal write favorite game. Each student instructed to identify self, animal and favorite game to group.
2	d. Continue to develop group involvement. e. Begin relaxation training. f. Begin awareness of self and others. g. Discuss non-assertive behavior.	Name game. Every member, in turn, names all other group participants. Counselor assists when necessary. Audio tape. Large muscle relaxation and a fantasy describing a child observing other children playing in a park are introduced. Group discussion. All activities are discussed following implementation.
3	h. Continue relaxation training and awareness of self and others. i. Begin to recognize non-assertive behavior. j. Discuss aggressive behavior.	Audio tape. Relaxation training and a fantasy describing a child involved in play with siblings in home. Group discussion. Informal behavioral contracts. An explanation of behavioral contracts was presented followed by discussion. Homework. Each child assigned responsibility to try to identify personal behavior to change.
4	k. Continue relaxation training and awareness of self and others. l. Begin to recognize aggressive behavior. m. Discuss assertive behavior.	Audio tape. Students becoming accustomed to relaxation and fantasy. No introduction of these exercises necessary now. Fantasy involves a conversation with parents. Videotape. Children view peers role playing interactions with parents. Homework. Students discussed assignment. Informal behavior contract. Each student identified behavior to change with counselor's help and verbally agrees to implement.
5	n. Continue relaxation training and awareness of self and others. o. Begin to recognize assertive behavior. p. Discuss non-assertive, aggressive and assertive behavior.	Audio tape. Fantasy involved interaction between teacher and student. Group discussion becoming less counselor-oriented. Videotape. Students view peers role playing with teacher. Homework. Discuss efforts to fulfill informal contracts in home. Many

Table 9-1 (Cont.)

Session	Objectives	Activities
		students frustrated. Counselors encourage and reinforce. Informal behavior contract. Contracts renewed to include interaction with teacher.
6	q. Continue relaxation training and awareness of self and others. r. Recognize non-assertive, aggressive, and assertive behavior in self and others. s. Discuss formal behavior contracts and role playing.	Audio tape. Fantasy involved interactions between classmates. Videotape. Students view inappropriate behavior and assertive behavior between peers. Homework. Discussed experiences with teachers and renewed informal contracts to include classmates.
7–11	t. Continue relaxation training and awareness of self and others. u. Introduce role playing of non-assertive, aggressive, and assertive behavior with parents, teachers, and classmates. v. Introduce written behavioral contracts. w. Recognize feelings in self and others resulting from non-assertive, aggressive, and assertive behavior. x. Recognize personal rights and responsibilities when interacting with others.	Audiotape. Relaxation and fantasy experiences continued. Role play. Introduced first before the group and followed same progression of interactions as fantasies: parents, teachers, and classmates. Videotape. After rehearsing role plays before group and discussing, role plays were videotaped and then played back. Behavioral contracts. A form including the child's name, an agreement to perform the identified assertive behavior, and child's signature was used. Group discussion. Focused on feelings of self and others and rights and responsibilities in human interactions.
12	y. Closure	Discuss group experience and summarize individual's growth and development. Complete self-report instrument.

animal pictures and posted them on the bulletin board in the meeting room. Next the counselor reviewed the purpose of the group by saying, "We have agreed to meet in this group to learn to work and play better with other children. To learn these skills we need to help each other by talking in the group and sharing our thoughts and feelings." To close this group session, the counselor explained that in the next meeting, each time children made verbal contributions they would receive candy.

Reinforcement Procedures

Anticipating that shy children would be reluctant to interact verbally, the counselor had decided to implement a reinforcement procedure in the second session. A fixed-ratio reinforcement schedule would be used initially: each time a child made an appropriate verbal response he or she would receive a small piece of candy. The candy served as a primary reinforcer for desired behavior, with group interaction and praise a secondary reinforcer.

With the introduction of reinforcement, most children began to interact verbally. Before the fourth group session, the reinforcement was changed to a variable-ratio schedule, in which the number of appropriate responses necessary for reinforcement varied, so that children received both primary and secondary reinforcers whenever the counselor believed they remained "on task" verbally. By the eighth session, the use of all primary reinforcement had been phased out. Secondary reinforcement was continued throughout the group sessions.

Relaxation and Guided Fantasy

Sessions 2 through 12 began with an audiotaped relaxation and guided fantasy experience designed from an example by Wittmer and Myrick (1974). The tapes were developed to help children learn to relax and become more comfortable in the group and to get in touch with their thoughts and feelings in as nonthreatening a way as possible. A hierarchy of anxiety-producing fantasy situations was developed that included (from least threatening to most threatening): an experience in the park, watching others play, talking with parents, initiating requests from parents and siblings, playing with siblings, talking with teachers, initiating requests from teachers, talking with classmates, and playing with classmates.

Before each tape was played, children were instructed to relax and to listen carefully. The lights were turned off while the tape played. As children learned to relax, the relaxation tape was abbreviated. Guided fantasy was introduced immediately after each relaxation experience. For example, in Session 3, the counselor said:

> Now imagine that you are a ball. (Pause) You are lying in a grassy backyard. You hear voices and then realize that the neighborhood children are approaching your house. Imagine, they are about to play a game with you. What kind of game will they play? (Pause) Someone picks you up and holds you. How does it feel? (Pause) Suddenly, you are thrown high into the air. You soar high, high up. What do you see? How do you feel? (Pause) You float slowly to

the ground. The game is over and the children leave. You are left behind as the children enter the house. How do you feel being left out and alone? (Pause) As you turn you notice the children returning. It feels good knowing that you will soon be playing again. (Pause) One, the game is over. Two, open your eyes. Three, you are back in the counselor's office ready to work.

A brief discussion followed each fantasy. This discussion focused on students' thoughts and feelings about the fantasy. The counselor asked, "What happened before the fantasy scene?" "What occurred in the scene?" "What will happen next?" "What would you do in the scene?" "Has anything like this happened to you?"

Behavior Contracts

After the fantasy exercise in Session 3, the counselor initiated a discussion about social behavior and how one's own behavior affects the behavior of other persons. Both pleasant and unpleasant behavioral outcomes were examined. Next, the counselor described what a behavioral contract was and how contracts might be useful in the group. Group members were then asked, "What are some behaviors you might want to change?" For those children who were reluctant or unable to respond to this question, the counselor suggested some behaviors for them to consider. These suggestions were based on information shared previously in the group. The session closed with the counselor's recommendation that children identify an assertive behavior they would work on at home before the next meeting.

Formal behavior contracts were implemented in the remaining sessions of Phase 1. These contracts focused on the children's assertiveness at home with parents and at school with teachers and classmates. To complete the contract successfully, each child had to perform the behavior and have the appropriate person sign the contract. For successful completion of a contract, children were awarded 10 minutes of free play following the group session. A brief discussion about the contracts and children's success or failure at assertiveness was held before free play. Those children who were unsuccessful in completing the contract returned directly to their classrooms.

The children identified behaviors such as asking parents' permission to help around the house, asking teachers for help with school work, and asking classmates' permission to play with them. The following is an example of one behavioral contract.

I, Karen, will perform the behavior written below with classmates.
Behavior: I will ask Susan to play with me after lunch.
Signed: Susan S.

Video Models, Role Play, and Focused Feedback

Following relaxation and fantasy exercises in Sessions 1 through 6, the group viewed a videotape of children modeling nonassertive and assertive interactions with adult authority figures and peers. Two videotaped vignettes presenting nonassertive and assertive interactions with parents, teachers, and children were played and discussed, as in the following examples:

Nonassertive Behavior in a Classroom Situation

Teacher: Class, you have your reading assignments to do while I work with this group. (to the group) Children, how do you resemble the characters in the story? (Several children raise their hands.) Mary, what do you think?

Mary: John is like Juan. He never says anything in our group and he never plays with anybody.

George: Yeah, Mary's right.

Teacher: John, how do you feel about that? (John sits quietly and says nothing.)

Assertive Behavior in a Classroom Situation

Teacher: Class, you have your reading assignments to do while I work with this group. (to the group) Children, how do you resemble the characters in the story? (Several children raise their hands.) Mary, what do you think?

Mary: John is like Juan. He never says anything in our group and he never plays with anybody.

George: Yeah, Mary's right.

Teacher: John, how do you feel about that?

John: (hesitates) Well, I agree, but it's not that I don't want to play. I guess I'm afraid to ask the other kids and they don't ask me.

Nonassertive Behavior in a Second Classroom Situation

Teacher: Children you may work together on your social studies assignments. (Two students quickly team up.)

First Student: I'll look in the encyclopedia. You draw the map.

Second Student: O.K., maybe Jane would like to help us, too. She is so smart.

First Student: Yeah! But I bet she won't.

Second Student: I guess you're probably right. (Jane is working nearby and overhears this conversation.)

First Student: It was a good idea though.

Assertive Behavior in the Second Classroom Situation

Teacher:	Children you may work together on your social studies assignments. (Two students quickly team up.)
First Student:	I'll look in the encyclopedia. You draw the map.
Second Student:	O.K., maybe Jane would like to help us, too. She is so smart.
First Student:	Yeah! But I bet she won't.
Second Student:	I guess you're probably right. (Jane is working nearby and overhears the conversation.)
Jane:	(Joining the other two) Do you mind if I work with you? It's such a long assignment, we could help each other.
First Student:	Terrific! We were just coming to ask you.

The discussion focused on the nonassertive and assertive behaviors and feelings of the models. These activities and discussions provided additional help for students in identifying specific nonassertive behaviors.

In Sessions 7 through 9, group members were asked to role play the same situations they had previously viewed on videotape, involving parents, teachers, and classmates. Volunteers were selected and discussion followed each role play. During discussion, actors, and observers were encouraged to interpret underlying feelings in the role play, such as anger and hostility toward the adult authority figures as well as rejection from peers. As a result, children began self-disclosing similar feelings and experiences.

Sessions 10 and 11 followed a pattern similar to previous sessions. In addition, group members were videotaped while role playing the same situations they had experienced earlier. Some children created role plays of personal situations involving their own lives. After role playing, the tape was viewed and discussed. Group members' behaviors were emphasized and these behaviors were compared with those of the peer models.

The last session of Phase 1 was used to effect closure before the holiday. The group members were encouraged to express what they liked and disliked about the training. Most members said they enjoyed role playing and videotaping the most. In addition, members were asked to identify what they had learned. A few children said that they learned to relax. Children also mentioned that when they asserted themselves with others, sometimes they were successful but at other times they were not successful.

Phase 2

As a result of the work accomplished in Phase 1, several guidelines were followed in Phase 2 (Sessions 13 through 18). First, it was decided to continue using the relaxation tape because it provided a stimulus for children to get ready to work in the group. Second, the children's willingness to verbalize their thoughts and feelings in the group had increased to the point that reinforcement for appropriate verbal contributions was no longer necessary. Last, the verbal sophistication of the children interacting in the group had developed to the point that it was no longer necessary to plan exercises to encourage discussion.

The children continued to request to role play their personal experiences and discuss these experiences in the group. The children also indicated a desire to continue behavioral contracting and receiving free-play reinforcement for their efforts. The free-play time had indeed become very active. This was viewed positively by the counselor.

RECOMMENDED RESOURCES

Books

BERNSTEIN, D. & BORKOVEC, T. *Progressive relaxation training: A manual for the helping professions.* Champaign, IL: Research Press, 1973.

This manual describes specific relaxation procedures appropriate for therapists, counselors, and social workers. It contains information on kinds of problems and situations for which relaxation exercises are appropriate. The arrangement of the physical environment for relaxation training is also described as well as possible problems in training. A record illustrating wording, intonation, sequencing, and timing of a relaxation training session accompanies the manual.

CAUTELA, J. & GRODEN, J. *Relaxation: A comprehensive manual for adults, children, and children with special needs.* Champaign, IL: Research Press Catalog, 1982.

This manual features using relaxation training techniques with exceptional children. The first part teaches adults to learn to relax. The second part describes methods for teaching relaxation techniques to other adults and older children. Part three adapts relaxation training to younger children and children with special needs.

EPSTEIN, G. *Waking dream therapy.* New York: Human Sciences Press, 1981.

This book provides a guide to the clinical use of dreams, daydreams, and fantasies. The therapeutic process of reliving a dream in counseling and carrying it out through directed fantasy exercises is employed.

Audiotapes

COTLER, S. & GUERRA, J. *Self-relaxation training.* Champaign, IL: Research Press Catalog, 1982.

This tape introduces deep muscle relaxation and guided fantasies. It can be used by therapists as an adjunct in therapy or by persons wishing to learn to relax alone.

KEAT, D. *Self-relaxation program for children.* Harrisburg, PA: Professional Associates, 1977.

This tape provides a step-by-step process for helping children learn to relax. It provides simple introductory exercises to assist children in understanding what is expected of them and includes material which helps children increase the use of their senses. In addition, most of the experiences encourage children to creatively use their imaginations to finish fantasies that have been started.

Soaring with Jonathan. Center for Inner Motivation and Awareness, P.O. Box 3561, San Diego, CA 92103.

This tape is based on the story Jonathan Livingston Seagull. It provides a fantasy that most children have little difficulty getting involved with and enjoying.

SUMMARY

The first section in this chapter focused on relaxation training and guided fantasy as preliminary or preparatory concepts or techniques for the use of other behavioral counseling techniques. The second section provided a description of the behavioral counseling techniques covert conditioning, cognitive behavior therapy, and assertion training, which are often used in conjunction with relaxation training and guided fantasy. A detailed description of a group assertion-training program for shy children was also provided as an example of the utilization of several of these behavioral counseling techniques together. A list of recommended resources concluded the chapter.

REFERENCES AND RECOMMENDED READINGS

ANDERSON, R. Using a fantasy-modeling treatment with acting-out fifth grade boys. Unpublished doctoral dissertation, University of Florida, Gainesville, June, 1975.

———. Using guided fantasy with children. *Elementary School Guidance and Counseling*, 1980, 15(1), 39–47.

BANDLER, R. & GRINDER, J. *The structure of magic (Vol. I).* Palo Alto, CA: Science and Behavior Books, 1975.

BENSON, H. *The relaxation response.* New York: William Morrow, 1975.

BERNSTEIN, D. & BORKOVEC, T. *Progressive relaxation training: A manual for the helping professions.* Champaign, IL: Research Press, 1973.

BOSWELL, J. Helping children with their anger. *Elementary School Guidance and Counseling,* 1982, 16(4), 278–287.

BOWER, S., AMATEA, E., & ANDERSON, R. AT with children. *Elementary School Guidance and Counseling,* 1976, 10(4), 236–245.

BOYD, J. & GRIEGER, R. Rational-emotive group work with children. In J. Duncan & J. Gumaer (Eds.) *Developmental groups for children.* Springfield, IL: Charles Thomas, 1980.

CAUTELA, J. & BARON, M. Covert training: A theoretical analysis. *Behavior Modification,* 1977, 1, 351–368.

CRABBS, M. Fantasy in career development. *Personnel and Guidance Journal,* 1979, 57(6), 292–295.

DAVIS, D. Sense relaxation with children. *Elementary School Guidance and Counseling,* 1969, 3, 304.

DEFFENBUCHER, J. & KEMPER, C. Counseling test-anxious sixth graders. *Elementary School Guidance and Counseling,* 1974, 9, 30–34.

DILLEY, J. Mental imagery. *Counseling and Values,* 1975, 19(2), 110–115.

ELLIS, A. Can we change thoughts by reinforcement? A reply to Howard Rachlin. *Behavior Therapy,* 1977, 8, 666–672.

FLOWERS, J. & BOORAEM, C. Imagination training in the treatment of sexual dysfunction. *Counseling Psychologist,* 1975, 5(1), 50–51.

GRAZIANO, A. & DEAN, D. Programmed relaxation and reciprocal inhibition with psychotic children. *APA Proceedings,* 1967, 253–254.

GRODEN, G. & CAUTELA, J. Behavior therapy: A survey of procedures for counselors. *Personnel and Guidance Journal,* 1981, 60(3), 175–180.

GUMAER, J. & VOORNEVELD, R. Affective education with gifted children. *Elementary School Guidance and Counseling,* 1975, 10(2), 86–94.

———. & LEONE, S. Assertion training in group counseling for shy children revisited: A follow-up report. *Virginia Counselor's Journal,* 1982, 10, 12–20.

GUNNISON, H. Fantasy relaxation technique. *Personnel and Guidance Journal,* 1976, 55(4), 199–200.

———. Fantasy door approach: Merging the left-right hemispheres. *Personnel and Guidance Journal,* 1982, 60(7), 403–405.

HENDRICKS, G. & WILLIS, R. *The centering book.* Englewood Cliffs, NJ: Prentice Hall, 1975.

———. & ROBERTS, T. *The second centering book.* Englewood Cliffs, NJ: Prentice Hall, 1977.

HOLMES, D. & HORAN, J. Anger induction in assertion training. *Journal of Counseling Psychology,* 1976, 23, 108–111.

KEAT, D. Broad spectrum behavior therapy with children: A case presentation. *Behavior Therapy,* 1972, 3, 454–459.

KELLY, G. Guided fantasy as a counseling technique with youth. *Journal of Counseling Psychology,* 1972, 19, 355–361.

KOCHENDOFER, S. & CULP, D. Relaxation group intake procedure. *Elementary School Guidance and Counseling,* 1979, 14(2), 124.

KOEPPEN, A. Relaxation training for children. *Elementary School Guidance and Counseling,* 1974, 9, 14–23.

KRUMBOLTZ, J. & THORESEN, C. *Behavioral counseling: Cases and techniques.* New York: Holt, Rinehart, & Winston, 1969.

LAZARUS, A *Behavior therapy and beyond.* New York: McGraw-Hill, 1971.

————. *In the mind's eye: The power of imagery for personal enrichment.* New York: Random House, 1978.

————. & ABRAMOVITZ, A. The use of emotive imagery in the treatment of children's phobias. *Journal of Mental Science,* 1962, 108, 191–195.

LEONE, S. & GUMAER, J. Group assertiveness training with shy children. *School Counselor,* 1979, 27, 134–141.

LEUNER, H. Guided affective imagery (GAI): A method of intensive psychotherapy. *American Journal of Psychotherapy,* 1969, 23, 4–22.

LITTLE, S. & JACKSON, B. The treatment of test anxiety through attentional and relaxation training. *Psychotherapy: Theory, Research and Practice,* 1974, 11(2), 175–178.

LUPIN, M. *Peace, harmony, awareness: A relaxation program for children.* NY: Teaching Resources Corp., 1977.

McBRIEN, R. Using relaxation methods with first grade boys. *Elementary School Guidance and Counseling,* 1978, 12(3), 146–152.

MEICHENBAUM, D. *Cognitive behavior modification.* New York: Plenum, 1977.

————. & GOODMAN, J. The developmental control of operant motor responding by verbal operants. *Journal of Experimental Child Psychology,* 1969, 7, 553–565.

————. Training impulsive children to talk to themselves: A means of developing self-control. *Journal of Abnormal Psychology,* 1971, 77, 115–126.

MORGAN, J. & SKOVHOLT, T. Using inner experiences: Fantasy and daydreams in career counseling. *Journal of Counseling Psychology,* 1977, 24, 391–397.

OWEN, D. & WILSON, Jr. Cowboys and butterflies: Creative uses of spontaneous fantasy in career counseling. *School Counselor,* 1980, 23(2), 119–125.

PULVINO, C. & HOSSMAN, C. Mental imagery in counseling: A case analysis. *School Counselor,* 1976, 24(1), 44–47.

RASHBAUM-SELIG, M. Assertive training for young people. *The School Counselor,* 1976, 24(2), 115–122.

ROSSMAN, H. & KAHNWEILER, J. Relaxation training with intermediate grade students. *Elementary School Guidance and Counseling,* 1977, 11(4), 259–266.

ROZMAN, D. *Mediating with children: The art of concentration and centering.* Boulder Creek, CA: University of the Trees Press, 1975.

SCHNEIDER, M. & ROBIN, A. *Turtle manual.* Stony Brook, NY: Psychology Department, State University of N.Y., 1974.

SCHWARTZ, C. TM relaxes some people and makes them feel better. *Psychology Today,* 1974, 39–44.

SEILER, G. Yoga for kids. *Elementary School Guidance and Counseling*, 1978, 12 (4), 229–237.

SHAFFER, J. The experience of the holistic mind. In A. A. Skeikh & J. T. Shaffer (Eds). *The potential of fantasy and imagination*. New York: Brandon House, 1979.

SINGER, J. *Imagery and daydream methods in psychotherapy and behavior modification*. New York: Academic Press, 1974.

———. *The inner world of daydreaming*. New York: Harper & Row, 1975.

———. Fantasy: The foundation of serenity. *Psychology Today*, 1976, 37, 32–34.

WEIL, G. & GOLDFRIED, M. Treatment of insomnia in an 11 year old through self-relaxation. *Behavior Therapy*, 1973, 4(2), 282–284.

WITTMER, J. & MYRICK, R. *Facilitative teaching: Theory and practice*. Pacific Palisades, CA: Goodyear, 1974.

WOLPE, J. *The practice of behavior therapy*. (2nd ed.) New York: Pergamon Press, 1973.

WOODY, R . *Psychobehavioral counseling and therapy: Integrating behavioral and insight techniques*. New York: Appleton-Century-Crofts, 1971.

Part II

COUNSELING CHILDREN IN GROUPS

Chapter 10

Child-Centered
Group Counseling

AT BIRTH CHILDREN become members of a group. Initially, as a group member of the family unit, children begin to live and learn who they are in a group, what behaviors are acceptable, and what behaviors are not deemed appropriate. Most family groups provide for and protect the vulnerable infant, yet are supportive of the child's desire to examine the surrounding environment and to learn new behavior. As a result, these families encourage the child to grow from a position of total dependence at infancy toward increasing independence.

With family assistance, children learn to become social beings and incorporate their unique selves into family group norms. As children become more self-confident, they begin to initiate play with other children and expand their social world to their peer group. While interacting with the family and peer group, children are constantly testing their knowledge and physical skills. It is through the interpersonal relationships in these two groups that children develop their self-identities and learn the skills necessary to cope with life. Quite naturally, as children grow, they depend less on the family group and more on their peer group to satisfy their self-needs. Recently, I returned home from an extended business trip. Upon entering the house, I asked my 4-year-old son, Jeff, "Did you miss me?" As he ran toward the door, his reply was, "Gee no Dad, I've been playing with my friends. See you later, I gotta go." At that moment, I realized the transition of social need satisfactions from family to peers had occurred.

The degree to which children develop their sense of self-worth and become self-fulfilled depends on the degree to which they experience predominantly positive interactions in their two early group encounters. Children who value themselves and those important others in their lives become "group-adjusted." They are secure and feel they belong in their groups. These children have learned the necessary skills by which they will successfully integrate themselves into various other groups throughout their lives. What happens to those children who are not so fortunate?

It makes sense that group counseling be the preferred mode of therapeutic intervention for those children who are not group-adjusted. In his early writing, Faust (1968) stressed that group counseling was preferred because

> ... much of what is learned by children (and adults) is learned in groups, so new learning and 'unlearning' might well be effected via groups, perhaps with maximum results. (p. 140)

GROUP COUNSELING

What is group counseling? Several definitions of group counseling are available in the literature. The definition which best embodies my own thinking is offered by Gazda, Duncan, and Meadows (1967).

> Group counseling is a dynamic, interpersonal process focusing on conscious thought and behavior involving the therapy functions of permissiveness, orientation to reality, catharsis, and mutual trust, caring, understanding, acceptance, and support. The therapy functions are created and nurtured in a small group through the sharing of personal concerns with one's peers and the counselor(s). The group counselees are basically normal individuals with various concerns which are not debilitating to the extent of requiring extensive personality change. The group counselees may utilize the group interaction to increase understanding and acceptance of values and goals and to learn or unlearn certain attitudes and behaviors. (p. 306)

From this definition, it becomes apparent that the global goal of group counseling is to provide opportunity for personal growth and problem solving of children. As I view it, group counseling is therefore either *growth-centered,* focusing on helping children maximize their personal resources to cope more effectively with their daily lives; or *problem-centered,* focused specifically on remediating personal conflicts in children's lives which, if unresolved, will impede healthy future development. All children can benefit from growth-centered group counseling in which they examine self (values, attitudes, feelings, and behaviors) in relation to developmental life topics such as friendship, drugs, sex, or death. Growth-centered group counseling helps to prepare children to handle potential personal crises of a developmental nature. Problem-centered group counseling is, on the other hand, only appropriate for selected individuals who are currently experiencing similar personal concerns such as academic failure, obesity, divorce, and various behavior disorders. It is directed toward preventing personal crises from becoming problematic to the extent of debilitating the continued development of the individual child.

Historical Perspectives

Shortly after the turn of the century, Jacob Moreno provided the impetus for working with children in therapeutic groups. He used psychodrama—a technique which he encouraged children to act out their fantasies. Later, Slavson (1943) initiated activity-group therapy with children in which the therapist remained apart from the children in a passive role as the children engaged in various games, art activities, crafts, and outdoor activities. Shortly thereafter, these play activity concepts were developed more completely in 1947 by Virginia Axline as described in her book *Play Therapy* (1974).

Insight therapies such as psychoanalytic, Adlerian, and Rogerian predominated as group counseling with children developed through the next two decades. Not until the 1970s, as discussed in Chapter 8, were behavioral counseling techniques accepted widely for use in group work on a large scale (Rose, 1975; Stockton, 1980). Today a wide variety of strategies are used with children in group counseling. However, it appears that most group therapies involve the direct transfer of individual counseling techniques to a group context depending primarily on the counselor's training (Lakin, Lieberman, & Whitaker, 1969). Stockton (1980) points out that group leadership training is about 10 years behind individual counselor training in that there exists several training models with little evidence to support their use.

The Value of Group Counseling

Aside from the obvious economics of a therapist being able to work with more clients in less time, group counseling provides a lifelike representation of children's everyday world. The small group situation is a microcosm of the child's real world. Children interact in group therapy; share their lives and receive feedback from peers about their feelings, thoughts, and behavior. They relate interpersonally and learn to identify effective and ineffective social skills. Children learn about themselves by hearing other children's perceptions of them. They learn how they are similar and different, and that it is all right to be unique. Children learn they must conform and cooperate in some instances, but also that original and creative thinking is appreciated and supported. They are able to reality-test their ideas and behavior in a safe climate without interference or retribution. In a sense, group counseling recreates the therapeutic conditions of the fully functioning family or peer groups to which the child may or may not have been a member. Thus, the therapy group provides children with a basic sense of love, security, and belonging in which life can be explored. These values are idealistic and should be thought of as such.

I wish to caution readers in their exuberance for group counseling and the blind use of group therapy with children. Research has been inconclusive. Abramowitz (1976) reported on the effectiveness of group therapy with children. He found that one-third of the studies he examined produced positive results, one-third mixed results, and one-third generated no expected outcomes. In addition. Parloff and Dies (1977) reported that groups had not been successful with adolescent delinquents. I therefore encourage readers to be well trained and proceed slowly and cautiously.

KEY CONCEPTS

Because it would be impossible to adequately cover the topic of group counseling in three chapters, my intent is to present material that will supplement the expertise of those who have had an introductory group therapy course and who intend to work with children in groups. My further assumption is that all readers of this material have been or will be exposed to additional group counseling resources. Key concepts that are generalizable to both growth-centered and problem-centered counseling groups will be emphasized in the remainder of this chapter. These concepts include ethics, group dynamics, organization and implementation, and stages of development. Key concepts such as those involved in forming groups which are particular to either growth-centered or problem-centered group counseling will be discussed in those respective chapters.

Ethics

Often therapists who work with children forget, overlook, or fail to abide by the same ethical codes of professional conduct that they would use with adults. This is not to say or imply that these counselors are unprofessional in their behavior, but I would caution therapists not to make assumptions about children or take them for granted in the counseling arena. Several renowned professional organizations have published ethical codes for group workers. In 1969, the National Training Laboratories (NTL) published a booklet titled "Standards for the Use of the Laboratory Method" in which they incorporated seven principles from the American Psychological Association's (APA) Ethical Standards of Psychologists (1967), considered appropriate for group trainees. Recently the Association for Specialists in Group Work (ASGW) published a special issue of the journal on ethics which includes the text of the Association's "Ethical Guidelines for Group Leaders" (Roberts, 1982, p. 175–179). Most authorities who write about group counseling have also stressed ethical considerations (Corey & Corey, 1982; Duncan & Gumaer, 1980; Hansen, Warner, & Smith, 1976). In addition to adherence to the ethical guidelines mentioned, group counselors of children need to answer several specific questions to ensure children's rights and protection in groups.

1. *As a leader, is it necessary to screen and prepare children for group membership?* Yes, initial expectations for group member conduct presented in an interview, at the level of a child's comprehension, is a valuable asset to beginning the group. Most children are referred by adults for group therapy and may not want the experience. If after explaining who will participate and what is likely to occur, children do not agree to try it out, it is their personal right not to be involved. I recognize in some situations group counseling is mandated. However, in these situations where children are forced to participate, resistance is very high and unless overcome quickly little learning occurs and the potential for harm is greater.

2. *Do I need to seek and obtain parental approval?* Yes, by law parents are responsible for children and need to approve and be knowledgeable about therapy for their children. This parental contact has three potential advantages beyond direct services for the child. First, informal consent provides a degree of protection for the counselor when working with children. Secondly, it generates a line of communication between counselor and parent which may lead to greater parental involvement on behalf of the child. Lastly, in many instances, parents do not realize what therapy is about and counselors will have the additional opportunity to inform their public regarding role and function. Although most parental consent will be obtained via the mail, an invitation for a personal meeting and further discussion with the group counselor should be included in a letter. A sample letter is provided in Appendix D.

3. *Is it necessary for me to have supervised training with children in groups before working alone with children in groups?* Yes, working in group therapy with children is frequently distinctly different than with adults. For example, children do not generally verbalize as well and have a lessened capacity to communicate directly. They, therefore, need to be provided a medium through which they can communicate successfully with other children and the counselor. In addition, although many group theories, techniques, and strategies are appropriate across age groups, many are not. More specific information to answer this question is provided in Chapters 11 and 12 in the sections on formation of groups.

4. *Do I explain confidentiality to children?* Yes, the issue of confidentiality needs to be introduced in the initial interview and reviewed in the

introductory phase of the first group session. Children may not understand the term confidentiality, but they can comprehend that "what is discussed in the group is the group's secret and must not be talked about anywhere else. Group business stays in the group room." If children want to discuss group experiences, they can be encouraged to share things or events in general but nothing specific about others and told absolutely not to use names. For example, a group member could say, "One of the boys acted out in group today," but not say, "John was unruly." Should family members ask for information from a group member, it is permissible for that group member to discuss what he or she did in the group but not reveal specific information about other group members.

5. *Do I establish expectations for behavior? Yes*, it is my opinion that children need to know their limits. My preference is to originate this issue in the interview and review it in the first session by mentioning to the children, "You have all been in groups before. What rules are necessary for us to have a successful group?" Most of the time children will readily share behaviors they have learned not to demonstrate. For example, "Don't interrupt." My bias is to restate these ideas from a negative, don't do, behavior to a positive, do, behavior. For example, "Wait until a person is finished talking." Typical limits for group discussion children have contributed are: (1) one person talks at a time, (2) remain seated, (3) listen to others talk, (4) stick to the topic, (5) be ready to talk and participate, and (6) respect what others say.

6. *Once the group has begun, is it all right for a child not to participate or to quit the group? Yes*, at no point do I consider it ethical to force or pressure a child to participate either in group therapy itself or any of the exercises and activities that may be introduced in the group counseling sessions. However, I do believe it is the counselor's responsibility to suggest the benefits of participation to reluctant group members and to encourage them to participate. If a group member should desire to terminate involvement in the group, I suggest the leader encourage the child to reconsider the decision and think about it until the following group meeting. At this meeting the group member's request to exit may be brought before the group and discussed openly. Sometimes other children in the group will pressure a reluctant child to participate. Confrontations from peers can be very helpful. Again, however, the counselor must protect the individual's right not to participate. A child who refuses to participate continuously is probably not ready for group therapy. Many children need to be seen individually in counseling before experiencing group counseling. In many cases, a natural transfer from individual counseling to group counseling occurs. Sometimes a child may receive individual counseling and group counseling concurrently, which can also facilitate the transfer process.

7. *Once the group has begun, is it ever appropriate to remove a group member? Yes.* If an individual group member refuses to participate over several sessions, the therapist must reexamine whether or not the group counseling situation is appropriate for the individual and whether or not the individual's resistance is impeding his or her development or that of other group members. If so, the nonparticipatory group member must be removed. Also, if at any time the counselor feels that negative group behavior of an individual is physically or psychologically harmful to other group members, or detrimental to the progress of the group as a whole, the therapist may choose to remove the disruptive child from the group for a small time, the entire meeting, or permanently, if necessary. In addition, I feel it is necessary for counselors to remove children who have used alcohol or drugs directly prior to the group meeting. Children should be made aware of the counselor's expectations for their interaction and involvement in the pregroup interview as well as the rules for proper conduct in a group. These expectations and limits for behavior may need to be reinforced throughout the life of the group.

8. *Should children be informed about all specialized exercises to be used in the group? Yes,* many specialized exercises such as relaxation training and fantasy can be as frightening to children as they are to adults. In many instances, "lead-up activities" can be planned to help prepare children for potentially threatening group activities. For example, before being asked to directly confront other group members, children can be prepared indirectly by practicing confronting a classmate, teacher, or family member who is not present in the group through an empty-chair activity.

9. *Should I develop and monitor goals for individuals within the group? Yes,* although it is important to develop and to work toward accomplishment of group goals, it is also important for individuals within the group to work toward specific personal goals. Group members need to be informed in the preliminary interview of group goals, and, as the group moves into the working stage, be assisted by the group leader and other group members to identify personal goals. I recommend group counselors keep case notes on individual members and the group. Several examples of the development of group goals and objectives and of individual goals are provided in Chapters 11 and 12.

10. *Should I inform children of time parameters in the group? Yes,* as part of your expectations for children to be at the group meeting on time, and to help them learn responsibility, they need to know exactly when the group will begin and when it will end. Children also need to know the number of group sessions that they will attend. Being informed about time constraints also helps to prepare children for closing each group session and for terminating the group. Toward the end of each session, I usually

let children know that we have about 10 minutes remaining in the group before it is time to stop. In addition, I begin to prepare for group termination at the beginning of the group by saying, "We will meet for 15 sessions. Our first session is today and our last is planned for Wednesday, November 17." As we near our last session, I begin to remind the children by saying, "We have three sessions remaining." By informing children of time parameters, the leader helps them to get emotionally ready for exiting and discontinuing the group.

Group Dynamics

Group dynamics has been defined as the interactive forces operating within a group (Glanz & Hayes, 1967, p. 274) which influence group member's behavior. Yalom (1975) identified 10 curative factors involving group dynamics which lead to positive outcomes in group therapy: imparting of information, instillation of hope (belief in personal control of behavior), altruism, universality (understanding others have similar feelings), corrective recapitulation of the primary family group, development of socializing techniques, imitative behavior, interpersonal learning, group cohesiveness, and catharsis. Because no definitive agreement exists regarding these factors by experts, group dynamics remains a loosely defined concept in group counseling. Perhaps the only agreement among group experts that can be reached at this time is that group dynamics exist and that they can be either therapeutic or destructive forces. It is, therefore, the group leader's responsibility to help establish and maintain the positive elements and conditions of a group and to recognize and interrupt harmful forces.

I often ask students in my group counseling courses "What conditions would have to exist in our class group for you to self-disclose your innermost secrets and confront classmates directly?" The list of terms generated invariably includes trust, caring, understanding, acceptance, willingness of others to do the same, involvement over time, an "act of God," and never. This exercise forces students to realize that unless certain constructive conditions (group dynamics) are in place in a group, the group will be an ineffective therapeutic environment. It also makes painfully clear to potential group leaders that not all persons are ready for group therapy, nor will they ever be ready. The difficult question is "How do we as group counselors create and maintain these constructive group forces?" It is my opinion that the first step for all potential group therapists is to participate in and experience a counseling group as a member. Once group dynamics are experienced personally, then didactic course instruction on organization, planning, theory, techniques, and other group-leader skills becomes more meaningful.

Group Organization

The success or failure of any counseling group begins with the therapist's ability to organize and plan effectively. Too often novice counselors assume that their enthusiasm for and belief in group counseling and their desire to be helpful to children are enough to ensure success. This is not true. The counselor's willingness to plan extensively and organize carefully before the group actually meets increases tremendously the probability of a group's success. These preliminary plans and organizational practices need to be developed in light of sound, theoretical principles and based, as much as possible, on research findings. A few group experts have recognized and emphasized this need for organization (Duncan, 1974; Yunker, 1970). Ohlsen (1967) and Duncan and Gumaer (1980) have explained thoroughly procedures for organizing group counseling with children.

Because the vast majority of therapy groups for children are implemented in either school or agency settings and several professionals are responsible in these environments for the overall learning and development of children, it is highly desirable that counselors begin to organize by *communicating* their ideas, philosophy, and rationale for group therapy throughout their work setting. Therefore, the first step in organization is to "sell" the concept to colleagues and potential clients. By gaining collegial cooperation, counselors minimize the possibility of their institutional peers sabotaging their group efforts later on. Examples of sabotage include not sending children to group because schoolwork is unfinished and purposely scheduling more attractive competing activities at the same time as the group. By informing children, counselors generate interest in groups, establish early rapport with children, and diminish their fear and misunderstanding. As counselors inform their publics about the benefits of group therapy, it is important that they begin step two of the organizational process, which is *identifying* potential client populations.

Counselors may begin to solicit cooperation from their peers in a staff development meeting. If so, this is also an opportune moment to ask colleagues to identify children who may benefit from therapy and to identify problematic topics for children in their care. When discussing group counseling with children in classrooms or in assembly, counselors can administer simple needs-assessment surveys. For example, as a school counselor, I have entered each grade level classroom and asked children to list the five biggest problems they have at the moment from most serious to least serious. This list is generated anonymously to ensure as great and accurate a response as possible. Next, I tabulate the lists and select the problems listed by most children as most serious at a particular grade level and offer group counseling on those topics where teachers have also indicated the need.

Another method is to administer a class sociogram. This process only takes a few minutes of class time and identifies readily those children who are perceived negatively or positively by peers. I use four statements, three positive and one negative, and ask children to list the three most preferred classmates for each statement with the first choice being most preferred. For example, classmates I would most like to work on a project with are; classmates I would most like to play with are; classmates I would most want to invite to my birthday party are; and classmates I like least are. It is best to try to include statements that elicit information from a variety of school and home social situations in which interpersonal relationships are important.

Once children for group counseling are identified, a third step and essential part of group organization is begun, thorough *planning*. To plan efficiently, counselors need to consider the following:

1. *The length of the group counseling program.* Most research has indicated that for group counseling to be minimally effective with children, at least 10 sessions are necessary. I would personally recommend 15 group meetings.

2. *The time of day and days of week.* Decisions regarding these factors depend heavily on the age of the children and type of counseling group. Both of these considerations will be discussed in the next two chapters. Practical experience has also demonstrated that children are usually not accessible for group therapy in the morning school hours. This time is usually reserved for teaching academic subjects. To avoid conflicts with academics, it seems best that counselors block out 45 minutes to one hour time slots in their schedules in the early afternoon following lunch and plan two sessions per week on an every-other-day basis (Monday and Wednesday or Tuesday and Thursday). Friday is often a day for which special activities are planned.

3. *The setting.* It is important that the group room be attractive, large enough to accommodate 8 to 10 movable chairs (but small enough to encourage cohesion), carpeted, and private. Many children often desire to sit on the floor and appear to disclose more readily in this position. In addition, many activities dictate either sitting or lying on the floor. Carpeting and several soft pillows can accommodate these needs.

4. *The plan for individual group sessions.* In my group counseling classes, students are instructed to write a group counseling proposal which they later are encouraged to implement as a first group counseling experience. The proposal consists of: (a) an introduction, which states the need for counseling children on a particular topic, (b) a rationale, which includes a review of the literature citing theoretical approaches and group procedures which have been used successfully with the particular concern, (c) a 10-session structured plan for each potential session of the group, and (d) a method of evaluation. This organization provides many students with

additional confidence before implementing the group. Students are cautioned that the written plans for the individual sessions are to be used only as guidelines. Further, students are reminded that a primary consideration for planning these sessions is that they be based on developmental group theory and include the various stages of group process. These stages are discussed later in this chapter.

Here are a few guidelines for planning individual group counseling sessions:

a. I recommend each session be organized around two or three specific objectives stated to meet the developmental goals of the group. The goals are general statements for the group's direction. Objectives are specific statements for children's participation and group process for each day.

b. Several strategies or activities should be planned to meet each objective. These strategies should be designed to encourage the development of the necessary conditions for group progress. Although the combination of children's readiness and willingness and group-counselor response and planning skills ultimately determine how well the group progresses, activities, based on sound theory, will help create the opportunity and atmosphere for developing children's self-awareness, self-exploration, and self-understanding in the group. It will also help the leader control the movement of the group.

c. When implementing this plan, students evaluate its content after each session, discuss which activities worked well, which were awkward but might be changed and tried differently, and which were inappropriate at that time and should be discarded. Students also evaluate their response skills and make case comments on individual child members as well as a statement to the group's overall progress. Several examples of session by session group counseling plans are shared with readers in the next two chapters on growth-centered and problem-centered groups.

5. *The interview to select children for participation.* Participant selection is the last step in group organization and perhaps the most important. Ohlsen (1969) observed that:

> By careful selection of clients a counselor can increase his chances of helping them. He must be free to accept only those clients whom he feels reasonably certain can be helped in his group, and preferably only those who request membership after they realize what will be expected from others in the group. (p. 105)

Although it is best to select participants from a pool, I am not implying that all children in the pool should be nor that they will be selected. I am suggesting that group therapists interview individually prospective group members to explain the group experience. This explanation should include the counselor's expectations for the child's participation including any behavioral limits, an idea of the kinds of activities in which the child will partake, and the names of other children who are being interviewed for membership in the group. If children are uncomfortable with any aspect of the interview, they should be placed on a waiting list for inclusion in a future group, scheduled for individual counseling, or referred. Naturally, the interview process must be greatly simplified for very young children.

Developmental Group Stages

To assist group members to have the most meaningful experience possible by planning effectively, therapists must understand how groups evolve. In the group counseling literature, four developmental group stages have typically been discussed: involvement, transition, working, and ending (Mahler, 1969); orientation and exploration, transition, working, and consolidation and termination (Corey, 1981). The nomenclature applied to a given stage describes the group's goals during that particular phase and characterize group member's behaviors. For my purposes, discussion regarding group counseling will focus on the following four developmental stages: establishment, exploration, work, and termination.

In the initial group stage, *establishment*, children are somewhat anxious and insecure about the group and its members. Children are excited about the group yet unsure. They may manifest these uncertainties by giggling, not attending, being late to group, or by mildly acting out. These behaviors are normal and should not be construed as disruptive. In this stage, children depend on the therapist. It is the counselor's responsibility to establish the group by getting children involved with each other so that they begin to experience the necessary conditions mentioned earlier (i.e., acceptance, trust, etc.). To establish the group, the therapist should concentrate on: (1) helping children understand the purpose(s) and structure of the group, (2) helping children get better acquainted, and (3) helping children to begin to become aware of feelings in self and others. To assist children to learn to discuss their feelings and behavior, it is also important that counselors understand and begin to plan for two fundamental interaction goals in the group: self-disclosure and feedback. Mahler (1969) described the following six stages of personalization, identified by Betty Berzon, that group members go through:

1. No personally relevant material is discussed.
2. There is an aloof, superficial manner in presenting facts about public aspects of themselves.

3. There is an "inward reference" for material, but the discussion does not move toward exploring the significance or meaning of the material.
4. There is increased emotional involvement on the part of group members in their own contributions.
5. There is a tentative probing and effort toward self-exploration and an inward search for discovery of new feelings.
6. Members are actively exploring their feelings, their values, perceptions of others, fears, and life-choices with emotional proximity to the material. (p. 83–84)

Figure 10–1 describes the "ideal" self-disclosure (personalization) process in the four developmental group stages. Throughout the establishment stage, the counselor should introduce only those activities which encourage self-disclosure at a superficial level. One of my favorite early group activities is the *personal shield* designed after an example provided by Simon, Howe, and Kirschenbaum (1972, p. 279). This activity requires that children be involved in using their imaginations, drawing, and self-disclosing. The personal shield can be used for all levels of self-disclosure. In addition, it helps children learn confidentiality in that the activity is designed so children draw symbols representing their disclosures and are instructed only to disclose as much as they wish.

To use the shield, a machine-duplicated personal shield is distributed and children instructed to draw in the appropriate section a symbol (picture) representing them. If necessary, a symbol can be defined as a picture that stands for something. Examples such as the American flag, stop sign, or handshake can be used to illustrate the definition. For superficial self-disclosure, the shield may be separated into four parts and children asked

Figure 10–1. Flowchart for Developmental Group Stages and Interaction Goals: Self-Disclosure and Feedback

Level of Personal Involvement	Group Stages			
	Establishment	Exploration	Work	Termination
Superficial				
Intermediate		(positive feedback)	(negative feedback)	
Deep				

to respond to the following questions in order in the respective sections of the shield.

1. What is your favorite school activity?
2. What is your favorite after school activity?
3. What is one thing you wish you had that you do not have?
4. What is one thing you have that you are most proud to own?

Once drawing is completed, children are asked to volunteer to share a part of their shield. Discussion is then facilitated related to these self-disclosures.

Because children often lack information about each member's behavior and generally have not achieved a sufficient level of comfort in the group, the feedback process is not initiated in this stage. Table 10–1 provides recommended objectives, activities, and counselor-response skills for the four developmental group stages. It is noteworthy to mention that many of the child-centered counselor response skills recommended in group therapy are also used in individual counseling. I feel that to be an effective group counselor, one must demonstrate effective counseling skills with individual clients. In addition, the group therapist's response skills referred to in Table 10–1 are *additive* throughout the developmental stages. Once the response skills are initiated in a given stage, they are continued, when appropriate, in all other stages.

The counselor response skills have been assigned to the developmental stages based upon my personal experience with children in groups and my efforts to teach and to monitor these skills in a systematic fashion with counselors in training. The skills are not my own but have been adapted for use with children from those identified by other authors (Dyer & Vriend, 1977; Gill & Barry, 1982; Lieberman, Yalom, & Miles, 1973; and Ohlsen, 1977). It is my desire that by classifying these skills in the developmental stages, readers will be able to assess their group work with children more accurately and gain greater competence. The classification system is not intended to be inflexible. In fact, in most cases, as counselors become more skilled and integrate these skills into their individual styles, responses suggested for implementation in later stages are used earlier. To further assist the reader, a checklist of group-counselor competencies is also provided in Appendix E.

The child-centered response skills in the first stages aid in developing acceptance, trust, and cohesion, and help children to become self-aware and self-accepting. Counselors use response skills initially to state and discuss the purpose of the group, their expectations for the group, and expectations for group behavior. As group discussion unfolds, therapists should reflect feelings of individual members, clarify group member's thoughts and feelings, and encourage sharing of more information by asking open-ended questions. Praise is often used to reinforce appropriate contributions by group members and to encourage reluctant children to

Table 10-1

RECOMMENDED OBJECTIVES, ACTIVITIES, AND COUNSELOR RESPONSE SKILLS FOR DEVELOPMENTAL GROUP COUNSELING STAGES

Group Stages	Objectives	Activities	Counselor Response Skills *

Establishment	1. To help children understand the purpose(s) and structure of the counseling group.
	2. To help children get better acquainted with group members.
	3. To help children become aware of feelings and behaviors.
	  a. Children will become aware that feelings exist.
	  b. Children will become aware that all persons possess feelings at all times.
	  c. Children will become aware that feelings are neither bad nor ugly. (Faust, 1969).
		1. Activities are designed to elicit "superficial" self-disclosure, or the sharing of nonthreatening information such as favorite hobbies or TV shows. Superficial self-disclosure most often involves talking about *things*.
		E.g.: Personal Shield
			1. State clearly group purpose and expected group behavior. *E.g.*: "You have agreed to meet in group counseling for 15 sessions to discuss your parents' divorce."
			2. Reflect child's feelings. *E.g.*: "Johnny, you were mad when Betty took your pencil."
			3. Clarify child's statements. *E.g.*: "Susan, I believe you mentioned your birthday will be next week and you are planning a party."
			4. Ask open-ended questions that elicit more information. Avoid closed questions that tend to get yes and no answers.
			E.g.: Open-ended question: "What happened on the way to school?"
			E.g.: Closed question: "Do you like cartoons?"
			5. Use verbal praise for appropriate group contributions and behavior.
			E.g.: "Sally, you helped the group a great deal today by sharing your experience."
			6. Summarize important material. *E.g.*: "We have discussed several things we like to do during and after school such as . . . ."
			
			(continued)

Table 10-1 (Cont.)

Group Stages	Objectives	Activities	Counselor Response Skills*
Exploration	1. To help children disclose feelings and experiences. 2. To help children become aware of and understand feelings and behavior in self and others.	1. To begin the group, some activities should be designed to continue to elicit "superficial" self-disclosure. 2. Other activities are incorporated to elicit "intermediate" levels of self-disclosure, or sharing of information such as likes and dislikes regarding parents, siblings, teachers, and classmates. Intermediate-level self-disclosure most often involves talking about *important persons* in the child's life. *E.g.:* Personal Shield 3. Feedback activities are begun. These activities provide children with the opportunity to hear how classmates perceive them. Focus on feedback in this stage is on *positive* behavior. *E.g.:* Unfinished sentences. ("One thing I appreciate /about ____ is ____."	7. Respond to salient nonverbal cues of group members. 1. Continued use of the seven responses from the establishment stage. 2. Pair feelings and behaviors. The counselor points out similarities and differences in children's feelings and behaviors. *E.g.:* "Billy and Joe both dislike fighting. Billy ignores others who call him names, while Joe asks the teacher to help." 3. Model positive feedback. *E.g.:* "Billy, you mentioned your concern for Joe. I'm pleased you want to help him with his work." 4. Elicit positive feedback from children to other group members. *E.g.:* "Joe, Billy helped you with your reading assignment. How do you feel about Billy and his help?" 5. Maintain silence when appropriate.

Work

1. To help children continue to share feelings and experiences.
2. To help children examine alternative ways of behavior.
3. To help children examine consequences for behavior.
4. To help children identify socially ineffective personal behaviors.
5. To help children become aware of socially effective behaviors.
6. To help children learn responsibility for behavior.
7. To help children learn self-control.
8. To help children learn effective decision-making skills.
9. To help children learn problem-solving skills.

1. Some activities should be designed to continue to elicit intermediate-level self-disclosure.
2. Other activities are used to elicit "deep"-level self-disclosure, or sharing of more psychologically threatening information such as feelings about personal inadequacy in school or phobias. Deep-level self-disclosure most often involves talking about subjects directly related to the individual *self*.
   E.g.: Personal Shield
3. Feedback activities are continued. Focus of feedback in this stage should be on both positive and negative behavior.
   E.g.: a. secret pooling
   b. unfinished sentences
   c. empty chair
   d. direct confrontation in group
   e. direct confrontation out of group
   These examples are listed from least threatening to most threatening for both the giver and receiver.

1. Continued use of the counselor responses from the establishment and exploration stages.
2. Elicit empathic responses from children directed toward other group members.
   E.g.: "Sue, how do you think Billy feels about failing the test?"
3. Elicit negative feedback from children to other group members. These verbal confrontations should be directed toward specific inappropriate behaviors. It is important that the child who receives negative feedback is developmentally capable of changing the identified behavior if so desired.
   E.g.: "Sue, Billy ruined your class display on purpose. How do you feel?"
   Sue: "Billy, when you ruined my work I got so mad I wanted to hurt you back."
4. Provide appropriate personal self-disclosure.
   E.g.: "Sometimes people feel so bad that they take out their feelings on other people. I remember last week when I had car trouble and got stuck in traffic.

(continued)

Table 10-1 (Cont.)

Group Stages	Objectives	Activities	Counselor Response Skills*
			I got to group and the first thing I did was yell at you. It wasn't your fault at all."
			Appropriate self-disclosure will enhance group trust, cohesiveness, and encourage reluctant students to contribute.
			5. Interpret underlying feelings. *E.g.*: "Billy, somehow I think that failing this one test is not all that is bothering you. Could it be that not doing well in school makes you feel bad about yourself?"
			6. Focus on individual behavioral change. *E.g.*: "Billy, there are several reasons children do not do well in school. With the group's help, let's list those things you do well and those things you are not doing to help yourself."
			7. Set goals for change. *E.g.*: "Billy, we have discussed several things you could do to change your work habits. Now is the time to decide which one(s) you want to work on first."

| Termination | 1. To help children put new learnings into practice.
  a. Children will make responsible decisions.
  b. Children will express feelings in socially effective ways.
  c. Children will begin to change inappropriate behavior to appropriate behavior. | 1. Activities should be designed to return the group to the "intermediate" and eventually to "superficial" self-disclosure levels. Children need to be prepared to move to less-facilitative classroom environments. Should they happen to expose their "deep" feelings in a nonfacilitative environment, it may prove damaging.
2. Activities should be designed to continue expressing feelings and giving feedback.
3. Activities should be planned to *practice* making decisions, solving problems, and implementing behavior change in group.
  E.g.: Role play, simulation
4. Activities should be planned to help transfer personal behavior change for action out of group.
  E.g.: Behavior contracts
5. Evaluate.
  E.g.: Self-evaluation and strength bombardment. | 1. Continued use of counselor response skills from previous three developmental stages.
2. Provide appropriate support.
  E.g.: "Billy and Joe, I have noticed you helping one another with your school work several times this week. Keep up the good work."
3. Give appropriate advice and information.
  E.g.: "John, although you have made some effort to talk with your teacher, I think we should reexamine your approach. It isn't working. Other children with your problem have been successful by. . . ." |

*Counselor response skills are additive. Once initiated in a group stage, they are continued throughout the life of the group.

interact more often. Counselors may also summarize to review important material, to begin to ready the group to close, and to prepare the group for the next meeting.

In the second stage, *exploration*, children are no longer anxious about a new experience but do experience anxiety and defensiveness resulting from a fear of greater personalization. It is frightening for children to self-disclose beyond a superficial level. They fear they will be judged, misunderstood, or that they may harm loved ones. Children have begun to open up but are not yet secure about their position in the group. When threatened, some children may attempt to change the focus of the group by acting out, story-telling, withdrawing, or claiming boredom. They are at-tempting to control the group and move it in a safer direction. However, as trust, acceptance, and cohesion continue to develop, children receive greater assurances and support for their involvement in the group. They learn that other children in the group have the same fears and that they are as much alike as they are unique. Gazda (1978) stated that group members' self-disclosure at a deeper level than "historical" information initiated the transition stage. The therapist's function is to plan appropriately so that children are gradually involved in *intermediate* level self-disclosures and to help children explore and understand the relationship of feelings and behavior in self and others. The intermediate level of personalization is characterized by discussion about important persons in a child's life. It is necessary to point out that children will also value a pet at this level. When using the personal shield for intermediate self-disclosure, the following questions might be asked:

1. What is something you did recently with a member of your family that you enjoyed?
2. What is something you have not done with your parents that you want to do?
3. What was the best time in your life?
4. What was the worst time in your life?

The last two questions tend to lead toward deeper disclosures and move-ment from the exploration to the work stage. Naturally, all questions used with the personal shield are constructed to accommodate the purpose of the group and its developmental goals.

To cement the group's movement into the exploration stage, *positive feedback* activities are introduced. Feedback, or confrontation, can be either positive or negative in valence. In either case, children giving and receiving feedback will feel discomfort because they are not accustomed to the process. Counselors can reduce this discomfort, and reduce additional group resistance, by teaching children the feedback process in a systematic fashion. I introduce and explain feedback to children by saying, "Often we wish to express our thoughts and feelings to group members yet we do not know how to put them into words. Feedback is a way of helping others know how you feel about something they are saying or doing." Next, a duplicated sheet is distributed containing a feedback sentence for each child in the group. The sentence includes addressing each child by name, describing the particular child's positive behavior and telling how this behavior makes me feel. Another sheet is handed out with only group member's names included in the sentences and children are instructed to complete each sentence for all other group members. Quite often children need help in identifying behavior specifically and in describing their feelings. For younger children, I only model feedback. Children who are aged nine or older have successfully learned to use the model presented.

A word of caution seems appropriate for the exploration stage. The group will develop no faster than the willingness of its slowest member to participate. For instance, Mahler (1969) identified several individual characteristics which lead to additional group resistance: the "odd guy," the "easily hurt individual," and "the openly hostile" person. In this stage, therapists must be particularly aware of individual differences in group members, demonstrate patience and understanding, be encouraging and reinforcing, be flexible, yet maintain a clarity of original purpose and control of the group. In addition to the seven counselor response skills introduced in the establishment stage, counselors are encouraged to pair (link) children's feelings and behaviors, model pleasant feedback, and elicit positive feedback from children to other group members.

The third stage, *work*, is characterized by children's sharing of intimate thoughts and feelings. Anxieties about the group have been overcome and children have developed an attitude of caring and sensitivity toward one another. A feeling of security and a sense of belonging have developed. Group members recognize their individuality and the need to focus their energy on significant personal problems. It is a time in the group when children develop the willingness and the courage, and make a commitment, to take action to bring about desired behavioral changes.

Mahler (1969) described the working stage as "the essential life of a group" (p. 152). The group has achieved a level of security which allows for productive personal growth of individual group members. The counselor's tasks are many and include helping children to (1) continue to self-disclose at a deep level, (2) examine alternative ways of behaving, (3) examine consequences for behavior before initiating behavior, (4) identify socially ineffective and effective behaviors, (5) learn to assume responsibility for behavioral choice, (6) learn self-control, and (7) learn effective decision-making and problem-solving skills.

Although intermediate level self-disclosures continue to be important in the work stage, activities are designed specifically to encourage *deep* level self-disclosure. When children self-disclose at a deep level, they are talking directly about themselves, not others or events. To continue with the personal shield activity, the following questions are asked:

1. What is something about yourself that you like?
2. How would your parents, teachers, or peers describe you?
3. What is something about yourself that you hate?
4. What is one thing about yourself you want to change?

Positive feedback activities may be continued to reinforce and encourage group members. However, it is important that children begin to realistically examine their ineffective behaviors. To accomplish this purpose, counselors need to implement negative feedback in this stage. Stockton and Moran (1980) reported on the use of verbal feedback in counseling groups. Their report indicated that "Research findings have consistently indicated that positive feedback early in the group experience is more readily accepted and leads to more change than negative" (p. 11). In addition, the research findings reviewed suggested the positive to negative feedback sequence to be most effective in counseling groups and that it was best to reserve negative feedback for later stages of a group.

To help readers make negative feedback a more constructive learning process in groups with children, I suggest you examine carefully the following 10 rules for confrontation in groups proposed by Egan (1970):

1. Confront in order to manifest your concern for the other.
2. Make confrontation a way of becoming involved with the other.
3. Before confronting, become aware of your bias . . . .
4. . . . proportion your confrontation to what the relationship will bear.
5. . . . try to take into consideration the possible punitive side effects of your confrontation.
6. Try to be sure that the strength and vehemence of your confrontation and the areas of sensitivity you deal with are proportioned to the needs, sensitivities, and capabilities of the confrontee.
7. Confront behavior primarily; be slow to confront motivation.
8. Confront clearly . . . .
9. Remember that much of your behavior in the group can have confrontational effects (e.g., not talking to others . . .).
10. Be willing to confront yourself honestly in the group. (pp. 334–335)

Because children have a difficult time understanding these rules as they are written, I have simplified many of the rules and eliminated others to aid in their comprehension. When introducing negative feedback to children, I teach the following:

1. Confront to help not to hurt.
2. Confront to talk about a problem not to get even (revenge).
3. Before confronting, ask yourself how you would feel if someone made the statement to you.
4. Confront behavior which can be changed.
5. Be specific when describing the behavior.
6. Be willing to be confronted.

The concept of negative feedback can create discomfort and defensiveness in group members. As a result, learning activities should be introduced which are structured to move from least threatening to most threatening in the group. The activity order which has proven most successful with children has been: (1) secret pooling, (2) unfinished sentences, (3) empty chair, (4) direct negative feedback in the group, and (5) direct feedback to persons out of the group.

Secret pooling is an activity which is easily structured. Children are asked to write anonymously an adjective on paper which describes one or more group member's behavior. No names are written with the adjectives. The papers are folded and handed to the counselor. As adjectives are read one at a time by the therapist, children are encouraged to guess who the adjective describes and provide a supporting statement for the guess. For example, John raised his hand and when called upon said, "I think 'antsy' describes Joe. He has a hard time sitting still in group and in class." Secret pooling poses a limited threat to children in that:

1. Children are writing anonymously and cannot be identified with their adjectives. It is important that the counselor distribute paper and pencils so that children cannot be identified by the paper's size and color, by color of ink, or by differing textures of pen and pencil marks.
2. Children are guessing who the adjective describes and trying to provide a reason for their guess. Other children in the group may concur with the statement or reject it.
3. Adjectives used often describe the behavior of several group members.
4. The therapist is in control and chooses whether or not to read a particular adjective. Not all adjectives must be read.
5. The counselor can structure the writing and reading of adjectives to include positive as well as negative feedback. Research has demonstrated that negative feedback is received better when preceded by positive feedback.

Unfinished sentences, like secret pooling, can be structured to include positive and negative feedback. As indicated in Table 10–1, the exploration stage, the therapist distributes a duplicated sheet containing several sentences with blank spaces for the child's name and specific behavior. It becomes only necessary for the counselor to change the word *appreciate* in the example to *dislike* to manipulate the unfinished sentence from positive feedback to negative feedback. Children are instructed to complete the sentences about group members. The sentences can be written anonymously and read by the therapist or read by the children. The latter is more threatening and defense-posturing. Because children are curious people, if the activity is done anonymously and the counselor decides not to read all the statements, it is critical that the sentences are destroyed (not just thrown away) following the group. This prevents group members from searching the wastebasket later and attempting to identify who said what.

Empty chair is a gestalt technique which forces children to confront indirectly an important person in their lives. An empty chair (pillow) is included in the group. Children are instructed to think of a person in their lives, outside the group, to whom they would like to give positive or negative feedback. Volunteers are then selected to place this person's image in the empty chair and speak directly to the chair while giving the person feedback. Although the designated recipient of feedback is not present, this activity can create a great deal of emotional catharsis for the child. Children repress frequently deep emotions related to loved ones for long periods of time. When counselors encourage the release of this material, they must be prepared to help the child, and other group members, cope with the experience. I also feel that it is imperative *all* group members participate in this activity, or some form of it, before confronting directly in the group. Experience has indicated the empty chair activity is more threatening than secret pooling or unfinished sentences because it requires children to own what they say to persons they care about. It therefore provides the bridge between feedback activities that are anonymous and indirect to those that are owned and direct. Once this transition in group posture has been made, children are ready to confront each other directly in the group and to begin to prepare to confront others directly outside the group.

To facilitate in group learning and the transfer of training for children outside the group, therapists should continue to use response skills from the establishment and exploration stages. During this stage, counselors should also initiate six additional response skills: eliciting empathic responses from one child to another, eliciting negative feedback from one child to another, providing appropriate counselor self-disclosure, interpreting underlying feelings, focusing on behavior change, and helping children set personal goals for change.

The final developmental stage, *termination*, is initiated when children begin to practice new learning (group behavior) in their everyday lives. Children experience greater self-awareness and self-responsibility. They become goal-directed and actively work toward making behavior changes which can impact their lives in a positive direction. Children begin to become more fully functioning and socially effective beings.

Activities in the termination stage may include:

1. Practice for desired behavioral changes. I prefer role playing, simulation exercises and videotaping. These activities might also be introduced in the working stage. These activities are described in greater detail in the next two chapters.

2. Encouragement and support from other group members for attempting behavior change.

3. Planned transfer of behavior learned in the group to action out of the group. Behavior contracts have worked well to accomplish this growth.

4. Evaluation of children's efforts. Children need to learn how to assess their work honestly and accurately.

5. Movement toward closure. It is the counselor's responsibility to ensure that children are ready to return to the real world without the support of the group. It is helpful to plan purposely to move away from deep levels of self-disclosure and to increase positive feedback while minimizing negative feedback.

Two activities I prefer to use in closing a group are self-evaluation and strength bombardment. These activities tend to provide a synthesizing experience for children in that they involve an integration of all the work accomplished throughout the different stages of group development. Evaluation of self honestly and accurately begins with self-exploration, awareness, and self-understanding. This assessment process continues as children receive both positive and negative feedback from respected others as to how effective they are in their change efforts and interpersonal relationships.

Self-evaluation involves children taking stock of their strengths and weaknesses and identifying, with the aid of the group, how they plan to take advantage of their strengths and to work toward removing shortcomings. Children are instructed to write on paper two strengths and two weaknesses. Readers may find that it is easier for children to identify weaknesses than strengths. When children experience difficulty in getting started, pair up group members and have partners help one another. Once writing is completed, group members take turns reading their strengths and weaknesses to the group. After a child finishes talking, other children feedback as to their agreement and disagreement. Following this exchange, children are instructed to complete the unfinished sentences: I plan to use my strengths: to _____. I plan to work toward improving my weaknesses: _____ by _____. The discussion process is then repeated. If group time will not allow for completion of both positive and negative self-evaluation, therapists can either reduce the number of items to be identified or separate the activity in half whereby group members would focus on strengths in one session and weaknesses in the next. Counselors might copy the sentences (minicontracts) completed by children and use them in follow-up of each child's progress out of group.

Strength bombardment is my favorite activity to end the group. All group members are involved in helping each other appraise themselves positively. No negative comments are allowed. Beginning with a volunteer, all children in the group are asked to sit next to the therapist in a "special" seat. By sitting next to the child, I am able to touch, or hug the child at any time. Other group members are then given the opportunity to make at least one positive feedback statement to this child. The focus child may not speak, only listen, until all group members have shared their perceptions. Once the go-around is completed, brief discussion is allowed before going on to the next child. Depending on the abilities of the children, I may or may not begin the feedback process to model for the group member. If modeling is not necessary, it is best to allow the children to express their thoughts first to avoid suggesting a "mind set" on a child to other group members. Once all group members have had a turn, it is important to discuss how the children felt about their experience. It is especially important that all children in the group have the opportunity to participate in this activity. If extra time is needed, counselors should plan ahead to accommodate the activity.

Counselor responses in the termination stage include all those presented in the first three stages. In addition, therapists should provide appropriate support and advice. Examples of these two skills are provided in Table 10–1.

RECOMMENDED RESOURCES

Books

COREY, G., COREY, M, CALLANAN, P., & RUSSELL, J. *Group techniques.* Monterey, CA: Brooks/Cole, 1982.

This book provides techniques for preparing groups and the four developmental stages of groups. It is intended, in general, for practitioners in human services fields and particularly for those in counseling.

KOTTLER, J. *Pragmatic group leadership.* Monterey, CA: Brooks/Cole, 1983.

This book is designed for those who are already familiar with the theory and research of group counseling. It is for counselors who wish to integrate interdisciplinary knowledge, a wide range of useful skills, and accepted theories into a universal model of helping people in groups.

SCHAEFER, C., JOHNSON, L., & WHERRY, J. *Group therapies for children and youth.* San Francisco: Jossey-Bass, 1982.

This book provides a practical and comprehensive handbook of group therapies for children from age 4 through adolescence. It encompasses all major theoretical approaches and should benefit professional clinicians of all disciplines. It consists of abstracts of articles which focus on practical how-to information including developmental perspectives on children's groups and specific group treatments for particular disorders.

Journals

The Journal for Specialists in Group Work. Association for Specialists in Group Work, a division of the American Personnel and Guidance Association, Two Skyline Place, Suite 400, 5203 Leesburg Pike, Falls Church, VA 22041.

The official journal of the Association for Specialists in Group Work is published on a quarterly basis in February, May, August, and November. It publishes full-length articles on group research, innovations and ideas, and working with groups.

Small Group Behavior. Sage Publications, Inc., 274 South Beverly Drive, Beverly Hills, CA 90212.

This journal is an international and interdisciplinary journal presenting research and theory about all types of small groups, including but not limited to therapy or treatment groups. It contains full-length articles, book reviews, up-to-date bibliographic listings, and news of significant professional activities and meetings. The journal is published on a quarterly basis in February, May, August, and November.

SUMMARY

This introductory chapter on group counseling began by providing a brief introduction to and rationale for group counseling with children. A definition for group counseling was provided; distinctions were drawn between two types of counseling groups, growth-centered and problem-centered; and historical perspectives were presented, as well as the value of group counseling for children. The second part of the chapter focused on the key concepts of ethics, group dynamics, organization, and implementation, and on the developmental stages of groups. Objectives, activities, and recommended counselor response skills were discussed for each group stage. The chapter concluded with several recommended resources.

REFERENCES AND RECOMMENDED READINGS

ABRAMOWITZ, C. The effectiveness of group psychotherapy with children. *Archives of General Psychiatry,* 1976, 33, 320–326.

AMERICAN PSYCHOLOGICAL ASSOCIATION. *Casebook on ethical standards of psychologists.* Washington, DC: APA, 1967.

AXLINE, V. *Play therapy.* Boston: Houghton Mifflin, 1974.

COREY, G. *Theory and practice of group counseling.* Monterey, CA: Brooks/Cole, 1981.

———. & COREY, M. *Groups: Process and practice.* (2nd ed.) Belmont, CA: Brooks/Cole, 1982.

DUNCAN, J. Group counseling with adolescents in the school setting. In J. Cull & R. Hardy (Eds.) *Counseling high school students: Special problems and approaches.* Springfield, IL: Charles C Thomas, 1974.

———. & GUMAER, J. *Developmental groups for children.* Springfield, IL: Charles C Thomas, 1980.

DYER, W. & VRIEND, J. *Counseling techniques that work.* New York: Funk & Wagnalls, 1977.

EGAN, G. *Encounter: Group processes for interpersonal growth.* Belmont, CA: Brooks/Cole, 1970.

FAUST, V. *The counselor-consultant in the elementary school.* Boston: Houghton Mifflin Co., 1968.

GAZDA, G. *Group counseling: A developmental approach.* (2nd ed.) Boston: Allyn & Bacon, 1978.

———, DUNCAN, J., & MEADOWS, M. Group counseling and group procedures— report of a survey. *Counselor Education and Supervision, 1967, 9,* 305–310.

GILL, S. & BARRY, R. Group focused counseling; Classifying the essential skills. *Personnel and Guidance Journal,* 1982, 60(5), 302–305.

GLANZ, E. & HAYES, R. *Groups in guidance.* (2nd ed.) Boston: Allyn & Bacon, 1967.

HANSEN, J., WARNER, R., & SMITH, E. *Group Counseling: Theory and process.* Chicago: Rand McNally, 1976.

IVEY, A. Demystifying the group process: Adapting microcounseling procedures to counseling in groups. *Educational Technology,* 1973, 13, 27–31.

LAKIN, M., LIEBERMAN, M., & WHITAKER, D. Issues in the training of group psychotherapists. *International Journal of Group Psychotherapy,* 1969, 19, 307–325.

LIEBERMAN, M., YALOM, I., & MILES, M. *Encounter groups: First facts.* New York: Basic Books, 1973.

MAHLER, C. *Group counseling in the schools.* Boston: Houghton Mifflin Co., 1969.

NATIONAL TRAINING LABORATORY. *Standards for the use of laboratory method.* Rosslyn Station, VA: NTL Institute Programs, October 1969.

OHLSEN, M. Counseling children in groups. *The School Counselor,* 1967, 15, 343–349.

———. *Group counseling.* New York: Holt, Rinehart & Winston, 1969.

———. *Group counseling.* New York: Holt, Rinehart & Winston, 1977.

PARLOFF, M. & DIES, R. Group psychotherapy outcome research 1966–1975. *International Journal of Group Psychotherapy,* 1977, 27, 281–319.

ROBERTS, A. Ethical guidelines for group leaders. *Journal for Specialists in Group Work,* 1982, 7, 174–181.

Rose, S. *Treating children in groups.* San Francisco: Jossey-Bass, 1975.

Schaefer, C., Johnson, L., & Wherry, J. *Group therapies for children and youth.* San Francisco: Jossey-Bass, 1982.

Simon, S., Howe, L., & Kirschenbaum, H. *Values clarification.* New York: Hart Publishing Co., 1972.

Slavson, S. *An introduction to group therapy.* New York: Commonwealth Fund, 1943.

Stockton, N. Behavioral group counseling. *Journal for Specialists in Group Work,* 1980, 5, 189–195.

Stockton, R. The education of group leaders: A review of the literature with suggestions for the future. *Journal for Specialists in Group Work,* 1980, 5, 55–62.

—— & Moran, K. The use of verbal feedback in counseling groups: Toward an effective system. *Journal for Specialists in Group Work,* 1980, 5, 10–14.

Yalom, I. *The theory and practice of group psychotherapy.* (2nd ed.) New York: Basic Books, 1975.

Yunker, J. Essential organizational components of group counseling in the primary grades. *Elementary School Guidance and Counseling,* 1970, 4, 172–179.

Chapter 11

Growth-Centered
Group Counseling

MOST OF THE RECENT LITERATURE on group therapy with children has reported use of theory and techniques for helping troubled children. Little evidence exists that indicates the effectiveness of group counseling as a method to help children learn about developmental crises and how to cope effectively with these normal life events. In fact, in the last decade, these concerns have been handled in most schools and agencies in classroom situations by teachers who have had little or no training in these areas (Borton, 1970; Brown, 1971; Gorman, 1974; Weinstein & Fantini, 1970).

All children, including those considered "normal," need opportunities to explore and examine their values, beliefs, and decisions as they become more independent. To ensure the proper conditions for exploration of these private matters, group counseling is the environment of choice. To differentiate this type of counseling group from one which would include troubled children, I have labeled the two types of group situations growth-centered group counseling and problem-centered group counseling. The remainder of this chapter includes a definition of growth-centered group counseling, the value of growth-centered counseling groups, key concepts in the formation of this type of group, and detailed examples of growth-centered counseling groups.

Growth-centered group counseling involves the structuring of the necessary conditions, dynamics, interpersonal processes, and therapeutic functions of a counseling group. Group members are normal children who use the group structure and interactions to explore and examine personal values, beliefs, attitudes, and decisions to gain greater awareness, understanding, and acceptance of self and others. Growth-centered counseling groups are structured to help children realize and utilize their inner resources to cope with developmental problems and lead more self-fulfilled lives.

The Value of Growth-Centered Group Counseling

In order for children to prepare themselves for their adult lives, they need to learn who they are, how they think, what they believe, and how they relate to others. Everything children do, every decision they make or action they take, is based on the collective interaction of their values, beliefs, attitudes, feelings, and behaviors. All these factors are examined when therapists are helping children in growth-centered group counseling toward greater self-awareness, self-understanding, self-responsibility and self-worth.

Children encounter developmental concerns every day of their lives. They need to learn what and how to think, believe, and behave for themselves in a variety of situations. Growth-centered group counseling creates the atmosphere for children to capitalize on their inner energies to enhance their personal growth. Children are given opportunities to discuss their thoughts, feelings, and behaviors and compare themselves with others who are at about the same age and place in life. Out of these discussions, a sense of acceptance, caring, support, and encouragement is developed, enhancing feelings of security, self-assurance, and belongingness, which are all essential factors leading to higher levels of personal growth. Once children gain greater personal insight and better understand how others think, feel, and behave, they are more aware of themselves and their environment and are living more realistically. This increased self-awareness and reality leads in turn to greater self-understanding, which helps children gain more control of their lives and better organize for effective day-to-day living. Children who are in control and well-organized tend to be more self-confident and responsible and make better choices. They believe in themselves and undertake tasks readily without fear and, as a result, experience more success and less failure. Through reinforcement of these efforts, they continue to develop greater levels of self-esteem. From this point, children's development can become a positive, personal cyclic force leading from greater self-awareness and self-understanding to increased self-confidence and responsibility to development of more personal skills and self-esteem continuing to even higher levels of awareness. Once in place, this positive personal growth cycle has potential to endure throughout life.

KEY CONCEPTS

In organizing for group counseling, therapists must be aware of fundamental differences between growth-centered and problem-centered groups. Beyond the differences of purpose and goals of the groups lie several other key organizational considerations which influence the formation of the group and the ultimate outcome of the group experience. The type of group, the purpose of the group, and its goals should, however, act as a guide when considering these additional organizational factors in group formation. Mahler (1969) described 10 steps in the formation of a counseling group, and Duncan and Gumaer (1980) discussed 13 organizational parameters for growth-centered experiences. I have taken the liberty to combine these authors efforts and discuss what I consider to be only the crucial elements in forming a growth-centered counseling group that were not discussed in Chapter 10. These four components include: selection of group members, group size, length and frequency of sessions, and duration of the group. I have also included evaluation as a key concept in this chapter because it is applicable for both growth-centered and problem-centered groups.

Selection of Group Members

For growth-centered groups to be effective, it is my belief that participants be selected from a volunteer pool. I realize in many agencies children are required to participate in group therapy. However, it has been my experience that forced participation tends to create disruptive influences that can lead to harmful experiences. If children are not ready for group counseling, and many are not, they should not become part of a counseling group. In these instances, individual therapy should be a treatment of choice.

Ohlsen (1970) wrote, "By careful selection of clients a counselor can increase his chances of helping them. He must be free to accept only those clients whom he feels reasonably certain can be helped in his group. . . ." (p. 105).

Once children have volunteered and been interviewed, balancing factors of age, sex, prior acquaintance, and personality predominate. A good rule of thumb is to include children in groups who are about the same age or grade level. It is best not to place children in counseling groups who are more than one year or one grade apart. For example, a child who is 8 years old in the third grade may work well in a group with 7- or 9-year-old children who are in the second grade or fourth grade respectively. Usually the 7-year-old child will not function well with 9-year-old children or vice versa.

Many authors (Dinkmeyer & Caldwell, 1970; Keat, 1974) suggest same-sexed groups for children in grades one to six. I feel that learning to recognize and function with sexual differences is a natural part of children's development. By and large, children live and learn in mixed sex households and mixed sex classrooms. It makes little sense to me that we disrupt this pattern until children reach an age (preadolescence) where contact with the opposite sex in group could increase anxiety to the detriment of group members. I would also recommend racial integration of children's groups for the same reasons. The membership of growth-centered counseling groups should reflect, as much as possible, the community environment outside the group. However, it is crucial to remember that balance, and not integration, is the key factor. Ideally, a group of eight children would include four boys and four girls, two of each sex being black and two white. It would be poor group formation to include one girl with a group of seven boys or one white child with seven blacks. Remember, however, that perfect balance in groups is rarely, if ever, achieved. The group therapist's task is to work toward creating less imbalance in groups.

Once age and sex have been considered, counselors must weigh the effects prior acquaintance and personality differences will have on the success of the group. Some children work well together in groups, some do not. For example, to place a child who is disliked by most others in a growth-centered group could lead to scapegoating. In the individual interview, children should be asked whether or not they can work with other children who are also potential group members. Some control for balancing, identifying liked children and disliked children, can then be exercised by the leader. Therapists must be very careful not to include in the group children who have such dissimilar backgrounds or divergent personalities that communication is impaired and the group unable to function.

Group Size

Because growth-centered groups depend on the quality and depth of discussion generated by members, it is imperative that a minimum of four participants be maintained. With fewer than four children, the range of thought that is offered in discussion is limited. With six to eight group members, the variety and the scope of material discussed is greatest. With more than eight children, some members may avoid participation and involvement, whereas others may dominate more easily. In fact, with large numbers, the counselor's role may change to be more like a teacher and the group may interact more like a classroom group including all of the inherent problems of class populations. With more than eight children in a group, it becomes extremely difficult for therapists to control environmental factors, group dynamics, and group process that influence the group in a positive or negative direction.

Group size should be determined after examining several variables including the purpose of the group, age of children, developmental level, and time available. One rule of thumb to use as a guide is the younger the children, the smaller the group. Children between the ages 5 and 8 are less mature, are not as well developed in verbal skills, and tend to be distracted more easily than their older counterparts. As a result, it is best for growth-centered groups with these ages to be confined to a maximum of four to six children. The smaller the group the more individual attention the counselor can give to the children. Older, more mature, children will work well in growth-centered groups of six to eight.

As a part of group size, the issue of an open or closed group needs to be examined. Once the group is established, it is unwise to include new members. The addition of children changes the nature and dynamics of the group. It forces the group to regress and work toward including the new member. All the necessary conditions for group development must be reestablished with new membership. Closed groups are easier for therapists to organize, to establish, and to control. Children also benefit in that they gain greater levels of security and belongingness.

Length and Frequency of Sessions

Planning for the length and frequency of growth-centered group sessions depends on two basic factors, time available and age of children. Reality has indicated that many groups must be scheduled into an already established time frame, such as a school activity period, which counselors cannot control. In this case, counselors need to reconsider the number of children to be in their group. The length of each session should allow a minimum of five minutes of talking time for each child excluding therapist talk. For example, a 40-minute time period could accommodate adequately no more than six children at five minutes each—a total of 30 minutes—and a counselor at 10 minutes. Unfortunately, therapists tend to talk twice as much as any one child in a group and usually more often than necessary. One must recognize this negative tendency and plan to accommodate it.

If counselors have the luxury of planning without institutional time restrictions, I would recommend a minimum of one group session and a maximum of two group sessions per week. As mentioned in Chapter 10, when meeting twice a week, practical experience has demonstrated that alternating days are best (Monday and Wednesday or Tuesday and Thursday). In most agencies, Friday is a day set aside for special activities. It behooves counselors not to plan groups on Friday because children could be placed in a compromising situation which forces them to choose between group counseling and other more attractive activities, like play.

Generally, it is best for younger children to meet more frequently for a shorter period of time. For example, one-half hour twice a week with four 6-year-old children is adequate, whereas one hour twice a week with eight 12-year-old children would suffice. Should only one session a week be planned, additional time for discussion must be arranged. Children's lives are full of eventful happenings. Many things will occur and build up in a week's time that will need to be discussed in group. In the above examples, therapists might double the time allotments for each group to one hour for the four 6-year-olds and two hours for the eight 12-year-old children. This time frame may seem excessive for many readers. However, group breaks can be planned, and it is in the interests of children and the counselor to provide more time initially than might be necessary. Once groups are working, there exists a tendency for therapists to allow them to run beyond the prearranged time frame. I believe counselors need to learn to end groups at the designated time no matter what content is being shared. On the other hand, a nonproductive group session can be terminated early.

The above comments should be read as guidelines. More often than not, institutional restraints will dictate the length and frequency of group meetings, and therapists will have to learn to be flexible and creative in their planning. I want to encourage readers not to give up on group counseling because it seems you cannot get adequate meeting time, but rather to learn to live with reality and experiment within the constraints of the institution with time periods to see what works best for you and the children in your setting.

Duration of the Group

It has been my practice to ordinarily establish the number of sessions a counseling group will meet prior to beginning the group. This practice seems especially appropriate for group counselors who are working in settings in which children are available for therapy on a limited basis, which may be predetermined by court decisions or the school calendar. For example, in schools, counselors have about seven weeks without interruption from the first week of October to the beginning of Thanksgiving holidays. It will usually take the counselor the month of September to get organized and for children to become acclimated to the school climate. Following Thanksgiving, it is a few short weeks to the Christmas holidays and most schools become heavily involved in special programs. As a result of the school's fall and winter calendar, it seems reasonable that school counselors' planning time for leading groups requiring more than 12 sessions is immediately before Thanksgiving and after the Christmas holidays.

Little research evidence exists regarding the optimum number of group counseling sessions for any particular type of group. Some authors have identified 10 counseling sessions as a minimum number (Dinkmeyer & Muro, 1971; Mahler, 1969). It has been my experience that 10 sessions are not adequate to facilitate lasting change in children's behavior. However, 10 to 15 sessions have been sufficient to effect change in children's level of self-awareness and self-understanding and ultimately attitudinal change, which is one of the primary purposes of growth-centered counseling groups.

At times, counseling groups may be formed for special reasons which will not require 10 or more sessions. Examples might include a group for the orientation of new children to school who are not especially fearful or problem-ridden and a group for the discussion of personal hygiene for girls who have begun menstruation. In both these instances there exists specific but limited concerns and the goals for the groups could be accomplished in four to six extended sessions of one hour or more. For these unique growth groups, therapists might plan one session for introduction to the topic and establishment of the group, one to two sessions for exploration of the topic, two to three sessions for working, and one session for termination. For most growth-centered counseling groups heterogeneity of membership and issues is advantageous. However, for the unique, brief growth-centered groups homogeneity of topic and membership works best.

Although I try to structure the number of group counseling sessions early, situations do arise which necessitate changing the purpose or focus of a group briefly and extending the duration of the group to accomplish established goals. Flexibility is therefore an important characteristic for group therapists to possess. Counselors can demonstrate flexibility by putting aside their planned agendas and focusing on more pressing, immediate needs of group members. For example, a graduate student in group counseling practicum was leading a growth-centered counseling group for adolescent females on friendship when one member committed suicide. In supervision, the student was encouraged to interrupt her original direction and focus the next few group sessions on death and the loss of a friend. Although the student was quite distraught herself, she was able to face the issue and help her group accept and learn from the unfortunate circumstance before returning to the original purpose.

In addition to the previous example, therapists can never realistically predict when they might become ill or be forced to miss a group session themselves because of a personal crisis. It is easier for counselors to organize for one or two sessions more than seem necessary in the beginning than to try and build in additional time after the group has already begun. Practicality has indicated that over an extended time, one or two group sessions will have to be cancelled and either made up or eliminated.

Evaluation of Self and the Group

Evaluation can and should encompass many aspects of a therapist's role. As the "measurement" expert, counselors are often assigned the role of testing coordinator in schools and agencies. Parts of this function include: coordinating all the state-mandated achievement testing, providing inservice test training for staff members, serving as chairperson of test evaluation committees to select the "best" tests for a particular population, and serving as the coordinator of screening services for pupil evaluation for special education services. With all these evaluation responsibilities, I am not surprised when therapists resist evaluating themselves or their group experiences. However, counselors can ill afford not to evaluate their effectiveness to provide documentation for supervisors, staff members, parents, and children. The economics of our times dictate that public institutions and agencies be above all cost-efficient, productive, and accountable. Therapists who assume that their clientele accept blindly their abilities to help and that they value these above other professionals' helping capacities are unrealistic. Counselors need to protect their positions by collecting and disseminating evidence of their helping skill.

Regardless of the need to be accountable and the realistic possibility of losing jobs, therapists are in the business of helping children to bring about change in attitudes or behavior. As a result, counselors need to formulate methods to periodically review the effectiveness of their intervention strategies and the impact of these techniques on children's thinking and behavior. In the beginning of this book, the counselor's ability to assess individual client needs was discussed. The simplest way to accomplish this task when working with group counseling is to identify group goals and to plan specific, clear objectives for each group session and group activities to meet these objectives. These objectives and activities should be planned using developmental group theory and lead to the accomplishment of group goals. By putting these statements in writing, it is then possible to measure, with appropriate instrumentation, a group member's thinking and behavior before and after group intervention. This pregroup and postgroup group assessment is simplistic and not without contamination. However, it does provide therapists a source of information which connects their behavior to group goals, and a cause-and-effect relationship can be argued for counselors' impact on group members. At the very minimum, a postgroup assessment of children's feelings about the group experience should be conducted by the therapist. In addition, as mentioned in Chapter 10 under the guidelines for planning individual group counseling sessions, a session-by-session subjective evaluation should be made by group counselors of their skills, the activities used, individual group members' performance, and overall group progress. This evaluation can be kept as a brief written commentary in diary or log form. Some excellent resources on using tests in counseling and measures of attitudes are included in the recommended readings section (Crabbs & Crabbs, 1977; Goldman, 1971; Goldman, 1978; Robinson & Shaver, 1973; Shaw & Wright, 1967).

GROWTH-CENTERED GROUP EXAMPLES

As an elementary school counselor, I had the opportunity to organize and lead several growth-centered counseling groups with children ranging in age from 5 to 13. The following examples of growth-centered groups were all planned, implemented, and evaluated by me with children in the schools. I chose to share these particular examples because they represent positive group experiences on important developmental issues to both primary-grade-level children and intermediate-grade-level children. The activities used can be modified and adapted easily by readers to accommodate the developmental level of most children. This first example, the friendship group, is structured systematically and specifically for readers to include goals, objectives for each session, group activities, evaluation methods, and counselor anecdotes. Because both examples, are reprinted in part they provide general descriptions.

Example 1. *The Friendship Group* *

This particular group was implemented with eight fifth-grade children. Ten group sessions were planned once a week for 45 minutes. Some of the group goals were to (1) increase children's knowledge of self, (2) increase children's knowledge of classmates, (3) increase children's awareness and understanding of feelings in self and others, and (4) increase children's friendships.

Session 1

Objectives: 1. To establish the group by getting children involved.
               2. To get acquainted.
               3. To become aware of the concept friendship.

* Gumaer, J. Affective education through the friendship class. *The School Counselor*, 1976, 23(4), 257–263. Reprinted in part with permission of The American Personnel and Guidance Association.

Activities: 1a. Counselor asked, "Is there anyone in the group who can name everyone else?"

      b. Draw a picture of an animal that describes you as a person. Cut it out. Write your first name on the front and two reasons you selected this animal on the back.

      2. Guessing game—counselor collected animals and asked children to guess who made what animal. Game continued until all children were identified with their respective animals.

      3. Counselor asked, "Can anyone describe what a friend is?"

Anecdotes: Not one child was able to give both first and last names for all others. One example of a child's animal pictures was a dog because "I am fast and like to play with people." Children enjoyed the guessing game and wanted to share all their reasons. They described a friend as someone who "plays with you," "talks to you," and "helps you with schoolwork or when you are hurt." I emphasized that in order to be friends, we must get to know and understand one another better.

Session 2

Objectives: 1. To continue to get acquainted.

      2. To self-disclose at a superficial or intermediate level.

      3. To become aware of self as a friend.

Activities: 1a. Each child was given an opportunity to name everyone in the group.

      b. Volunteers were asked to name group members and identify each member's animal.

      c. One child was allowed to attempt to name all group members, their animals, and provide one reason for each group member's animal choice.

      2. Unfinished sentences were distributed; for example: Friends like me when _____. The best thing I like about me as a friend is _____. Something I did for a friend was _____.

Anecdotes: Most children were able to name everyone in the group. Most children associated names with animal pictures. A few children remembered reasons for animal choice. Unfinished sentences created a good deal of discussion that the children seemed to enjoy.

Session 3

Objectives: 1. To continue becoming involved.

      2. To continue self-disclosure at superficial or intermediate level.

      3. To become aware of others as friends.

Activities: 1. As an introductory activity to all remaining sessions, volunteers practiced naming and sharing something they had learned about other children.

      2. and 3. Unfinished sentences were again distributed, such as: Friends help me when _____. Something a

friend did for me was _____. Some things that
are different about my friends are _____. One
of the best times I had with a friend was _____.

Anecdotes: Group doing well. Nothing unusual.

Session 4

Objectives: 1. To begin to self-disclose at an intermediate or deep level.
              2. To initiate positive feedback.
              3. To become aware of and understand feelings in self and others.
              4. To relate feelings to friendship.

Activities: 1, 3, and 4. Personal shield—draw symbols for the following: a time
              my friends and I were happy, a time my friends and I were angry,
              a time my friends and I were confused, and a time my friends and I
              were frightened.

              2, 3, and 4. Feedback sentence—consisted of addressing the person by
              name, describing the person's behavior, and telling how the
              behavior makes one feel. Counselor initiated children's use of the
              sentence by saying, "Often we wish to express our pleasant feelings
              to our friends, yet we don't quite know how to put them into
              words. Learning to express feelings requires practice. Let's take a
              few moments and, using the feedback sentence, express pleasant
              feelings to others in the group."

Anecdotes: Animated discussion throughout the entire session. All children ex-
              pressed that pleasant feedback made them feel good and that they
              wanted to say nice things to other children in return.

Session 5

Objectives: 1. To continue to self-disclose at an intermediate or deep level and
              give positive feedback.
              2. To continue awareness and understanding of feelings in self and
              others.
              3. To continue to relate feelings and behavior to friendship.

Activities: 1, 2, and 3. Pantomime — A deck of three-by-five-inch index cards
              with one feeling word written on each card was introduced. The
              therapist selected one and instructed the group to guess the feeling
              as he acted it out. Once the feeling was identified, children were
              encouraged to disclose a time in their lives they felt this way and
              what might have caused the feeling. The activity continued with
              each child acting out feelings.

              1, 2, and 3. Charades — the counselor divided the group into two
              teams. Using the same set of cards, he moderated the game with a
              stopwatch. The game was repeated and discussion followed focus-
              ing on teamwork, cooperation, and sportsmanship.

              3. As a culminating activity, the therapist asked, "How does your be-
              havior and feelings influence friends?"

Anecdotes: Children very animated and spontaneous in role play. Activities were fun and generated excellent discussion. The last question was difficult for the children to answer. One child said, "If I act nice, I feel good and kids like me. If I don't, they won't."

Session 6

Objectives: The same as Session 5.

Activities: Counselor introduced this session by saying, "Usually when we are first getting to know a friend, we share things about ourselves that are not too important. However, to really understand each other and become close friends, it is necessary to disclose our deeper thoughts and feelings." Children were then encouraged to share:
1. A time in my life I was troubled and had no one to talk to was _____ .
2. The worst time in my life was _____ .
Discussion followed each activity. The therapist concluded the group by saying, "Last week we played games in group and had fun. We want friends in our life to share in our good times, but we also depend on friends when we are having problems. What is one problem you might want a friend to help you with right now?"

Anecdotes: A drastic change in mood from previous week. It was expected. Children very thoughtful and considerate.

Session 7

Objectives: The same as in Session 6.

Activities: Children were instructed to write a one-paragraph story about a time in their lives. The story had to contain a minimum of five feeling words. A personal example was provided by the counselor for the children to emulate.

Once completed, the children's stories were read to the group. Children identified feeling words, and the counselor emphasized the importance of identifying and understanding feelings in self and friends.

Anecdotes: Children resisted writing. Some experienced difficulty with feeling words, but all completed the assigned task and participated.

Session 8

Objectives: 1. To continue the objectives of Sessions 5, 6, and 7.
2. To introduce negative feedback.
3. To begin readiness for termination.

Activities: 1. Letter writing. Counselor introduced the session by saying, "Often we have thoughts and feelings about our friends. Yet, we do not express ourselves to them. Let's write a friendly letter to a person outside the group." An example of a friendly letter was provided, including heading and salutation. Children were encouraged to describe their feelings about events in the letters.

2. Feedback sentence. Using the sentence introduced in Session 4, children were encouraged to select and give another group member first positive, then negative, feedback. To begin, the therapist modeled the experience. The activity continued until everyone, counselor included, had received positive and negative feedback. Discussion focused on feelings when receiving negative feedback from friends and behavior alternatives when receiving negative feedback.

3. Summarization. Therapist reviewed group's progress to date and emphasized that only two sessions remained.

Anecdotes: Counselor mailed all children's letters. Children indicated it was easier to give negative feedback than receive it. They mentioned, "I got mad," "I wanted revenge," "I wanted to leave," "it was not true," and "right on."

Session 9

Objectives: The same as Session 8.

Activities: 1. Role Play. Counselor separated the group in half and instructed one group to develop a skit and be ready to act out, "Some ways to make new friends," and "Some ways to understand and help current friends." The second group was assigned the topics, "Some ways to improve friendships," and "Things one should not do with friends."

2. Role Play. The entire group worked to develop dramas related to, "Family as friends."

Following role plays discussion focused first on the feelings and behaviors of characters in the role play. The therapist then asked the children in the group, "Have any of these experiences happened to you?" Lastly, the counselor focused on the children's feelings of immediacy in planning and presenting the role plays.

3. Summarization. Counselor again reinforced the group's progress and pointed out that this was the next-to-last session.

Anecdotes: Children participated in role play readily and enjoyed it a great deal. Children quiet when reminded of upcoming termination. One child asked, "Do we have to stop?" Counselor's reply was, "Yes, we must stop the group."

Session 10

Objectives: 1. To provide support and encouragement to group members.
2. To evaluate the group.
3. To close the group.

Activities: 1. Strength bombardment. For a description of this activity, readers are referred to the discussion in Chapter 10 on termination.

2. Children were asked to complete a post group questionnaire which contained five descriptive statements related to their perceptions of friendship. They expressed their opinions by responding on a five-point Likert-type scale ("strongly agree" to "strongly disagree").

3. Following completion of the questionnaire, the therapist asked children for additional reactions to the group experience. Children were highly positive in their comments. They appreciated especially the sharing of thoughts and feelings and making new friends.

Anecdotes: On the postgroup questionnaire, 88 percent of the children agreed or strongly agreed to the first statement—"I feel this group helped me know more about myself." Only one child disagreed. Children agreed 100 percent to the second statement—"I feel this group helped me know more about others." To the third statement — "I feel that I have made more friends as a result of the group" — 75 percent of the children agreed, one was uncertain and one disagreed. One hundred percent of the group concurred with the last two statements, "I feel other children would enjoy this kind of group," and "I would be willing to participate in another counseling group."

Example 2. *Peer Facilitated Groups* *

The Peer Facilitator

The peer facilitator is a child trained by a counselor to work with other students. He is able to begin a small-group discussion and to use the facilitating responses of clarifying, reflecting, and giving feedback. The child can encourage other group members to explore their ideas and feelings. The peer facilitator can also help the counselor demonstrate concepts presented for discussion in a classroom. In brief, he is a leader of other children who is prepared to facilitate discussion among his peers.

Some fundamental steps for developing a program using peer facilitators are:

1. Select students who are potential facilitators;
2. Teach them facilitating responses;
3. Introduce human relations and social adjustment topics to the peer facilitator's group for practice and discussion;
4. Present the same topics in the classroom, using peer facilitators as assistants in role playing and demonstrations; and
5. Organize small classroom discussion groups which are led by peer facilitators.

* Gumaer, J. Peer facilitated groups. *Elementary School Guidance and Counseling,* 1973, 8(1), 4–11. Reprinted in part with permission of the American Personnel and Guidance Association.

In the beginning, the counselor administered a classroom sociogram and, with the aid of the teachers, identified students who appeared to be leaders. He reviewed their cumulative records and gathered additional information such as test scores, family history, previous academic performance, and teacher comments. The counselor also observed in the classrooms and interviewed children in order to make their acquaintance and to further assess the children's potential as peer facilitators.

A potential peer facilitator may be a child who others prefer to be with and to have as a friend. A quiet child who is willing to help others might be a better helper than one who is outgoing and outspoken. A child who has some academic difficulties, yet performs well on the playground and is a leader of games, may also offer possibilities as a peer facilitator.

Preparing the Peer Facilitator

The counselor selected eight 11-year-old peer facilitators, including an equal number of boys and girls, blacks and whites, to meet for 12 group-training sessions. The sessions were scheduled for one-half hour each day over a three-week period. The counselor generally began each session with a 15-minute presentation related to group leadership such as facilitating group discussion and being a good listener. The group then practiced discussion and listening skills.

Session 1

In the first training session, the children seated themselves in a circle, with blacks sitting next to whites and boys next to girls. The group got acquainted. The counselor asked for a volunteer to introduce himself and to name other members in the group. Each child was given an opportunity to name all the other members in the group. This procedure created familiarity and thereby fostered group cohesiveness. The counselor then encouraged the group to discuss the question, What is a leader? Some of the ideas expressed were: A leader "takes charge," "makes decisions," "shows the way by providing an example for others," and "helps others learn."

As the meeting progressed, guidelines for group discussion were identified and established. The basic rules agreed upon were: (a) one person speaks at a time; (b) raise your hand before speaking; (c) it is okay to express any thought or feeling; (d) when talking, make it brief; and (e) be a good listener. The trainees began to ask questions such as: "What do I do when someone refuses to talk? What if a fight starts?" The group briefly discussed the counselor's, teacher's, and facilitator's role in these and other possible situations. The total program was clarified, and all the children agreed to participate in additional training sessions and eventually in the classroom.

Session 2

During the second training session, the trainees learned more about facilitative responses. This skill session encouraged self-disclosure, improved listening habits, and increased the number of helping responses. The group began sharing information about relatively safe topics, such as "what I like and dislike about school: and "what are your favorite hobbies?" In one skill exercise, the students listed five things that no one else in the group knew about them. No child was forced to discuss items, but everyone was encouraged to talk about themselves and the experience of writing the list.

Session 3

In the third session the counselor asked the group, "What is meant by listening? What are some ways to show that you are listening?" He emphasized that group members should look at the person who is talking and listen to what is being said. To practice listening, the counselor randomly chose group members to repeat what someone had said.

A clarifying response was then explained as one way to help group members understand better or to make the picture of shared information more complete. For example, "Bob, let me see if I'm following you. You said that your team won the game after you hit a homerun?" "Joe, it seems that you don't want Tommy to bother you."

A reflecting response was illustrated as being analogous with the reflection from a mirror. A mirror provides the observer with an image of himself. Likewise, the facilitator reflects by repeating that which another has expressed while also pointing out the feelings which the speaker might be experiencing. For example, "Bob smiled when he said that his team won the game last night. You were excited, Bob, to win the game."

Session 4

In the fourth session, children were introduced to the idea of effective feedback. Feedback was explained as a way of letting someone know how you feel about something he is saying or doing. The sentence pattern described in the Friendship Group was used to assist in learning the concept. To practice feedback, the counselor divided the children into triads with one child talking, one facilitating, and one observing and giving feedback. The roles were then rotated giving each child a chance to experience all three roles.

Sessions 5 & 6

In the fifth and sixth sessions, a review of previously presented material was made with special attention to practicing facilitating skills. The remaining group sessions dealt with the discussion of special topics, such as majority and minority groups, stereotypes, prejudice, and decision-making in problem situations such as name calling, teasing, and fighting.

Session 7

In the seventh training session, students defined the concepts of majority and minority. They also identified various types of minorities within the group. Some children had sneakers and others had shoes; a few of the girls wore dresses while most of the group wore pants; and more members had long hair than short hair. These observations were related to the discussion. The group then completed a worksheet which required each member to identify pictures of minority groups. As the discussion progressed, each child also identified himself as a member of a particular ethnic group.

Sessions 8 through 11

In the eighth and ninth sessions, stereotypes, prejudices, and discrimination were defined and discussed. Stories such as "How Different Are We?" (Limbacher, 1969) and "After You, My Dear Alphonse" (Jackson, 1968) were read, and the group was asked to identify the stereotypes and prejudices involved. The children also related painful conflicts they had experienced in school resulting from the intolerance of others, such as being called "nigger" or "redneck," being left out of games because of sex or color, having money stolen, being sexually assaulted, and being discriminated against by teachers.

During the next two sessions, the group members further explored their values, attitudes, and feelings and examined alternative ways of behaving. Role playing was used to facilitate personal involvement and insight. In one instance, a boy and girl walked into the group holding hands, while another child teased them for being boyfriend and girlfriend. The situation was replayed four times. Four alternative ways of behaving in the situation were explored, including ignoring, threatening, fighting, and seeking adult assistance. Following each episode, the counselor asked the group to describe what had happened and how the persons felt. The group members enjoyed role playing when the counselor involved himself, too.

The counselor also presented cases studies of children with anecdotal information. In one case a 13-year-old girl had been suspended from school for physically hurting smaller children by pinching and hitting them. During the discussion of the case, the counselor modeled the facilitating responses previously presented and used the feedback response pattern.

Session 12

In the final training session, students listened to the record "Black and White," as sung by Three Dog Night, worksheets with the words of the song were distributed, and the group discussed the song's meanings. On one occasion, the counselor and group sang along.

The Peer Facilitator in Classroom Groups

After training, peer facilitators were scheduled to lead classroom groups for one-half hour each day for 15 days. The classroom groups were racially mixed and selected according to the counselor's and teacher's perceptions of which children seemed to work best together. It was assumed that each ethnic group needed a facilitator with whom they could identify. Therefore, when possible, each group was assigned one black and one white peer facilitator.

During the first classroom presentation, the counselor explained that each day he would make a brief presentation on a human relations topic followed by a demonstration and small group discussion. The counselor introduced the eight peer facilitators as a part of the demonstration team and small group discussion leaders. The peer facilitators then used the middle of the room to demonstrate how to form a circle for discussion. The rest of the class was asked to observe what happened. A discussion immediately followed during which several children noticed that black students were sitting next to white students. One child in the classroom pointed out that boys were also sitting next to girls. The classroom was then divided into four groups, with each group assigned a part of the room.

The topics and activities presented to the class were essentially the same as those presented during the peer facilitator training sessions and included guidelines for group discussion, self-disclosure, listening, feedback, majorities and minorities, stereotypes, prejudice, discrimination, name calling, teasing, and fighting.

The counselor, for example, introduced the topic of minority groups by asking the class, "What is a minority group?" A general discussion ensued in which the class identified and compared the general characteristics of various minority groups. As the discussion progressed, the counselor asked some of the peer facilitators to form a line in the front of the room. The class identified the minorities within the demonstration group. The class was then divided into small groups and continued the discussion about personal similarities and differences.

Each class presentation and demonstration required approximately 15 minutes. The small group discussions usually lasted another 15 minutes. However, the time for discussion varied and depended on the children's depth of involvement in the discussion. During small-group discussions, the counselor and teacher occasionally met with a group, observed the interaction, encouraged class members who hesitated to participate, and assisted group facilitators who were experiencing difficulty.

After the facilitators worked in their discussion groups, they met as a group with the counselor in his office. The facilitators expressed their concerns and feelings about the experience, discussed possible changes in procedure, and reacted to each other and individuals in the classroom groups. The facilitators also helped develop facilitative strategies such as seating in groups children who did not get along. They also made recommendations for future class presentations such as improvising situations with parents, teachers, and administrators. The counselor scheduled additional meetings for those who wanted or needed individual help.

Evaluation

A preprogram and postprogram questionnaire using a Likert-type scale was completed by the teachers. Data suggested that the children became "more attentive" and "more active" in class discussions and in some cases "more thoughtful and sensitive to others." Some of the children's comments were:

"What I like about this is that we have fun talking about our ideas and feelings."

"I like what we are doing because we are learning some things I never knew."

"I like feedback. It helps me stay out of fights when someone is bugging me."

"I like feedback because you can tell a person how you really feel about certain things."

"I like it because it's fun."

"I don't like it because you sit next to girls."

The peer facilitated group program dealt with interpersonal relationships in the elementary school, but it might also be attempted with older children and applied to such school related concerns as drug use and abuse, the broken home, sex education, career development, and student-teacher relationships.

RECOMMENDED RESOURCES

Books

JONES, J. & PFEIFFER, W. *The annual handbooks for group facilitators.* University Associates, Inc., 7596 Eads Avenue, La Jolla, CA 92037.

These books provide readers with a collection of information, techniques, methods, and activities for group work. The contents include sections on structured experiences, instrumentation, lecturettes, theory and practice, and resources.

SIMON, S., HOWE, L., & KIRSCHENBAUM, H. *Values clarification.* New York: Hart Publishing Co., Inc., 1972.

This book contains 79 strategies designed in a standard format to assist group leaders with values clarification of group members. The format contains a stated purpose for the activity, a step-by-step procedure for implementing the activity, a to-the-teacher (group-leader) component which makes suggestions for processing the activity, and additional suggestions.

Programmed Materials

BALL, G. *Innerchange.* Human Development Training Institute, Inc., 7574 University Avenue, La Mesa, CA 92041, 1977.

This kit addresses adolescent concerns and contains a leader's manual which will help familiarize readers with the instructional units of the program and instructions on how to use the materials. The innerchange instructional units include activities deemed introductory, moderately challenging, and advanced in nature to help children develop personal awareness, mastery, and social interactions.

DINKMEYER, D. *Developing understanding of self and others.* (DUSO Kit D-1). American Guidance Service, Inc., Circle Pines, MN 55014, 1970.
———. *Developing understanding of self and others.* (DUSO Kit D-2). American Guidance Service, Inc., Circle Pines, MN 55014, 1973.

DUSO Kit D-1 was designed for use with children in primary grades K through 3. DUSO Kit D-2 was developed for intermediate grades. Both DUSO programs use an inquiry, experiential, and discussion approach to learning. Each program consists of sequentially planned activities designed to help children cope with the developmental tasks of social and emotional growth. Each DUSO program is organized around eight major themes. DUSO Kit D-1 includes activities on understanding self, feelings, others, independence, goals and purposeful behavior, mastery, emotional maturity, and choices and consequences. DUSO Kit D-2 includes activities focused toward self-identity, friendship, responsible independence, self-reliance, resourcefulness and purposefulness, competence, emotional stability, and responsible choice making.

DUPONT, H. & DUPONT, C. *Transition.* American Guidance Service, Inc., Circle Pines, MN 55014, 1979.

Transition is a set of programmed materials to aid the social–emotional development of children aged 12 to 15. It includes five units: communication and problem solving, encouraging openness and trust, verbal and nonverbal communications of feelings, needs, goals, and expectations, and increasing awareness of values in which children participate in activities which generate discussion about experiences common to adolescence. Each unit contains 14 to 22 activities.

DUPONT, H., GARDNER, S., & BRODY, D. *Toward affective development.* American Guidance Service, Inc., Circle Pines, MN 55014, 1974.

This program was designed for use with children grades three through six. It is divided into five sections comprised of 21 units and 191 lessons. The purpose of the program is to promote psychological and emotional maturity. The five major sections and objectives of the program are (1) reaching in and reaching out, to assist children to extend their openness to experience; (2) your feelings and mine, to help children to recognize and label feelings; (3) working together, to develop skills of cooperation, (4) me: today and tomorrow to help children focus on their unique characteristics and careers; and (5) feeling, thinking, and doing, to help children learn problem-solving behavior.

PALOMARES, U. & BALL, G. *Magic circle: An overview of the human development program.* Human Development Training Institute, La Mesa, CA, 1974.

Magic circle was developed to provide affective educational experiences for children ages 4 to 12. The program consists of a series of systematic and sequentially planned activities focused on self-understanding (awareness), mastery (self-confidence), and human relations (social interaction). Some of the program's objectives include to improve children's self-concept, to increase children's respect for others, to improve interpersonal skills, to understand emotions in self and others, and to assume responsibility for one's behavior.

SUMMARY

The first section of this chapter provided an introduction, rationale, and definition of growth-centered group counseling. The second focused on the key concepts, selection of group members, group size, length and frequency of sessions, duration of the group, and evaluation, which are important considerations in the formation of growth-centered groups. The third provided two examples of growth-centered groups: the friendship group and peer-facilitated group. The last section provided several recommended resources, including books and programmed materials.

REFERENCES AND RECOMMENDED READINGS

BORTON, T. *Reach, touch, and teach.* New York: McGraw-Hill, 1970.

BROWN, G. *Human teaching for human learning: An introduction to confluent education.* New York: The Viking Press, 1971.

CRABBS, S. & CRABBS, M. Accountability: Who does what to whom, when, where, and how? *School Counselor*, 1977, 25, 104–109.

DINKMEYER, D. & CALDWELL, E. *Developmental counseling and guidance: A comprehensive school approach.* New York: McGraw-Hill, 1970.

—— & Muro, J. *Group counseling: Theory and practice.* Itasca, IL: Peacock, 1971.

DUNCAN, J. & GUMAER, J. (EDS.) *Developmental groups for children.* Springfield, IL: Charles C Thomas, 1980.

GOLDMAN, L. (ED.) *Research methods for counselors.* New York: John Wiley & Sons, 1978.

——. *Using tests in counseling.* (2nd ed.) New York: Appleton-Century-Crofts, 1971.

GORMAN, A. *Teachers and learners: The interactive process in education.* Boston: Allyn & Bacon, 1974.

GUMAER, J. Affective education through the friendship class. *The School Counselor*, 1976, 23(4), 257–263.

——.Peer facilitated groups. *Elementary School Guidance and Counseling*, 1973, 8(1), 4–11.

JACKSON, S. *Prejudice: The invisible wall.* New York: Scholastic Book Services, 1968.

KEAT, D. *Fundamentals of child counseling.* Boston: Houghton Mifflin, 1974.

LIMBACHER, W. *Here I am.* Dayton, OH: Pflaum/Standard, 1969.

MAHLER, C. *Group counseling in the schools.* Boston: Houghton Mifflin, 1969.

OHLSEN, M. *Group counseling.* New York: Holt, Rinehart & Winston, 1970.

ROBINSON, J. & SHAVER, P. *Measures of social psychological attitudes.* Ann Arbor, MI: Institute for Social Research, The University of Michigan, 1973.

SHAW, M. & WRIGHT, J. *Scales for measurement of attitudes.* New York: McGraw-Hill, 1967.

WEINSTEIN, G. & FANTINI, M. (EDS.) *Toward humanistic education: A curriculum of affect.* New York: Praeger, 1970.

Chapter 12

Problem-Centered
Group Counseling

IN THE PREVIOUS CHAPTER, the comment was made that most of the existing research on group therapy with children dealt with troubled children. I want to clarify this statement so that readers will not be misled into thinking that there has been a strong professional effort in researching problem-centered group therapy with children. Quite the contrary: for example, although the number of group items reported in two detailed literature reviews demonstrated an increase of more than 150 percent from 308 items in 1976 (Lubin, Reddy, Stansberry, & Lubin, 1977) to 748 items in 1981 (Silver, Lubin, Miller, & Dobson, 1981), the total number of group items reported in these reviews related directly to counseling children slipped from 14 to 12 for the respective years. A further examination of publication trends on group counseling and therapy over the past six years indicated that a small percentage of this literature (an average of approximately 2.5 percent annually) focused on children (Lubin, et al., 1977; Lubin, Reddy, Taylor, & Lubin, 1978; Lubin, Lubin, & Taylor, 1979; Silver, Lubin, Silver, & Dobson, 1980; Silver, et al., 1981). It would, therefore, appear that a dearth exists in the quality and quantity of literature related to problem-centered group counseling of children.

This paucity of research might simply indicate that few mental health professionals are reporting their group therapy experiences with children in the literature. However, it might also indicate that those counselors who are working with children in problem-centered groups are not doing so in an organized, systematic fashion that can be readily documented and published. If the latter statement is accurate, it would imply that many therapists who are working on a "hit-and-miss" basis with children in problem-centered groups are being less successful than they might be. It has been my experience that problem-centered groups need more structure and organization than growth-centered groups and that counselors need to demonstrate more consistency in behavior when working with troubled children. It also seems apparent that more professionals who counsel children in groups need to work harder at sharing their expertise. The remainder of this chapter consists of a definition of problem-centered group counseling, key concepts related specifically to the formation of this type of group, and three detailed examples of problem-centered groups.

Problem-centered group counseling, like growth-centered groups, involves the structuring of the necessary conditions, dynamics, interpersonal processes, and therapeutic functions of a counseling group. However, group counselees are troubled children who are currently experiencing similar personal conflicts or attempting to cope with similar past personal conflicts which, if not resolved, will impede subsequent healthy growth and development. In problem-centered groups, therapists focus on the remediation of children's personal conflicts and inadequacies. Problem-centered groups, therefore, are highly structured, organized, and controlled by the counselor.

The atmosphere of the group must be ordered so that children learn to know what to expect from the therapist at any given time and in turn what is expected of them at all times. This regulation of the group provides children the consistency in their group lives that often is missing elsewhere. No guesswork is required by the child as to consequences for behavior, whether it is positive reinforcement or punishment. Consequences for behavior are established early in the group, spelled out to the children, and maintained and managed by the counselor. In problem-centered groups, therapists assume greater responsibility for all aspects of their group's functioning than they would in growth-centered groups. It has often been my experience that once children complete successfully a problem-centered group, they are then ready to participate in a growth-centered group.

KEY CONCEPTS

As indicated in Chapter 10, "Child-centered Group Counseling," there are many aspects of group therapy that can be generalized to both growth-centered and problem-centered counseling groups for children. As a result, it is important to make a greater differentiation between the two types of groups beyond definitions. In Chapter 11, I discussed in detail four components in forming growth-centered counseling groups: selection of group members, group size, length and frequency of sessions, and duration of the group. Evaluation was also discussed because it is an important concept to both types of groups, but may vary somewhat in application to each type group, as is indicated in the group examples provided. The following discussion of the four elements as they relate to problem-centered groups for children is an attempt to further explicate the distinctions between the two types of groups.

Selection of Group Members

Unlike growth-centered groups, children are usually referred for problem-centered group counseling by others, either teachers or parents. In many cases, the courts or institutions also require group therapy as part of a remedial training program for youthful offenders. Because many children are other-referred or required to attend group, this type of group counseling demands that the therapist spend longer periods of time in the establishment stage, building relationships and levels of trust between and among group members. In addition, anxieties and resistances will be higher for these children; therefore, it takes more time in the exploration and working phases of the group to overcome the discomfort.

Although group therapy may be mandatory for some children before release from an institution, it is important for counselors to interview and screen all prospective participants. Balancing of group members is even more critical in problem-centered group therapy. For example, a graduate student in counseling organized and planned a group for delinquents in her work setting; the administration decided who would be in the group. It consisted of boys ages 12, 13, 14, and 17, and two girls, 12 and 15. The oldest boy was aggressive physically and verbally. He threatened, intimidated, and verbally abused all other members, including the female counselor. This boy should not have been admitted to this group and, once identified as a harmful member, should have been removed. Unfortunately, this action was not taken until the therapist confronted the administration and insisted upon his removal (either the boy was removed or she would stop the group).

Much damage had already been done to the group, some of it irreparable. Even in situations where children are required to participate in group therapy, the counselor must maintain the power and the control in deciding who enters what group and when. In the previous example, the older boy should have received individual counseling until a more appropriate group could be arranged.

All of the factors identified and discussed in Chapter 11 for balancing in growth-centered counseling groups should be considered for balancing problem-centered counseling groups. Additional thought should be given by the therapist to personality differences of prospective members. In the earlier example, it was improper to place shy children with an aggressive child. The timid children were easily dominated and became more submissive and fearful whereas the aggressive child continued to use bullying as an inappropriate method to express unfulfilled needs. Troubled children may possess one or more personality flaws. As a prerequisite to the interview, counselors must prepare or acquaint themselves thoroughly with each child's case history before making decisions after the interview regarding placement in group therapy. To protect further, counselors could also interview adults who are influential in the child's life. Some children are skilled tacticians at manipulating truth and reality to fit the situation. Even the most experienced therapist can be fooled some of the time. A few final words and rules of thumb to follow in selection of members for problem-centered groups are to try to keep the personalities of children and problem behaviors as homogeneous as possible. If you are uncomfortable with the diversity of personalities and concerns of children available for your counseling groups—do not run the groups—trust your feelings and intuitions. If you have no group experience, gain experience by leading several growth-centered groups prior to attempting a problem-centered group. When first attempting problem-centered groups, be sure you are supervised or have access to skilled consultation.

Group Size

The personality and behavior of the troubled child dictate that a problem-centered group consist of fewer children than a growth-centered group. These children need more individualized attention. My general recommendation is that a problem-centered group can be formed and led effectively with a minimum of three children and should not exceed a maximum of six children. Younger or less mature children and children who are experiencing immediate crises or problems of greater severity need to be in smaller sized groups (three to five). Older, more mature, children or children who are coping, in part, with their problems can function in larger sized groups (four to six).

It is also my belief that problem-centered groups should always be closed. Once membership is identified and selected and the group has begun work, no new members are allowed. Experience has shown that pressure often is brought to bear on counselors by parents and other professionals to admit just one more child after the group has begun. It is best to stand firm and state that, "The group is closed. The child will be placed in the next available, proper group setting. Until that time, I will be happy to meet individually with the child or find a suitable referral." If you compromise either the limits of group size or the issue of opening or closing your groups, you increase dramatically the probabilities for group disruption and diminish significantly your opportunities for helping.

Length and Frequency of Sessions

For problem-centered groups, the length and frequency of sessions is usually longer than growth-centered groups. If counselors are forced to schedule this type group into preestablished time schedules that are unchangeable, they must select the size of the group to "fit" the time available. The length of each session should allow a minimum of 10 minutes of talking time per child, excluding therapist talk; five minutes for getting ready to start; and 10 minutes for clean up when necessary. For example, a one-hour period of time would accommodate comfortably three children (30 minutes), the counselor (15 minutes), and cleaning up (15 minutes). It is wise to remember that these children often arrive late and become reluctant to leave the group. You might ask, "What can I do in 30 minutes twice a week?" My reply is "not much," unless you have three very mature young children who are verbal and nonresistant. Do not delude yourself into thinking you can lead effectively a problem-centered group in such a short time frame. In some situations, growth-centered groups are the only groups that can be realistically formed.

If you are able to establish your own time constraints for problem-centered groups, I would recommend a minimum of two group sessions per week and a maximum of daily group meetings. Depending on their concerns, younger children need generally to meet for shorter periods of time more frequently. For example, a group of four 8-year-old children focused on divorce may meet for one hour on Monday, Wednesday, and Friday. Whereas, the same type group for the same number of 12-year-old children might be planned for 1½ hours twice a week. Children who are disruptive or who experience problems in managing and controlling other behaviors, such as abusing alcohol, drugs, and eating habits, may need to meet on a daily basis.

Oftentimes counselors will be able to compensate for some loss in length of sessions by increasing the frequency of their meetings—as well as by reducing the numbers of participants. To the previous question, "What can I do in 30 minutes twice a week?" I responded somewhat negatively. However, the probabilities for a successful group experience are increased when the question is changed to read, "What can I do in 30 minutes five times a week?" The therapist and children now have a total of two and one-half hours of group time each week instead of one hour. Some time will be lost each day to beginning and ending the group in the short 30-minute time frame, but this loss will be absorbed in additional meetings. Generally, the group counselor who meets for shorter periods of time more frequently will need to be better prepared and exercise more control and direction than the group therapist who meets a group for longer periods of time less frequently.

Creativity and flexibility are two important characteristics for group counselors to possess. In many agencies where therapists attempt to implement problem-centered groups in restricted time frames, these characteristics must be used to their upper limits—to manipulate the length and frequency of group meetings and establish adequate time frames. The bottom line is whether the counselor can meet the purpose of the group and accomplish its goals in the time available. If your response is no, do not begin the group. You will only be setting yourself and the children up for a limited and possibly harmful experience. If your reply is maybe and you are relatively inexperienced as a leader, the answer remains the same. If, on the other hand, you say maybe and you have led several other problem-centered groups, go ahead and try the group.

Duration of the Group

Simply stated, problem-centered groups are continued until the purpose and the goals of the group have been accomplished. Unlike growth-centered groups, problem-centered groups require typically more than 15 sessions to observe significant and long-lasting behavioral change in children. However, like growth-centered groups, most problem-centered groups are scheduled with a pre-fixed number of group sessions prior to meeting. In this case, counselors must set realistic, obtainable goals for individuals and the group. For example, a five-week group composed of six obese adolescent females might initiate group therapy by establishing individual goals for weight loss of two pounds per week with an overall group goal for weight loss of 10 pounds per week. At the end of five weeks, it would be expected that individuals lose 10 pounds each and the group loss be at least 50 pounds. Should some children not meet their goals, it is likely others will exceed expected outcomes. As a result, individual failure is not tied directly to nor sufficient for group failure and vice versa. If counselors and counselees desire greater gains, the group can be rescheduled or continued with expanded goals. No doubt the identification and establishment of individual and group goals constitute the single most important determining factor of group duration. However, it is also influenced by other considerations, like personality characteristics of children and environmental factors.

In most problem-centered groups, the personal attitudes and work motivations of group members are extremely low at the outset of the group. With many problem-centered groups, counselors will establish secondary goals, attempting to influence negative attitudes of children in a positive direction. For instance, in the previous example, supplementary goals may be identified to improve children's self-esteem and attitudes toward healthy foods and adequate exercise. Some readers will argue these conditions need to be met prior to weight loss. I will not address this issue of which comes first, "the chicken or the egg" (weight loss or attitude change) of this example. What is important for group therapists is to recognize that it takes longer in group to mold the negative and often divergent personal characteristics of children referred for problem-centered groups.

One might confound the issue of duration further by considering the impact of home environments and parental attitudes on children's ability to lose weight. If parents are obese too, they likely will not support their children. In addition, parents who are not at home cannot monitor the refrigerator or snack habits of their children. Obese children may also use eating as a source of nurturance for loss of parental love or to control anxiety induced by a disruptive home. It would not be unreasonable for counselors to write tertiary goals to try to have an effect on the attitudes of parents and change their involvement with their obese children or to include parents, home, and family as topics for additional group sessions with the children in this problem-centered group. These multiple considerations and decisions group therapists encounter when forming problem-centered groups increase the duration. With the number of elements to be examined and analyzed in this type of group, it is impossible to identify a particular number of counseling sessions that will meet satisfactorily the entire problem or set of problems. Counselors must treat each group as a separate and discrete entity. My best advice is that therapists can expect problem-centered groups to need and to utilize at least twice as much time to fulfill the requirements of each developmental group stage discussed previously. What follows are descriptions of two problem-centered groups. Goals, objectives, specific activities, and evaluation strategies are highlighted for each group.

PROBLEM-CENTERED GROUP EXAMPLES

The following problem-centered groups were planned, implemented, and evaluated in the public schools. These groups are representative of troubled populations counselors will encounter in a variety of institutions and agencies. Although all of the examples have been published as journal articles, and are being reprinted in part with permission in this text, I have attempted to ensure as much consistency in style as possible from the description of one group to the next.

Example 1. Behavioral Group Counseling and Schoolwide Reinforcement Program with Obese Trainable Mentally Retarded Students*

Eleven children, eight females and three males, were referred to the counselor for help in controlling a weight problem. The students, aged 11 to 21, possessed IQ scores ranging from 25 to 55 as measured by a recent administration of the Wechsler Intelligence Scale for Children. Students' height ranged from 53 inches to 65 inches, while their weights ranged from 117 pounds to 219 pounds. A child who was 20 pounds overweight was considered obese. The counselor met individually with the referred children to explain the program. All of the 11 students agreed readily to participate.

Procedures

After consultation with the counselor, the school nurse agreed to work with these students one-half hour each Monday and Wednesday to teach them what foods to eat in maintaining a healthy diet and how to exercise and "burn off" calories.

During these sessions, the nurse reviewed the school lunches emphasizing proper portions of each food and distributed a form, "What I ate today." Students were then instructed to take it home, fill it out with their parents' assistance, and bring the completed form to class to be reviewed the following week. This task helped get parents involved, encouraged parents to plan a balanced diet at home, and helped point out what the students should and should not be eating.

The nurse also obtained the cooperation of cafeteria workers and had them, at the students' request, provide fruit to replace dessert, and low calorie vegetables to replace high calorie starches. Students were also taught how to do physical exercise in class and were encouraged to ride bikes, take walks, and to do other physical activities.

The counselor next discussed the purposes and procedures for the program with teachers in a faculty meeting. It was decided the students would meet in group counseling for 14 weeks once each week for 50 minutes on Friday during the same time period scheduled with the nurse on Mondays and Wednesdays.

Behavioral Group Counseling Sessions

Specific plans were followed which consisted of objectives and brief descriptions of activities. Each counseling session began with weigh-ins

* Gumaer, J. & Simon, R. *Education and Training of the Mentally Retarded*, 1979, 14(2), 106–111. Reprinted in part with permission of the Division on Mental Retardation, The Council for Exceptional Children, 1920 Association Drive, Reston, VA.

and concluded with reinforcement (choosing activity cards) for those students who achieved target weight.

Throughout the group sessions, the counselor encouraged self-disclosure and discussion, responded to students' thoughts and feelings ₅bout eating behaviors, pointed out similarities and differences in students' feelings and behaviors, and helped students explore consequences for overeating. The TMR students were extremely non-verbal and the counselor had to direct discussion almost entirely. In addition, it was necessary to respond to many non-verbal cues. For example, as one student puffed air into her cheeks, the counselor responded, "Patty, do you mean that your face is chubby?" Patty replied, "No, fat." A brief outline of each counseling session's objectives, activities, and counselor anecdotes follows:

Session	Objectives	Activities	Anecdotes
1	(a) Get to know one another. (b) Begin group discussion.	Imaginary friend. Students cut out pictures of persons they would like for a friend from magazines and pasted them to construction paper. Each student then discussed their picture with the group.	Counselor began discussion with "What were some reasons you chose this picture as a friend?" Most students nonverbal; counselor asked many open-ended questions. No one selected a fat person.
2	(c) Continue to develop group involvement. (d) Begin self-awareness.	If I could be anybody. Students painted on construction paper a picture of who they would like to be. The pictures were shared and discussed.	Many of the pictures represented a friend or parent. No one painted a fat person. Counselor directed group and responded to many non-verbal cues.
3	(e) Discuss being thin.	If I were skinny. Students were directed into two groups. Each group was instructed to dramatize one of two situations: at the pool, at the school dance.	Children seemed to enjoy role play and imagining they were thin. Much laughter and applause at end. Students verbalized difference between "skinny" and "fat."
4	(f) Recognize and discuss obesity.	Seeing myself. Students instructed to look at themselves in a full-length mirror. Each student shared something liked and	Counselor elicited positive feedback from group members. Members encouraged each other, for example, "You can do it."

Session	Objectives	Activities	Anecdotes
		something he/she would like to change.	Obesity discussed in a positive way.
5	(g) Recognize and discuss obesity in self.	Myself. Students were instructed to draw a picture of themselves using the mirror for help. A discussion followed focused on obesity.	All pictures were realistic and indicated obesity. Students modeled repeatedly in front of mirror.
6	(h) Discuss feelings on being obese.	Ugly remarks. Using puppets as a projective device each student told his/her feelings when called "fat."	Students' comments were realistic, e.g., "I'm fat. It hurts to be called fat." The puppets stimulated self-disclosure. Many students were non-verbal but made faces.
7	(i) Discuss feelings of being obese.	Role play. Students dramatized two situations: (a) children on the playground. No one wanted Mary on their team. She was too "fat" and couldn't run. (b) Overheard adults talking about how awful it was for a child to be so fat.	Students very realistic in portrayals. Students made up their own situations and shared times in their lives similar things happened.
8	(j) Recognize personal responsibility for obesity.	Christmas dinner. Counselor asked children to close eyes. A fantasy describing the preparation, aromas, and eating of Christmas dinner was presented. Children discussed what they experienced.	Students identified proper portions of different food groups to eat and agreed they were responsible to refuse second helpings. Many students felt ashamed for eating so much. All students said they enjoyed fantasy.
9	(k) Recognize personal responsibility for obesity.	Christmas dinner. Members shared what they ate on Christmas day.	Some confessed they overate and ate improper foods; others remained on their diets.

Session	Objectives	Activities	Anecdotes
10	(l) Review food groupings.	Circle fantasy. Each student was given a dittoed sheet with a large circle in the middle and imagined what the circle was. As foods were mentioned, they were discussed.	All students stated the circle was some kind of food such as apples, pie, oranges, cake, potatoes, etc. Many discussed desserts followed with "But I shouldn't eat that."
11	(m) Express feelings on losing/ gaining weight.	Here and Now. A discussion was begun by the counselor asking, "How did you feel when you got on the scales today?" "How do you feel when taking your I.D. card home?"	Counselor encouraged confrontation. For example, "John what do you think about Susan's diet?" Students received positive and negative feedback.
12	(n) Recognize what personal sacrifices are necessary to reduce.	Discussion. Each student verbalized what to do to lose weight. For example, eat less and/or exercise more.	All students understood what was necessary for weight loss, but expressed difficulty in giving up things liked, especially in the beginning.
13	(o) Express feelings on losing weight.	New clothes. Several students discussed their shopping experience to buy new clothes, selecting what they wanted, looking for smaller sizes, wearing their clothes and hearing compliments.	Most parents had bought new clothes for children prior to this session. Everyone participated. Some students verbally expressed feelings of excitement, pride and guilt.
14	(p) Closure	Fashion show. Students invited classmates, teachers, and parents to the school auditorium. All members wore a new outfit and modeled one at a time.	Great excitement for everyone. Each student received tremendous applause as he/ she modeled.

Schoolwide Reinforcement Program

Students were weighed at the beginning of each group counseling session. The weight was recorded on a cardboard bar graph that resembled a thermometer with actual weights at the bottom and projected weight goals at the top. A weekly target weight, a minimum of one-half pound weight loss, was established for each student. These target weights were arranged according to body build and successively approximated to the long-range goal weights. The weekly target weights were written on group identification cards and given to students. Each Friday at weigh-in, students who had reached their weekly goal in weight loss were praised by the counselor and allowed to color in the amount of the loss on the thermometer. Students in the group also recognized and reinforced each other's success with applause. Students were then issued another identification card in a different color with a new target weight and the amount of weight lost during the previous week.

The new identification cards were taken by the students to their teachers who reinforced them for reaching their target weights with praise and with participation in special activities such as free time at a learning center in the classroom, overnight use of school games at home, or a special weight-watcher snack. Students who failed to lose weight received no recognition and were given notes to take home explaining their lack of progress. In addition, a fashion show, to be presented in school assembly, was planned for students who maintained desired weight losses.

The special activities, praise, and coloring served as immediate secondary reinforcers. The fashion show provided a long-term social reinforcer. All schoolwide reinforcement procedures were in effect during the group counseling sessions and continued after closure of the counseling group with the teacher's and parent's assistance.

Parental Involvement

The counselor sent a letter to parents of the referred students explaining the behavioral group counseling and schoolwide reinforcement program objectives and how often the group would meet. In addition, the letter explained the identification cards and forms that the parents would see. Parents were also asked to reinforce their children for successful weight loss with praise and to call the counselors at school if they had any questions.

The counselor recognized the general value of following up with parents to increase involvement and the value of involving parents of the retarded in a group setting as indicated by Ramsey (1967). Four group discussion sessions for the parents of the subjects were scheduled once every other week over eight weeks. Discussion in these sessions focused on helping parents express feelings about their children and how to reinforce their children for maintaining a healthy diet and weight loss. At least one parent from each family attended all the sessions.

Evaluation

An examination of personal records in the school indicated that the TMR students in the study had each gained between 10 and 20 pounds each academic year. An examination of Table 12–1 indicates that these 11 students, after participating in behavioral group counseling and a schoolwide reinforcement program, lost a combined total of 87 pounds in 14 weeks. This was a mean weight loss of 7.9 pounds per student. Nine of the 11 students lost weight, with the most weight loss by one student being 30 pounds. Two students gained weight, a female (13 pounds) and a male (6 pounds). It is interesting to note that the two students who gained weight dropped from the behavioral program.

A three month follow-up indicated there was no gain in height by any student when compared to heights prior to program intervention. Yet, all students who continued the reinforcement program in class maintained their weight loss. These eight students lost an additional 30 pounds. A follow-up weight was unavailable for one student who had graduated from school. However, the teacher indicated that this student had reached her long-range target goal. It is noteworthy that the two students who dropped from group counseling and the reinforcement program continued to gain weight, a combined total of 32 pounds or an average gain in weight of 16 pounds per person over three months. There appeared to be no apparent sex differences in students' ability to lose weight.

Example 2.   Developmental Play
in Small Group Counseling
with Disturbed Children*

For lack of better training, many teachers have resorted to behavioral counseling strategies to minimize class disruptions while using programmed teaching materials like Developing Understanding of Self and Others (Dinkmeyer, 1970, 1973) and Toward Affective Development (Dupont, Gardner, & Brody, 1974). This past year one such teacher asked for assistance with her class of eight disturbed children. While consulting with her, she indicated that she was tired of being a "heavy" with the children. I, therefore, suggested that we discuss how to implement a Developmental

* Gumaer, J. *The School Counselor*, 1983, in press. Reprinted in part with permission of the American Personnel and Guidance Association.

Table 12-1
SEX AND WEIGHT OF ELEVEN TMR STUDENTS BEFORE, AFTER,
AND THREE MONTHS FOLLOWING COUNSELOR INTERVENTION

				Weight		
STUDENT	SEX	BEFORE	AFTER	DIFFERENCE	3 MONTH FOLLOW-UP	DIFFERENCE
1	F	175	163	− 12	160	− 3
2	F	219	211	− 8	209	− 2
3	M	161	153	− 8	151	− 2
4	F	144	136	− 8	133	− 3
5	F	196	185	− 11	182	− 3
6	F	210	180	− 30	170	− 10
7[a]	F	128	116	− 12	—	—
8[b]	F	136	149	+ 13	166	+ 17
9[c]	M	214	220	+ 6	235	+ 15
10	F	162	148	− 14	145	− 3
11	M	117	114	− 3	110	− 4

[a] Student graduated; no three month follow-up weight available.
[b] Student withdrew from program after the fourteenth counseling session and closure of the counseling group.
[c] Student withdrew from counseling group after the tenth session at request of parent.

Play (DP) program (Brody, Fenderson, & Stephenson, 1976) with the class. DP was designed to help children experiencing personal detachment and other emotional, social, or learning difficulties to overcome these problems through the development of positive, loving interactions, and attachments with important adults who then serve as models for the children in learning how to relate to others.

Organization and Implementation

In consultation with the teacher, we discussed the value of DP and she became convinced that DP was an appropriate program for her children and that it would be helpful to her children. However, the program as described in the source book was impossible to implement with a class of eight children and two adults. The idea of asking one parent of each child to be involved was explored, but in all eight cases, after personal interviews, not a single parent agreed to participate. We, therefore, decided it might be best to attempt to implement the theoretical concepts of DP through small group counseling with these children. In a follow-up conversation, all the parents gave permission for their children to participate.

Although unsure of herself, the teacher agreed to lead a group of girls provided I planned the group sessions and that I would lead the group of boys at the same time and in the same room with her should immediate supervision be necessary. I consented and decided how to partition the room with movable coat closets so that one group would not disturb the other while working. It was then decided that the children would meet in group counseling for 12 weeks once each week for 45 minutes on Tuesdays beginning at 1 p.m. This schedule allowed children full participation in all academic subject areas and followed lunch which helped settle them down. It also provided 15 minutes before the groups met for preparation and 15 minutes after meeting for consultation and supervision with the teacher.

Group Members

This self-contained classroom for disturbed children consisted of four girls and four boys. All the children, aged eight to nine possessed IQ scores in the average range as measured by the Wechsler Intelligence Scale for Children–Revised. Students mean behavior scores as rated by teachers on the Devereux Child Behavior Rating Scale (Spivak & Spotts, 1966) was equal to or higher than the mean scores of 252 atypical children, in residential treatment centers, on 15 of 17 factors measured. The children in residential treatment centers were between the ages of six and 13 and their scores were cited as reference data in Table 1 of the [Devereux] manual. This earlier rating provided some degree of confidence that no children were in the group who were not characteristic of disturbed children thus insuring as much homogeneity in the groups as possible. Group counseling was explained to the children as a new program to help them understand themselves better. All children expressed a desire to participate. The Piers-Harris Self-Concept Scale (1969) was then administered before group counseling began.

Developmental Play Group Counseling Sessions

Specific plans were followed which consisted of objectives and brief descriptions of activities. In addition to implementing the planned activities, the teacher and I focused on key concepts of non-verbal communication which are of particular importance to DP: touching, spacing, and using facial language. Physical contact to encourage the children to experience themselves through other group members was planned for every DP session and modeled by the group leaders. Naturally in order for touching to occur, group members had to be seated in close proximity to one another. To implement the use of facial language to communicate with children, we made conscious efforts to smile and to make comfortable eye contact with all children through our initial greetings and by sitting on the floor with them. A brief outline of each counseling session's objectives, activities, and my personal anecdotes follows.

Session	Objectives	Activities	*Personal* *Anecdotes*
1	a. Get to know one another.	Draw an animal. Children discussed why they drew animal.	Counselor began discussion with "What was one reason you chose this animal?" All group members participated. One boy felt his picture wasn't any good and another said, "I'm a snake because I'm bad." Most of the children experienced difficulty in remaining seated and not interrupting discussion.
	b. Become acquainted with the group counseling situation.	Children moved like their animal and thought what it feels like.	
	c. Begin group discussion - introduce concept "to feel."		
2	d. Introduce basic rules for group discussion.	Counselor brought carpet squares to group. Children selected one and a place on floor to sit. This spot then became designated personal space. Introduced rules for discussion through a stuffed animal. Reinforced picture of animals from session one. Children closed eyes and touched the child (animal) on each side.	Counselor asked, "What are some rules we need in our group?" After going around the group to get opinion, the counselor said, "O.K., let's try just two. Whoever has this stuffed dog may talk. Everyone else must be quiet and listen, and unless told differently, everyone must remain on carpets."
	e. Select carpet piece and place.		
	f. Introduce stuffed animal.		
	g. Introduce verbal reinforcement and encouragement.		
	h. Begin physical contact (touching).		
3	i. Continue building group environment, focus	Reviewed names and animals. Closed eyes and	Children learned names and associated names with

Session	Objectives	Activities	Personal Anecdotes
	on feeling, and touching.	held hands (paws, etc.) of other animals. Closed eyes and imagined greeting friends on street, your parents at home.	animals. Children commented: It was warm, cold, sweaty. One boy said, "It pulled us together like glue." Greetings included: shake hands, hello, slap hands or high five for friends and hugs for parents. Feelings included: warm, loved, and sometimes pain when slapped. Children responded well to passing stuffed toy and encouragement for contributions.
4	j. Continue to develop group cohesiveness. k. Begin self-awareness: the body.	Group began with personal greetings. Described similarities and differences in animal bodies. Named body parts, touched body parts of child on left and right, described feelings.	Children more involved. The group moved in close around me. Everyone touched gently. Some anxiety present. Group agreed that some parts of body should only be touched by self or parents.
5	l. Continue self-awareness: the body and associated feelings.	Reviewed greetings, body parts. Paired up, traced partner's hands on one side of construction paper, feet on the other. Closed group by reading story	Children ready to work when I arrived. They enjoyed tracing. Much laughter present. I introduced the story by saying, "I often put my own little boy to bed at night by holding him on

Session	Objectives	Activities	Personal Anecdotes
		with child in lap.	my lap and reading a story. It helps him feel loved. I would like to close our group each time this way with one of you." Jimmy, the largest child (120 pounds) said, "I will but I'm too big, you can't hold me."
6	m. Continue self-awareness of body.	Paired up and traced partner's body on large paper. Filled in detail, colored, and cut out to hang on wall. Story.	Counselor elicited reinforcing and encouraging comments from group members. Jimmy, "Look at my ears, they're too big." Joe, "Everybody's different in some way. I'm hyperactive and take pills every day." Children animated as they work; anxious for turn in my lap. Eliminated stuffed toy. No longer necessary.
7	n. Begin self-understanding.	Examined body tracings and discussed.	Counselor encouraged group to cite positive points in appearance. Children identified feelings as part of the stomach, heart, and head. Children are touching in a gentle way on their own. A lot of hugging.
	o. Discuss physical self.	Discussed location of emotions in body.	
	p. Discuss emotional self.	Story.	
8	q. Continue self-understanding.	Discussed describing and ex-	Counselor provided both positive and

Session	Objectives	Activities	Personal Anecdotes
		pressing emotions. Examined behavior when angry, proud, and happy.	negative examples of socially appropriate expression of feelings.
			Children realistic and honest. For example with angry, "My teacher told another kid to shape up and leave me alone. I felt great." "I beat a kid up who was bugging me. It felt terrific." "Someone was teasing me. I put it out of my mind and found something fun to do."
9	r. Continue self-understanding.	It's O.K. to cry. Discussed words that describe feelings. Pantomimed feelings. Story.	Everyone very close in group. Two boys leaned on each other. Jimmy entered room and hugged me. Counselor pantomimed: scared, surprised, angry, and hurt. Children guessed to identify feeling. Counselor emphasized when you hurt, it's O.K. to cry and comforting to be held and touched softly. All boys sat in counselor's lap and hugged at end.
10	s. Continue self-awareness and self-understanding.	Reviewed feeling words. Fantasy: Close eyes imagine a per-	Children involved. Smacked their lips and said "yum" to ice cream. Offered

Session	Objectives	Activities	Personal Anecdotes
	How do feelings affect behavior?	son offering you ice cream, makes fun of you. How do you feel toward each person? What does the feeling make you want to do? What would you do? Finish story.	their favorite flavors. Frowned and made fists to the second image. Feelings ranged from great, hungry, excited for ice cream to awful and hate him for teasing. Children said they most often treated others like they were treated.
11	t. Understand how feeling affects behavior.	Role play. Counselor to group: "O.K., I'm mad! Everybody heads down and no talking. I want it quiet." Discussion. "Now I feel terrific. Let's go out and play together." Here and now. A discussion: For example, "Joe, how do you feel when Jimmy teases you, hugs you? What do you want to do?" There and then. A discussion: For example, "Mark, you mentioned your Dad never hugs you. What does he do when you hug him?"	At first children didn't believe me. I continued role play. They followed directions, appeared disappointed almost to tears. Each role play only lasted a few minutes. Discussion followed focused on my feelings and behavior and the impact of these. Counselor encouraged confrontation and feedback among group members. Group members responded to feelings. Everyone hugged.
12	u. Reinforce posi-	Go around.	Children excited

Session	Objectives	Activities	Personal Anecdotes
	tive experience of group.	Each group member said something positive to other group members.	and pleased. They responded to feelings and behavior. "Group hug." I encouraged them at
	v. Terminate.	Counselor asked, "How does it feel to hear these pleasant things? What does it make you want to do?" Photographed.	end to continue touching at home and with friends and teacher at school.
			Pictures distributed to group members.

Evaluation

One week following the last group therapy session, the self-concept scale was readministered. One boy failed to complete the instrument properly at this time. As a result, the total number of children whose pre- and post-group counseling self-esteem scores were examined was seven rather than eight. An examination of Table 12–2 indicates that these seven students, after participating in DP group counseling, increased their scores a total of 44 points (boys, 20; girls, 24). This was a mean increase in score of 6.3 points per child. Five of the seven increased their scores while two children, a boy and a girl, decreased in self-esteem. In this particular class of disturbed children, it appeared that developmental play in group therapy was a positive experience for most participants and helped the majority of boys and girls feel better about themselves.

Although the teacher was involved in the group counseling, she reported positively that learning which occurred in the group sessions generalized to the classroom. This transfer of training effect was apparent to her in the children's conversations with each other and their play. They demonstrated frequently warmth and caring toward each other by hugging and responding to feelings. The teacher also felt more relaxed with the children and relieved to be able to express her affection for them as well as be firm and a disciplinarian. It may well be that this teacher was the recipient of greater positive gains than the children.

Although evaluated in a simplistic fashion, this initial effort to use developmental play in group therapy with disturbed children appeared to have a positive impact both on the lives of the children and the teacher. It

Table 12-2
PRE- AND POST-ASSESSMENT SELF-ESTEEM SCORES
(N = 7)

Boys	Pre-Test Score	Post-Test Score	Difference
1	29	46	+ 17
2	37	45	+ 8
3	53	48	− 5
			Total + 20
Girls			
1	43	48	+ 5
2	36	50	+ 14
3	44	40	− 4
4	38	47	+ 9
			Total + 24

also became apparent that the concepts and activities of developmental play can be creatively adapted for use in small group counseling. There existed less personalized one-to-one contact between adult and child in the groups but all children valued their time in counseling and the levels of attachment that evolved.

RECOMMENDED RESOURCES

Books

APTER, S. *Troubled children/troubled systems.* New York: Pergamon Press, 1982.

This text presents a synthesis of ecological assessment and intervention strategies based on theories of community psychology.

DEUTSCH, C. *Broken bottles, broken dreams: Understanding and helping the children of alcoholics.* Totowa, NJ: Teachers College Press, 1982.

This book focuses on an understanding of what alcoholism is and is not, and what impact alcoholism has on family members. It also presents scenarios of persons helping in various roles, examines support groups, and explains how their methods work.

SCHAEFER, C., JOHNSON, L., & WHERRY, J. *Group therapies for children and youth.* San Francisco: Jossey-Bass, 1982.

This book was introduced and reviewed in the recommended resources section of Chapter 10.

SLAVSON, S. & SCHIFFER, R. *Group psychotherapies for children: A textbook.* New York: International Universities Press, 1975.

This book describes primarily Slavson's activity-group therapy techniques with children experiencing "minor" problems. It describes the use of play, materials, refreshments, and other activities as part of group therapy.

Films

Daddy doesn't live here anymore: The single-parent family. Human Relations Media, 175 Tomkins Ave., Pleasantville, New York, 1983.

This film discusses a four-part program including the changing family, when parents divorce, the lives of parents and children in single-parent households, and the special characteristics of the stepparent home.

My parents are getting a divorce. Human Relations Media, 175 Tompkins Ave., Pleasantville, New York, 1982.

This two-part program examines divorce in our society and some of the reasons behind the high divorce rate. It discusses problems children may encounter when parents divorce and problems of others in the family. Part one focuses on the separation and part two on adjusting.

Journals

Elementary School Guidance and Counseling. American School Counselors Association (ASCA), a division of the American Personnel and Guidance Association, Two Skyline Place, Suite 400, 5203 Leesburg Pike, Falls Church, VA 22041.

This journal is published by ASCA and focuses specifically on the interests of counseling practitioners who work with elementary school-aged children. It is published four times per year in October, December, March, and May.

The International Journal of Group Psychotherapy. American Group Psychotherapy, Association, Inc., by International Universities Press, Inc., 315 Fifth Avenue, New York 10016.

This journal is the official journal of the American Group Psychotherapy Association (AGPA). It is published quarterly in January, April, July, and October. For membership information, write AGPA, 1995 Broadway, 14th Floor, New York, NY 10023.

The School Counselor. ASCA, Two Skyline Place, Suite 400, 5203 Leesburg Pike, Falls Church, VA 22041.

This journal is the official publication of ASCA. It is directed primarily to the interest of counseling practitioners especially in school settings. Articles focus on implementing theory into practice in counseling, research, practical ideas and suggestions, and book reviews. It is published five times a year in September, November, January, March, and May.

SUMMARY

This chapter on problem-centered group counseling began with an overview of the paucity of research available in the literature related to the group counseling of troubled children. A definition of problem-centered group counseling was also provided. The second section of the chapter focused on key concepts of forming problem-centered counseling groups, including selection of group members, group size, length and frequency of sessions, and duration of the group. These concepts were presented so that readers could compare and contrast them with those of growth-centered groups. The third section of the chapter described two problem-centered groups in detail. The chapter concluded with a listing of recommended resources.

REFERENCES AND RECOMMENDED READINGS

BRODY, V., FENDERSON, C., & STEPHENSON, S. *Sourcebook for finding your way to helping young children through developmental play.* Tallahassee, FL: Department of State, 1976.

DINKMEYER, D. *Developing understanding of self and others* (DUSO Kit D–1). Circle Pines, MN: American Guidance Service, 1970.

———. *Developing understanding of self and others* (DUSO Kit D–2). Circle Pines, MN: American Guidance Service, 1974.

DUPONT, H., GARDNER, S., & BRODY, D. *Toward affective development.* Circle Pines, MN: American Guidance Service, 1974.

GUMAER, J. Developmental play in small group counseling with disturbed children. *The School Counselor* (in press).

——— & SIMON, R. Behavioral group counseling and schoolwide reinforcement program with obese trainable mentally retarded students. *Education and Training of the Mentally Retarded,* 1979, 14(2), 106–111.

LUBIN, B., LUBIN, A., & TAYLOR, A. The group psychotherapy literature: 1978. *The International Journal of Group Psychotherapy,* 1979, 29(4), 523–576.

———, REDDY, W., STANSBERRY, C., & LUBIN, A. The group psychotherapy literature: 1976. *The International Journal of Group Psychotherapy,* 1977, 28(4), 521–552.

———, REDDY, W., TAYLOR, A., & LUBIN, A. The group psychotherapy literature: 1977. *The International Journal of Group Psychotherapy,* 1978, 28(4), 509–555.

PIERS, E. & HARRIS, D. *Manual for the Piers-Harris children's self-concept scale.* Nashville, TN: Counselor Recordings and Tests, 1969.

RAMSEY, C. Review of group methods with parents of mentally retarded. *American Journal of Mental Deficiency,* 1967, 71, 857–863.

ROSE, S. *Treating children in groups.* San Francisco: Jossey-Bass, 1975.

SILVER, R., LUBIN, B., & MILLER, D. The group psychotherapy literature: 1981. *The International Journal of Group Psychotherapy,* 1982, 32(4), 481–554.

——— & DOBSON, N. The group psychotherapy literature: 1980. *The International Journal of Group Psychotherapy,* 1981, 31(4), 469–526.

———, SILVER, D., & DOBSON, N. The group psychotherapy literature: 1979. *The International Journal of Group Psychotherapy,* 1980, 30(4), 491–538.

SPIVACK, G. & SPOTTS, J. *Devereux child behavior rating scale manual.* Devon, PA: Devereux Foundation, 1966.

Chapter 13

Family Therapy: An Introduction to a Structural Perspective

Thomas Tavantzis

VIEWING CHILDREN'S PROBLEMS as residing within them is a model that has a long history in the counseling (therapy) of children. Diagnosing, probing, developmental history-gathering, understanding, and intervening are all focused on the individual child. This model has been predominant since the development of the Child Guidance Clinics in the early 1920s.

From the philosophical and social roots of the child guidance movement, social settings were considered to be largely responsible for problem behavior. First children, and then parents, mostly mothers, were seen at the clinics. At that time, appreciation of the internal psychological functioning of a child was a major step, although, as some experts note in terms of social response to childhood dysfunction, it was a conservative one (Levine & Levine, 1970). Furthermore, as psychoanalytic thinking took hold in the United States, Freud's emphasis on excluding family members from treatment further entrenched the individual model in most forms of psychotherapy. As philosophy was translated into practice in the midst of prevailing social realities, individual treatment in which the primary intervention was play therapy conducted by a psychiatrist or psychologist, became a fixture. Framo (1979) described how the model of individual treatment operated within traditional child guidance models:

> Even if both parents were seen, the focus on the child's problems; the social worker, who had to deal with the bulk of the pathology, would gradually become aware, for example, of marital or in-law problems, but she would be given the clear message by the rest of the psychiatric team that her therapy efforts were secondary. (p. 989)

A number of assumptions underlie the individually oriented model. It assumes that observation of the child at play by a therapist elicits a sample of a child's typical behavior. Related assumptions are that the child's problems are intrapsychic (within the child) and that isolated changes in the child's behavior will have positive effects, or at least no negative effects, on the family. These assumptions negate the child's role in a family social system.

Montalvo and Haley (1973) described several additional assumptions implicit in traditional theory and practice of play therapy that also handicap the therapist. When the therapist lacks an understanding of the ways children respond to their interpersonal context, and when one therapist is dealing with the parents while another therapist treats the children;

> . . . there is a chance of an influence on the family through the social worker's (therapist's) endeavors. However, there is also a chance that social workers and child therapists will be in covert conflict with each other about the family, taking sides in family struggles, and will merely replicate the conflictual situation that has produced a disturbed child. (p. 242–243)

While the traditional model was developed in the child guidance clinics, it was also followed in a variety of social institutional settings, including schools. Traditional, individual therapy of children, with an intervention model based on looking "inside" children for their problems, is still quite common.

Madanes (1981) provided another schema for viewing different therapeutic approaches. She distinguishes between therapies in several ways, but most useful here is her view that what differentiates;

> . . . the individual therapist from the family therapist is the concept of the unit that has the problem: whether it is one person, two people, or three people or more. By definition, psychodynamic therapy has a unit of one, since it is the therapy of the individual psyche. When one person is the focus, the therapy needs to center on that person's feelings, ideas, perceptions, and behavior. (p. 5).

A therapeutic family model for the child in social context requires a concept of the family unit which views the problem involving three or more persons.

Viewing the Child's Problem in Context

There have been several excellent descriptions of the various interrelated economic, societal, and scientific developments that gave rise to a family therapy movement (Broderick & Schrader, 1981; Guerin, 1976). Rather than provide a historical overview, implications of the family therapy movement will be discussed.

Family therapy has been called a revolutionary shift (Framo, 1979), and contrasts sharply with the traditional model of individual child therapy. Rather than viewing and intervening with children in isolation from the family, problematic children are viewed in the context of the family and the family in the context of its community. When family therapy is seen as just another method of working with the individual, it loses its revolutionary impact. It becomes individual therapy with family members. It is, rather, when family therapy is viewed as a way of conceptualizing phenomena that its revolutionary side is seen. For instance, one can conduct individual play therapy, but the therapist's understanding, interventions, and opportunities for success are enhanced if the therapist thinks from a family perspective (Montalvo & Haley, 1973). A family perspective assumes that the problem a child presents is a way of communicating and it is functional within the family's unique transactional reality.

Other assumptions center on the role of the therapist, who is a powerful participant in creating new realities for the child and family. The therapist's role requires regulating input and output during a family session. The therapist recognizes that social context is a creation that organizes not only the family's behavior but also the therapist's behavior in relation to the family. Counselors must realize that even as they intervene to alter family realities, they have already participated in the creation of the unit. Moving to a family perspective should influence how therapists think and then direct their actions in therapy. For instance, a child counselor, instead of searching in the child's symbolic play for the roots of the child's problem, recognizes, from a family perspective, that intervention into the family is necessary and views the child's play as actively communicating about the context. The therapist's role involves active participation in shaping a therapeutic context that will provide opportunity for the family to change. Family therapy, therefore, directs intervention towards relationships between family members, and between families and social institutions such as schools.

The last decade witnessed an explosion in writing, research, and clinical interest in family therapy. Several family therapy models evolved. This chapter focuses on Structural Family Therapy with children.

As Stanton (1981) said, "Two of the predominant modes within what have been termed 'systems' or perhaps more accurately, 'communication' approaches to family therapy are the 'Structural and Strategic' types."

This chapter emphasizes the Structural model and its integration and application as reflected in the author's current work setting. It might be useful to indicate that elements of the Strategic school, particularly Haley (1980) will become evident. I maintain that the two approaches are distinct but compatible. Stanton (1981) pointed out that:

> . . . their compatibility in many areas is not surprising, since a Strategic therapist, Jay Haley, was instrumental in the development of Structural family

therapy. Both Haley's Strategic model and the Structural approach place considerable emphasis on the hierarchical family organization, noting that aberrant hierarchies (such as cross-generation coalitions) are frequently diagnostic of family dysfunction. (p. 439)

Walbridge (1981), a Structural family therapy trainer, actively espouses the position that a counselor should be fluent in and able to work from both models. In my professional career, I have had the opportunity to train with several excellent clinical trainers-supervisors. While the trainer-supervisors differed a great deal theoretically, operationally for me there appeared commonalities, since all contained a systems focus, which included recognizing the influence of the social context on behavior, a greater concern with process than content, and a valuing of the interdependence of humans.

An additional impetus towards my choosing to work from a Structural model as my work with low- and middle-income, rural and urban families in Greece and in the northeastern United States. More specifically, as director of a small human services agency in Schenectady, New York, Parkhurst Parent and Child Center, I was able to integrate the Structural model into practice with children and families in crises. As trainer, educator, therapist, consultant, and supervisor, I experienced an understanding of the Structural model meshing it with an emerging personal style. More recently, Parkhurst launched an innovative project; Families Work, that provides home-based, short-term family therapy to families with children between 10 and 16 years of age, who are at imminent risk of placement in an institution. The Structural approach has been adopted.

Aponte and Van Deusen (1981) described in their book, *Families of the Slums*, a Structural Family Therapy Model developed from work with low socioeconomic families at an institution for boys. In this book, the two authors focused on client characteristics and a model based on those realities:

> The families they met at Wiltwyck were grappling with day-to-day survival, seeking real solutions to the real problems in their lives. They were poor. The urgency that poverty generates about obtaining the necessities of life inclines families to approach psychotherapy as a practical means for solving problems that are causing them trouble. When they enter therapy, they look to see that what is being done has a tangible relationship to their problem and that results are perceptibly forthcoming from their efforts. Therapies that depend heavily on talking about rather than talking directly to problems, that are aimed towards understanding and insight rather than action, that seek the expression of feeling instead of the integration of feeling with behavior, that aim to change attitudes about life and not the conditions of life are too removed from the pressures of the everyday problems of poor people and to be useful to them.
>
> Minuchin and his co-workers developed a therapeutic approach that was founded on the immediacy of the present reality, was oriented to solving prob-

lems, and was above all contextual, referring to the social environment that is both a part of and the setting for an event. The Structural orientation itself was shared by the exigencies of the social conditions of these boys from Wiltwyck School. (p. 310)

KEY CONCEPTS

Structure

Structure is basic to understanding the interrelationship of behavior in the family. Systems of family interactions or, better yet, transaction are regulated by rules. These rules govern behavior. Rules are revealed in the repeating, relatively enduring patterns of behavioral transaction. Patterns are the organization or structure of families. Rules are creations of the therapist that are useful in organizing redundancies (patterns) of transactional phenomena. As Minuchin (1974) observed, "repeated (family) transactions of how, when, and to whom to relate underlie the system" (p. 51). These patterns are the organization (structure) and constitute both functional and dysfunctional aspects of a system. When dysfunctional, they are the target of change; when functional, the target of counselor's support. A relatively enduring pattern in a family may involve, for example, a husband making a complaint to his spouse, who then turns and complains to an adolescent daughter about her behavior. Mother and daughter argue. Father withdraws. When this pattern is seen in a variety of content forms, one may infer a family rule; negotiation of difference between any dyad is unacceptable.

Boundaries

In the above example, when mother shifts away from father to child, she is also making a comment about how issues are resolved between mother and father. Boundaries are invisible borderlines that define relations in the family. Limits on who participates and how are defined by the concept of boundaries.

Boundaries are seen as existing on a continuum from *enmeshed* to *disengaged*. Enmeshed or overinvolved subsystems exist when people are in each other's business, or as one bright young family member said, clearly describing his own family enmeshment, "It's like Superman changing clothes in a telephone booth with three other people trying to help him." Enmeshment includes, among other behaviors, continual interruption of each member, one member speaking for another, and privacy equated with disloyalty to the family. When togetherness or belongingness are pursued by family members to the subsequent detriment of individuation, there are members participating in enmeshed subsystems. At the other extreme are subsystems that de-emphasize togetherness or interdependence and support an alienated version of individuality. Boundaries of disengaged subsystems are more impervious to communication in contrast to the looseness of enmeshing subsystems. Disengaged subsystems are low on interpersonal contact. Parents' and children's subsystems are probably quite disengaged when a child's continual truancy from school is unknown to the parents. Family members behave as if they have little to do with each other. For Minuchin (1974), "operations at the extremes of this continuum indicate areas of possible pathology" (p. 55).

While the continuum of enmeshment and disengagement may not approximate the complexity of family functioning (Hoffman, 1981) as well as might other concepts (Olsen, Sprenkle, & Russell, 1979; Wertheim, 1973), the author views the continuum as useful from a practical point of view. Family systems present complex organizations that act in powerful ways to reduce a therapist's influence. Cognitive maps, like Minuchin's continuum of engagement to disengagement, can help to create ways of distancing (or disengaging) the counselor in therapy, enabling him to maintain a therapeutic role. Moreover, the continuum is useful in orienting the therapist toward communication processes occurring between family members and between a family and its community.

Boundaries are also invisible barriers that regulate information across family systems and the surrounding social context. Families may have overly loose or rigid boundaries as far as permitting external input (friends, relatives, social agencies), into their system. One novice counselor, after a home visit to a family, was exasperated by how the family session was continually interrupted by neighbors dropping into the house. Both therapist and family had difficulty in defining the family system. Family health is related to clarity of boundaries between family members and the family and its context. The processes of belongingness and separateness are brought into sharp focus by the concept of boundaries. Interventions are shaped by the counselor's understanding of the operation of these processes in and across subsystems.

Subsystems

While subsystems have been introduced in the above discussion of boundaries, their significance in the family may not be clear. Participation in the various subsystems activates different behaviors and different experiences. The family is viewed as having a number of subsystems—husband-wife, mother-father, parent-child, siblings. For instance, the sibling subsystem provides experiences in peer-interaction, exploration, negotiation, cooperation, and competition. The types of experiences between siblings are seen as distinct from those occurring, for example, between parent-child subsystems.

Transactions in subsystems also need to reflect growth and development of the members over time. As members reach different developmental stages, behaviors need to change. The parent needs to provide different experiences to a small child than to a young adult. Support, maintenance, and activation of alternative transactions are provided to subsystems by the counselor. Recognition of the significance of subsystem integrity by a therapist is critical to improving the functioning of families.

Development

Families, like all living structures, maintain and change themselves. The concept of morphostasis suggests the "configuration of parts and processes that work together to produce the stability in the living structure, while the concept of morphogenesis suggests the change that occurs in living structures" (Durkin, 1981, p. 344). In family systems, morphostatic structures preserve function and morphogenetic structures transform function. Structures are preserved in the face of external and internal disturbances, while structure also changes in the direction of greater adaptiveness. An example of morphostatic structure might be evident when a 10-year-old demands a 10 o'clock curfew during school nights because that is what the child's friends are allowed. Parents respond by uniting and firmly continuing the 8 o'clock curfew, preserving their parental function and the status quo in the family. Morphogenesis, or change in structure, would be illustrated by the same example if, when reaching age 16, the child made the same request (unlikely as it may seem) and the parents responded by renegotiating the curfew rule, thereby acknowledging autonomy in the child.

Family life-cycle development (Haley, 1973b; Minuchin, 1974) has become a useful cognitive framework for viewing the complementary processes of morphogenesis and morphostasis. Problems are seen as arising from struggles to maintain a given structure (morphostasis) in the face of developmental changes (morphogenesis).[1]

Hierarchy

Implicit in much that has been described is the view that the family has a hierarchy of roles and power. Parents are higher in the hierarchy than children. Older children are higher than younger children (Haley, 1980;

---

[1]In the early years of the Family Therapy movement, change or morphogenesis was neglected, while morphostasis was studied. More recently, attempts have been made to examine the process of change in structure (Hoffman, 1981). Currently, theories of family therapy are increasingly dialectical as theorists recognize that family processes that maintain morphostasis have within them processes that are structure challenging—morphogenetic.

Madanes, 1981; Minuchin, 1974). Hierarchies that are confused or reversed are seen as creating symptoms. For example, when a disruptive boy is controlling his parents by virtue of his behavior, the hierarchy of parents in control of child is reversed. Placing the parents in control and blocking any attempts by the parents to relinquish their positions in the hierarchy removes the symptom.

TECHNIQUES AND SKILLS

As we have seen, Structural family therapy concepts offer a view of redundant processes or patterns that occur between family members. Processes or patterns within the family, and between family and its surrounding community, are ongoing. It is the therapist who, through a conceptual framework, freezes process (pattern) into structure in a family. Process can be compared to an ongoing videotaping of communication whereas discussion of structure freezes a single section of the videotape. Discussion of structure is, in fact, discussion of redundancy of patterns reified. Techniques and skills developed by Structural family therapists are conceived as ways of altering and creating alternate family structures.

Joining

The initial and ongoing task of the therapist is to follow and then lead the family into an alternate structure or reality. A basic but significant technique and skill to accomplish this task is joining. In joining, the counselor must enter and experience the family's reality and the family in turn must experience the therapist's understanding of their unique reality. Family members' experience of a joining operation should be a reduction of the counselor's strangeness. Acknowledged or nonacknowledged at its base, joining is a process that draws upon the shared humanity of therapist and family. This is a basic aspect of joining, for a counselor is provided an experiential data base about the family. In forming this base, a therapist experiences the family structure in the room and is freely pulled and swayed by the structure of a family.

To know a family in an experiential way requires security on the part of the counselor. It is necessary for successful family therapy that the therapist follow a family in its transactional process, so in turn, the family will follow the therapist into more functional organization and out of its painful and dysfunctional patterns. It is through joining operations that a base of trust develops, allowing the family to tolerate arousal that often times is discomforting as a family follows a counselor into developing alternate structures. Recognizing that structure, even if dysfunctional, is powerfully morphostatic, the therapist respects the family structure which is in place. At the same time, the goal is change.

For example, if, in the initial family interview, mother's role in the family is to control other members' contact with people outside the family, then this structure needs to be recognized and accepted. The therapist contacts mother in such a way as to gain permission to contact other members. Later in the therapeutic process, a challenge to this structure will need to take place.

Joining occurs at the family level by observing and respecting family organization but, equally important, by responding and resonating to individual members' realities. The word *resonating* here is used to describe the therapist's allowing a member's experience of the family and world to activate parts of the therapist's self. Allowing and recognizing activated aspects of counselor's self is a potent tool in understanding and changing families. Similarly, parts of a therapist's self left unactivated by the family may often be aspects that a counselor needs to bring into action to challenge, by difference, a dysfunctional reality.

Joining is an operation that trainees either have in their repertoire or seem to easily pick up. Unfortunately, however, joining alone does not alter dysfunction patterns. It is ongoing support provided by joining, balanced by structure-challenging operations, that leads to possibilities for more functional transactions.

Enactment

The Structural model is a therapy of experience (Aponte, 1981). A task of the therapist is to first activate in the session dysfunctional family patterns and then encourage the family to experience alternative coping processes. This, at times, is a rather difficult concept to translate into practice. It is particularly difficult for students trained in traditional techniques of counseling. Traditional models focus on gathering content about a problem related by members to a therapist, rather than on requesting a family to enact its problem. In the Structural model, diagnosis is an ongoing process, refined over time, leading to clearer and more focused interventions. The therapeutic context is defined as family + therapist + context, and new data is created. Moreover, trainees are frequently confused by the difference between role playing and enactment. Role playing involves a real or hypothetical situation where family members are asked to assume roles. Generally, enactment is activation of the ongoing family patterns in the consulting room (Minuchin & Fishman, 1981). For instance, a mother who complains of her three children being out of control begins to tell the counselor the history of the problem. Meanwhile, the children steadily begin to fight, argue, and generally create upheaval. Instead of focusing attention on mother's history-telling, the therapist could observe her efforts to control the children and their responses to her—in effect, their patterns of transaction. It would be even more helpful for information-gathering for the counselor to ask mother what she would like to do about her children, i.e., to enact the dysfunctional pattern.

Other times the therapist may have to activate an enactment by organizing family members. A counselor might say to mother and father, "I think it would be good for you and your husband to discuss the ways you agree on treating your son's rule-breaking." This directive asks the parents to hold a discussion within their parental roles. Additionally, what is unique for these parents is the focus by the therapist on their agreement where in the past their differences were usually highlighted.

Asking for all family members to draw together on a large piece of blank paper with crayons is yet another way of eliciting and organizing a family enactment (Tavantzis, 1982; Vassiliou, 1981). Asking this of a family in an initial session, or in a subsequent session, provides diagnostic information about family structure, sets goals for therapeutic interventions, and allows the family an opportunity to view themselves participating in a concrete yet ambiguous task to help themselves. This technique, use of drawings, is examined further in this chapter in "Stages and Process: Two Case Examples."

Enactments are fundamental to the conduct of Structural therapy. They provide concrete opportunities for therapist's interventions which block, modify, support, and alter transactions. At times a counselor may challenge a subsystem involved in an enactment that portrays a dysfunctional pattern by suggesting the participants find another way of discussing the issue. Frequently, a therapist may prolong an enactment while also pushing for an alternative; or support one side of the dyad in the enactment. There are a variety of interventions that may be indicated, based on the therapeutic goals. The question of what to do with an enactment once it emerges or is organized high-lights the significant role of the counselor as regulating, directing, supporting, and conducting the emotionality of a session.

Planning

In the Structural model, therapy is conducted in relation to a plan for the family developed by the therapist. Understanding of the family is a result of hypothesizing about symptom-maintaining patterns. Usually, as we apply Structural theory in the context of our Center, two therapists will have assessed the family in their home and a team meeting is then convened. Tentative hypotheses about the systemic functioning of the family are developed and then implemented in a family's therapy session (90 percent of which occur in the family's home).

In order to further encompass the family complexity into a concrete treatment plan, families are requested to have at least one therapy session within a one-way mirror room. At this point, the team gathers to observe therapist + family + context created.

Workable Realities

Within this model counselors help families to view their dysfunction in solvable terms. Often this means reorganizing how a symptom is viewed. For example, therapist says to parents, "Jean is not crazy, but rather needs your help to break her habit of staying out late."

Once a counselor shifts to viewing the task as one that focuses on a search for competence, it becomes easier to create or frame family problems in ways that allow members to experience success (Minuchin & Fishman, 1981). An example of this would be parents who present their child as beyond their control and crazy, expecting a counselor to "do something about their crazy child." A therapist might agree that the parents do in fact have a child who is difficult and misbehaving and that if they are interested in family therapy will help them cope more effectively with their child. This brief example contains the elements of creating a workable reality by not focusing on their crazy child but on helping them cope more effectively with a child who is difficult. The onus of responsibility is shifted back to the parents, the task of changing the child is now focused upon increasing parental competence and the therapist shifts from miracle-worker to consultant to the parents, while also joining with parents in a new reality.

Reframing

A counselor uses reframing of reality as a way of initiating the search for alternatives. For instance, a boy of 12 refuses to go to school. Mother sympathetically supports the child staying home by accepting his rather lame sickness excuses. Mother is alone and having son home is quite enjoyable as they watch the soap operas and play board games with each other. Alarmingly, the child has only been to school 15 days in six months. The response of school and probation officials is for placement of the boy in an institution.

The intervention with this family can be divided into three broad steps over a six-week period that redefine the relationship of this enmeshed mother-son dyad. The therapist asks the mother about her hopes for her son's future five years and ten years from now. Mother describes her desire for her son to go to college, get married and not be dependent on welfare. Counselor supports mother in her hopes and indicates she is a responsible mother. Counselor then assumes a puzzled pose and asks, "How is that going to happen? How is your dream going to be fulfilled? My guess is that your son wants to defeat you. So while you allow him to stay home and you both have fun together, you are allowing him to defeat you as a mother. You see he is about to be placed in an institution for at least 18 months." The second and major part of this intervention takes place in the following session two days later after mother and son are warned not to make any drastic changes. In this session, the therapist requests the mother to find out from her son how she allows him to manipulate her into staying home. The counselor is quite persistent in pursuing this theme in the session, thereby challenging the seeming closeness of mother and son that is in fact quite destructive for both. A final step takes place when the therapist suggests to a now angry mother that she has a right to have her dreams about her son fulfilled. In fact, she will have to buy her son an alarm clock and take him to school every day. Within two weeks, the son is attending school on a regular basis without mother, and mother is beginning to discuss her own interest in going back to school. While obviously all cases are not as dramatically successful, or as easy to document, this case illustrates how the operation of reframing of the mother-son reality and their acceptance of the reframing reorganizes and challenges a particular version of agreed-upon reality.

The therapist is "selling" a different reality to mother based on her wishes. Reframing is always highlighting an aspect of reality concealed by the constraints of the prevailing family structure. The task of a counselor is to modify and expand the constraints on perception self-imposed by the family.

Complementarity

Creating workable realities and also viewing a problem in units of three or more people reflects a therapist's way of thinking. Being able to think and view behavior of individual family members as complementary is essential. Individuals do not experience the interlocking system of relationships of which they are part. Rather experience is seen linearly, "my child is out of control," rather than, "my child's out-of-control behavior is activated by my becoming depressed." In this interdependent sequence, when mother shows signs of withdrawal and complains about her life, son behaves in ways that give her life meaning and she tries to control him. Son calms down, relieved that mother is still OK. Minuchin and Fishman (1981) describe complementarity as

> . . . being foreign to common experience. People generally experience themselves as acting and reacting. They say, "My spouse nags me." "My wife is overdependent." "My child is disobedient." From the castle of the individual self,

they see themselves as besieged and as responding to that siege. At a session with the Kingman family, composed of the husband and wife and a young psychotic daughter who is almost mute, the therapist asks the girl how long she has been in the hospital, and both parents answer simultaneously. He asks the parents why they answered when he asked their daughter a question. The mother says that the daughter makes her talk. The father explains that since the girl is always silent, they speak for her. "They make me silent," the girl contributes, with a vague smile.

Each of these people has a blind-man-with-the-elephant version of the same reality. Experientially, each of them is correct, and the reality that each defends is the truth. Yet many other possibilities exist in the larger unit. (p. 194)

A Nasrudin Hodja story, a folklore hero shared by the Mediterranean and Middle Eastern people, may help further clarify this concept:

Walking one evening along a deserted road, Nasrudin saw a troop of horsemen coming towards him. His imagination started to work; he saw himself captured and sold as a slave, or impressed into the army.

Nasrudin bolted, climbed a wall into a graveyard, and lay down in an open tomb.

Puzzled at his strange behavior, the men, honest travellers, followed him. They found him stretched out, tense and quivering.

"What are you doing in that grave? We saw you run away. Can we help you?

"Just because you can ask a question does not mean that there is a straightforward answer to it," said Hodja, who now realized what had happened. "It all depends upon your viewpoint. If you must know, however, I am here because of *you*, and you are here because of *me*."

Search for Strength

Structural therapy is an exploration for the patterns in a family that are functional: patterns that support belongingness and individuation. No assumption is made that all family patterns will change, but rather movement is toward economy of therapeutic effort. It also assumes that given an opportunity, family members are competent. In fact, even dysfunctional family patterns are attempts, albeit harmful and often destructive, at competence.

While difficult at times, the challenge of the therapist, and in turn of the family, is to recognize wells of unacknowledged resources within the family. A single-parent father, who saw his children viewed by officials as uncontrollable in school, felt his children did not acknowledge him as a father, and also felt he might potentially abuse his children. When confronted with his unrecognized strength by the counselor, the father became determined not to allow his children to be institutionalized as he had previously desired and demanded improvements in the children's lives by insisting the school provide necessary services. The therapist challenged the reality of an otherwise demoralized father. With this intervention, counselor and father began a process of returning father to an executive position in the family and in relation to the school.

All too frequently, the realities a family creates constrain the recognition of strengths within members. This is a challenge to a therapist; to search for competence in members.

Unbalancing

As a family operates to maintain dysfunctional patterns, they also operate to repel, in different degrees, information that would alter those patterns. Unbalancing, or introducing disequilibrium, (Vassiliou, 1981), is a therapeutic operation tantamount to dropping a 100-pound sack of potatoes on an evenly balanced seesaw in an attempt to disrupt a family's dysfunctional status quo. In unbalancing, a counselor behaves in unfair and undemocratic ways. Minuchin and Fishman (1981) describe three categories of unbalancing:

1. Affiliation with members, where the therapist uses self to join with one member to change a hierarchical position in the family. For example, a therapist may bring his or her position of expertness to the side of an over-extended mother, or to a father who is peripheral. For strength, the demands of a specific goal may require the therapist to join with a family member other helpers have found unsympathetic. Searching for the underlying human ties makes the joining possible.
2. Alternating affiliation, which is best seen in families that present a problematic adolescent. Here the unbalancing involves temporarily siding with the parents and their right to set rules for the youngster in the house, and alternately the adolescent's right to negotiate for increasing autonomy.
3. Ignoring family members, which requires an ability on the part of the counselor to act as though certain family members were not even present in a session. This planned ignoring will cause those being ignored to take some form of action in order to become recognized. Occasionally, these actions are directed at the therapist, but more often, they will be designed to get attention from other family members. In the latter case, an attempt to form a unit apart from the counselor, realignment of the family structure, is more readily facilitated.

In a family where the mother and 10 year-old son were extremely over-involved, the son exhibited most infantile behaviors while the mother encouraged him to continue. The therapist could not speak directly to the son without the mother taking over. Seeing the therapist's plight, the supervisor entered the room with the goal of helping to block the mother, thereby allowing the therapist to contact the son. Blocking involves verbal and nonverbal behaviors similar to those of a traffic officer. The mother became quite furious with the supervisor. Finally, the son was able to tell the mother, "Leave me alone, I can talk for myself."

Intensity

Intensity is a technique related to unbalancing in that the therapist attempts to deliver a message to the system. "Interventions for intensifying messages vary according to the therapist's degree of involvement" (Minuchin & Fishman, 1981, p. 118). Involvement is related to the degree the counselor accelerates the emotional import of the message. An example of intensity may be the repetition of an unpleasant "reality" to the family: "If you continue this behavior, your son (or daughter) will unfortunately be successful in the next suicide attempt." Intensity can be developed in a variety of ways. Yet in order to be therapeutic, it demands behavior on the part of the therapist that pushes the family's level of discomfort higher. This challenging tactic requires the counselor to be able to cope with uncomfortable feelings of his or her own. As discomfort in family members is increased, family members become angry and provoked. This leads into the breaking up of the status quo. Intensity operations require close observation of the family and openness to feedback as they reorganize. In effect, the therapist has precipitated a crisis.

Intensity is another technique, like unbalancing, that goes against the grain of polite, middle-class professionals. It also raises concern, and rightly so, when "done for the wrong reasons." Typically when this technique is used with families, we work with a team of family therapists with one counselor observing behind the one-way mirror, and the intervention strategy is planned during a team conference before the family session.

A Synthesis of Technique and Process

Dissecting an approach into techniques risks losing perspective on how a model applies over the course of therapy. Furthermore, it is also useful to integrate functions of technique into the larger purposes of Structural therapy. Figure 13–1 provides a schema for viewing a process of therapist-family transaction. Two dimensions are utilized, *Family Arousal Level* and *Family Structural Complexity Level*. The former refers to techniques that are meant to create discomfort within a family system (the clearest examples would be unbalancing and intensity), while the latter refers to movement of a family system to higher levels of structural complexity, a goal of therapy. T_1 through T_6 are meant to reflect differing moments in a relationship of therapist and family.

This schema is not a prescription for the application of the Structural model, but rather it is meant to illuminate the complexity of a process. For instance, joining techniques (T_1) provide the base for structure-challenging techniques (T_2), which are meant to induce higher levels of arousal. In leading a family, a therapist carefully follows how the system organizes to meet, challenge and reduce arousal. T_3 suggests a moment where counselor follows the family and rejoins them.

New techniques, when applied, can feel awkward and mechanical. A "map" such as Figure 13–1, that suggests the territory, may help the trainee. Working with families is complex and conceptual frameworks can be aids to look at the complexity.

Figure 13–1   A Schema of Structural Family Therapy Process

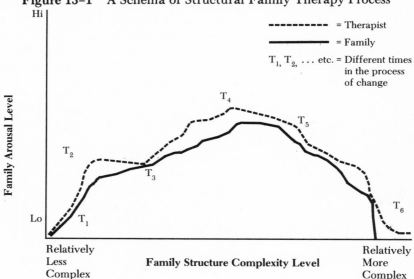

Larger System Issues

While not specifically addressed in the above overview, Structural thinking includes examining community systems (schools, work settings, welfare) as contributing to, exacerbating and/or maintaining dysfunctional patterns. Aponte (1981), in his discussions of therapy with poor families, continually emphasized the need for focus on organization or boundary issue: within the family and between family and community. Haley (1980), in *Leaving Home*, discussed the same issue: that a variety of "helpers" or agents of social control involved in a family themselves can create problems for the families. In our own experience in working with adolescents at high risk of, or being returned from institutionalization, we find that workers from other agencies have their own view of the problem and ways to solve it. Whenever possible, we believe it is beneficial to organize the helpers who have legal responsibility (child welfare worker or probation officer) while assuming a hierarchical position in relation to them and the family. This is not based on a belief that we have "a true" grasp on the family's problem, but in relation to families in crisis, delivering different messages only leads to feelings of less competence on the part of family members. As Aponte (1976) indicated, intrusion by agents of society is a fact of life for the poor. Therapists cannot ignore these agents in working with families. The significant question is how to organize these agents for the benefit of a family. This seems especially necessary in a society where prevailing government policies fail to do so.

The translation of the Structural model advocated herein also emphasizes an availability to the family in crisis, as opposed to therapy that is confined to seeing a family or its members once a week for an hour. In our practice of Structural Family Therapy, interventions occur in the settings where problems are seen at the time they occur: home, work, school, and other social institutions.

STAGES AND PROCESS
THROUGH TWO CASE EXAMPLES

While brief examples of a number of concepts, techniques, and skills have been provided throughout this chapter, a series of lengthier examples might be helpful in illustrating applications of the model. (Excellent transcripts of family therapy sessions are also to be found in a number of books—see Recommended Resources section of this chapter.)

J Family

In this case, the son, 16, was in placement in a group home. The referral came from the group home's agency and was a request to determine if the son could return home in the near future. The family, according to the referring worker, had exhausted all their resources and had successfully defeated two of their counselors. Our team discussed accepting this family and we decided to come in as consultants for a six-week contract with the family. Specifics of the case included the son who was failing in school and being violent in the home (throwing chairs against the wall, pulling the telephone off the wall) and the parents who felt son was disturbed and had sought and achieved institutional placement of him. Father was a self-described ex-alcoholic and businessman who had failed in a number of business ventures, and mother suffered from various psychosomatic problems. Both parents had succeeded in being identified by former therapists as not having any potential to change. Before the first session, the counselor was directed by her supervisor to question whether the family and she should work together and that both the family and she, in consultation with her supervisor, needed to arrive at a decision by the next session.

During the first session, the family demonstrated its rather rigid organization. Mother and son were extremely enmeshed (mother talked about her son's being in placement had interrupted their evening ritual of her brushing her son's hair). Father appeared disengaged from mother and son. The therapeutic hypotheses focused on the mother-son enmeshment, the lack of connections or disengagement in son-father, father-mother, and (indirectly) husband-wife relationships. The formulation by the supervisor and therapist was that son's symptomatic behavior enabled him to remain in need of his mother, and provided her relief from being alone. Father was effectively out of the picture, since he only came in to control his son and soothe his wife. Son, therefore, was enabling mother and father to have contact. In the first session, enactments by the family confirmed our formulations.

Mother would speak for son, and interfere in attempts by the counselor to activate the father-and-son relationship. Even when mother was blocked from interfering, father and son could not sustain a dialogue and son or father would turn to mother who would then triumphantly turn to therapist as if to say, "See, only I can talk to my son." During this first session, the counselor openly agreed that this family had problems and would raise questions about what, if anything, could be done. This tack was taken to avoid a struggle for power between family and therapist. By her behavior, the counselor willingly moved into a one-down position in relation to the family. At the end of the first session, the therapist agreed with the family as she instructed them to decide if they wanted five more sessions. The counselor softly added to the parents, "But you should realize that if you want Harry (the son) to return home, you may have to give up some of your ways of being together as a family. You, as mother, and you, as father, should very seriously discuss if your son is not better off in placement so things can remain the same." With this "soft"challenge, the therapist also mentioned that if they decided to come back, they would have to pick up their son from the group home and drive him to the session and not have the group home parent drive him. This intervention was a challenge and served to increase the family's discomfort.

The therapeutic team, knowing the family's success at defeating counselors was not interested in fighting with them. Rather the position of the team acknowledged a complementary aspect of their family reality; to remain as they were even if it was discomforting. By asking the family to pick up their child and bring him to therapy, the therapist issued a directive aimed at increasing parental subsystem interaction while keeping them responsible for their child. Child-care agencies often reinforce dysfunctional family patterns. One way they accomplish this is by allowing a family to give up responsibility for their offspring, further disrupting or reinforcing overly loose or rigid subsystem boundaries.

During the intervening days before the next scheduled appointment, the mother tried to contact the counselor by telephone to really describe Harry's problem and how it was the other parent's fault. All these attempts were recognized by the therapist who agreed that parents have tremendous influence on their children but that she should discuss her understandings with her husband.

In the next session, the family and counselor mutually agreed to five sessions. These sessions were quite intense. The basic therapeutic approach was to increase the level of discomfort with the goal of disrupting and creating a new response within this triad. The disengaged father was assigned all handling of responses to Harry's misbehavior. Father's behavior was reframed as competent, but lacking experience with his son; mother's behavior was reframed as tirelessly giving and frightened by her son's growing up; and Harry's behavior was viewed as caring about his mother. Harry, in an exchange with his father, was able to communicate his concern about past abuse and his doubt that he could trust his father to care for his mother when he really left home. This provided an excellent opportunity to challenge father to keep son out of his and and his wife's business, thus beginning to establish a much-needed generational boundary.

Tasks assigned in the session included having son behind the one-way mirror to observe how his parents needed to relearn how to be together while also illustrating how they could depend upon each other. Activating anger responses through intensity in the session by son toward mother was also an important feature of this brief intervention. This enactment illustrated how mother contributed to son's behavior. Son could receive a supportive response from mother only when he acted irresponsibly or in line with their past interaction as mother to young child, not as adolescent. Father was activated and asked to replace mother as disciplinarian of son.

In the last session, the change that we were working for occurred in the room. Mother and son were in a typical interaction, arguing without resolution, with son beginning to become exasperated, stammering, and becoming more hopeless. Father entered the interaction by firmly ending the mother-son interaction, while engaging son and negotiating rules for son's behavior. To punctuate the event, the supervisor entered the room and congratulated the father, then son. The last words to mother were, "Now you have a new challenge. You must support your husband in his relationship with your son."

While there are many complex issues involved in this case, it is presented here to illustrate a short-term, problem-focused Structural approach. Throughout the sessions, there were a variety of Structural interventions, each building on the other, but all were organized by the therapist's and supervisor's view of the problem, i.e., the current rigidly organized system of father disengaged and mother and son extremely enmeshed. Son's often violent and irresponsible behavior was viewed as maintaining and, at the same time, challenging the dysfunctional family structure. With this overly organized family, a small, but significant, change occurred in the last session. Father finally activated himself into breaking the mother-son enmeshment.

F Family

This second case example is presented to illuminate therapist interventions and, more significantly, the use of family drawings as a technique in the initial family therapy interview. I was asked to consult for a colleague on a family. John, 15, the identified patient, was presented as being disruptive at school and home, particularly in fighting with his sister, 8, and mother, 43. Father, 45, was described as distant.

> *Th:* My name is Dr. Tavantzis, and I've been asked to meet with you today. We will only meet once, and I hope that I can be helpful to you and your therapist, S. I would like to start by going around and finding out your names.
> *John:* I want to . . .
> *Mo:* John!
> *Th:* Would you like to start, Mom?

(In these opening moments, the counselor is very carefully following and experiencing the pull of the family. Observation partially entails nonverbal gestures [e.g., sitting], and the bid for opening the session. Purposefully starting ambiguously, the therapist is permitted to view a fragment of a pattern that becomes increasingly meaningful as time goes on: mother interrupting son is the way it appears here. Therapist acknowledges the hierarchy and follows mother who then relaxes as she is recognized.)

> *Mo:* My friends call me M——. John, our son, has a problem.
> *Th:* I realize that you really want to discuss how you've come here but names are important to me.

(Mother has made a second move to determine what happens—counselor insists on completion of the task. This has already impressed upon the therapist that in this family tasks may be continually disrupted, and he is starting to wonder how does one have a voice in this family.)

> *Th:* (To father) Your name is . . .

With the successful completion of naming, the therapist introduces drawing which is intended to accomplish the statement of problem and the enactments of the problem.

> *Th:* As a way to help you and myself know you better—Please all of you draw on one sheet of paper together.
> *Mary:* I don't want to.
> *Th:* Feel free to draw anything.

(Son begins to write the word F—— on the paper, changes his mind after getting a laugh from everyone, turns sheet over to start again. Therapist interferes and firmly, but supportively, insists he continue to use the same side. John begins to draw a river stream.)

> *Mo:* (To father): Are you going to draw or aren't you going to cooperate—as usual.

(Father remains silent except to grunt, and reluctantly begins to draw. At the same time, Mary begins to complain that John is bothering her—even while she calmly receives and he calmly gives her a crayon she has requested. This cooperative element of their behavior is stored for future reference by the therapist. John's response is to "extend the stream" into the house Mary is carefully putting the finishing touches on. Her house includes a chimney with smoke coming out.)

> *Mary:* Stay on your own side. Here, (draws a dividing line) don't cross that! (John, with a smile, proceeds to cross it. Mary shrieks.)
> *Mo:* Well (to father) aren't you going to do something about their fighting, you . . .
> *Fa:* They are just bickering, leave them alone.

(Mother begins to respond, stops, gives children a glare, and continues to draw a large mountain. Her drawing covers one-third of the paper. Meanwhile, father has selected a small corner to draw a small, faint tree.)

After the drawing stage, the counselor asks each member to provide a title, a feeling that is evoked by the family drawing, and what it reminds them of in their recent experience (Tavantzis, 1982; Vassiliou, 1981).

> *Mary:* A mess. That's my title—and mad, it makes me feel mad.
> *Th:* And what does it remind you of?
> *Mary:* John going over my line . . . in this drawing. He never leaves me alone . . . gets into my things.

(John's behavior seems to be a metaphor for how the parents are with each other—specifically, he gives a mirror image of mother in relation to the family. Mother interrupts Mary by arguing with father. Therapist interrupts them and brings them back to the current task.)

> *Th:* We will get to that (refers to arguing), but right now Mrs.——, tell me what you drew—and give it a title.

Mo: Confusion unlimited . . . sad . . . my family is falling apart (voice starts
to accelerate in loudness), he doesn't do anything. He is always un-
cooperative. I drew a mountain scene that reminds me of fresh air.

Th (To John): What do you see?

John: Everything is stupid—that's my title. And, I feel smart.

Th: John, how does this remind you of your family?

John: Bunch of stupid people, except Dad; sometimes he leaves me alone.

(Mother enters the conversation in a loud way yelling, "He doesn't
care that's why." Both children cover their ears. Therapist blocks mother
from continuing her behavior and turns to Mary.)

Th: You seem about ready to cry (mother begins to shout). It is unfortunate,
you miss the point (with your daughter). You behave contradictorily—you
say you want a cooperative family, but you undermine them from hearing
you when you shriek that way.

(Mother quiets down, but the pattern of dysfunction is further
clarified. A rule that is emerging is completion of any negotiation between
two people must be avoided. The counselor in response continues to move
to complete this stage. The therapeutic process is itself becoming a new experience for members in completing a task.)

Th (To father): You have been quiet in this uproar. What do you see in this
picture?

Fa: Ridiculous! My wife's mountain takes over the whole page.

(Siblings begin to argue between themselves. Mother requests father
to control them. Therapist insists on calmly continuing the transaction
with father in part to give him status and also to probe how immovable is
his disengagement. The sibling quarrels are viewed as a mirror image of
husband-wife disagreements.)

Fa: I would like more space in the drawing, but she gives no space
. . . no room.

(Here a significant feature of the drawing process is illustrated.
Father can use the drawing as a metaphor for his relationship to his wife
and the counselor can also actualize this metaphor repeatedly during a session or over several meetings.)

Th: Can you make room for yourself?

Fa: She takes over the whole space.

Th: You were content with that small space while you wanted to use more—

Fa: Yeah, but I am content.

(Therapist raises the complementary aspect of father's behavior while
challenging him.)

Fa: I guess I didn't want to change anything (refers to drawing).

Th: (Shifts from drawing to father's current experiences.) What do you have
that allows you to be content?

Fa: I have other things going for me. My work.

(The first half of the session is over. The counselor has obtained each member's view of self and family. Enactments of the family dysfunction have occurred. The drawing process has quickly provided a concrete illustration of the family structure. The middle stage of this interview focused on probing and creating intensity in the father-mother and husband-wife dyads.)

Th: (To father): Are you satisfied with what you have in this family?
Fa: I am reasonably content.
Th: I think you two (mother and father) need to discuss your situation. (Turns their chairs to face each other.)
Mo: (Complaining) You never stay home, you are buying antiques, always thinking about your deals.

(Father remains silent and then laughs. Counselor decides to intensify the interaction.)

Th (To mother): That the way it is? You scream, he stays out, and on and on. You are stuck. Do something different.

(John and Mary start to become uncomfortable and try to distract the therapist.)

Th: Let's draw a line between adults and kids. The kids are fine, they become upset when they see you two can't work it out.

(Their drawings suggest that their needs are not being met. John's "stream" needs structure so he can successfully channel his behavior, while Mary's drawings indicate her wish for security in the midst of the current upheaval.)

Th: Try to find a way to talk with each other.

While the session continued for another half hour, for the purpose of this chapter, the focus is on the use of the family drawings. For instance, the size of mother's drawing in contrast to father's provided the counselor with a concrete illustration that formed a hypothesis about their complementary interaction, i.e., mother complained about father's noninvolvement while providing little space for him to enter into any transaction. Father, for his part, saw little room for himself while his wife loomed large over him. He confined himself to a marginal role in the family in which he was content. Necessarily, from mother's perspective, she had to assume a major role in the family since the children are seen as "out of control," while father, who didn't see a problem, remained marginal. Their actual drawings, their behavior during the drawing phase and afterward, all provided confirmation at different levels of their relationship issues. In this family, as is often the case (Madanes, 1981), the symptoms of the family, the children's constant quarreling and especially John's disobedience, were similar to caricatures of issues between the father and mother.

Mother's enmeshment with the children needed to be blocked, while also blocking father's use of the children to argue with his wife. The therapeutic focus needed to be on parental and spousal relationships.

RECOMMENDED RESOURCES

HALEY, J. *A Modern Little Hans*. Philadelphia Child Guidance Clinic.

This is a 60-minute black-and-white videotape of therapy of a family with the presenting problem being a boy's fear of dogs. Mariano Barragan is therapist, while J. Haley provides the live supervision and narration for this training tape. It is a good introduction to Structural Family Therapy.

HALEY, J. & KIRSCHNER, S. *Heroin My Baby*. Family Therapy Institute, Chevy Chase, Md.

This tape illustrates Haley's model of working with a family who have a problem of a young adult leaving home. Excerpts of the complete therapy of the family of a heroin addict are used.

LIFTON, W. & TAVANTZIS, T. *Just like a family* (two-part film). Produced at SUNYA, 1978. (Available for rental from APGA.)

This film used a session in the life of a counseling group to discuss the dramatic changes and their impact on the family in America. The need for developing surrogate families—heterogeneous, ongoing family-like support systems for individuals—is introduced.

MINUCHIN, S. *Taming Monsters*. Philadelphia Child Guidance Clinic.

This is a videotape of Minuchin consulting with a family where the presenting problem is an out-of-control 5-year-old little girl. Excellent illustration of the techniques of enactment, unbalancing, and creating change within the consulting room. Also, fine example of the use of play in context of the Structural model.

MONTALVO, B. *A Family with a Little Fire*. Philadelphia Child Guidance Clinic.

Structural family therapy with a one-parent family where the presenting problem is the daughter's tendency to set fires. Sessions reveal a repetitive series of sequences with son, as a parental child, and interactions between mother and daughter.

PAPP, P. *Making the Invisible Visible: A Tape on Family Sculpting*. Nathan W. Ackerman Institute Training Tape, New York, 1974.

Sculpting is a technique that requires a troubled family to create a picture of their troubled relationships. In this videotape, Papp presents her approach, an interview and then a commentary on the conceptual model and family dynamics.

SUMMARY

This chapter on family therapy was divided into five major sections. The first provided a brief overview of the individual versus family systems perspective and a rationale for the latter. The second provided an introduction to the Structural model and defined and described key concepts: structure, boundaries, subsystems, development and hierarchy. The third part contained a description of various techniques and skills, including concrete examples. The fourth section provided two case examples of the application of a Structural perspective and included one example of the family drawing technique in therapy. The last section was a list of recommended resources.

REFERENCES AND RECOMMENDED READINGS

ACKERMAN, N. *The psychodynamics of family life.* New York: Basic Books, 1958.

———. *Treating the troubled family.* New York: Basic Books, 1966.

APONTE, H. Organizing treatment around the family's problems and their structural bases. *Psychiatric Quarterly,* 1974, 48, 8–12.

———. Underorganization in the poor family. In P. Guerin (Ed.), *Family therapy: Theory and practices.* New York: Gardner, 1976, (a).

———. The family-school interview. *Family Process,* 1976, 15, 303–310, (b).

——— & VAN DEUSEN, J. Structural family therapy. In A. Gurman & D. Kniskern (Eds.) *Handbook of family therapy.* New York: Brunner/Mazel, 1981.

BANDLER, R., GRINDER, J., & Satir, V. *Changing with families.* Palo Alto, CA: Science & Behavior Books, 1976.

BATESON, G. *Mind and nature.* New York: E. P. Dutton, 1979.

BATESON, G. *Steps to an ecology of mind.* New York: Ballantine Books, 1972.

BLOCH, D. (Ed.) *Techniques of family psychotherapy.* New York: Grune & Stratton, 1973.

BOSZORMENYI-NAGY, I. & SPARK, D. *Invisible loyalties.* New York: Harper & Row, 1973.

——— & FRAMO, J. (Eds.) *Intensive family therapy.* New York: Hoeber/Harper & Row, 1965.

BOWEN, M. *Family therapy in clinical practice.* New York: Jason Aronson, 1978.

BRODERICK, C. & SCHRADER, S. The history of professional marriage and family therapy. In A. Gurman & D. Kniskern (Eds.), *The handbook of family therapy.* New York: Brunner/Mazel, 1981.

BUCKLEY, W. Society as a complex adaptive system. In W. Buckley (Ed.) *Modern systems research for the behavioral scientist.* Chicago: Aldine, 1968.

DELL, P. Researching the family theories of schizophrenia. *Family Process,* 19 1980.

DURKIN, J. Foundations of autonomous living structure. In Durkin (Ed.) *Living groups: Group psychotherapy and general system theory*. New York: Brunner/Mazel, 1981.

ERICKSON, M. & HALEY, J. (Ed.) *Advanced techniques of hypnosis and therapy*. New York: Grune & Stratton, 1967, 395–397.

———, ROSSI, F., & ROSSI, S. *Hypnotic realities*. New York: Irvington Publishers, Inc., 1976.

FRAMO, J. Family theory and therapy. *American Psychologist*, 34, 1979, 988–992.

GRINDER, J., et al. *Patterns of the hypnotic techniques of Milton H. Erickson, M. D.* Cupertino, CA: Meta Publications, 1977.

GUERIN, P. (Ed.) *Family therapy: Theory and practice*. New York: Gardner, 1976.

GUERIN, P., JR. Family therapy: The first twenty-five years. In P. Guerin (Ed.) *Family therapy: Theory and practice*. New York: Gardner, 1976.

HALEY, J. *Strategies of psychotherapy*. New York: Grune & Stratton, 1963.

———. (Ed.) *Advanced techniques of hypnosis and therapy: Selected papers of Milton H. Erickson*. New York: Grune & Stratton, 1967.

———. Approaches to family therapy. *International Journal of Psychiatry*, 9, 1970, 233–242.

———. A review of the family therapy field. In J. Haley (Ed.), *Changing families*. New York: Grune & Stratton, 1971.

———. Family therapy: A radical change. In J. Haley (Ed.) *Changing families*. New York: Grune & Stratton, 1971.

———. We're in family therapy. In A. Ferber, M. Mendelsohn & A. Napier (Eds.) *The book of family therapy*. New York: Science House, 1972, 113–122.

———. Strategic therapy when a child is presented as the problem. *The Journal of the American Academy of Child Psychiatry*, 1973a, 12, 641–659.

———. *Problem solving therapy*. San Francisco: Jossey-Bass, 1976.

———. Ideas that handicap therapy with young people. *International Journal of Family Therapy*, I, 1979, 29–45.

———. *Leaving home: The therapy of disturbed young people*. New York: McGraw-Hill, 1980.

HOFFMAN, L. Enmeshment and the too richly cross-joined system. *Family Process*, 1975, 36, 457–458.

———. Breaking the homeostatic cycle. In P. Guerin (Ed.) *Family therapy: Theory and practice*. New York: Gardner Press, 1976.

———. *Foundations of family therapy*. New York: Basic Books, Inc., 1981.

JACKSON, D. The study of the family. *Family Process*, 1965, 4, 1–20.

———. *Therapy, communication and change and communication, family and marriage*. Palo Alto, CA: Science & Behavior Books, 1967.

———. (Ed.) *The question of family homeostasis:Communication, family and marriage*. Palo Alto, CA: Science & Behavior Books, 1968.

KANTOR, D. & LEHR, W. *Inside the family*. San Francisco, Calif.: Jossey-Bass, 1975.

KLEIN, N., ALEXANDER, J., & PARSON, B. Impact of family systems intervention on recidivism and sibling delinquency: A model of primary prevention and program evaluation. *Journal of Consulting and Clinical Psychology*, 1977, 45, 469–474.

LAING, R. *Self and others*. New York: Pantheon Books, 1969.

LANGSLEY, D. & KAPLAN, D. *Treating families in crisis*. New York: Grune & Stratton, 1968.

LENNARD, H. & BERNSTEIN, A. *Patterns in human interaction*. San Francisco: Jossey-Bass, 1970.

LEVINE, M. & LEVINE, A. *A social history of the helping professions*. New York: Appleton-Century-Crofts, 1970.

LIFTON, W. & TAVANTZIS, T. Facilitating surrogate families. *Journal of the Association of Specialists in Group Work*, 1979, 4, 104–109.

——— & MOONEY, W. The disappearing family: The role of counselors in creating surrogate families. *Personnel and Guidance Journal*, 1979, 58, 161–165.

MADANES, C. & HALEY, J. Dimensions of family therapy. *Journal of Nervous and Mental Disease*, 1977, 165, 88–98.

———. Protection, paradox, and pretending. *Family Process*, 1980, 40.

———. *Strategic family therapy*. San Francisco: Jossey-Bass, 1981.

MALCOLM, J. A reporter at large: The one-way mirror. *The New Yorker*, 1978, 40.

MARUYAMA, M. The second cybernetics: Deviation-amplifying mutual causal processes. In W. Buckley (Ed.) *Modern systems research for the behavioral scientist*. Chicago: Aldine, 1968.

MINUCHIN, S., et al. *Families of the slums*. New York: Basic Books, 1969.

———. *Families and family therapy*. Cambridge, Mass.: Harvard University Press, 1974.

——— & FISHMAN, C. *Family therapy techniques*. Cambridge, MA: Harvard University Press, 1981.

MONTALVO, B. & HALEY, J. In defense of child therapy. *Family Process*, 1973, 227–244.

NAPIER, A. with WHITAKER, C. *The family crucible*. New York: Harper & Row, 1978.

OLSEN, D., SPRENKLE, D. & RUSSELL, C. Circumplex model of marital and family systems: Cohesion and adaptability dimensions, family types, and clinical applications. *Family Process*, 18, 1979, 3–28.

PAPP, P. (Ed.) *Family therapy: Full-length case studies*. New York: Gardner Press, Inc., 1977.

RISKIN, J. & FAUNCE, E. An evaluative review of family interaction and research. *Family Process*, 1972, 11, 365–455.

RUESCH, J. & BATESON, C. *Communication: The social matrix of society*. New York: W. W. Norton, 1951.

SATIR, V. *Conjoint family therapy*. Palo Alto, CA: Science & Behavior Books, 1964.

SELVINA PALAZZOLI, M., et al. *Paradox and counterparadox*. New York: Jason Aronson, 1978.

———. Why a long interval between sessions. In M. Andolfi & I. Zwerling (Eds.) *Dimensions of family therapy*. New York: Brunner/Mazel, 1980.

——. Hypothesizing-circularity-neutrality. *Family Process*, 1980, 19, 3–12.

——. The problem of the referring person. *Journal of Marital and Family Therapy*, 1980, 6, 3–9.

SLUZKI, C. & RANSOM, D. (Eds.), *Double bind: The foundation of the communicational approach to the family*. New York: Grune & Stratton, 1976.

SPECK, R. & ATTNEAVE, C. *Family networks*. New York: Vintage Books, 1974.

STANTON, M. An integrated structural/strategic approach to family therapy. *Journal of Marital and Family Therapy*, 1981, 427–439.

——. Strategic approaches to family therapy. In A. Gurman & D. Kniskern (Eds.) *Handbook of family therapy*. New York: Brunner/Mazel, 1981.

TAVANTZIS, T. Family counseling, family drawings and the initial interview. *Journal of the Association of Specialists in Group Work* (in press), 1982.

VASSILIOU, G. Overcoming barriers to communication in group therapy with total strangers. In L. Wolberg & M. Ronson (Eds.) *Group and family therapy—1980*. New York: Brunner/Mazel, 1980.

—— & VASSILIOU, V. Outlining the synallactic collective image and technique as used within a systemic-dialectic approach. In J. Durkin (Ed.) *Living groups*. New York: Brunner/Mazel, 1981, 216–227.

VOGEL, E. & BELL, N. The emotionally disturbed child as the family scapegoat. In N. Bell & E. Vogel (Eds.) *The family*. Glencoe, IL: Free Press, 1980, 382–397.

WALBRIDGE, I. *Personal communication*. Schenectady, New York, 1981.

WATZLAWICK, P., BEAVIN, J. & JACKSON, D. *Pragmatics of human communication: A study of interactional patterns, pathologies and paradoxes*. New York: W. Norton, 1970.

——, WEAKLAND, J., & RISCH, R. *Change: Principles of problem formation and problem resolution*. New York: W. W. Norton, 1974.

WEAKLAND, J., RISCH, R., WATZLAWICK, P. & BODIN, A. Brief therapy: Focused problem resolution. *Family Process*, 13, 1974, 141–168.

WERTHEIM, E. Family unit therapy and the science and typology of family systems. *Family Process*, 12, 1973, 361–376.

WHITAKER, C. Psychotherapy of the absurd. *Family Process*, 14, 1975, 1–16.

Part III

CONSULTATION FOR HELPING PROFESSIONALS

Chapter 14

Consultation Procedures

ALTHOUGH CONSULTATION as a mental health service began in the early 1950s, it did not receive general acceptance in clinical and educational professions as a helping strategy until 1963 when Congress passed the Community Mental Health Center Act. This act provided specifically that consultation would be a necessary component of developing community mental health programs. The legislation recognized and encouraged strongly that the helping professions needed to shift from problem remediation to problem prevention (Kurpius & Robinson, 1978). The one individual who can be credited with providing the major impetus to the consultation movement during this period is Gerald Caplan. Caplan (1970) focused his early work on the theoretical bases of maintaining a healthy relationship between consultant and consultee in individual consultation, including developing the relationship, using effective levels of anxiety, destroying destructive stereotypes, developing additional insights, suggesting strategies for change, and reinforcing productive work efforts. Caplan differentiated between individual and organizational consultation, but devoted little of his effort toward identifying specific training procedures for consultants.

Training counselors as consultants became a major professional issue in the late 1970s. The American School Counselor Association (1977) policy statement included consultation as part of the school counselor's role, the Association for Counselor Education and Supervision (1977, 1978a, b) made definitive statements regarding consultation skills training, and several articles were published suggesting training modalities (Cochran,

1980; Dinkmeyer & Carlson, 1977; Gallessich & Ladogana, 1978; Randolph, 1980). In a survey involving 31 percent of the existing counselor training programs, Miles and Hummel (1979) reported that 44 percent of these programs offered courses in consultation and that the counselor as consultant was ranked second only to counseling as a major counselor responsibility.

Consultation as part of the counselor's role has therefore made a rapid and significant impact on the profession. Yet, much work needs to be accomplished to refine it as a legitimate, effective helping function. As Kahnweiler (1979) reported in addressing consultation needs for the future, consultation models and techniques must contain specific parts which are practical and applicable, existing training programs must become competency based, while more programs develop consultation courses, and more outcome research is recorded to demonstrate consultation makes a difference as an intervention technique.

The Purpose of Consultation

Consultation is not counseling, therapy, or supervision. It is a separate, quite distinct, method for a helping professional to provide *indirect* service to a client population through *direct* service to a consultee. Counseling is a direct, dyadic, interchange between counselor and client regarding a problem the client is experiencing. The focus in this relationship is entirely on the client's situation. Consultation, like counseling, is a dyadic relationship between the consultant and the consultee but differs dramatically in that the primary focus of the interaction between consultant and consultee is on a third person(s) or variable such as child, classroom management, or developing family rules in the home. Supervision, on the other hand, also involves a dyadic relationship but one person (supervisor) is in an authoritarian position which includes responsibility for evaluating the quality of work performance of the other person. Professional lines of major responsibility are clear in all three instances: counselor to client, consultant to consultee, supervisor to agency or institution.

Consultation can be further differentiated from therapy by examining the clientele and basic objectives of each. In counseling children, the primary client is the child. In rare instances, therapists of children may become involved in counseling relationships with adults such as a child's teacher or parents. The fundamental objectives for counseling are to establish a relationship in which the client feels free to make an extensive exploration of self, encourage and support the client's personal psychological growth, and assist the client with appropriate behavioral change. Unlike counseling, the consultant's clientele consists predominantly of adults who work with children: teachers, parents, administrators, law enforcement personnel, psychologists, psychiatrists, social workers, medical doctors, and other referral sources. Therapists may work as consultants with children but very infrequently. I have established the following basic objectives of my work as consultant to be to:

1. Establish a relationship in which the consultee will readily express job-related concerns.
2. Lead the consultee toward new insights about *professional* self.
3. Encourage personal *professional* growth in the consultee.
4. Evaluate the consultee's situation, and stimulate the consultee to develop ideas for positive changes in performance.
5. Suggest specific techniques and strategies to help create positive change.
6. Model appropriate behavior.
7. Provide inservice training, information, and informational resources.
8. Evaluate progress.

Although the several distinctions offered between counseling, supervision, and consultation may have helped readers to clarify the concept consultation, it has not been defined. Dinkmeyer and Carlson (1975) provide a definition of consultation that incorporates most of my personal opinion.

> Consultation, as we view it, is a process in which the consultant is available to the consultee in order to produce change in the system, growth for the consultee, or an improved relationship with the consultee's client. The consultant relationship is based upon the necessary and sufficient conditions for a helping relationship: empathy, genuineness, concreteness, respect, and confrontation. Beyond the relationship, the consultant must understand a pragmatic theory of human behavior which can be applied in the consultation process. The consultant is capable of working with the consultee individually or in a group. He has an orientation that is concerned with perceptual meanings, beliefs, and creating an atmosphere for change. The consultant is able to develop a collaborative, clarifying, confrontative relationship in which the consultee looks at specific behaviors of the client, his own responses, and the consequences of the interaction. Together, consultant and consultee consider alternatives and the consultee decides, plans, and makes commitments (p. xvi).

The Value of Consultation

In the late 1960s, Begal (1967) reported to the Canadian Commission on Emotional and Learning Disabilities in Children that 1.5 American children in 10 suffered mental health problems. This figure was documented later by Couchman (1974) when he indicated that approximately 15 percent of the population in the United States required assistance from mental health professionals. In addition, the passage of Public Law 94–142, the Education of Handicapped Children Act, in 1975, and its subsequent implementation in the schools in 1977, created a massive public awareness regarding handicapping conditions in children and the mandate to public schools to educate these children in the least restrictive environment. What does this information mean? Let us consider a numeric example based on some hypothetical data.

The average class size per school is between 20 and 30 children. In a school with 25 classrooms (i.e., between 500 and 750 children and one counselor), a minimum of 75 children will require direct counseling assistance. It is almost impossible and certainly impractical to attempt to service these children through individual appointments in a less-than-40–hour work week. If group therapy were used, it would indicate a minimum of 15 groups of five children each which would seriously restrict the counselor's involvement in other guidance activities such as helping to screen handicapped children for proper school placements.

As educational challenges to public institutions and agencies increase, with reduced financial support, administrators and therapists are confronted with difficult decisions. How do they meet the children's needs most effectively? Counselor educators such as Faust (1968) and Dinkmeyer and Caldwell (1970) recognized that counselors' time would be limited and advocated they work toward including consultation as part of a developmental guidance approach in the schools. By working as a consultant to the 25 teachers in the classrooms mentioned in the previous example, counselors could impact positively on all children in the school.

Another way to look at this same issue is to consider that one distraught teacher is likely to create a dysfunctional classroom environment with 20 distracted children. As consultant to this teacher, the counselor can help change the lives of 20 children and one adult. Thus, therapists in agencies and institutions who assist other professionals with problems, can impact the overall environment through a "ripple effect." Unfortunately, one serious drawback regarding the value of consultation, as Kahnweiler (1979) made clear in his historical review of consultation, is that research related to consulting practices has lagged far behind the development of consultation theory, rationale, models, and techniques. In four professional journals surveyed from 1969 to 1978, only 19 research articles were published related to consultation; of these, only 12 indicated the relative effectiveness of consultation.

KEY CONCEPTS

Adopting a Theory of Consultation

As with individual counseling and group counseling, it is my belief that therapists must practice consultation from a theoretical base. Since no singular theory of consultation has evolved, most counselor education programs instruct students in consultation theory by adapting existing counseling theory to the practice of consultation. I have found this method of training acceptable in as much as students are able to integrate successfully their knowledge of counseling theory to their practice of consultation. Students are encouraged to adopt a theoretical position which is uniquely their own. This learning exemplifies an approach which Brammer and Shostrom (1982) have labeled "creative synthesizing."

> The "creative" element comes in when the counselor not only puts together concepts and practices from other theories in new ways, but also transforms them into ideas and methods which have continuing relevance for himself . . . .
> The "synthesis" element comes into the theory-building process as counselors strive to integrate in incremental fashion what appear to be separate ideas and uncoordinated methods (p. 36).

To elucidate this creative synthesizing process, let us examine consultation from the two theoretical positions which predominate in this text, the person-centered process model and the behavioral model. Table 14–1 compares and contrasts the two models according to seven criteria: objec-

Table 14-1
CONSULTATION APPROACHES

Criterion	Person-Centered Process Model	Behavioral Model
Objective:	Problem resolution	Same
Etiology:	Psychodynamic conflict	Learned maladaptive behavior
Approach for a solution:	Insight via introspection and information	Reinforcement by conditioning
Consultant's role:	Nondirective Nonauthoritative Avoid therapeutic input Facilitator of process Collaborator Resource person	Directive Authoritative Instigate therapeutic input Evaluator, supervisor Same Same
Types of responses:	Response to feelings Clarifying Interpreting Questioning Supporting	Giving direction Reinforcing Informing Evaluating Judging
Consultee's role:	Involving Informing Exploring Elaborating Analyzing	Same
Responsible person:	Consultee	Consultant and consultee

tive, etiology, approach for solution, consultant's role, types of response, consultee's role, and responsibility for outcomes. Readers can quickly recognize that the two approaches are dramatically different other than the two criteria objectives and consultee roles.

How does the consultant synthesize different theoretical models? Egan (1982) presents a three-stage eclectic model for the skilled helper: exploring and clarifying the problem, developing new perspectives and setting goals, and acting, which includes identifying alternative strategies for problem resolution, implementing a program, and evaluating programs. For the most part, I remain person-centered in the first two stages. It is the third stage (acting) that allows integration of a variety of theories and techniques for helping the consultee, depending on the consultee's situation. Before we examine the consultation process further, it is important that readers realize that, in most instances, therapists are not asked to consult immediately. Therefore, it is important that counselors communicate their role to their constituencies and work gradually toward building their consultant image.

Building the Consulting Role

To enhance public relations efforts in your setting, you need to be available and visible to teachers, parents, administrators, and other professionals who may use consulting services. The following recommendations will help to build the consultation image.

1. *Plan and schedule to be with faculty or staff during the day.* As a consultant, spend the first hour of each day talking with teachers about their problems. Other times during the day that are available include immediately after school, during planning time, and during lunch. In addition, teachers may sometimes welcome you into their classrooms for a chat while children work at their desks.

2. *Avoid isolation in an office.* Toward the end of each day, move throughout the building and stop to talk with faculty who are willing and interested in your help.

3. *When asked, respond honestly and openly to important questions such as institutional policy or role expectations.* With the introduction of many special-education programs and teachers, one of the most difficult tasks you will handle is to help regular classroom teachers understand that special-education teachers work hard even though they have fewer children assigned to them. Another important issue is to help both administrator and teachers understand that you support discipline but you are not an agent for punishment.

4. *Treat faculty as professional equals.* A collegial relationship in

which all parties work together toward common goals is most beneficial.

5. *Avoid using professional jargon in conversations.* No one likes to feel they are being talked down to.

6. *Remember that success experiences with a few faculty will encourage others to be involved with you.* Identify those persons with whom you seem to relate best and begin consulting with them. These faculty will quickly pass the word via the "grapevine" as to how helpful you have been.

Assessment of Self and Others

As mentioned previously, when initiating any consulting relationship, therapists must have a thorough knowledge of their consultation role, theory, and techniques. It is also extremely important for a consultant to know self in this role so that you can model self-confidence and ego strength when working with adults who are experiencing self-doubts. If you are not as comfortable working with adults as you are with children, then it behooves you to de-emphasize your consultation role until you gain sufficient skills and more experience. Lastly, you will increase your opportunities for success by consulting initially with persons who are experiencing conflicts in areas of life that you are knowledgeable, experienced, and capable of helping.

Like yourself, each faculty and staff member in your school or agency is a unique individual who possesses different personality characteristics and abilities to cope with stress and anxiety. It is the consultant's responsibility to identify consultees' "psychological positions" and begin at the level where they are functioning. In addition to different personalities, all faculty have distinct abilities and capacities to contribute to the system. The consultant's assessment of consultee includes discovering faculty strengths, as well as weaknesses, so that the individual's strengths can be reinforced frequently and recognized publicly while remediating weaknesses. I often ask consultees if they would mind my sharing with other faculty a particular item of their work I found beneficial to children. I have never been refused and by simply asking the question smiles appear on many persons' faces who appreciated this simple recognition of their efforts. Many faculty commented how refreshing it was to hear about their colleagues in a positive manner for a change rather than "gossiping" or "griping." They also would frequently, at a later time, go to the teacher's room to examine the project or process under discussion. As a result of this broadcasting effort, a cross-communication system can begin which provides cross-fertilization of positive thinking and excellence in performance.

In addition to identifying psychological position, and strengths and weaknesses of the faculty, the consultant should determine consultees' educational and philosophical orientations for working with children. It is important to have this information so that consultants can "match" their recommendation for change with the ideological positions of consultees. For example, some teachers and parents are absolutely opposed to the use of behavioral intervention strategies with children and when these are mentioned as possible alternatives, they became incensed. The remainder of a session may then be spent on rebuilding or redefining the relationship. To avoid similar unpleasantries in consulting, readers should consider three additional rules of thumb:

1. *Never reject a potential consultee.* When making "rounds," you might encounter teachers who are experiencing crises with a particular child. To say, "I can't see Billy today," or "My schedule is full now, but . . . " are rejecting responses. Teachers will not hear past the first part of these statements.

2. *Take the time to show you care.* Consultants must stop and listen to consultees, respond to their concerns, and explain specifically when and what can be done.

3. *Not all faculty want a consultant's help.* Although you are beginning your consulting activities with those persons with whom you are most comfortable, remember you may encounter some faculty who are frightened of "outsiders" and do not desire to share of themselves or their ideas. Consultants need to work with those persons who are willing, offer their services to those who are not, but accept the possibility that some persons will find your services aversive.

Personal experience has also demonstrated that persons experiencing stress and anxiety seek help. The type of help sought is usually either related to a need for information or a crisis. As a result, I have classified consultation into three distinct categories: informational, crisis and developmental.

Informational Consultation

Informational consultation occurs when a consultee requests specific information from the consultant. Gazda et al. (1977) discuss four classifications for helpee statements to assist mental health workers to perceive what it is the helpee is seeking: requests for information, requests for action, requests for understanding/involvement, and inappropriate communication. These categories and descriptions supplement my thinking on consultation types. For example, a request for information by a teacher might be, "Johnny is taking Ritalin for hyperactivity. I would like to know more about the drug and its side effects." In this situation, the consultant acts as a resource person and does one of three things: provides the information with a verbal response, shares the information from the *Physicians Desk Reference* (see "Recommended Resources" in Chapter 1) or other office literature, or if the information is not accessible immediately, refers the teacher to an appropriate resource outside the school. A fourth alternative might be for the consultant who does not possess the information to offer to take action and obtain the information and relay it back to the teacher. Information can be extremely helpful. Sometimes it is all that is necessary to increase consultee's understanding of a client enough to reach a solution. However, I offer a word of caution. As with therapy, in consultation, the presented request is not always the issue that needs to be addressed. For many potential consultees, requests for information are made when they are unsure as to how to initiate a request for action or understanding and involvement.

Crisis Consultation

Crisis consultation occurs when a consultee seeks help with a problem which requires immediate attention. It is a request for the consultant to perform a physical act to assist the consultee. For example, a teacher asked for help regarding a boy who, on several occasions, became ill immediately after eating lunch. The following is part of the dialogue between the teacher and consultant:

> *Consultee:* Can you help me? Johnny vomits almost every day after lunch. He's obviously not physically ill because his mother had him checked out recently by a doctor. I don't know what to do.
>
> *Consultant:* It is obvious you are extremely worried about Johnny. It is a difficult situation, one in which I need more information. Let me observe him at lunch today, and we can meet afterwards to discuss it.
>
> *Consultant:* (After lunch.) Well, he did it again, but I learned a lot. While observing Johnny, I noticed three important things about his lunch behavior. First, he is gulping his food by the mouthfuls. In fact, it only took him three minutes to devour his entire lunch. Second, when he finishes his lunch, he grabs parts of other children's food which he also eats rapidly. Finally, he is extremely active for the remainder of the lunch period. He crawled under the table, and got up two other times to poke children.
>
> *Consultee:* I agree, but what can I do?
>
> *Consultant:* Let's work on this together. I will contact the mother and the family physician today. Could you try sitting Johnny at the end of the table where he has minimal contact with the other children? This move may re-

duce his activity and provide him less chance of getting food from other children. Together, we might also teach a class lesson on nutrition, something about good eating habits.

Consultee: OK. You take care of the seating arrangements, too, and I'll plan the health lesson.

Consultant: Great! We can begin tomorrow.

Like informational consultation, crisis consultation may require only one session or it may involve several sessions where a model for consultation is implemented and strategies for intervention are discussed, implemented, and evaluated.

Developmental Consultation

Developmental consultation, in contrast to the other two types of consultation, is a continuous educational program with a preventative focus. The consultant takes an active, developmental role in the institution or agency's total program. In developmental consultation, the consultant works with faculty and staff to integrate counseling and guidance principles into the agency climate or school curriculum. For example, as a developmental consultant, I have helped teachers write classroom units for the psychological and affective education of children in content areas such as feelings (Gumaer, Bleck, & Loesch, 1975), friendship and values (Ackerman & Gumaer, 1976), racial understanding (Gumaer, 1977), and extortion (Gumaer & Beale, 1977). In addition, developmental consultation may involve planning and implementing inservice workshops in which the consultant introduces, explains, and demonstrates counseling and guidance materials and techniques for classroom use (Myrick & Moni, 1972).

Developmental consultation should be an organized, systematic approach for helping. In an earlier article (Gumaer & Myrick, 1976), I described a step-by-step process model for developmental consultation. However, since that time, I have refined my thinking to include the following six steps: identifying and focusing the main issues, observing, facilitating exploration of the issues, hypothesizing and developing an intervention plan, implementing strategies, and evaluating, following up and reevaluating. This developmental consultation model fits nicely in Egan's helper model mentioned previously.

Step 1. Identifying and Focusing the Main Issues

Because the developmental consultant is an active individual and has the latitude in role to move about the building each day, it is important that the consultant focus a major portion of "making the rounds" on developmental concerns of the institution, faculty, and children. Examples of developmental concerns which have been encountered are: classrooms where counseling and guidance materials are not used, classrooms that are disorganized and mismanaged, classrooms that are experiencing interpersonal relationship problems, classrooms that are undergoing mainstreaming experiences, teachers who are distraught, teachers who are experiencing difficulty with classroom management, first-year teachers who feel inadequate or uncomfortable, and teachers who experience problems with certain types of children such as gifted, underachievers, or slow learners who are not eligible for special-education-program services. Once the consultant has identified a few key developmental issues of the institution, I recommend the issues be prioritized so that the most important concerns receive initial and immediate attention.

Step 2. Observing

After the initial interview, the consultant should observe the consultee, other persons involved in the situation, and the environment where the problem occurs. It is through observation that the consultant objectifies the consultee's perception of the situation. The consultant can log data on teacher-student or parent-child interactions which either supports what the consultee is reporting or refutes erroneous consultee impressions. In addition to observation, the consultant may find a personal interview with children helpful to compare and contrast their point of view with that of the observation and consultee reports.

Step 3. Facilitating Exploration of the Issues

This step involves the consultant's conscious use of three child-centered skills discussed in Chapter 2: listening, responding to feelings, and clarifying the situation. Because the skills were examined earlier in light of their use in a counseling sense, a brief description of their suitability in this consultation model will follow.

LISTENING. As in counseling, it is important initially that the consultant attend and listen to the consultee in order to facilitate catharsis of the consultee's emotions regarding the situation. The consultee must relieve self of an "affective overload" when discussing emotionally charged issues before being able to think clearly about the issue. Once emotions are defused, the consultant and consultee can plan constructively to change the situation. This attending and listening behavior by the consultant builds, enhances, and bonds the consultant-consultee relationship because the consultant is perceived by the consultee as a caring and helping person of all parties involved in the problem. The consultant also gains valuable information which can be compared with previous information and observations for consistencies and inconsistencies. The consultant also listens selectively for consultee's feelings.

RESPONDING TO FEELINGS. By responding to feelings, the consultant should encourage additional catharsis related to various aspects of the identified problem situation. However, the consultant must be extremely careful not to encourage an extensive and personal exploration of the consultee's self. The self-disclosure of the consultee should remain at the intermediate level as described in Chapters 2 and 10. Thus, the consultation relationship is developed and maintained by sharing feelings about others and things and avoiding a counseling relationship involving the disclosing of deep feelings about self. In addition to the catharsis experience, which usually involves ventilation of negative affect, the consultant should be sure to invite the consultee to express positive thoughts and feelings related to the concerns and reinforce the consultee's attitudes and behaviors believed to be in the best interests of the consultee. The consultant's response to feelings of the consultee indicates the consultant's accurate understanding of the situation to the consultee.

CLARIFYING THE SITUATION. Through clarification, the consultant indicates a desire to understand the entire problem and indicates to the consultee a recognition that no easy solution exists. When clarifying, the consultant may wish to identify and discuss specific consultee or child behaviors that seem to create the situation and to exacerbate or minimize the problem and those behaviors that might lead to positive change and remediation.

Step 4. Hypothesizing and developing an intervention plan

Together the consultant and consultee explore and examine various thoughts as to what precipitated the problem(s). After hypotheses regarding causation are generated and discussed, the consultant and consultee might develop a list of possible ways to deal with the problem. This list should be prioritized from the most likely cause(s) to least likely. Once causes are ranked, the consultation process should proceed with a discussion of methodologies for intervening in the situation. As each alternative method for change is produced, an examination of the potential consequences of implementation should occur. Naturally, it follows that the consultant helps the consultee select and plan specifically a "best fit" plan for intervention. This plan ought to include specific objectives for each method decided upon as part of the intervention and strategies to help meet each objective.

A case example should help delineate further the first four steps of the model. This particular situation depicts a classroom teacher's struggle to help a slow-learning child. The situation is common to most teachers in schools today, and is one in which I have been asked frequently to consult. What follows are edited excerpts of two 30-minute consultation sessions.

Step 1

Consultant: What is it you wanted to see me about this afternoon?
Teacher: There is a boy in my class I don't understand. Maybe you can help. He disturbs the class, won't concentrate and doesn't finish his work.
Consultant: Uh huh!
Teacher: It's not that he fights in class but he comes in from recess all stirred up and won't settle down.
Consultant: What is it that you notice specifically about his behavior when he comes in?
Teacher: He's usually running instead of walking. He always has negative comments for someone like, "I'll get you." It's mostly a verbal thing rather than physical fighting.
Consultant: How does it involve the other children?
Teacher: They seem to feel they have to respond to it. "I'll get my gang and get you."
Consultant: So. He's kind of a catalyst for negative behavior.
Teacher: Yeah! It's almost like he's proving himself. I really don't think he feels that great about himself and it's his way of making himself feel better.
Consultant: It sounds like you are really trying to understand him. And you don't have a grasp, right now, of what's really going on.
Teacher: Yeah! That would carry over though in terms of the work that he does because he wants me with him constantly when he's working. It's like he's saying, "I can't do it unless you help me."
Consultant: To give us a balanced picture, what are some of his strengths?
Teacher: OK. In class discussion, he has a lot to contribute. I feel he says some good things but it takes so long.
Consultant: Sounds like you really want him to succeed more than he is because you believe in him, but it's hard to wait.
Teacher: Yeah!

(About 15 minutes of consulting later.)

Consultant: Well, our time is up. I would like to do two things before we meet again. First, I would like to give him a brief intelligence test to get a picture of his general ability to begin the screening process for special-education placement if it becomes a relevant issue. Secondly, I would like to observe him on the playground and in your classroom. When can we start?
Teacher: Tomorrow.

Step 2

Consultant: I had a chance to test and observe Jim today. First, I would like to share the results and some of my observations with you and then together try to develop some ideas about the causes for his behavior.

The screening test revealed that he has an IQ score of 85, which places him in a slow-learner category. If it is accurate, and I have no reason to believe otherwise, it means he will not qualify for any of our special-education programs. A student must have at least a score of 90 to be considered for learning disabilities placement and a score of 70 or below for mental retardation. It appears he won't be able to do as well academically as you want, and without special services, the burden will be on you and Jim.

Teacher: What does this mean for Jim and me?

Step 3

Consultant: Well, let's review your concerns. You are worried about his self-concept. You feel his low opinion of self is related to how he performs in his schoolwork and how he gets along with other children.

Teacher: Yes.

Consultant: As I observed him, I noticed he was working with another boy.

Teacher: That wasn't unusual. Sometimes he does it and other times he won't. But, did you notice he erased a lot and said, "It's all wrong."

Consultant: I couldn't hear him but I noticed he looked around and was off task after a few minutes.

Teacher: Yeah. He does that a lot. He just gets started and quits.

Consultant: I also noticed that you went to him and praised him for his work and he responded well to you.

Teacher: That's just it. I can't be there all the time so he will work. There are other children, too. Part of it seems to be his inadequacy but part seems to be his just wanting my attention.

Consultant: It's like he needs to get other people involved with him and he needs your attention a lot. How do you feel when he does that?

Teacher: I have mixed feelings. I want to help him, but not too much. I want to give support, but I don't want to help him all the time. There are 26 other kids, and I can't spend all my time with him.

Consultant: It is frustrating.

Teacher: Yeah! It's like saying to him, "Look, I know you can do more, I wish you felt that way, too."

Consultant: Ah! Then you are really looking for ways to boost his self-confidence so he doesn't have to resort to fighting and doesn't always demand other's attention.

I think I'm beginning to understand some of the things

you are saying. You said you're worried about his self-concept, and you feel that affects his behavior in school, like completing his work by himself, like playing with others without getting in fights, and having things his way.

Teacher: That's right.

Consultant: As we work together, it's obvious to me how much you care for Jim and want him to do well. Yet, your efforts seem to be in vain and the harder you try, the more frustrated you get.

Teacher: Exactly! I've run out of things to do. It has become exhausting and exasperating. It just hurts so much to see someone his age give up.

Step 4

Consultant: I would guess Jim feels pretty much like you do. He might behave the way he does for attention or approval. Yet we can't rule out the possibility much of his work may be difficult and require him to spend more time on it than the average to above-average child and that he may not finish. However, I don't want to overlook his strengths. Many times we can eliminate causes for misbehavior and improve self-esteem by using a child's strengths. What are his strengths, again?

Teacher: He seems to do better in math than other subjects especially with computation problems. He is a leader, too.

Consultant: Let's begin to make a plan for Jim. These are things we've mentioned: (1) He has a goal for attention that seems to be caused by low self-worth. (2) He feels inadequate in certain academic areas, reading for example. (3) He has strengths in leadership and math computation.

Teacher: That's about it.

Consultant: OK. Let's generate a list of things we can do. You offer some ideas and I'll jump in with some, too.

Teacher: Something that might be helpful would be to team him up with another person. Where his skills are stronger than the other person. This would put him in a position of leadership and he could see he was able to do something better than another child. He would also feel good about himself as a helper.

Consultant: Yeah! That would sure work on his sense of inadequacy and you would be actively helping him build good feelings about self.

I would like to suggest he get attention at times he wasn't acting out but when he was on task and following instructions.

Teacher: Right. You're saying ignore his daydreaming, but when he's got his pencil in his hand and writing go over and say, "I'm glad to see you working so hard."

Consultant: Uh huh! Help him to learn to get attention for constructive work habits and not acting out.

(Consultation continued to completion.)

Step 5. Implementing Strategies

Because in developmental consultation the plan for intervention is a cooperative effort between consultant and consultee, it becomes a joint responsibility for it to be implemented successfully. Although the consultee has the major role of implementing the change procedures in the classroom or home, the consultant should work collaboratively with the consultee during implementation. The consultant can help by looking for unforeseen circumstances, obtaining needed resources, offering support, observing progress, and making additional recommendations. In many situations that involve parents, consultants will be unable to visit the home directly. However, the consultant should be available by phone and be accessible for continued consultation. In addition, when implementing new strategies, teachers and parents are often skeptical of their value. It behooves the consultant to recommend a gradual, small-scale initial endeavor to provide maximum probability of success and to allow careful evaluation before the procedure is adopted by the consultee as a matter of practice.

Step 6. Evaluating, Following up, and Reevaluating

With all the paperwork and other responsibilities teachers and parents face daily, a tendency exists to overlook the value of evaluation. However, even though data collection may appear to be a necessary evil, it is imperative to the successful consultation process. Evaluation can begin as early as the second step when the consultant observes. It is common practice to make observations and record behaviors systematically to obtain a "baseline" performance level of behavior, which then acts as a standard of comparison for additional chartings following interventions. It is my opinion that evaluations should occur before and after implementing strategies. Without precomparisons and postcomparisons, in some instances, it is difficult to demonstrate progress to the consultee. Too often teachers and parents expect "miracles" and want a total elimination of unwanted behavior overnight. Often, these consultees need evidence that small increments of change in the desired direction is progress to keep them involved and their interest high.

To obtain the greatest cooperation in evaluation, I will usually ask consultees first how and when they would prefer to evaluate before making recommendations. It is, therefore, necessary to determine not only the evaluation methodology with the consultee but also reasonable timing. For instance, once a procedure has been implemented, it might then be continued for one week and evaluated subjectively by consultant and consultee in a follow-up session. If at this time it appeared to be successful, it might be continued for a longer time period such as five weeks before objective evaluations such as charting or checklist were used again. Consulting sessions should be scheduled frequently to reevaluate progress and the strategies. Should a procedure prove ineffective, the consultant and consultee would then return to Step 4 in the developmental model to reinitiate the search for an effective method of remediation.

Consultation is an integral part of most mental health systems and can serve a vital role in the intervention and remediation of children's problems. As with individual counseling and group counseling, I would like to share with readers a checklist for consultation skills. Although not inclusive, Appendix F describes those consultation competencies I feel are absolutely essential to master the process.

RECOMMENDED RESOURCES

Books

ALPERT, J. & ASSOCIATES. *Psychological consultation in educational settings.* San Francisco: Jossey-Bass, 1982.

This casebook focuses on consultation in a variety of educational settings from elementary school to college. It highlights issues in the following consultation stages: entry, diagnosis, intervention, and evaluation. Of particular interest to readers will be the authors' sharing of personal experiences and their practical comments on successes and failures.

CARLSON, J., SPLETE, H., & KERN, B. (Eds.) *The consulting process.* Falls Church, VA: American Personnel and Guidance Association, reprint series No. 7, 1975.

In this book of readings, the editors have compiled a number of articles on every conceivable aspect of the school counselor's consulting process.

COOPER, S. & HODGES, W. *The mental health consultation field.* New York: Human Sciences Press, 1983.

This four-part book of readings focuses on models of consultation, processes of consultation, several issues in consultation (including transition points, accountability and ethics), and the evolution of consultation in helping professions.

DRAPELA, V. *The counselor as consultant and supervisor.* Springfield, IL: Charles C Thomas, 1983.

This book is unique in that it treats the concepts of consultation and supervision in a unified format. Section one presents the theoretical foundations of counseling, consultation, and supervision. Section two focuses on working with individuals and groups in consultation and supervision. The last section discusses the consultant's role as a change agent in institutions and the community.

DINKMEYER, D. & CARLSON, J. (Eds.) *Consultation: A book of readings.* New York: John Wiley & Sons, 1975.

This book of readings begins with several articles focused on the rationale for and theory of consultation. It next presents consultation as an approach for interacting with a total system and readers are introduced to a number of procedures for working with the system. Part three provides readings which detail specifics of various consultation processes. These processes are then applied to individual consultation, teacher groups, and parent and family groups in the remainder of the book.

GALLESSICH, J. *The profession and practice of consultation.* San Francisco: Jossey-Bass, 1982.

This handbook contains four parts which offer helping professionals basic information needed to establish and maintain an effective consulting practice. The first part examines social, institutional, and technological forces shaping modern consultation practice. Part two explains differences in major consultation approaches, then describes six distinctive models. The third part details steps common to all types of consultation and offers guidelines for each phase of the consultation process. The last part suggests ways to improve consulting services, professional ethics, and training programs.

Article

KURPIUS, D. A topical bibliography on consultation. *Personnel and Guidance Journal,* 1978, 56, 442–447.

This bibliography includes extensive listings for books and journals under the following topics: consultation theory and process, planned change, school and university, organization development, organization theory and practice, research and evaluation, and planning for the future.

SUMMARY

The first section of this chapter provided an introduction, rationale, definition, and discussion of the value of consultation. The second section emphasized the key concepts of adopting a theory of consultation, building the consulting role, assessment of self and others, informational consultation, crisis consultation, and developmental consultation. The third section focused on a developmental process model for consultation which included an example of its use. Several recommended resources on consultation concluded the chapter.

REFERENCES AND RECOMMENDED READINGS

ABRAMOVITZ, A. Methods and techniques of consultation. *American Journal of Orthopsychiatry,* 1953, 23, 126–133.

ACES. Standards for the preparation of counselors and other personnel services specialists. *Personnel and Guidance Journal,* 1977, 55, 596–601.

———. ACES guidelines for doctoral preparation in counselor education. *Counselor Education and Supervision,* 1978, 17, 163–166(a).

———. ACES position paper: Counselor preparation for career development/career education. *Counselor Education and Supervision,* 1978, 17, 168–179(b).

ACKERMAN, K. & GUMAER, J. Human sexuality: An affective classroom approach. *Journal of Counseling Services,* 1976, 11, 13–19.

ALPERT, J. & ROSENFIELD, S. Consultation and the introduction of social problem-solving groups in schools. *Personnel and Guidance Journal,* 1981, 60, 37–41.

ALTROCCHI, J., SPIELBERGER, C., & EISDORFER, C. Mental health consultation with groups. *Community Mental Health Journal,* 1965, 1, 127–134.

ANANDAM, K. & WILLIAMS, R. A model for consultation with classroom teachers on behavior management. *The School Counselor,* 1971, 18, 253–259.

ANDERSON, D. Counseling and consultation versus teacher consultation in the elementary school. *Elementary School Guidance and Counseling,* 1963, May, 267–285.

ARGYRIS, C. Explorations in consulting-client relationships. In W. Bennis, K. Benne, & R. Chin (Eds.) *The planning of change.* New York: Holt, Rinehart & Winston, 1961, 434–456.

ASCA. The role of the secondary school counselor. *School Counselor,* 1977, 24, 228–334.

AUBREY, R. Power bases: The consultant's vehicle exchange. *Elementary School Guidance and Counseling,* 1972, 7, 90–98.

BEGAL, M. U.S. Public Health Service Report to CELDIC Commission. National Institute of Child Health and Human Development. Ottawa, Canada: Governmental Document, 1967.

BENDER, D. Counseling, consulting, or developmental guidance? Toward an answer. *Elementary School Guidance and Counseling,* 1970, 4, 245–252.

BENNE, K. Some ethical problems in group and organizational consultation. *Journal of Social Issues,* 1959, 15, 60–67.

BERLIN, I. The theme in mental health consultation sessions. *American Journal of Orthopsychiatry,* 1960, 30, 827–828.

———. Mental health consultation in schools as a means of communicating mental health principles. *Journal of American Academic Child Psychiatry,* 1962, 1, 671–679.

———. Learning mental health consultation: History and problems. *Mental Hygiene,* 1964, 48, 257–265.

BINDMAN, A. Mental health consultation: Theory and practice. *Journal of Consulting Psychology,* 1959, 23, 473–482.

BLAHA, M. When and how the consultant can be used most effectively. *Educational Leadership,* 1952, 10(1), 96–100.

BOEHME, W. The professional relationship between consultant and consultee. *American Journal of Orthopsychiatry,* 1956, 26, 241–248.

BOWMAN, P. The role of the consultant as a motivator of action. *Mental Hygiene,* 1959, 43, 105–110.

BRAMMER, L. & SHOSTROM, E. *Therapeutic psychology: Fundamentals of counseling and psychotherapy* (4th ed.). Englewood Cliffs, NJ: Prentice-Hall, 1982.

BROWN, J. Pragmatic notes on community consultation with agencies. *Community Mental Health Journal*, 1967, 3, 399–405.

BURGGRAF, M. Consulting with parents of handicapped children. *Elementary School Guidance and Counseling*, 1979, 13, 214–221.

CAPLAN, G. *The theory and practice of mental health consultation.* New York: Basic Books, Inc., 1970.

CARLSON, J. Case analysis: Parent group consultation. *Elementary School Guidance and Counseling*, 1969, 4, 136–141.

———. Consultation: Facilitating school change. *Elementary School Guidance and Counseling*, 1972, 7, 83–89.

CHILDRESS, N. Group consultation with middle school teachers. *The School Counselor*, 1982, 30, 127–132.

CHRISTENSEN, O. Family education: A mode for consultation. *Elementary School Guidance and Counseling*, 1972, 7, 121–129.

CIAVERELLA, M. The counselor as a mental health consultant. *The School Counselor*, 1970, 18, 121–126.

COCHRAN, D. Contracting in consultation: Training guidelines and examples. *Counselor Education and Supervision*, 1980, 20, 125–131.

COHEN, L. Consultation as a method of mental health intervention. In L. Abt & B. Riess (Eds.) *Progress in clinical psychology.* New York: Grune & Stratton, 1966, 107–128.

CONVER, B. Principles of psychological consulting with client organizations. *Journal of Consulting Psychology*, 1947, 11, 227–244.

COOPER, L. Making the most of an educational consultant. *School Management*, 1971, 9, 16–17.

COUCHMAN, R. Counseling the emotionally troubled: A neglected group. *Personnel and Guidance Journal*, 1974, 52, 457–463.

DINKMEYER, D. & CALDWELL, E. *Developmental counseling and guidance: A comprehensive school approach.* New York: McGraw-Hill, 1970.

DINKMEYER, D. & CARLSON, J. *Consultation: A book of readings.* New York: John Wiley & Sons, 1975.

DINKMEYER, D. & CARLSON, J. Consulting: Training counselors to work with teachers, parents, and administrators. *Counselor Education and Supervision*, 1977, 16, 1972–177.

DOWD, E. & MOERINGS, B. The underachiever and teacher consultation: A case study. *The School Counselor*, 1975, 22, 263–266.

DURSTIN, R. & BURDEN, C. The counselor as a behavioral consultant. *Elementary School Guidance and Counseling*, 1972, 7, 14–19.

EGAN, G. *The skilled helper: Models, skills, and methods for effective helping.* (2nd ed.) Monterey, CA: Brooks/Cole, 1982.

EISDORFER, C. & BATTON, L. The mental health consultant as seen by his consultees. *Community Mental Health Journal*, 1972, 8, 171–177.

EISENBERG, L. An evaluation of psychiatric consultation service for a public agency. *American Journal of Public Health,* 1958, 48, 742–749.

ERGEHARDT, L., SULZER, B., & ALTEKRUSE, M. The counselor as a consultant in eliminating out-of-seat behavior. *Elementary School Guidance and Counseling,* 1971, 5, 196–204.

EVANS, D. Problems and challenges for the mental health professional consulting to a community action organization. *Community Mental Health Journal,* 1973, 9, 46–52.

FAUST, V. *The counselor consultant in the elementary school.* Boston: Houghton-Mifflin, 1968.

FRANKEN, M. The consultant role in elementary school guidance: Helping teachers increase awareness of behavior dynamics of children. *Elementary School Guidance and Counseling,* 1969, 4, 128–135.

FROEHLE, T. Systematic training for consultants through competency-based education. *Personnel and Guidance Journal,* 1978, 56, 436–441.

FULLMER, D. Family group consultation. *Elementary School Guidance and Counseling,* 1972, 7, 130–136.

—— & BERNARD, H. *The school-counselor consultant.* New York: Houghton-Mifflin, 1972.

GALLESSICH, J. & LADOGANA, A. Consultation training programs for school counselors. *Counselor Education and Supervision,* 1978, 18, 100–108.

GARRETT, A. The use of the consultant: Psychiatric consultation. *American Journal of Orthopsychiatry,* 1956, 26, 234–240.

GAUPP, P. Authority, influence and control in consultation. *Community Mental Health Journal,* 1966, 3, 205–210.

GAZDA, G., ASBURY, F., BALZER, F., CHILDERS, W., & WALTERS, R. *Human relations development: A manual for educators.* (2nd ed.) Boston: Allyn & Bacon, 1977.

GIBB, J. The role of the consultant. *Journal of Social Issues,* 1959, 15, 1–4.

GLIDEWELL, J. The entry problem in consultation. *Journal of Social Issues,* 1959, 15, 51–59.

GRIFFITH, C. & LIBO, L. *Mental health consultants: Agents of community change.* San Francisco: Jossey-Bass, 1968.

GUMAER, J. Racial understanding through affective education. *The School Counselor,* 1977, 24, 171–177.

—— & BEALE, A. Counselor in the classroom: The guidance drama. *The Guidance Clinic,* 1977, 6–9.

——, BLECK, R., & LOESCH, L. Affective education through role playing: The feelings class. *Personnel and Guidance Journal,* 1975, 8, 604–608.

—— & MYRICK, R. Developmental consultation can be systematic. *The Guidance Clinic,* 1976, February, 4–6.

——. & VOORNEVELD, R. Affective education with gifted children. *Elementary School Guidance and Counseling,* 1975, 2, 86–94.

HAYLETT, C. & RAPOPORT, L. Mental health consultation. In L. Bellak (Ed.) *Hand-*

book of community psychiatry and community mental health. New York: Grune & Stratton, 1964, 319–339.

HUME, K. Counseling and consulting: Complementary functions. *Elementary School Guidance and Counseling,* 1970, 5, 3–11.

JARVIS, P. & NELSON, S. Familiarization: A vital step in mental health consultation. *Community Mental Health Journal,* 1967, 3, 343–348.

JOHNSTON, J. & FIELDS, P. School consultation with the "classroom family." *The School Counselor,* 1981, 29, 140–146.

KACZKOWSKI, H. The elementary school counselor as consultant. *Elementary School Guidance and Counseling,* 1967, 3, 103–111.

KAHNWEILER, W. The school counselor as consultant: A historical review. *Personnel and Guidance Journal,* 1979, 57, 374–379.

KAUFMAN, I. The role of the psychiatric consultant. *American Journal of Orthopsychiatry,* 1956, 26, 223–233.

KRANZLER, G. The elementary school counselor as a consultant: An evaluation. *Elementary School Guidance and Counseling,* 1969, 3, 285–288.

KURPIUS, D. (Ed.) Consultation I and II. *Personnel and Guidance Journal,* 1978, 56, (Whole Nos. 6 & 7).

KURPIUS, D. & ROBINSON, S. An overview of consultation. *Personnel and Guidance Journal,* 1978, 56, 321–323.

KUZNIAR, J. Teacher consultation: A case study. *Personnel and Guidance Journal,* 1973, 52, 108–111.

LEWIS, M. The effects of counseling and consultation upon sociometric status and personal and social adjustment of 3rd grade pupils. *Elementary School Guidance and Counseling,* 1970, 5, 44–52.

———. Elementary school counseling and consultation: Their effects on teachers' perceptions. *The School Counselor,* 1970, 18, 49–52.

LIBO, L. Multiple functions for psychologists in community consultation. *American Psychologist,* 1966, 21, 530–534.

LIPPITT, R. Dimensions of the consultant's job. *Journal of Social Issues,* 1959, 15, 5–12.

———. A study of the consultation process. *Journal of Social Issues,* 1959, 15, 43–50.

LISTER, J. The consultant to counselor: A new professional role. *The School Counselor,* 1969, 16, 349–354.

LOMBANA, J. A program-planning approach to teacher consultation. *The School Counselor,* 1979, 26, 163–170.

MALE, R. Consultation as an intervention strategy for school counselors. *The School Counselor,* 1982, 30, 25–31.

MANN, P. Accessibility and organizational power in the entry phase of mental health consultation. *Journal of Consulting Psychology,* 1972, 38, 215–218.

MANNINO, R. & SHORE, M. The effects of consultation: A review of empirical studies. *American Journal of Community Psychology,* 1975, 3, 1–21.

MARCHANT, W. Counseling and/or consultation: A test of an educational model in the elementary school. *Elementary School Guidance and Counseling*, 1972, 7, 4–5.

MAYER, R. Behavioral consulting: Using behavior modification procedures in the consulting relationship. *Elementary School Guidance and Counseling*, 1972, 7, 114–120.

McBEATH, M. Consulting with teachers in two areas: Grief and mourning: Relaxation techniques. *Personnel and Guidance Journal*, 1980, 58, 473–476.

McGEHEARTY, L. Consultation and counseling. *Elementary School Guidance and Counseling*, 1969, 3, 155–163.

McGreevy, C. Training consultants: Issues and approaches. *Personnel and Guidance Journal*, 1978, 56, 432–435.

MICKELSON, D. & DAVIS, J. A consultation model for the school counselor. *The School Counselor*, 1977, 25, 98–103.

MILES, J. & HUMMEL, D. Consultant training in counselor education programs. *Counselor Education and Supervision*, 1979, 19, 49–53.

MOE, E. Consulting with a community system: A case study. *Journal of Social Issues*, 1959, 14 (2), 28–35.

MOEK, S. & MUHICH, D. Some problems and parameters of mental health consultation. *Community Mental Health Journal*, 1972, 8, 232–239.

MORACCO, J. Counselor as consultant: Some implications for counselor education. *Counselor Education and Supervision*, 1977, 16, 73–75.

MORRISON, A. Consultation with group processes with indigenous neighborhood worker. *Community Mental Health Journal*, 1970, 6, 3–12.

MUSANTE, G. & GALLEMORE, J. Utilization of a staff development group in prison consultation. *Community Mental Health Journal*, 1973, 9 (3), 224–228.

MYRICK, R. & MONI, L. The counselor's workshop: Teacher in-service workshops. *Elementary School Guidance and Counseling*, 1972, 7, 156–160.

NAGLER, S. & COOK, P. Some ideological considerations underlying a mental health-consultation program to the public schools. *Community Mental Health Journal*, 1973, 9 (3), 244–252.

NELSON, R. & ROOP, P. Should consulting include classroom observation? *Elementary School Guidance and Counseling*, 1972, 7, 137–142.

NEWMAN, R. *Psychological consultation in the schools: A catalyst for learning.* New York: Basic Books, 1967.

NORMAN, E. & FORTE, T. A study of the process and the outcome of the mental health consultation. *Community Mental Health Journal*, 1972, 8, 261–270.

PALMO, A. & KUZNIAR, J. Modification of behavior through group counseling and consultation. *Elementary School Guidance and Counseling*, 1972, 6, 258–262.

PANCVAZIO, J. The school counselor as a human relations consultant. *The School Counselor*, 1971, 19, 81–87.

PAPANEK, G. Dynamics of community consultation. *Archives of General Psychiatry*, 1968, 19, 189–196.

PARKER, B. The value of supervision in training psychiatrists for mental health consultation. *Mental Hygiene*, 1961, 45, 94–100.

———. Some observations on psychiatric consultation with nursery school teachers. *Mental Hygiene,* 1962, 46, 599–666.

PIETROFESA, J. & PIETROFESA, D. The counselor's role as a consultant in familial sexual development. *The School Counselor,* 1976, 23, 339–345.

RANDOLPH, D. Teaching consultation for mental health and educational settings. *Counselor Education and Supervision,* 1980, 20, 2, 117–124.

——— & HARDAGE, N. Behavioral consultation and group counseling with potential dropouts. *Elementary School Guidance and Counseling,* 1972, 7, 204–209.

——— & SABA, R. Changing behavior through modeling and consultation. *Elementary School Guidance and Counseling,* 1973, 8, 98–108.

RAPOPORT, L. (Ed.) *Consultation in social work practice.* New York: National Association of Social Workers, 1963.

RITCHIE, M. Parental consultation: Practical considerations. *The School Counselor,* 1982, 29, 402–410.

ROBBINS, R., SPENCER, E., & FRANK, D. Some factors influencing the outcome of consultation. *American Journal of Public Health,* 1970, 69, 524–534.

SCHEIN, E. *Process consultation: Its role in organization development.* Reading, MA: Addison-Wesley, 1969.

SCHMIDT, J. & ATLAS, J. Teacher-parent communication: A consulting model. *The School Counselor,* 1976, 23, 346–352.

——— & MEDL, W. Six magic steps of consulting. *The School Counselor,* 1983, 30, 212–216.

——— & OSBORNE, W. Counseling and consulting: Separate processes or the same? *Personnel and Guidance Journal,* 1981, 60, 168–171.

SEASHORE, C. & VAN EGNAOND, E. The consultant trainer role in working directly with a total staff. *Journal of Social Issues,* 1959, 25, 36–43.

SIGNELL, K. & SCOTT, P. Mental health consultation: An interaction model. *Community Mental Health Journal,* 1971, 7, 288–303.

SPLETE, H. The elementary school counselor: An effective consultant with classroom teachers. *Elementary School Guidance and Counseling,* 1971, 5, 165–172.

——— & BERNSTEIN, B. A survey of consultation training as part of counselor education programs. *Personnel and Guidance Journal,* 1981, 59, 470–472.

STEIN, H. Discussion on workshop: The use of the consultant. *American Journal of Orthopsychiatry,* 1956, 26, 249–252.

STEPHENS, T. Psychological consultation to teachers of learning and behaviorally handicapped children using a behavioral model. *Journal of School Psychology,* 1970, 8(1), 13–18.

STILLER, A. Presenting: The consultant to counselors. *The School Counselor,* 1974, 21, 342–349.

STRINGER, L. Consultation: Some expectations, principles, and skills. *Social Work,* 1961, 6(3), 85–90.

SWENSON, C. Social impact of consultation. *Professional Psychology,* 1971, 2, 324–345.

Tilles, S. Understanding the consultant's role. *Harvard Business Review*, 1961, 39, 87–99.

Ulmer, R. & Kapperman, S. An empirical study of the process and outcome of psychiatric consultation. *Journal of Clinical Psychology*, 1970, 26, 323–326.

Walton, R. *Interpersonal peacemaking: Confrontation and third party consultation.* Reading, Mass: Addison-Wesley, 1969.

Westling, D. & Joiner, M. Consulting with teachers of handicapped children in the mainstream. *Elementary School Guidance and Counseling*, 1979, 13, 207–213.

Whitley, A. & Sulzer, B. Reducing disruptive behavior through consultation. *Personnel and Guidance Journal*, 1970, 48, 836–841.

Wigtil, J. & Kelsey, R. Team building as a consulting intervention for influencing learning environments. *Personnel and Guidance Journal*, 1978, 56, 412–416.

Zaffrann, R. Using the workshop in consultation training. *Counselor Education and Supervision*, 1979, 18, 304–311.

Appendix A

Case Study Outline

Name: Date:

Age:

I. Presenting problem
   A. Parental perceptions

   B. Child perceptions

II. Circumstances of birth
   A. Were there unusual conditions of delivery?
   B. Were both parents present?
   C. Was prenatal care followed?
   D. If not, what were parents' behaviors before delivery that might influence child's development? (E.g.: excessive drugs or alcohol; smoking; improper nutrition.)

III. Motor development
   A. At what age did the child sleep through night?
   B. At what age did the child walk, talk, obtain bladder and bowel control?

C. Can child skip, hop, and run?
D. Are there other problems with coordination?

IV. Medical history
   A. What childhood illnesses were contracted?
   B. Does the child experience any chronic disease?
   C. Is the child on any medication?
   D. Does the child experience any recurring medical problems?
   E. What is the overall energy level of the child?
   F. Are there any deficiencies in vision or hearing?
   G. Has the child had a recent physical examination?

V. Diet
   A. Has the child been a good eater?
   B. Are there any significant feeding problems?
   C. Does the child eat sufficient amounts of protein, fats, carbohydrates, green and yellow vegetables?

VI. Social development and peer relationships
   A. What was the age and reactions of the child to his or her first play situations?
   B. Is the child a leader, a follower, or both, in play with peers?
   C. What kinds of toys/games does the child enjoy most?
   D. Does the child self-initiate play while alone/with others?
   E. Does the child prefer playing with children of the same sex, opposite sex, or both?
   F. Are the preferred playmates of the child older, younger, or about the same age?
   G. How well does the child compete and cooperate in play?

VII. Emotional development
   A. Is the child able to express emotions?
   B. What is the child's overall temperament?
   C. What are the child's feelings toward self?
   D. How does the child feel toward family, friends, teachers?
   E. Are there any excessive fears?
   F. Does the child experience unusual or persistent dreams or nightmares?

VIII. Family history and relationships
   A. Parents
      1. Are they living together, separated, or divorced?
      2. Are they alive, deceased, or incarcerated?
      3. Do they have any chronic or fatal disease?
      4. Are they experiencing any personal mental health problems?
   B. What are the occupations, education levels, and personal incomes of parents?
   C. Siblings
      1. What are ages and sex?
      2. What are similarities and differences in children?

   3. What are the children's strengths/weaknesses?
   4. What responsibilities do the children have in the home?
 D. Parent-child relationships
   1. With which parent does the child identify most?
   2. What things does the child do with each parent or both?
   3. What specifically does the child do that pleases the parents?
   4. What specifically do the parents do to please the child?
   5. What are the family rules for the household?
   6. How does the child respond to discipline?
   7. What are the parental methods of discipline?
   8. What is most perplexing about the child to the parents?

IX. School/academic history
 A. What are the child's present and past reactions to school?
 B. What are the child's relationships with teachers (male, female; black, white; classroom, other activities)?
 C. What is the current classroom atmosphere (self-contained, open, team teaching)?
 D. What are child's academic strengths and weaknesses?
 E. What is the child's attendance record?
 F. What school activities interest the child?
 G. What test scores are available on the child (I.Q., achievement, aptitude)?

X. General impressions and comments

Appendix B

Individual Counseling Competencies Checklist

	Observed	Unobserved
I. Academic competencies		
A. Demonstrates a knowledge of counseling theory.	_____	_____
B. Demonstrates a knowledge of counseling procedures and techniques appropriate to a particular theory.	_____	_____
C. Possesses knowledge of child growth and development.	_____	_____
D. Demonstrates application of knowledge of counseling theory and child growth and development in planning for therapy.	_____	_____
II. Counseling competencies		
A. Facilitation phase		
1. Greeting is warm and friendly.	_____	_____
2. Attending: maintains appropriate eye contact, looks at client without staring, does not look around.	_____	_____
3. Posture: facing client, relaxed, not	_____	_____

	Observed	*Unobserved*
fidgeting, leaning slightly toward child.		
4. Voice tone and facial expressions genuinely pleasant and warm.	_____	_____
5. Encourages child by issuing open invitation to be involved.	_____	_____
6. Demonstrates listening skills, is able to restate content of child's message.	_____	_____
7. Responds to surface feeling of child.	_____	_____
8. Uses silence effectively.	_____	_____
9. Clarifies child's content and feelings of child's message.	_____	_____
10. Uses open questions to encourage child to explore concern.	_____	_____
11. Supports and encourages client behavior that enhances therapy.	_____	_____
12. Summarizes significant content and feelings of session.	_____	_____

B. Transition phase

13. Responds to intermediate-level feelings.	_____	_____
14. Responds to deep-level feelings.	_____	_____
15. Interprets child's content and feelings to provide insight into self.	_____	_____
16. Uses counselor self-disclosure appropriately.	_____	_____
17. Uses closed questions to be concrete.	_____	_____
18. Personalizes child's content and feelings.	_____	_____

C. Action phase

| 19. Responds with immediacy. | _____ | _____ |
| 20. Uses confrontation appropriately. | _____ | _____ |

	Observed	Unobserved
21. Helps client by initiating action.		
22. Assists client in problem identification.		
23. Assists client exploration of alternative behaviors.		
24. Assists client exploration of consequences to behaviors.		

D. Termination phase

	Observed	Unobserved
25. Summarizes counseling session and prepares child for future sessions.		
26. Ensures child's emotional readiness to exit counseling.		
27. Gives appropriate "assignments" or "homework" to child.		
28. Demonstrates effective closure by maintaining time limits of each session.		
29. Demonstrates personal readiness to "let go" or give up client.		
30. Provides appropriate advice.		

Appendix C

Bibliotherapy Reference List

Coping with Human Death

Alexander, A. *Trouble on treat street*. Atheneum, 1974.

Armstrong, W. *Sounder*. New York: Harper & Row, 1973.

Arundal, H. *The blanket world*. Nashville: Nelson, 1973.

Bartoli, J. *Nonna*. New York: Harvey House, 1975.

Beckman, G. *Admission to the feast*. New York: Holt, Rinehart & Winston, 1971.

Bernstein, J. *Loss: And how to cope with it*. New York: Seabury, 1977.

Bernstein, J. & Gullo, S. *When people die*. New York: Dutton, 1977.

Blue, R. *Grandma didn't wave back*. Franklin Watts, 1972.

Brooks, J. *Uncle Mike's boy*. New York: Harper, 1973.

Cleaver, V. & Cleaver, B. *Grover*. Philadelphia: Lippincott, 1970.

Clewes, D. *Storm over Innish*. Nashville: Nelson, 1973.

Dixon, P. *Promises to keep*. New York: Atheneum, 1974.

Dixon, P. *May I cross your golden river?* New York: Atheneum, 1975.

Donovan, J. *I'll get there. It better be worth the trip*. New York: Harper, 1969.

Duncan, L. *I know what you did last summer*. Boston: Little, Brown & Co., 1973.

Farley, C. *The garden is doing fine*. New York: Atheneum, 1975.

Fassler, J. *My grandpa died today*. New York: Human Sciences Press, 1971.

Greene, C. *Beat the turtle drum*. New York: Viking, 1976.

Greenfield, E. *Sister*. New York: Crowell, 1974.

Grollman, E. *Talking about death: A dialogue between parent and child*. Boston: Beacon Press, 1976.

Hunter, M. *A sound of chariots*. New York: Harper, 1972.

Jones, A. *So, nothing is forever*. Boston: Houghton-Mifflin, 1974.

Klagsbrun, F. *Too young to die: Youth and suicide*. Boston: Houghton-Mifflin, 1976.

Lee, M. *Fog*. New York: Seabury, 1972.

Lee, M. *The skating rink*. New York: Seabury, 1969.

LeShan, E. *Learning to say good-by: When a parent dies*. New York: Macmillan, 1976.

Lund, D. *Eric*. Philadelphia: Lippincott, 1974.

Mathis, S. *Listen for the fig tree*. New York: Viking, 1974.

Morgan, A. *Ruth Crane*. New York: Harper, 1974.

Platt, K. *Chloris and the creeps*. New York: Chilton, 1973.

Rinaldo, E. *Dark dreams*. New York: Harper & Row, 1974.

Shecter, B. *Across the meadow*. Garden City, NY: Doubleday, 1973.

Smith, D. *A taste of blackberries*. New York: Crowell, 1973.

Stein, S. *About dying: An open family book for parents and children together*. New York: Walker, 1974.

Stolz, M. *By the highway home*. New York: Harper & Row, 1971.

Stolz, M. *The edge of next year*. New York: Harper & Row, 1974.

Viorst, J. *The tenth good thing about Barney*. New York: Atheneum, 1971.

Zolotow, C. *My grandson Lew*. New York: Harper & Row, 1974.

Coping with Divorce and Parental Separation

Adams, F. *Mushy eggs*. New York: Putnam Press, 1973.

Blue, R. *A month of Sundays*. New York: Watts, 1972.

Blume, J. *It's not the end of the world*. New York: Bradbury Press, 1972.

Cameron, E. *To the green mountains*. New York: Dutton, 1975.

Gardner, R. *The boys and girls book about divorce*. New York: Science House, 1971.

Klein, N. *Mom, the wolfman and me*. New York: Pantheon, 1972.

Klein, N. *It's not what you expect*. New York: Pantheon, 1973.

Lexau, J. *Me day*. New York: Dial, 1971.

Newfield, M. *A book for Jodan*. New York: Atheneum, 1975.

Rogers, H. *Morris and his brave lion*. New York: McGraw-Hill, 1975.

Smith, D. *Kick a stone home*. New York: Crowell, 1974.

Stanek, M. *I won't go without a father*. Chicago: Whitman, 1972.

Accepting Stepparents and Stepfamilies

Bradbury, B. *Those Traver kids*. Boston: Houghton-Mifflin, 1972.

Childress, A. *A hero ain't nothin' but a sandwich*. New York: Coward, 1973.

Gardner, R. *The boys and girls book about stepfamilies*. New York: Bantam, 1982.

Green, P. *Ice river*. Reading, MA: Addison-Wesley, 1975.

Greene, C. *I know you, Al*. New York: Viking, 1975.

Mazer, H. *Guy Lenny*. New York: Delacorte, 1971.

Pevsner, S. *A smart kid like you*. New York: Seabury, 1975.

Rockwell, T. *Hiding out*. Scarsdale, New York: Bradbury Press, 1974.

Wells, R. *None of the above*. New York: Dial, 1974.

Accepting Relocation

Alexander, M. *Sabrina*. New York: Dial, 1971.

Amos, B. *The very worst thing*. New York: Parents' Magazine Press, 1972.

Bach, A. *They'll never make a movie starring me*. New York: Harper, 1973.

Baldwin, A. *A friend in the park*. N.Y.: Four Winds, 1973.

Binzen, B. *First day in school*. Garden City, NY: Doubleday, 1972.

Blume, J. *Then again, maybe I won't*. Scarsdale, NY: Bradbury Press, 1971.

Breinburg, P. *Shawn goes to school*. New York: Crowell, 1973.

Brink, C. *The bad times of Irma Baumlein*. New York: Macmillan, 1972.

Clifton, L. *Good, says Jerome*. New York: Dutton, 1973.

Cormier, R. *The chocolate war*. New York: Pantheon, 1974.

Gray, G. *Sore loser*. Boston: Houghton-Mifflin, 1974.

Hickman, M. *I'm moving*. Nashville: Abingdon, 1974.

Kantrowitz, M. *Good-bye Kitchen*. New York: Parents' Magazine Press, 1972.

Kantrowitz, M. *Willy bear*. New York: Parents' Magazine Press, 1976.

Lewis, T. *The dragon kite*. New York: Holt, Rinehart & Winston, 1974.

Lystad, M. *That new boy*. New York: Crown, 1973.

Mann, P. *The secret dog of little Luis*. New York: Coward, 1973.

Martin, P. *Be brave, Charlie*. New York: Putnam, 1972.

Mathis, S. *Sidewalk story*. New York: Viking Press, 1971.

Phipson, J. *Polly's tiger*. New York: Dutton, 1974.

Robinson, C. *New kid in town*. New York: Atheneum, 1975.

Rockwell, H. *My nursery school*. New York: Greenwillow, 1976.

Schulman, J. *The big hello*. New York: Greenwillow, 1976.

Tobias, T. *Moving day*. New York: Knopf, 1976.

Wallace, B. *Victoria*. Chicago: Follett, 1972.

Wells, R. *The fog comes on little pig feet*. New York: Dial, 1972.

Wolde, G. *Betsy's first day at nursery school*. New York: Random House, 1976.

Yep, L. *Dragon wings*. New York: Harper, 1975.

Zolotow, C. *Janey*. New York: Harper, 1973.

Letter of Permission for Group Counseling Participation

School/Agency Heading

Date: _____

Dear Parent:

Your son/daughter has been referred by _____ and selected as a candidate for one of several counseling groups to be conducted by me this fall. Each group will consist of six children who will meet with me for 40 minutes on Monday and Wednesday at 2:00 p.m. for seven weeks. The focus of these sessions will be on learning to get along with other children and making friends.

During these sessions, children will be involved in group discussions, role playing, and other similar activities. It is my desire that children who experience these counseling sessions have the opportunity to express their thoughts and feelings and to learn new skills for developing and enhancing their interpersonal relationships. I have discussed this experience with your son/daughter who has indicated a desire to participate.

If you are supportive of your child's participating in this group counseling experience, please sign the letter where indicated below and return it to me. If you would like additional information about the counseling group, please feel free to call me at work. The number is _____. Should you desire a personal appointment, it can be arranged with your call.

I look forward to working with your child in group counseling.

Sincerely,

I give permission for ____(child's name)____ to participate in the group counseling experience described in this letter.

_____
(parent's signature)

Checklist for Group Counseling Skills

I. Organizing the group (communication)	Not observed	Unsatisfactory	Satisfactory
1. I have communicated the need for and value of group counseling to my supervisors, colleagues, and children.	_____	_____	_____
2. I have surveyed adults and children to determine children's group counseling needs in my school/agency.	_____	_____	_____
3. I have communicated to children opportunities for participation in group counseling.	_____	_____	_____
4. I have developed a pool of potential child clients for counseling groups.	_____	_____	_____
5. I have interviewed children for my counseling group.	_____	_____	_____
6. During each interview, I have stated the purpose of the group, expected roles of group members, and the			

	Not observed	*Unsatisfactory*	*Satisfactory*
names of other children who may be in the group.	_____	_____	_____
7. If child indicates an interest in counseling, I have received parental (guardian) permission.	_____	_____	_____

II. Organizing the group (formation)

8. I have established specific guidelines for selecting group members based on balancing factors such as sex, age, personality differences, and developmental levels.	_____	_____	_____
9. I have established an appropriate-sized group based on the type of group, age, and developmental level.	_____	_____	_____
10. I have established an appropriate frequency of group meetings based on the type of group and perceived group needs.	_____	_____	_____
11. I have established an acceptable minimum number of sessions for my group.	_____	_____	_____
12. I have established an adequate meeting time based on children's and institutional needs.	_____	_____	_____
13. I have selected and arranged an appropriate setting for group counseling.	_____	_____	_____
14. I have made preliminary plans including goals, objectives, and activities for my counseling group.	_____	_____	_____

15. For evaluative purposes, I have administered appropri-

	Not observed	Unsatisfactory	Satisfactory
ate pretests to children, parents, or teachers.			

III. Establishing the group

16. I have stated clearly the purpose of the group, my role, and my expectations for children's behavior.

17. I have encouraged group involvement (superficial self-disclosure) by implementing appropriate group activities.

18. I have responded to children's surface-level feelings.

19. I have clarified children's thoughts, feelings, and behaviors.

20. I have asked open-ended questions to elicit more information from children.

21. I have provided verbal praise for appropriate group contributions and behavior.

22. I have summarized important material during group and at the close of group sessions.

23. I have responded to nonverbal cues of children.

IV. Exploring with children

24. I continue to use skills from the establishment stage.

25. I have planned and provided group activities to encourage self-disclosure at an intermediate level and to introduce positive feedback.

26. I pair feelings and behaviors

	Not observed	Unsatisfactory	Satisfactory
by pointing out similarities and differences in children's feelings and behaviors.	_____	_____	_____
27. I have modeled positive feedback.	_____	_____	_____
28. I have elicited positive feedback from children to other group members.	_____	_____	_____
29. I have maintained silence when appropriate.	_____	_____	_____

V. Working with children

30. I have continued to use responses from the previous two stages.	_____	_____	_____
31. I have planned and provided group activities to encourage self-disclosure at a deep level and to introduce negative feedback.	_____	_____	_____
32. I have elicited empathic responses from children toward other group members.	_____	_____	_____
33. I have elicited negative feedback from children toward other group members.	_____	_____	_____
34. I have provided appropriate personal self-disclosure.	_____	_____	_____
35. I have responded to underlying feelings of group members.	_____	_____	_____
36. I have provided appropriate interpretation of underlying feelings.	_____	_____	_____
37. I have helped group members identify and focus on individual behavior change.	_____	_____	_____
38. I have helped group members examine alternatives and			

	Not observed	*Unsatisfactory*	*Satisfactory*
consequences for behavior change.	_____	_____	_____
39. I have helped group members set specific goals for behavior change.	_____	_____	_____

VI. Terminating the group

40. I have continued to use responses from the previous three group stages.	_____	_____	_____
41. I have helped group members implement their learning outside the group.	_____	_____	_____
42. I have provided appropriate encouragement and support.	_____	_____	_____
43. I have provided appropriate advice and information.	_____	_____	_____
44. I have evaluated the group and the individuals in it.	_____	_____	_____
45. I have evaluated myself.	_____	_____	_____

Appendix F

Checklist for Consultation Competencies

I. Preparing Self and Others	Not observed	Unsatisfactory	Satisfactory
1. Develops a rationale for consultation.	_____	_____	_____
2. Describes and clarifies the consultation service to administrators, faculty, and staff.	_____	_____	_____
3. Identifies personal strengths and limitations.	_____	_____	_____
4. Is aware of personal values and bias and how these might influence consultation process.	_____	_____	_____
5. Is flexible with and visible to consultee populations.	_____	_____	_____
6. Responds openly and honestly to consultee questions regarding role.	_____	_____	_____
7. Possesses adequate information about consultee populations. (E.g.: ethnic, racial,			

357

	Not observed	Unsatisfactory	Satisfactory
and socioeconomic backgrounds.)	_____	_____	_____
8. Identifies personal strengths and weaknesses of consultee population.	_____	_____	_____
9. Describes role of consultant and consultee clearly to prospective consultee.	_____	_____	_____

II. Building the Consulting Relationship

	Not observed	Unsatisfactory	Satisfactory
10. Demonstrates empathy, respect, and warmth.	_____	_____	_____
11. Develops trust and rapport and reduces anxiety by listening, responding to feelings, and clarifying the situation.	_____	_____	_____
12. Encourages consultee to explore the situation in detail.	_____	_____	_____
13. Recognizes the type of consultation request.	_____	_____	_____
14. Collects data related to the situation.	_____	_____	_____
15. Evaluates data and information presented by consultee.	_____	_____	_____
16. Recognizes consultee defenses and resistance to change.	_____	_____	_____
17. Encourages independence in consultee by reinforcing ability to cope with the situation.	_____	_____	_____
18. Models emotional stability, enthusiasm, self-confidence, and professionalism.	_____	_____	_____
19. Maintains a collegial relationship with consultee.	_____	_____	_____
20. Analyzes the entire situation			

	Not observed	*Unsatisfactory*	*Satisfactory*
and prepares hypotheses with supporting rationale.	_____	_____	_____

III. Hypothesizing and developing a plan

21. Communicates hypotheses with rationale to consultee.	_____	_____	_____
22. Elicits consultee's opinions.	_____	_____	_____
23. In collaboration with consultee, lists probable causes of concern.	_____	_____	_____
24. Prioritizes the listed concerns.	_____	_____	_____
25. Generates and discusses alternative strategies for intervention to fit primary concerns.	_____	_____	_____
26. Generates and discusses consequences to the alternatives.	_____	_____	_____
27. Helps develop behavioral objectives for the plan.	_____	_____	_____
28. Provides information, materials, and other resources necessary in preparing the plan.	_____	_____	_____
29. Assists in developing a formal evaluation methodology for the plan.	_____	_____	_____
30. Reinforces the consultee's ability to implement the plan.	_____	_____	_____

IV. Implementing a plan

31. If necessary or requested, models implementation of strategies.	_____	_____	_____
32. Supports consultee implementation of plan.	_____	_____	_____

	Not observed	*Unsatisfactory*	*Satisfactory*
33. Recognizes subjective assessments of the situation are necessary and ongoing activities.	_____	_____	_____
34. Schedules and plans to be accessible to the consultee.	_____	_____	_____
35. Identifies sources of interference to intervention, if any exist.	_____	_____	_____
36. Obtains additional resources to implement a chosen alternative.	_____	_____	_____
37. Begins to terminate the relationship.	_____	_____	_____

V. Evaluating and ending

38. Evaluates the plan.	_____	_____	_____
39. Provides formal evidence of progress to consultee.	_____	_____	_____
40. If plan works, terminates relationship. If not, reinvests self.	_____	_____	_____

Author Index

Subject Index